IMPERIALISM AND THE ORIGINS OF MEXICAN CULTURE

COLIN M. MACLACHLAN

IMPERIALISM
AND THE ORIGINS
OF MEXICAN CULTURE

HARVARD UNIVERSITY PRESS
Cambridge, Massachusetts
London, England
2015

First printing

Library of Congress Cataloging-in-Publication Data
is available from the Library of Congress

ISBN: 978-0-674-96763-2

To my mestizo son, Alexander Mariano Romero MacLachlan,
with the wish he will always take pride in his Indo-European legacy

Contents

IMPERIALISM AND THE ORIGINS OF MEXICAN CULTURE

Prologue

Y INTEREST IN EMPIRES is both intellectual and experiential. It began at birth in Singapore City in the early 1930s,
when Singapore functioned as a crown colony and British
Malaya was lumped together as the Straits Settlements, a term that conveyed the notion of permanent colonies. My parents lived in a separate
commercial world, one that did not survive Imperial Japan's ambitions
in the early 1940s. The 1930s, the era of the Great Depression, marked a
downward spiral of imperial functionality as demand for commodities
fell. The age of political-economic imperialism had ended already, although the various imperial capitals hesitated to act to spin off what in
modern terminology constituted underperforming assets.

When empires function as intended, they serve to harness the latest
technology and organize resources and markets for the benefit of their
advanced centers. Empires have a vested interest in order as a means
of assuring supplies of raw commodities and sustaining demand for
manufactured goods. To justify their presence, imperial powers impose
controls over local customs that are disruptive in economic ways or
violate what the imperial center determines to be civilized behavior.
Violence, particularly intraregional wars and intragroup conflict and
piracy, were usually promptly suppressed. Certain practices provided
moral justification for intrusion that hardened into imperial superiority.
Indigenous religious practices were assumed to be primitive or im-
moral, a judgment arrived at usually without any serious theological
examination. Pressing the indigenous population to accept various

1

replacements was, in a sense, not that different from carrying off idols to "Rome the Church of the World," in the words of Emperor Constantine.

My family's thoughts about empires were molded half a step ahead of the Japanese army. The family barely escaped the fall of Singapore and divided into two contingents, perhaps because of visa difficulties. My father went on to the United States to procure oil-field equipment for Middle Eastern oil fields still under British control. The rest of the family—my mother, older brother Alan, and I—somehow skirted the outer edges of British imperial defeat. We escaped to Vancouver, Canada, where the mental condition of my mother required hospitalization. My brother and I were temporarily placed in a state orphanage until a foster home provided a happier interlude for us as the war dragged on. After our mother had recovered sufficiently, we embarked for the doubtful security of South Australia, where we had relatives. In Australia, we expected to be invaded by Japanese armies at any moment. As far south as Melbourne, air-raid trenches appeared, though their number seemed inadequate and they were filled with trash. The radio played the U.S. Marine Corps hymn incessantly to prop up morale, but realists had less hope.

General Douglas MacArthur, ordered to escape from Corregidor, attempted to land at Darwin in the extreme north of Australia only to find it under Japanese air attack.[1] Consequently, his party flew on to establish headquarters in Brisbane in 1942. The Japanese bombed Darwin some sixty times from the initial attack in December 1941 to November 1943. As the supreme Allied commander in Australia, MacArthur was shocked to learn that very few Commonwealth troops could be mustered to defend what was then still very much a dependency. Surprisingly the Australian government saw the Americans as quasi-invaders.[2] Australian troops were poorly trained and equipped, with many of Australia's experienced soldiers deployed to block the Japanese from invading India. Few experienced Australians manned the lines. Meanwhile, the wisdom of the British surrender of Singapore without any land resistance remains subject to debate.[3] Commonwealth soldiers soon filled Singapore's Changi internment camp.

Adolescents, including my brother and I, joined the Royal Australian Air League with the unstated notion that we were apprentices, depending on how the war went: perhaps boy soldiers in waiting. On the personal level, we moved around out of necessity; our stricken mother continued to experience serious breakdowns. Consequently, we moved from Caulfield, a district in Melbourne, to Upper Fern Tree Gully to stay with relatives. Upper Fern Tree Gully was a rural agricultural district some thirty-two miles or so upcountry whose one-room schoolhouse remained our intellectual home until we returned to Bombay. Somewhat oddly to us, we were referred to as "the Canadians." We wondered perhaps for the first time who we were and where we belonged.

The threat of Japanese invasion ended in mid-August 1942, the result of the American victory at Guadalcanal and the naval battles of the Coral Sea and decisively the American victory at Midway. Once the supply lines were secure, little luxuries such as chewing gum from the United States delighted us. The Saturday film matinees opened with screen renditions of "God Save the King" as we stood in respect. We eagerly awaited a showing of the serial action adventures of Captain Midnight leaping from an airplane to carry the day.[4] The actual physical war never intruded except when we visited a nearby military hospital or pored over newspapers that printed photos of those who had been killed in action.

As is often the case in war, the Japanese army and navy had different strategies for what parts or ports of Australia should be occupied. While the enemy army hoped to consolidate its holdings in the Asian landmass with Singapore as an anchor, the navy preferred a few well-situated ports to mount a blockade of supplies and troops from the United States as a defensive outer ring.

With the surrender of Japan in 1945, my brother and I returned to Bombay, soon renamed Mumbai, crossing India by train on the five-day journey to our boarding school at Kodaikanal in the cool hill country of South India. As we passed through the Indian heartland, we observed numerous communist flags flying in every village along the way. We realized that control of British India had slipped out of colonial hands. On Indian Independence Day, August 15, 1947, the Union Jack came down at our school as we stood at attention. Indian students, invited on campus to witness the historic event, lined up and sang while the regular student body, mainly American missionary children, looked on. As British subjects by birth, yet never having lived in the United Kingdom, we had a sense of being cast adrift by a mother country we never knew. Crumbling empires encourage others to step forward to pick up the pieces. Other European empires experienced similar sharp, violent, imperfect, and difficult adjustments. The Asian Pacific War and the destruction visited on the imperial centers in Europe by the Axis stripped away the illusion of European military and economic superiority. Psychologically broken empires cannot be easily restored, if they can be restored at all.

In 1948, we embarked from Ceylon, now Sri Lanka, and passed through the Suez Canal. Our ship, the HMS *Chinese Prince,* took on a group of British Tommies at Suez who had elected to be demobilized in Canada as landed immigrants. We proceeded on to Halifax, Canada, then to New York, the new center of economic global power. One suspects that Roman centurions would have recognized the debris of war washing abundantly ashore in both ports.

At the time, the United States, the only superpower in the world, emerged as the new Rome. For centurions as well as for me, military service became the means of entering the new society. In my late teens, I enlisted into the U.S. Marine Corps. Upon my discharge three years later, I did not receive land to cultivate as in ancient Rome, but with the benefit of the GI Bill, I enrolled in William and Mary College to cultivate my mind. Because the cost of that institution was high, I accepted the advice of a fellow student and enrolled in the less expensive Mexico City College, an American institution in that metropolis. There I was struck by fate of a once magnificent empire of the New World as I lived and studied atop the ruins of Tenochtitlan, destroyed and rebuilt as Mexico City by Hernán Cortés. Because I was enchanted by Mexico and its history, I later enrolled in the University of California at Los Angeles for graduate work in Latin American history. Although my doctoral dissertation and my subsequent publications have focused on other topics, I continued to ponder the evolution of empires, with extensive reading spanning decades and efforts to understand their construction and disintegration. *Imperialism and the Origins of Mexican Culture* is the result of that preoccupation.

Introduction

THIS IS THE STORY of two imperialisms—that of Indo-Mexico as it developed in the valleys of Mesoamerica and that of Spain in the Old World and in New Spain, now Mexico. The transatlantic contact created a unique Mestizo culture as the two cultures fused in the sixteenth century. This work is also an account of the historical experience that created their civilizations and gave rise to their empires. Each empire had a long history, from tribal origins to overarching political entities that spread far beyond their earlier borders to encompass and absorb other cultures and language groups. Each empire, with justification, thought itself to be the carrier of a great civilization. As many others did at different times, the peoples of the two civilizations turned to a religious explanatory framework to understand their existence, to organize life at all levels, and of utmost importance, to legitimize their sociopolitical structures. In the case of Spain, the cultural impact of Muslim Al-Andalus (Land of the Vandals) from 711 to 1492 remained strong, long after the fall of Granada to Christian forces, the same year Castile reached the Western Hemisphere. The Christian West's fear of the Muslims, reinforced to the point of hysteria by the fall of Constantinople to the Ottomans in 1453, remained in play until the Western naval victory of Lepanto in 1571 stabilized religious borders. Consequently, it may only be a slight exaggeration to suggest that three imperial cultures met at Tenochtitlán in 1521.

When empires meet, the encounter is often violent. Among the consequences of defeat is the imposition of the victor's cultural agenda,

5

sometimes with benign intent but ignoring the two sides' differing historical trajectories that in the end determine how they fit together and to what extent. Spain saw the Western Hemisphere as a "New World" in spite of the existence of ancient civilizations. Nevertheless, the Indo-Mexican historical experience could not be swept aside, nor, subsequently, could that of other American civilizations as Spain's empire expanded beyond North America.

Civilizations emerge from a common human process, but neither at the same rate nor exactly in an identical manner. The basic components that make civilizations possible regardless of time and location are the elaboration of an explanatory imagination (religion), fixed settlements, occupational specialization, experiential knowledge, order, and security—not necessarily in that order. Civilizations require the allocation of sufficient material surplus to free a percentage of the population, often a priestly class, to generate knowledge and consequently a culture.[1] These elements, together with a multitude of hard-to-define peripheral notions, create civilized cultures. Civilizations and their cultures are not static; change, however, is usually measured and often generational. Foreign imperialism speeds up the pace and alters the cultural direction, sometimes radically. A victorious imperial power is changed also by territorial expansion, as was Rome, whereas subject civilizations are transformed to the point that their culture is replaced in part but usually not completely. If the object of imperialism has elaborated its culture in isolation from the broader universe, as did Indo-Mexico, the arrival of imperial intruders is a traumatic shock: mental confusion went both ways as Spain and Indo-Mexico struggled to place events in an understandable context.

At a certain point (ca. 100 BC), a settled culture emerged in Indo-Mexico. Although not static, it provided the foundation for incremental changes over time. European imperialism interrupted that process and destroyed much of these cultural foundations, while imposing its own on its new subjects. The imposition of a culture formed by a different historical experience altered the trajectory of the now imperial dependency; the fusion of elements from both sides, but not in equal measure, depended on a number of factors. Although the racial definition of a Mestizo is a person born to Indian and European parents, a better definition of a Mestizo is a person who functions within a modified culture drawn from both the indigenous and European historical-cultural experience: in short, those who embrace cultural *mestizaje* and organize their personal life and behavior accordingly. The extent of such borrowing must be substantial but not necessarily evenly balanced or complete.[2] Biology is less important than the acceptance of a culture introduced by the imperial power mixed with elements from Indo-Mexican culture. Indo-Mexico's demographic disaster, to be discussed in the following pages, tipped the balance toward European elements, creating Mexico's Mestizo culture.[3]

The Mexican essayist Agustín Yáñez (1904–1980) singled out the imposition of language as the key transformative violence associated with imperialism, a process that involves a "pre-existing language . . . in contact with a new reality" that results in "thoughts inconceivable in Spain."[4] Religion and language are perhaps the two most important cultural elements in that they express a unique consciousness that governs all else. Spain contemplated Indo-Mexico through its medieval lens, whereas Mexico's cultural mosaic was shattered into incoherent fragments, much of which survives along with archaic Castilian elements in Mexico's culture.

As the neomaterialists have suggested, people invent culture in order to manage themselves as well as to interact as a group.[5] When circumstances and needs change, so does a people's culture.[6] Change inevitably is an uneven process both embraced as well as resisted and one that proceeds at a different pace depending on complex interactions. The parts do not always mesh together smoothly, nor are they equally weighted. Excessively delayed modifications can result in rigidity, lingering contradictions, and collapse of cultural centers that fail to respond. Both Indo-Mexico and Europe experienced that process in a similar but not an identical way, nor at the same time. As cultures come in contact with each other, they function as two-way prisms used by both the imperial power and the subordinate side to attempt to understand each other. The reality perceived by one is not necessarily the reality of the other.

To understand the formulation of Hispano-Mexico, the history and culture of both Spain and Indo-Mexico must be examined from primitive tribal times through the transformative sixteenth century. Religion constituted the driving force across Indo-Mexico and Spain as well as much of Eurasia. As a response to practical explanatory necessity, the motivation was the same, but the explanations differed, though not entirely; the prominent role of the sun is but one shared example. Spiritual beliefs once elaborated and codified tend to be fairly static: it is easier to incorporate new gods (representing new ideas) than to eliminate established deities, allowing less useful gods to fade into the background. Consequently, active religions rest on layered foundations that unwittingly or not preserve aspects of prior beliefs extending back into prehistory.[7] Both Indo-Mexico's and Europe's sociopolitical structures were tied to the external spirit world. Sacred rituals acknowledged the source of authority and power and reaffirmed popular support and the legitimacy of temporal political authority. Both theocracies had a prolonged tribal history in the course of which religion, language, and their accompanying social paradigms became central tools in the elaboration of their civilizations. Along the way, the tribes absorbed others who contributed aspects to create increasingly complex cultures. To a remarkable extent, the process in both Europe and Indo-Mexico followed a similar path. Nevertheless, Spain as the intruding imperial power imposed its history and culture on that of Indo-Mexico, suppressing but not completely destroying indigenous culture or replacing it fully with that of Castile.[8] In the end, an acceptable compromise (not a balance and not an ideal one) emerged, combining elements drawn from both Indo-Mexico's and Spain's historical experience.

Indo-Mexico's civilization emerged long before the Mexica (subsequently, the Aztecs) arrived in the Valley of Mexico. Although a large number of languages were, and still are, spoken, several languages already had established regional dominance, albeit with various dialects: Nahuatl, Mayan, Tarascan, Zapotec, and Mixtec stand out. Several had the potential to become the dominant language across Mesoamerica. Along with language came political groupings and civilizations that over time became a broader Mesoamerican culture.[9] Trade, war, plunder, and tribute added a dynamic political element. Nevertheless, the record of Indo-Mexico's civilized progress is murky; successive civilizations emerged to be destroyed, in turn, leaving only tantalizing clues in the ruins. Our knowledge improves as we move closer to modern times. The civilization and city of Teotihuacán (100–750) with roots in unknown tribal groups had a population of over 100,000 and appears to have survived for some seven centuries.[10] Its successor, the Toltecs, transmitted the foundational culture across what is now Mexico and northern Central America. With the fall of Tula, the Toltec capital in 1168, refugees mixed with other groups to establish urban concentrations, eventually forming cities that consciously preserved as much of Toltec civilization as possible.

In the era of this study, Indo-Mexico and Spain evolved separately and in isolation from each other until 1519. Nevertheless, the process was similar but, of course, not the same. As the European author of the thirteenth-century *Song of the Saxon Wars (Chanson des Saisnes)* perceptively observed, people of European culture should know "the matter of Britain, the matter of France, and the matter of Rome the Great."[11] What he meant was that certain events, mythological or real, formed Europe's historical experience and its culture. The "matter" of Britain involved the semimythical King Arthur and his knights, their behavior in battle, and the elaboration of a personal code of honor. That of France rested on the feats of Charlemagne and the constant internal conflicts among the Carolingian nobility that created a political and economic mosaic. The "matter" of Rome the Great referenced the cultural membrane through which westward-migrating tribes passed through willingly or reluctantly, including the religion bequeathed to Europe as a whole. He could have noted Christianity as yet another "matter" but likely assumed that all understood its centrality. All these matters constituted the building blocks of a generalized western European Christian culture that evolved into an empire of belief.

In Indo-Mexico, a similar selection of "matters" may be discerned: that of Teotihuacán, Tula, Tezcatlipoca, Quetzalcóatl, and Huitzilopochtli and the central importance of human sacrifice and the values of a warrior caste. Such matters referred to both the continuity of civilization and its sudden collapses and rebirths—the importance of an integrated duality but not one of ridged opposites, such as good and evil, so that their gods were ambivalent and unpredictable. The matter of human sacrifice in return for the debt of human existence, an obligation that could never be satisfied, referred to the bloody keystone of religious beliefs. More positively, those shared historical beliefs recalled the glories of Teotihuacán and Tollan (Tula), paid homage to the skills of the Toltec, and kept alive the notion of re-creating a lost civilization. The matter of Huitzilopochtli spoke of war unending. The Aztecs and other chieftaincies, each with a strong memory of their tribal origins, relied on and responded to such formative matters, as Europe did with its history.

At the time of the arrival of the Europeans, Tenochtitlán had a population of at least 150,000, making it one of the largest cities in the world. Demographic growth, tribute, and plunder had begun to distort social, political, and economic structures. In Indo-Mexico, tribute empires had reached their limits by the mid-1400s. Without a reworking to establish mutual advantage, the cost of deploying an army to enforce tribute collection when necessary became burdensome as well as ineffective. Moreover, the demand for continuous large-scale human sacrifice with a premium on warriors captured in battle made it difficult to end a destructive reliance on war. These factors—tribute, plunder, and war—molded social, political, and economic institutions, but religion provided the overarching context for all civilized activity.

In the struggle to conceive what modifications might be introduced, Indo-Mexico could not rely on a fully elaborated history: a disadvantage that could not be compensated for easily. Contact with the past is a crucial element in the intelligent elaboration of human society—then as now. Indo-Mexico grappled with a past filled with disastrous destruction of civilizations that left fragments of knowledge, often gathered together and preserved in myths, and material advances picked out of the rubble. Myths contain some factual information and provide imagined scenarios that create an intellectual context for decision making but are not as useful as fully recorded history.[12] Fleeing refugees transferred living knowledge, technology, and manual skills as they dispersed across a region, but in an ahistorical manner.[13]

As Indo-Mexican empires expanded, plunder and tribute served to transfer wealth. Trade, although useful and more rationally distributed, did not provide the infusion of capital that force provided. The close association of tribute with political domination makes it difficult to cultivate mutual advantage. The fruits of raiding and plundering in primitive economies are distributed more or less equally among the victors but emphasize consumption over production, resulting in scarcity. The plunderers live well, at least for the moment, while the sacked struggle to regroup. A more effective arrangement is to levy tribute that year after year is dispatched in return for being left more or less alone. Tributaries gathered together under a dominant power constituted a primitive empire.

The Mexica, even before they assumed the directive head of the Aztec Confederation, struggled to consolidate their empire politically and to ameliorate some of the strain on subject groups by regularizing tribute, in effect transforming it into a predictable, if still resented, tax in the absence of mutual advantage.[14] Nevertheless, a tribute empire, although seemingly static, is a transitory imperial stage. Subordination by force, together with a host of less obvious unwilling interactions between the center and its subjects, creates hostility and resentment and nourishes rebellion. Those who are so subordinated are ever in search of the means to escape the yoke, just as the Mexica had earlier in their history. Prosperity, to be sustained, requires a shift to mutual advantage/interdependence: a much more difficult system to manage with implications, perhaps unacceptable, for existing power relations. Moreover, a regulated tribute empire provides a temporary solution only to the political tensions that accompany domination but does not address overconsumption at the center and scarcity among the tributaries. Trade in Mesoamerica had been carried on for centuries but not on a sufficiently large enough scale to integrate and weave together tribal economies, although in the fourteenth century a significant increase in trade had the potential to do so. More problematic, the flow of wealth to an imperial center attracts in-migration that eventually challenges existing political institutions and internal integrity.

In Mesoamerica, only the nobles and priests were taught how to read and interpret the codices' hieroglyphics; the political elite were also the knowledge elite. Just how many codices existed is unknown, in part as a result of destruction by the early Christian missionaries, or perhaps they were burned or buried to avoid seizure by the Spaniards. The ones that survived, often taken as interesting souvenirs, are few. An estimate of at least 50,000 in all of Indo-Mexico might be at the low end of the range. Bernal Díaz, a participant in the initial Spanish conquest, personally observed a storage office stuffed with codices recording tribute conditions, the type of goods to be dispatched to Tenochtitlán, and perhaps much more.[15] Priests would have had access to codices to keep track of rites and holy days.

The majority of the population was illiterate: their access to stored knowledge depended on the nobility, who created, selected, and determined what information would be conveyed to the people and in what form. Although useful politically, control of knowledge limits the individualism necessary for innovation; that, of course, may be the point.[16] Knowledge sharing remained a face-to-face activity. Indo-Mexico relied extensively on an oral tradition as a means of social indoctrination rather than to stimulate intellectual advances. Recitation of orations, the *huehuetlatolli* (meaning "wisdom of the ancients"), required memorization and ritualized presentation, both of which encouraged a fixed mold of expression that acted to restrain the play of ideas. The initial paradigm of received wisdom repeated orally cannot be easily displaced.[17]

Living knowledge, such as contemporary tribal, administrative, and social organization, including the administration of justice, could be observed by the incoming generation and then copied, refined, and passed along but not accompanied by an explanation of why seemingly slight but unrecorded and accumulatively transformative changes might have been made over an extensive period of time. Impressive but unbalanced advances in fields that can be captured in symbols, such as astronomy and mathematics, fully testify to Indo-Mexico's genius. Just as the development of Babylonian mathematics relied on tables, Indo-Mexico recorded tables for the same purpose, independently elaborating the major concept of zero. Symbols give rise to thoughts that, in turn, influence language and how people use it to think and consequently act, but those less tangible, abstract elements that make up the intellectual milieu are not so easily captured. In addition, the limited number of minds with access to complex thought and procedures retards innovation.[18] Abstract knowledge cannot survive without being recorded or disseminated. If it is not immediately useful to a sufficient number of individuals, it dies with its author.

While the transmittal of past knowledge can be accomplished in skeletal forms by a variety of methods, the most important form of conveyance from previous to active generations is a fully developed writing system able to capture abstract notions rather than suggestive shadows of ideas. The absence of deep pools of abstract ideas bequeathed and recorded by prior civilizations makes change incremental.

The need to record had been recognized. Mesoamerica employed several methods depending on the subject to be recorded: pictographic (visual representation), ideographic (symbols that presented an idea), and phonetics so that hieroglyphic symbols could be read counterclockwise to express the sound of the spoken word.[19] Subject matter captured in pictographic representations was weighed toward divine organization, including time and its passing, omens, calendars of sacred events, required rituals, names, chronicles to war, disasters, and the gods and their avatars and functions. Secular pictographs recorded tribute lists, artisanal methods, parental responsibilities, property divisions, and other matters deemed important to document. It is possible that some phonetic element such as the pronunciation of place names were included.[20] That the Roman alphabet introduced by the Spaniards was rapidly adopted in Mesoamerica indicated a realization that simple phonetic characters worked better than pictographic or ideographic representations. What is significant is how close Mesoamerica had come to a system of effective recording and, subsequently, how quickly the literate population adopted Roman letters.[21]

On the eve of the European arrival, Indo-Mexico had reached a crucial socioeconomic and political moment in its civilized evolution. Change appeared to be imminent in the central valleys. The Aztecs suffered a series of demoralizing defeats on the battlefield. Adding to military setbacks, the Aztecs struggled with an overextended empire and delayed rationalization of imperial-tributary economic relations. Internally, increasingly rigid status differentiation, particularly under Montezuma II, apparently designed to reverse the emergence of social groups not tied directly to the political system, also unsettled society. Growing Aztec domination of the Triple Alliance, suggesting an amalgamation of its imperial partners, presaged a significant but uncertain geopolitical rebalancing. The increasing number of nobles with independent resources and a merchant class and luxury craftsmen unable to deploy their earned resources openly and politically indicated growing pressure for structural modifications. Movement toward private property, noble status disconnected from function, and a rational market economy including symbolic value (money) had occurred already and likely would have followed the same basic human trajectory as in Europe had time not run out. Many of the same forces in play in the central valleys impacted Mesoamerica in general.

Collectively, Mesoamerica required a "great awakening" and perhaps the emergence of a prophet.[22] The possibility of a charismatic individual able to override centuries of tribal beliefs, to negate the value of untold human sacrifices, and to establish a new divine explanatory structure able to transform an existing society would seem to be almost impossible. Nevertheless, as the myth of Quetzalcóatl portended, such a prophet could emerge and found a new religion or radically modify the existing one. The mythical Quetzalcóatl was reported to sacrifice butterflies and small animals, not humans, perhaps indicating a collective wish to move beyond human offerings. The prophecy that he would return to destroy those who did not share his beliefs seems to be a subliminal wish common in many religions. Subsequently, Quetzalcóatl's rejection of human sacrifice appealed to the friars looking for signs that Saint Thomas had preceded them. Bernardino de Sahagún pictured Quetzalcóatl with a bishop's miter, a staff, a surplice, and sandals.[23] Time to modify religious notions in isolation would not be possible as Europe entered the New World. Just how different were these European elements from those of Indo-Mexico?

Indo-Mexico's henotheism recognized one supreme god but did not exclude other gods. Europe's somewhat ambivalent monotheism at the moment of New World contact retained aspects of polytheism in the form of mediators—most notably Jesus, the Virgin Mary, recognized saints (an ongoing process), and patron saints (assigned to a distinct group), all able to intercede with the supreme deity.[24] In both Christian and Indo-Mexican theology, the supreme deity functioned as a creator who had not been created and, consequently, without the degree of objectification that characterized deities in subordinate divine positions. That the two theologies differed in the degree of order imposed on their respective pantheons is obvious. Christianity had a divine hierarchy that extended down to the faithful at the bottom in a chain of authority difficult to contest. Moreover, Christianity required belief, not ethnic membership—a feature shared with its immediate competitor, Islam, but not Judaism, which required birth by a Jewish woman. Christianity as a revealed religion attempted to escape from human history, although it built on Judaism, as did Islam.[25]

Christianity had an aggressive, defined missionary impulse traceable to the gospel that recorded Jesus's declaration, "all authority in heaven and on earth has been given to me"; thus, "Go, therefore make disciples of all nations; baptize them in the name of the Father and of the Son and of the Holy Spirit."[26] The notion of an active effort to create a religious monopoly implied political control: in short, an expansionist empire of belief with strong universal ambitions. Castile, as a bearer of a culture formed around Christianity, envisioned such an empire in the New World.

When Christianity came in contact with Indo-Mexican religion, both belief systems were challenged by the experience.[27] A sudden assault on a people's cultural foundations, even if a replacement is offered, is traumatic. It is not clear that the Europeans understood the shock that stunned indigenous societies.[28] In the minds of the missionary friars, Indo-America represented the last of the world's isolated pagans—a reprise of the early days of Christianity as it sought to displace Roman polytheism.[29] It had a direct connection with the end of the earthly world and the arrival of the heavenly kingdom on earth as prophesied.

Religion is, by its nature, divisive—believers as opposed to nonbelievers. When reasonably articulated religions meet, particularly monotheistic ones with more or less settled orthodoxies, compromise is difficult. In contrast, polytheism's pantheon is, in essence, never complete. Each of the many gods represents aspects of the divine cosmos; consequently, each represents only a part of the whole of the human puzzle. Roman Catholicism did not totally reject polytheism, as the use of patron saints suggests, nor did it eliminate all aspects of ancient religions in its struggle to create a "universal commonwealth of believers."[30]

In spite of the evidence before the eyes of Christians, as well as the wonder, even admiration, they expressed on occasion, they framed the indigenous populations of the New World as organized but preferred to see them as uncivilized. The elements they selected to support that conclusion, all on the surface true, were savage religions, perpetual warfare, and an economy that depended heavily on plunder and tribute rather than mutual advantage. What their initial analysis missed was Indo-Mexico's progress, until they began to compare pre-Roman and Roman Hispania with Indo-America and concluded that the Western Hemisphere represented an isolated and, consequently, neglected portion of the world. In fact, two distinct civilizations had collided that were on the same path toward modernity but not at the same rate. Previously barbaric parts of Europe and Spain had taken similar steps toward civilization, and Iberia suffered through the Roman conquest of the tribes.[31]

Eurocentric interpretations of the encounter and the clash of cultures that followed set in place a simplistic paradigm of an advanced civilization descending on an exotic collection of territorial groupings still emerging by varying degrees from tribalism. Hernán Cortés (in his letters), his secretary Francisco López de Gómara, Gonzalo Fernández de Oviedo, Toribio de Benavente (commonly called Motolinía), Bernardino de Sahagún, Bartolomé de las Casas, and others mixed positive portrayal of the indigenous population with sufficient negatives to justify their own presence as well as to support the legitimacy of Spain's claims. The perceived need to bring the indigenes into the community of believers provided the sweeping rationale in which all else, both negatives and positives, had a supporting role. Clerical intellectuals following the pope's lead made the case that the Indo-American population was worthy of Christianization and the monarch's benevolent rule. In effect, their level of civilization could be tolerated.

Several contradictory subparadigms were in play: one that may be labeled that of the benevolent-intent legitimizers and the other that of settlers who viewed Indo-America as a frontier whose population and resources were there to be economically exploited in the interest of permanence and a viable economy. Of the two paradigms, the latter was more in tune with the Spanish experience. As Frederick Jackson Turner noted in his influential study referring to a different frontier in another time, a frontier is both an institution and a state of mind.[32] Of the two conflicting views, the settlers understood that different civilizations had come in contact and took advantage of the opportunities provided by their superior political situation. They left the question of Spain's legitimate claims for the schoolmen to debate and proceeded to reap the fruits of the new frontier.

European settlers focused on the obvious assets—land, minerals, and labor—with pro forma support for the religious transformation so important to the missionary friars and, politically, to the monarchy. The benevolent legitimizers placed the Indians culturally in a more favorable context, reaching a high point with Juan de Palafox y Mendoza's work the *Virtudes del Indio (De la naturaleza del Indio),* written in the early 1640s.[33] Palafox extolled their fidelity, obedience, patience, and intellectual abilities, among other positive attributes. Both paradigms, that of the settlers and that of favorable clerics, posited the existence of a moldable Indian, although the settlers relied on coercion to a far greater extent. The high level of tension between paradigms led to exaggerated rhetoric, alienation, and a barely averted revolt by those who depended on Indian labor.

Plunged into the future by the Europeans, Indo-Mexico failed to meet expectations. In addition, the circumstance surrounding the conquest, the decapitation of the Aztec Empire, left only a weakened Indian authority to defend, only marginally successfully, a civilization collectively discredited by defeat at its putative center.[34] As a practical consideration in spite of perceived differences, the philosophical gap between the two civilizations was not unbridgeable.[35] In a fashion similar to that of competing empires in Mexico, Castile had struggled to dominate a fractious Iberia.

As the sociocultural pioneer Sir Ernest B. Tylor asserted, humans appear to evolve along the same lines regardless of time and place, but to what extent and always in the same way?[36] Are human beings hardwired to evolve in a similar manner? Noam Chomsky posits the notion that development of languages is one such universally implanted impulse;[37] there may be many more, such as religion. As one identifies similarities, it is important to remember that pronouncing them similar is not identifying them as the same. Nevertheless, the gray area between similar and the same is where hybridization takes place.[38] The various elements of pre-Spanish Indo-Mexico had to be fitted with those of a Castile just emerging from the conclusion of the Reconquista with the fall of Granada in 1492. The fusion of cultures would not be easy. Hernán Cortés, as bound to his historical experience as the Mexica-Nahua to theirs, set the initial paradigm on the Indo-Spanish frontier. In reality, both sides were forced into innumerable compromises.

The religiously based cultures that came in contact in the early sixteenth-century Americas had been formulated over the centuries for much the same reasons and purposes. Although not synchronized chronologically, their sociopolitical and economic trajectories followed the same general path; in effect, they could talk to each other. Consequently, Indo-Mexico broadly understood the utility of European notions and adopted as well as adapted them as macrosolutions to some of the problems that it faced—a tacit collective response that explains the rapidity with which Indo-Mexico accepted key elements, but certainly not all Castilian innovations, in the immediate postcontact period.[39]

Spain had been well prepared to acquire a transatlantic empire. The focus on Spain's overland Reconquista and the natural tendency to contrast it to Portugal's maritime experience distorts the reality. Castile did not remain landlocked and, consequently, not a suitable candidate for a transatlantic empire. Sea routes and trade had long been a fixture of the Carthaginian, Roman, and later Byzantine empires, including their coastal settlements on the Iberian Peninsula.

Castile had become a maritime power to the extent that France and England competed to form a maritime alliance with the kingdom. The Treaty of Toledo (1368) decided the contest: the French supported Henry of Trastámara's claim to the Castilian throne in return for a military alliance. A combined Castilian-French fleet defeated the English at La Rochelle in 1372. Three years later, the English lost twenty-three ships to the Castilians. Castile's shallow-draft galley fleet raided the English coast with regularity. Large war galleys carried ten men at arms, thirty archers, and a crew of a hundred. They swiftly landed raiding parties and withdrew equally as fast with their plunder, leaving economic destruction behind. By 1389, the dynastic issues had been settled, and Castile ended raiding officially, although unemployed mariners likely made the transition to freelance piracy.[40]

The labor market for sailors was a Mediterranean and coastal North Atlantic one. Genoese, Castilian, Basque, and Galician sailors worked aboard any vessel in need of their services, including those of Portugal. Experience and maritime expertise was generalized.[41] Sailors in the ensuing century developed considerable experience with Atlantic currents and wind patterns, making the more-than-1,000-mile voyage to Guinea and the Canaries by going south-southwest.

Castile's transatlantic imperial role became feasible as the outcome of the Reconquista became clear and appeared irreversible. The discovery of a chain of islands far across the Atlantic, confusingly called the "Indies" and subsequently Indo-Mexico and Peru, did not mean that the focus on expansion along the North African littoral had been shelved or that Spain had redirected attention from the Mediterranean or its hostile engagement with Islam.[42] Although sufficient maritime strength made the New World empire viable both economically and politically, it should be kept in mind that Spain's survival depended on its political, military, and financial agility in the European theater, which, in turn, depended on its extractive relationship with its empire, as exemplified by the policies of Carlos V and Felipe II on into the succeeding centuries.[43] This reality reflected the amount of attention and resources devoted to the New World.

Empires are by their nature psychological and transcendental, encapsulating many different entities under the imperial banner. At the highest level, they require loyalty but not organizational uniformity. Carlos V's long list of active kingships, dukedoms, counts, and other political titles, along with a few that fell into the realm of romantic nostalgia, personified late medieval emperors. Emperor Carlos V functioned within a Christianized European world with well-defined religious competition to the east. Just when the pieces that made up Spain's worldview appeared set in place, the concept of the known world came cascading down as Indo-Mexico and, subsequently, Inca-Peru came into focus. As to be expected, an amazed Spain reacted by updating its notion of the world, revisiting the biblical prophesies, and contemplating the possibility that the apocalypse might be near. That a psychologically surprised Spain initially mismanaged its American empire in the early sixteenth century should not be surprising. That it recovered quickly is to its credit.

The search for imperial purpose by a medieval theocracy had to be framed in religious terms before more mundane consideration could be addressed. Spanish Catholicism had reached its zenith in 1492. Its religious world was perceived as a duality split between Christianity and Islam, with a few peripheral peoples in sub-Saharan Africa. As a fully elaborated system with a fixed perception of the world, Spanish Catholicism had limited flexibility. Understandably, reactionary rigidity approached orthodox intellectual tyranny until the Renaissance slowly but progressively softened Spanish Catholicism.

Suddenly, the perceived world expanded bewilderingly to encompass an untold number of organized and civilized peoples across the Atlantic. Since Spain was charged by the papacy to introduce Christianity in the new discoveries, in return for recognition of its territorial claim, efforts had to be made as soon as possible to uphold the Crown's obligations. Consequently, organized evangelization (introduction of Christian culture) began on a small scale in 1524 with the arrival of twelve (Christian symbolism) Franciscan friars, followed by an equal number of Dominicans in 1526. Meager reinforcements arrived in 1533 as seven Augustinian missionaries arrived. Collectively, such a small contingent could only make an inadequate contribution to the overwhelming task of conversion. The dispatching of missionaries constituted a political act by the Crown, useful to indicate that Spain took its religious obligations seriously and to keep Europeans as well as Indo-Mexicans off balance in the crucial early period of the conquest. It should be kept in mind that Carlos V had to deal with the Protestant Reformation, among other difficult and politically distracting issues, during the same time.

Just what the friars faced soon became evident. A dialogue in 1524 between Franciscan missionaries and an indigenous priest, perhaps organized by Cortés, not without bias, defended the validity of Indo-Mexican beliefs.[44] The Indian theologian laid out his view convincingly enough. His central points could have been understood immediately. The longevity of belief and the fact that it had been passed down over generations and, moreover, that it had preserved the people led to the question of why Indo-Mexicans should break an ancient compact with the gods. Just how many others held these views cannot be determined.[45] It seems likely that most Indo-Mexicans preferred not to risk an abrupt change when confronted by an ill-understood theology.

Collectively, the friars focused on the population in the central basin. Concentrating on the former Aztec Confederation made sense. What occurred in the central basin had an impact throughout Mesoamerica. The resort to mass baptism with virtually no instruction in the faith, which could be rationalized under frontier circumstances, did not result in practicing Christians but added to the religious confusion. Those who submitted to superficial baptism may have done so as a means of making protective contact with the intruders. Honoring the Virgin Mary or Jesus among their other gods accomplished the same objective: it added to the pantheon, and it did not overturn their belief structure.

Meanwhile, Cortés noted the eagerness of the population to identify with the new religion. In reality, he misinterpreted their willingness to recognize useful modifications and politically accept new gods associated with the conquerors. It is possible that a self-serving Cortés obliquely suggested that he could guide his charges. Meanwhile, on the basis of earlier divine predictions, Cortés could be seen as the new Quetzalcóatl with sufficient legitimacy to hold the Indo-Mexican empire together and extend it. Mexico was less a "spiritual conquest" than a tactical marketplace of self-selected and accepted possibilities. Indo-Mexico adapted to, rather than adopted, the Euro-Hispanic religious culture.

An unprepared, consequently confused population faced overwhelming uncertainty. The appearance of Europeans, the rapid overthrow of seemingly permanent empires, the discrediting of Indo-Mexico's religious explanations and with them society's legitimacy altered the Indo-Mexican reality, but with no immediate understanding of what would happen next, the future could not be imagined. The confusion inflicted by the conquest and its assault on an established religion cannot be overestimated.[46]

Drawing Indians into Christianity required an institutional replacement of the well-ordered indigenous priestly structure and its extremely full calendar of religious events. Although it is impossible to determine the percentage of the indigenous population that had been employed in the priesthood and how many others had peripheral religious roles, it is obvious that it must have numbered in the many thousands across Mesoamerica. The Spaniards could smash religious structures and idols, but Castile did not have sufficient resources to substitute a full-blown Christian clergy for the indigenous one. Instead, Spain destroyed the legitimacy of the indigenous clergy for political reasons well before it could be replaced. Consequently, the handful of friars functioned more like agents of the new regime than priests.[47] Franciscan Juan de Zumárraga received the nomination as the first Hispano-Indo-Mexican bishop in 1527 before the new political structure could be unfolded in its preliminary form. Episcopal authority at the time extended to a very small number of individuals; nevertheless, Bishop Zumárraga, fresh from witch-hunting among the Basques, set the initial tone of the Christianization effort in both its positive and negative aspects. Thirty-eight years after the fall of Tenochtitlán (1559), the number of missionaries totaled 801—though reinforced by the Creole sons of the early settlers, still an insignificant number.[48] That this represented a high point became evident as the Crown put in place a secular hierarchy and laid out parishes manned by secular priests well before it was warranted.

The Crown, reacting to Spain's dire fiscal problems, appeared to be more interested in Indo-Mexico's economic potential, in particular, silver mining. Consequently, commercialization of Indo-Mexico occurred with a rapidity approaching that associated with plunder. Five years after the fall of Tenochtitlán, a decree of 1526 established state ownership of all land and subsoil deposits. Taxes on an array of activities, including creation of monopolies, slave trading, and tribute extracted from Indians, provided a new revenue stream. At a certain point, the Crown lowered Indian tribute but in 1556 increased the rates. Exploitation of silver deposits appeared to be of more concern than the demographic disaster overtaking Indo-Mexico.

Epidemic diseases arrived with the intruders and mirrored the Eurasian experience. Disease in Indo-Mexico, as in Europe, drastically changed the sociodemographic equation in the New World and consequently played a crucial role in the development of a Mestizo nation: Indo-Mexico's population numbered in the millions at the time of contact with Europe, clearly the demographically dominant population. In the absence of disease, Spain would have been a colonial intruder regime at best, perhaps able to act as the political and cultural arbitrator over well-established populations with their own worldview but not able to do much more.[49] It did not happen. In central Mexico, the population fell from an estimated twenty-five million (at the time more than Spain and France combined) to one million over the first century of European contact. Indo-Mexico plunged into a demographical disaster accompanied by social disintegration. Social unraveling caused by mass deaths likely mirrored that of Europe when an unknown number of people reverted back to pre-Christian practices until the threat had passed. Social organization and behavior in Indo-Mexico, in general, deteriorated in the face of the conquest, uncertainty, and devastating disease.

Subsequently, Alonso de Zorita simplistically blamed social deterioration on the example set by many Spaniards for what appeared to be the self-destructive behavior of the Indians. He came closer to the truth when he quoted an informant who, when asked why his people had such bad habits, replied, "because you don't understand us, and we don't understand you and don't know what you want. You have deprived us of our good order and system of government."[50] The inability of the indigenous population to understand fully what had happened and why caused a collective psychological trauma, particularly in central Mexico. In less accessible regions, the population could hold on to many of its old beliefs and legitimacy much longer and slowly rationalize the disaster and work out an acceptable relationship with the new rulers.

Within the first half century of contact with Europe, pre-Cortésian Indo-Mexico had seemingly all but vanished, its culture not yet replaced by a Mestizo culture, although the trajectory had been set. Within a generation, a culture weighted toward the values and religious beliefs of Europe, but with significant carry forward of indigenous elements, emerged.[51] Colonial cities functioned as emerging Mestizo cultural centers surrounded by Indian towns and villages that sought with mixed success to retain their languages and the remnants of an indigenous culture. One should keep in mind that Mestizo is both a biological and a cultural term. Although the mixture of Indian and European resulted in a new racial category, one could be a cultural Mestizo by adopting elements of European culture (most importantly language) while retaining religious fragments, words, customs, and food from the indigenous side. Borrowing went both ways, although it was biased in favor of European elements, particularly in the cities.

Conflicting Prisms

The clash of empires engenders vivid notions of large armies locked in bloody death struggles; a single battle that decides the fate of both the victor and the defeated and determines the nature of the world they will live in is too simplistic a vision. Nevertheless, epic encounters such as the fall of Troy in ancient times and the medieval destruction of Tenochtitlán are forever imprinted on the historical imagination. Yet calamitous events are as much beginnings as endings. Empires are more than valiant soldiers, inspiring leaders, and grateful monarchs. Empires are constructed culturally as well as physically. Incorporation within an empire following a conquest requires time and the passage of several generations as well as the acceptance of the utility of the new modes of thought that accompany imperialism. The process is not immediate or easy, nor is it necessarily complete.

Indo-Mexico experienced a violent clash of cultures in the sixteenth century that made mutual understanding problematic at best. Just how much both sides actually comprehended cultural implications embedded in different languages and religions is difficult to determine with confidence. The disruption caused by the intruders after 1519 was massive; the attempts to erase Indo-Mexico's history almost succeeded. In reality, we are still struggling to unravel the sociointellectual processes that underpinned pre-Spanish Indo-Mexico's cultures in spite of impressive modern scholarship and new techniques. The why, not the how, is the problem.

The many pre-European codices destroyed by fearful Spanish clerics and others intent on eliminating what they viewed as satanic obstacles to conversion complicates historical reconstruction. One is shocked how quickly major elements of a long, complex history disappeared after the destruction of Tenochtitlán. The physical evidence crumbled and disappeared or lay abandoned, no longer protected by sacredness, awaiting the labor of modern archeologists to uncover buried fragments and anthropologists to tell us what we see.

The intangibles of history are harder to recover. Among the most valuable surviving sources are the descriptions of Indo-Mexico society, its beliefs and customs, gathered by European friars from native informants. Collectively, they allow for a workable view of Indo-Mexican civilizations but with important caveats; mainly, did they get it right? Recording oral speech in written form can be problematic, made even more so by its rendering in a different language in the Roman alphabet. The way knowledge is organized, put into categories, associated, and presented differs. Euro-Hispanic literacy allowed for manipulation of words and changes in their order and other adjustments necessary to engage in syllogistic reasoning. Written translations of oral presentations tend to make explicit what may have been implicit in speech or to miss it entirely.[52] Just as oral and written presentations are not the same, neither are literate and semiliterate cultures.[53]

Nevertheless, those who elaborate a mental framework, whether literate or not, select and create patterns that come together as a philosophical matrix that guides them as they expound their worldview. Consequently, European observers reported what they saw through their own cultural prism and placed Indo-Mexico in a familiar context.[54] Rome, the obvious comparison, subdued and introduced the Celts and Celt-Iberians to an advanced civilization and laid the foundations of Europe in general. Judaism and Islam had a more contemporary influence, both negative and positive, that underpinned the notion of Christian unity threatened by unbelievers. Spaniards retained a vivid perception of their progress from primitive times and did not hesitate to point out similarities with Indo-Mexican customs, including human sacrifice, the eating of human flesh, and other sinful proclivities, as did Gonzalo Fernández de Oviedo. In a similar blunt fashion, José de Acosta, in his *Historia natural y moral de las Indias* (1590), noted that before one judged the Indians harshly, a critic should acknowledge the same or similar things engaged in by the Greeks and Romans.[55] Understandably, Spanish schoolmen compared Indo-Mexican henotheism to Roman polytheism, which (more or less) had been overwhelmed by Christianity in the course of the centuries. In at least one colonial document, the *macuyltepanpixque* (a fiscal officer) was referred to as the equivalent of a Roman centurion (lower-ranking officer in charge of discipline); some reports refer to indigenous temples as mosques and Indians as "*alarabs.*"[56] Cortés, searching for a frame of reference, described the clothing of Indo-Mexico as *almaizales* (Moorish light veils), their colorful blankets as *alquiceles* (Moorish cloaks), and their temples as *mezquitas* (mosques).[57] Father Bartolomé de las Casas wrote somewhat later and with evident admiration, "One does not need witnesses from heaven . . . to demonstrate that these were political peoples with towns, large inhabited places, villas, cities and communities," a description that could have just as easily been applied to Roman Spain.[58]

The indigenous reality that existed at the time of the European contact must be separated in some fashion from the perceived reality. Did the Castilians fully comprehend what they saw? To them, Indo-Mexico appeared to be a mosaic of city-states along the lines of ancient Greece; in fact, it was a collection of tribal chieftaincies, of different language groups, each with a sense of uniqueness but with distinct elements of shared historical myths. Europeans' misinterpretation of what was before their eyes caused problems as they organized their new subjects by urban, not tribal, concentrations.[59] On the positive side, the interpretive use of the Greek model at the lower political levels resulted in the retention of Indian self-government overlaid by the model of imperial Rome at the vice-regal level.[60]

Did European interrogators ask the right questions, and did their interlocutors understand what they wanted to know? Native informants, usually drawn from the indigenous nobility, responded in ways that could be seen as devious or positive. That they understood what their interlocutors preferred to hear is clear, but we do not know the extent to which they accommodated them. Informants may have been tempted to be self-serving in the hope of regaining a degree of prestige. Indigenous historians, writing in the newly introduced phonetics, may have responded in a similar manner. Another possibility, a more positive explanation, is that the indigenous intellectuals who served as informants sought to construct a synthesis to make sense of their new reality. To what extent sixteenth-century Indo-Mexicans understood the nature of the Spanish monarchy is difficult to determine. It is likely some assumed that the king represented a deity who dwelled across the sea, perhaps like Quetzalcóatl. An invisible, distant focus of authority and power may have provided a psychological, if not physical, unity to override linguistic and tribal divisions.[61]

That the missionary friars sought to convey a Euro-Hispanic worldview to their potential converts seems obvious. The friars struggled to explain medieval European theological concepts to recent converts, whereas their confused followers continued to draw on the traditional indigenous meanings and consequently understood matters differently—a problem soon realized by the friars. The decision to avoid using what appeared to be equivalent indigenous gods or religious terms indicated an admirable degree of sophistication.

To what extent the Spaniards and the Indians could lay aside their distinct paradigms in order to comprehend each other remains in question. It would seem impossible to do so completely. If there is one possible exception, it is the impressive investigative work of Sahagún, written in Nahuatl in the newly introduced Roman script with the title in Spanish translation: *Historia general de las cosas de Nueva España*. He began his work around 1540 and completed it in 1569. He arrived in Mexico in 1529 and thus witnessed the progressive collapse of Indo-Mexican culture. The *Historia general* was not published in his lifetime and was lost for several centuries until 1777; it is an encyclopedic account of pre-Spanish Indo-Mexico. Sahagún used elderly informants, assisted by several of his former students, and checked facts as much as possible; in many respects, he functioned as a modern researcher, but not entirely. He naively accepted and recorded a description of a robbery involving an orderly group marching to music to the target, carrying the elbow of a woman who had died during her first childbirth, before departing the robbers sat down for a feast.[62] One would have expected the victim's husband to have been on guard.

A transcendental problem for both sides was fitting their respective histories together in some fashion. Indo-Mexico had little choice but to accept inclusion in Spain's history; Diego Durán in his *History of the Indians of New Spain*, one of the standard sources for pre-Spanish Mexico, demonstrated European self-absorption, noting that Moctezuma II came to power in 1503, the "same year that . . . the Spaniards conquered the island of Cuba, . . . the same year the great Turkish Sultan Selim was Crowned."[63] That the Castilian monarchy favored a simplified indigenous history that elevated European concerns and implied a rescuing mission followed a common response to justify imperialism.

The New-Old Frontier

As the conquering power, Castile viewed Mexico as an imperial appendage in an all-embracing and continuous Christian frontier war against unbelievers and as an extension of a similar campaign concluded in Spain in 1492.[64] Nevertheless, the monarchy understood that the Indo-Mexican frontier was different in ways both obvious and much less so. Cortés named his conquest "New Spain," indicating geological similarities as well as its political connection with old Spain. Religious notions placed Indo-Mexicans in revealed history as among the last pagans to be exposed to Christianity, a sign of the approaching final stage before the apocalypse. The imposition of European history validated by victory overrode an Indo-Mexican history delegitimized by defeat and subordination.

From an immediate political-psychological standpoint, Spain found it necessary to convey to its new subjects the trauma of its Christianized war against Islam and its rejection of Judaism, which had reached a high point just as the Western Hemisphere entered the known world. Reenactments of the missionary play *Moros y Cristianos,* introduced very early in the contact and still performed in our own time, were hugely popular then and are somewhat less so now.[65] In a performance in Tlaxcala, the friars, using Indian actors, re-created a wildly fanciful reenactment of the conquest of Jerusalem in AD 70. They included scenes depicting the punitive massacre of the Jews by the Roman commander Titus. The imaginative script placed the fall of Tenochtitlán and Jerusalem in the same category, suggesting God's punishment for grievous sins in both cases. Oddly, a Cortés character played a sultan in the extravaganza.[66] That the friars felt it necessary to slip Mexico into European history may be explained, at least in part, because both the physical and psychological struggle with the Muslims and the Jews remained an active one that had not played itself out, as the frequent updating of scripts of *Moros y Cristianos* suggests.[67]

A symbolic battle between Moors and Christians staged for an Indo-Mexican audience across the Atlantic drew a psychological line beyond which the friars dared not step but one they felt compelled to share. In a certain sense, *Moros y Cristianos* brought Indo-Mexico up to date on Spain's anguish. In a similar fashion, the unenforceable prohibition of New Christians (suspected crypto-Jews and Muslim converts) from immigrating to the New World symbolically introduced a social poison concocted in Spain.[68] The missionary friars sought to be included in the elaboration of a hybrid Indo-Spanish history: significantly, the trauma of Indo-Mexico remained unaddressed but real. How each side understood each other's anguish is not so obvious. Indo-Mexicans could not openly draw obvious parallels between their defeat and destruction and that visited on Spain, which they now supposedly lamented. The hostility directed by the friars toward Islam and Judaism formed defensive elements of Spanish Catholicism in its new setting. On a deeper level, as Américo Castro posits, Christian Spain understood, but could not face, the extent to which it had been Islamized or deal with the bitter fruit of the division between Old and New Christians that perversely preserved Sephardic and Muslim remnants.[69]

Spain, almost at the moment it made contact with the Western Hemisphere, seemingly would have had little energy or time to devote to its developing empire. The aftermath of the fall of Constantinople in 1453 shocked the Christian world and seemingly threatened its existence. The high point, the fall of Granada in 1492 (not the Antilles), immediately dashed by the Moorish revolts of 1493 and 1497 and, subsequently, the Comunero revolt of 1520–1521, disappointed the monarchy. Moreover, European unity appeared threatened by the Protestant Reformation. The ongoing tension caused by the decision to impose religious uniformity as a precondition for political unity led to disruptive policy choices that negatively impacted the economy and social stability. Carlos V's expensive political ambitions required more money than the economy could generate. Meanwhile, the Ottoman offensive threatened to turn the Mediterranean into a Muslim lake. Unrest and eventually revolt (1567) in the Netherlands plunged the monarchy into more debt. The victory over the Ottoman fleet at the Battle of Lepanto in 1571 put an end to the invasion threat but did little to alter the dismal downward trajectory. Spain's understandable preoccupation with American gold and silver must be placed in the context of its desperate fiscal situation and massive bankruptcies.

Constructing a Usable Past

Modern scholars are uneasy reading back in time too broadly; nevertheless, they provide likely possibilities, but in the end, they must speculate prudently and venture an interpretation. The paucity of pre-European records, particularly thoughtful exegeses by those who elaborated their worldview in isolation from the wider world, understandably results in high levels of speculation and uncertainty.[70] It is important to understand as much as possible Mexico's pre-European experience and what the Hispanicization of Indo-Mexico meant, as well as to understand the historical process of Romanization and Islamization of Spain long before the New World entered the imagination. For Indo-Mexico, we rely on the work of archeologists, art historians, and ethnohistorians, including many of the early friars, and generations of historians to reconstruct with some precision the culture encountered by the Europeans in the early sixteenth century. For the European side of Mestizo culture, a wealth of scholarship exists that enables historians to reconstruct much, but not all, of Euro-Spain's philosophical trajectory.

In recent times, the insights of a generation of historical sociologists have added useful theory that helps to clarify and narrow possibilities. How one understands history is not fixed or impervious to continuing influences and new concepts. Intellectual interaction with continuing scholarship results in constant shifting of historical composites, although with many recognizable "facts" that seem to pass through various versions untouched.[71] The historian must put it all together in some fashion—not a simple task. The Mexican intellectual Edmundo O'Gorman, in his imaginative work the *Invention of America,* suggests the process of fleshing out intellectual concepts and, with luck, avoiding "metaphysical wrestling."[72]

The present work sets out Indo-Mexico's evolution alongside that of Euro-Spain, so that their amalgamation in the Mexican setting can be better understood. In a macro sense, Hispano-Indo-Mexico became an heir to a lengthy historical process including early Iberian tribalism,

Rome, the Visigoths, Spanish Islam, Judaism, and Western civilization, in general. In a micro sense, cultural resistance guaranteed that Indo-Mexico did not disappear, although it submerged, at least temporarily.[73] What transferred from Europe and what did not are equally as important to our understanding. A receiving civilization has the final say regardless of external pressure or force. It selects, absorbs, and preserves or rejects often based on unarticulated needs, although a dependency's rejection has to be done prudently. Mexico's version of Catholic Christianity is perhaps the most obvious example of acceptance mixed with rejection.

Both Indo-Mexico and Spain evolved in a similar fashion, but their trajectories were many centuries apart until 1519—an indication that empires and human civilizations encounter similar opportunities and obstacles and find similar solutions for their times. In that respect, Noam Chomsky may have underestimated the extent that humans are hardwired.

Modern Mexicans largely are orphaned from their indigenous parental past and are perhaps inescapably the adopted children of western European history.[74] The upward trend in the number of Mestizos of both categories (cultural and biological) indicates the rate of acculturation in colonial New Spain. Mexico proceeded on an accelerated path to becoming an integral part of the western European world, albeit with some exotic features. Modern Mexicans are Mestizo by default or biology.

That the simple biological division between Spaniards and Indians did not last could not have been a surprise. The conquistadores received women as gifts and likely took what they favored. In New Spain, Mestizos were incorporated into the small European community still involved in the last stages of the conquest when every man counted. It seems evident that many assumed that Mestizos represented an initial frontier phenomenon that would soon fade. By the 1540s, Mestizos had become a separate racial-cultural group, rather than just a few incidental offspring of Indians and Spaniards. Indian villages that were able to tolerate a few Mestizos raised in their culture could not accept the growing number. Vice-regal authorities with only weak control in rural areas attributed disorders in the countryside to these outsiders. Alleged negative traits ascribed to Mestizos limited their opportunities, although social barriers became more difficult to sustain as their numbers increased.[75] In 1536 and 1563, the Crown, urged by missionaries, prohibited Mestizos and vagrants from living in Indian villages. Finally, in 1600, all outsiders were barred from living in indigenous villages with the sole exception of Mestizos raised by their Indian mothers. Social rejection by both Indians and Europeans made Mestizos rootless and encouraged them to seek livelihoods in the cities or to exploit hapless villagers. By the turn of the century, impoverished and socially detached individuals of all races functioned as cultural Mestizos.

Mestizos became associated with street loungers, con men, and petty thieves. Marginal city dwellers were lumped together as *leperos* (social lepers), a category that inadvertently acknowledged Mestizo acculturation at the lower social level. Eventually, out of necessity, Mestizos were made somewhat socially acceptable by stressing that their good traits came from their European blood and their failings were indigenous.[76] Even when it became evident that bicultural knowledge and skills were useful, Mestizos could not shake the stereotype that endured through the seventeenth century—until it became impossible to maintain. If one could pass as a Creole, it made sense to do so. Race and class claims in New Spain, as befitting a frontier, were what one could get away with under the circumstances. Frontiers allow for social flexibility. A reasonable command of Latin made one into a *letrado* (a learned individual) or perhaps a priest. Artisan guilds might restrict obvious Mestizos to journeymen status, but racial origins often could not be determined. With increasing numbers, Mestizos became a defined group, socially the most dynamic. Indian culture was in retreat; consequently, it made little sense to identify with indigenous culture. Indians moving into cities who claimed Mestizo status avoided paying tribute or participating in labor drafts, representing a step toward the privileges that fell to Spaniards. Mestizos made up the racial and cultural center, able to draw on both Indian and European notions as well as to absorb those who sought to escape from indigenous restrictions and tribute. The growth of the Mestizo population was an indicator of the spread of a modified culture.

The gap between Creoles (those born in Mexico who claimed European blood) and Mestizos closed as urban demographics and self-identifications changed the game. Mestizos tended to drop social markers and to assume those of the perceived higher-status Creoles. By the eighteenth century, the Mestizos were the fastest growing segment of the population. Just how many had moved on to claim Creole status is unknown. In the eighteenth century, demand for Creole status prompted a revenue-starved monarchy to sell certificates of whiteness (*cédulas de gracia al sacar*). Just how much social impact such a certificate had is difficult to judge, but when combined with wealth, it likely did not matter.[77] The degree of acceptance of Mestizo culture varied by class, not race. Eventually, few Mestizos could function effectively apart from the cultural reality; if they chose to do so, they remained foreigners. Europeans immigrants and their children had little choice but to adopt Mexico's hybrid creation if they wanted to be Mexicans.

This study is an interpretive one that examines the history of pre-Columbian Indo-Mexico as well as the historical background of Spain and the hybridization that took place after the fall of Tenochtitlán in 1521. The various components of this study should be approached not as a segmented history but rather as a continuum that places Indo-Mexico, Europe, and Spain on the same road to modernity, but not, of course, in sync. One can identify the historical similarities that, in the sixteenth century for Indo-Mexico, represented a medieval present and, for Europe as it entered the Renaissance and confronted the Protestant Reformation, represented the immediate past. A Mestizo culture emerged as an uneven composite of both articulated and unarticulated Euro-Spanish culture anchored in the pre-1492 European experience mixed with Indo-Mexican cultural survivals detached from their philosophical foundations—a medieval mentality lightly touched by the early Renaissance that reached Indo-Mexico in 1519. Imperial Spain succeeded in jolting Indo-Mexico into the universal sixteenth century, albeit in traumatic fashion.

Chapter 1 deals with the emergence of a historical people in Mesoamerica as they moved through various stages from small groups to tribes to settled chieftaincies. It examines their historical similarities and differences in order to understand how, why, when, and where they evolved—a process guided by explanatory religious systems that created distinct Indo-Mexican civilizations.

Chapter 2 examines the formulation of Euro-Spanish culture, whose roots are deep in the past, tempered politically, economically, and culturally by Rome; shaken by the collapse of polytheism; and remolded by Christianity. Chapter 3 examines the impact of the Muslim conquest from 711 that almost extinguished Christian Spain. Weak Visigoth remnants clung to survival on the wrong side of the natural defensive barrier of the northern mountains, with little prospect of sustained help from their coreligionists. After more than 700 years, Islam left a deep cultural imprint. Spanish religiosity resulted from the unique circumstance that no other region of the Christian West faced: physically and psychologically cut off from Europe by the Pyrenees and confronted by an enemy that expanded from an established center in the Muslim East. The traumatic experience reached a political but not a culture conclusion in 1492. The long campaign to drive the Moors out of the Iberian Peninsula molded the Spanish character on the very eve of Castile's arrival in the Western Hemisphere.[78] Stubborn tenacity and suspicious intolerance grew out of a struggle inevitably cast in a religious context.

Chapter 4 traces the formation of a Euro-Indo-Mexico—a process distorted by the terrible mortality extracted by epidemic diseases and the deurbanization of the indigenous population that followed. As authority slipped from indigenous hands, the rallying of Indo-Mexico became impossible. Imperialism, among the various ways, both positive and negative, in which it changes and modifies the people it engulfs, imposes its own unique history on its victims. In the case of Indo-Mexico, what happened in Europe over a millennium before Cortés destroyed Tenochtitlán in 1521 played a crucial role in the remolding of indigenous Mexico. By putting in place a Christian paradigm, Spain redirected radically Indo-Mexico's historical trajectory. The process as it unfolded across the Atlantic required Spain to make some adjustments to its worldview also, but it did so from a position of assumed cultural superiority. Castile severed Teotihuacán and Tollan (Tula) from Indo-Mexico's active historical memory after 1521, to be replaced, in part, by Greece, Rome, Constantinople, and Jerusalem. Destruction, replacement, and amalgamation created Mestizo Mexico.

1

Mesoamerican Civilizations
The Evolution of Mesoamerica

INDO-MEXICO PROVIDED the canvas on which imperial Spain superimposed its historical experience. Consequently, in order to understand the process of the creation of a hybrid Mestizo culture, one must begin with an examination of the important elements of pre-Columbian Mexico that existed prior to the European intrusion. All organized human existence appears to follow a similar path from small groups huddled in caves or under rock formations to more complex conglomerations over time. Early groups were migratory in both Europe and Indo-America. Humans likely began as gatherers before becoming hunters as well as gatherers, followed by settled agriculture and interaction, hostile or otherwise, with others. The elaboration of religion is the key element that makes civilized progress possible. Seeking to explain and control one's environment is the first step in the elaboration of culture in a collective sense. The intent of spiritual practices in a universe created by gods is the same in spite of the different forms those practices take among others. No human group is unique; consequently, we should not be surprised that the path toward civilization is similar and, on occasion, virtually the same. The encounter in 1519 was not one of Martians with Earthlings, in spite of the initial shock and confusion.

The roots of early Mesoamerican civilizations are lost in prehistory and can only be partially and painstakingly uncovered by archeologists. Their discoveries tend to indicate that early humans were not as primitive as modern society prefers to imagine. Nevertheless, in the absence of recorded histories, one can only speculate broadly. The origin of these early migrants to the Americas is the subject of debate. Many specialists believe that the Western Hemisphere's early populations crossed a Bering Sea land bridge from Asia, perhaps following migrating herds. Others suggest that there was more than one migration route, including those who argue that Polynesian navigators from the Asia Pacific region, perhaps observing migratory birds, reached the coast of what is now South America.[1] Just how long ago such a population movement occurred is another unresolved question. Most geneticists and archeologists agree that Native Americans are descended from Siberians who crossed into America 26,000 to 18,000 years ago via a land bridge over the Bering Strait. But although genetic analysis of modern Native Americans lends support to this idea, strong fossil evidence has been lacking. Now a nearly complete skeleton of a prehistoric teenage girl, with an intact cranium and preserved DNA, newly discovered in an underwater cave in the Yucatán Peninsula, establishes a clear link between the ancient and modern people. Writing in the journal *Science,* the researchers report that they analyzed mitochondrial-DNA genetic material passed down through the mother that was extracted from the skeleton's wisdom tooth by divers. Their analysis reveals that the girl, who lived at least 12,000 years ago, belonged to an Asian-derived genetic lineage seen only in Native Americans.[2] Older sites with evidence of human habitation, which point to a much longer time frame for the presence of humans in Meso- and South America, are being excavated by teams of archeologists and other specialists. At the same time, material from sites excavated in the twentieth century is being reevaluated to determine if new and previous claims of habitation ranging from 25,000 to 50,000 years ago can be substantiated.[3] If the northern land bridge served as the principal population conduit, experts in migration studies estimate that it would have required some 18,000 years to spread the population throughout the Americas as successive waves of migrants crossed into the Western Hemisphere. Similarly, linguistic evidence from the Americas suggests that the older dates are credible; some 140 different languages and 1,200 dialects are spoken, more than anywhere else in the world.[4] If these experts are correct, the Yucatan excavations indicate that migrations into the Western Hemisphere began some 40,000 years ago. Although the debate remains unresolved, new dating techniques and comparative analysis is broadening our under-standing of the peopling of North and South America.[5]

Skeletal remains indicate that these hunters and gathers were well nourished, tall, and generally healthy. Given a plentiful supply of game, they must have enjoyed leisure time, a prerequisite for the development of civilizations. Indigenous peoples of Mexico began to breed maize plants selectively around 8000 BC. In 7200 BC, climate change resulted in drier conditions that, coupled with population increases, set the stage for the development of fixed agriculture and pottery. The transition from hunting and gathering supplemented by root agriculture to settled agricultural villages with the ability to support artisanal pro-duction took some time.[6] Evidence shows a marked increase in pot-tery working by 2300 BC and the beginning of intensive maize farming between 1800 BC and 1500 BC.

Between 1800 BC and 300 BC, complex cultures began to form. Many matured into advanced pre-Columbian Mesoamerican civilizations such as the Olmec, Zapotec, Maya, Izapa, Teotihuacán, Mixtec, Huastec, Purepecha, Totonac, Tarascan, Toltec, and Mexica (also called Aztec), which flourished for nearly 4,000 years before the first contact with Europeans. According to postconquest accounts gathered from native informants by the Franciscan friar Bernardino de Sahagún, three foun-dational civilizations preceded that of the Mexica-Aztecs who domi-nated central Mexico when the Spaniards arrived in the Western Hemi-sphere. The three dominant civilizations were the Tamoanchán, perhaps the Gulf Coast Olmec, followed by Teotihuacán and the Toltec: a trans-mission chain of civilized complexity from the Olmecs to the ultimate beneficiary—the Aztec and other contemporary groups.[7] We know the cultural development of present-day Mexico was far more complex.

The Olmecs were an ancient pre-Columbian people living in the tropical lowlands of south-central Mexico, roughly in what are the modern-day states of Veracruz and Tabasco on the Isthmus of Tehu-antepec. Their immediate cultural influence, however, extended far be-yond this region as a result of trade and conquest. The Olmecs flour-ished during the Formative (or Preclassic) Period, dating from 1600 BC to about 400 BC. Olmec peoples continued to inhabit the region, how-ever, until 100 BC. This Olmec culture is currently considered the pro-totype civilization of Mesoamerica. The Olmecs may have been the first Mesoamericans to build ceremonial centers. Three ceremonial sites dominated Olmec culture during various periods: San Lorenzo (1600–900 BC), La Venta (900–600 BC), and Tres Zapotes (500–100 BC). These centers originally had only a few permanent residents, including priests and rulers and their staffs. Most of the population continued to live in disbursed settlements and came to these protocities to participate in religious ceremonies, public works projects, trade, and public events. Gradually, ceremonial centers evolved into cities with temples, elite housing, large plazas, housing blocks to accommodate other urban residents, and markets and artisan production sites.

Discoveries in the early twenty-first century, though, have persuaded experts that the Olmecs were the originators of some of the most important aspects of Mesoamerican civilization. Olmec artifacts provide the first evidence of many of the Mesoamerican religious themes and architectural, social, and political structures central to later civilizations. What we know about the Olmec political and social system is based on archeological remains and informed conjecture. That they were a politically organized chieftaincy seems clear: only a highly organized group could have built cities and produced the large stone sculptures that distinguish them; the stones had to be transported from sixty miles away by hand, perhaps utilizing rafts to reach their destination. From very recent evidence, it seems possible that Mesoamerican ball games, calendars, mathematics, astronomy, and even written script had their origins in Olmec times.[8]

Other regions of southern Mexico, including Oaxaca in southeastern Mexico and the Yucatan Peninsula, developed in a similar trajectory during the Formative Period. In contrast to the Olmec culture, however, in the Classic Period (1200 BC–AD 100), militarism and belligerent domination of distant groups became a central feature of Mesoamerican political dynamics. By the early Classic Period, around 200 BC, the Zapotecs, who inhabited the highland valleys of Oaxaca, attained military and political control of the region. They established their capital at Monte Albán, which dominated the area from 250 BC to AD 700. The city developed extensive trade and cultural relationships with the Olmecs, the Mayans, and the city of Teotihuacán in the Valley of Mexico. Whereas Olmec writing has been verified by symbols found in 2002 and 2006, dating from 650 BC and 900 BC, respectively, Zapotec writing dates from about 400 BC. The earliest known writing in the Mayan script dates from about 250 BC, but the script is thought to have developed at an earlier date.[9] Other Mesoamerican cultures began to demonstrate significant advances and borrowings from other cultures,[10] although debate continues about the role of the Olmecs, Zapotecs, and Mayans in the development of the concept of the zero and the calendar. Three calendars utilizing an overlapping system were important elements of a number of Mesoamerican cultures by AD 100: the *Long Count,* a chronological system that began on a specific date in the distant past, which probably commemorated some important actual or mystical event; a 360-day calendar divided into eighteen periods of twenty days with five days added at the end of the year to align it to the solar year; and a 260-day ritual calendar divided into twenty periods of thirteen days. These are but two examples of the intellectual vibrancy that typified Mesoamerican societies.[11]

The remarkable city of Teotihuacán in central Mexico (ca. 100 BC–AD 750) became the largest city in the Americas during the Classic Period, with an estimated population of 120,000 to 200,000 spread over eight square miles. It was a thriving center of religion and culture, as well as manufacturing, trade, and commerce. The city eventually controlled the trade routes in Mesoamerica. Impressive civil and religious structures dominated the city; their remains continue to awe modern visitors. The priest-rulers who governed the city also carried out grand religious pageants and ceremonies that often involved human sacrifices. Two pyramids dedicated to the sun and the moon, some 200 feet high and covered with frescos, were placed on the wide street of the dead that cut through the city, complemented by another broad east-west thoroughfare, which provided the urban axis. Residents lived in apartment-like structures; the city must have resembled a human anthill. The economy, built on trade and a tribute system, attracted merchants, craft workers, porters, and religious pilgrims. Goods produced in Teotihuacán made their way to virtually every corner of Mesoamerica and perhaps beyond. As was characteristic of Mesoamerican religion, a pantheon of gods was venerated. The cult of Quetzalcóatl (plumed serpent) appears to have reached its distinct form in the city. Although Teotihuacán's influence waned over time and the city was abandoned, its religious and secular accomplishments continued to influence subsequent Mesoamerican development.[12]

The successor group, the Toltecs, arrived in the central valley in the ninth century AD, conquered the Otomies of Culhuacán, and subsequently established the Toltec city of Tollan (Tula) in 698. The Toltecs adopted important elements of Teotihuacán's civilization, including the cult of Quetzalcóatl, while adding aspects of their own. The Toltecs were a militarized chieftaincy, as evidenced by the architecture of Tula's Temple of the Warriors. Military orders such as those of the Coyotes, the Eagles, and the Jaguar knights provided the professional core of Toltec armies. Their conquest empire extended across a large swath of Mesoamerica, including south to Oaxaca, a colony in Mayan territory at Chichén Itzá, and a northern ring of settlements to protect the central valley from barbarians (*Chichimecas*) moving southward from the arid north. Toltec traders traveled into what is now the American Southwest for turquoise and into Central America for quetzal feathers.[13]

Somewhere along the way, the cult of Quetzalcóatl was transformed into a moral death struggle personified by the plumed serpent as virtue and with evil in the form of Tezcatlipoca, the feared smoking mirror, who supported human sacrifice and warfare. According to one of several myths, Quetzalcóatl was seduced at the instigation of Tezcatlipoca, resulting in a gross violation of his priestly status. A disgraced Quetzalcóatl left Tula and traveled to the Gulf Coast, where he sailed away on a serpent raft, vowing to return and destroy his enemies. Another version is that he set himself on fire. The notion of an avenging return appears to have had the most currency. The myth has aspects of expulsion similar to that of Adam and Eve, as well as a threatened apocalyptic ending.[14]

The Toltec empire experienced the same fate as Teotihuacán before it. Drought in the north propelled desperate waves of Chichimecas against the city of Tula, relentlessly crippling its economy, physically demolishing its grandeur, and forcing the survivors to become refugees. The last paramount Toltec chief, Huémac, abandoned the city, moving deep into the Valley of Mexico, where he committed suicide. Toltec remnants gradually mixed with other groups and exited history. Violence once again had served to disperse cultural fragments widely across Mesoamerica.[15]

An idealized characterization of the Toltecs emerged that presented them as a people who excelled in the arts and fine crafts, as well as in commerce, architecture, and agricultural sciences. Indo-Mexicans had a valid claim to being their heirs. For the Aztecs, the Toltec mantle served as a means of legitimizing their imperial ambitions. In the great

Templo Mayor, the Mexica kept objects, some 7,000 gifts offered to the gods, including many from tributaries. Of more significance were masks from Teotihuacán and the Olmecs who preceded the Toltecs, but not one item from the Mayans or the Tarascans. The Mexica used the sacred compound to integrate an imagined past and into a religiopolitical imperial culture.[16]

The Mexica Road to Empire

The progression of the seminomadic Mexica from a difficult existence in the arid north to central Mexico represented a pattern previously followed by many others. The great basin of central Mexico, which today includes the Federal District, the Mexican states of Mexico, Morelos, Hidalgo, Puebla, and Tlaxcala, is an area of 2,500 square miles, bounded by low hills in the north and high mountains to the east, west, and south. Most of it is at an elevation of over 7,000 feet with a corresponding temperate climate. Reasonably well-watered valleys with alluvial soils subdivide the central region. It functioned as one of the world's cradles of civilizations along the lines of the lower Tigris-Euphrates river valley.

How long ago the Mexica started their journey and from where and why is a mystery. We know that Nahuatl is a Uto-Aztecan language related to indigenous groups in what is now the American Southwest. The Mexica claimed to have originated in a place called Aztlán. Did their mythical Aztlán actually exist, or did its invention become necessary to anchor a fabricated history?[17] It is fairly safe to speculate that chronic hunger, drought, and famine provided the motivation to migrate from what archeologists have designated as "arid America" to an adjacent region with small but well-watered spots referred to as "oasis America." Survival in most of arid America, with the exception of the higher elevations of mountain ranges and the scattered oasis locations, depended on gathering, hunting, or fishing more than on agriculture. Those who inhabited the semidesert high plateaus collected mesquite seeds, pine nuts, acorns, and other useful seeds, as well as cacti pads and fruit, and used the multipurpose agave to produce clothing, pulque, and mescal. The occasional deer, small rodents, rabbits, and grasshoppers provided some variety. Hunting and gathering bands need between one and four square miles to support one individual; in the arid north, it might require even more; consequently, they formed small bands rather than tribes.[18] That so much is unknown suggests that the Mexica's physical and cultural journey required innumerable generations and many stops along the way. As they moved out of arid America into a more favored region able to support larger groups, they evolved into a tribe. They likely had become a semiagricultural people before they arrived in the Valley of Mexico.[19] They may have also settled for a considerable time on the outer fringes of the central valleys. As the Mexica came in contact with others, they adopted new gods to add to their pantheon and established some important links with past civilizations. They incorporated other groups into their tribal structure as they moved southward and resources became much more abundant. At a certain point, probably before they arrived in the central valley, the tribal leadership evolved into a chieftaincy: institutionally on the same political level as others in the Valley of Mexico. This organizational level made it possible to negotiate with similarly led groups, while still maintaining a separate identity. By now the Mexica were not Chichimecas but *Tamime:* a designation for tribes that hovered between a nomadic existence and settled agriculture but recognized as moving toward civilization.[20]

Where cities are founded depends on topography, a reality that results in their political and economic importance.[21] The manner in which cities are constructed and then reconstructed, organized, reorganized, and controlled reflects a succession of cultural influences. Tribal groups must establish a physical focal point, be it a sacred mountain, a well-watered valley, or an advantageous place on a river. Necessary functions—religious, political, social, and economic ones—must be brought together in one spot to be effective; as clans develop into tribes, they may be joined by other clans, perhaps attracted by power, wealth, or both, to form a larger demographic amalgamation ruled by a chieftainship. To mark a city's connection with the gods, a divine myth is employed—an eagle perched on a cactus in the case of Tenochtitlán or, in Europe, Rome's wolf nursing two human twins. The notion of founding twins also appears in the *Popol Vuh* of the Quiché Maya.[22]

A city-based chieftaincy would be stronger than its rural counterpart because of its concentrated population and a diversity of interconnected activities that form a unifying social and economic network. Militarily, it would be less vulnerable than a tribe spread across a thinly populated countryside. Managing larger populations with diverse functions required a directive political organization: a paramount chief. Initially, in warrior societies, the paramount chief was elected in some fashion; probably the obvious candidate was chosen by popular consent. He surrounded himself with family members and lesser chiefs and their dependencies, as well as warrior clients, creating a political foundation that could be extended beyond one population center. Powerful chieftaincies established a level of dominance over other such entities sufficient to demand tribute and cooperation or to form alliances.[23] Shared cultural elements across a wide swath of Mesoamerica facilitated interaction and amalgamation under dominant chieftaincies. Nevertheless, it remained an unstable arrangement that depended on the leadership's military success. Control over others, rather than displacement and seizure of land, laid the foundation of Indo-Mexican empires.

In the Valley of Mexico, an assortment of chieftaincies vied for dominance. The limited amount of arable land bounded by mountains in all directions made for geopolitical tension and war.[24] Xaltocan, at the northern end, confronted Texcoco, on the eastern shore of the lake system. Azcapotzalco in the west and Culhuacán in the southern part completed an uneasy geopolitical arrangement but one that attracted newcomers willing to be subordinate mercenaries. The Tepanecas, a Nahuatl-speaking group that preceded the Mexica, entered the valley in the late twelfth century. When the Mexica arrived (ca. 1253) in central Mexico, they shared the same language and worldview as the Tepanecas. They became tributaries in the service of Azcapotzalco: one of the cities of the Tepaneca empire. The Mexica settled on the lakeshore at Chapultepec. The Tepaneca empire reached its zenith under its paramount chief, Tezozomoc (d. 1426), dominating the central Valley of Mexico and spilling over into parts of the Toluca and Morelos valleys. The Valley of Mexico was a Nahuatl-language region with the exception of the Otomí, a relatively recent arrival from the north. Although different tribes occupied the valley, each with a strong sense of its history and separateness, language provided the interconnecting cultural links.

For the Mexica, surviving the shifting geopolitics of the Valley of Mexico would not be easy. The Mexica in the service of Azcapotzalco were defeated by Culhuacán and subjected to a quarter century of abject domination. The god Huitzilopochtli, a fabricated protector of the

Mexica, provided guidance as they sought to escape from the Culhua. The Tarascans, who prized the hummingbird's sacred feathers, may have inspired the creation of Huitzilopochtli. The Mexica transformed the divine bird into their war god, Huitzilopochtli, meaning "hummingbird on the left," to guide their imperial ambition. Although theologians linked Huitzilopochtli with other gods, the myth that he had killed his mother provided a symbolic break that signified his attachment to one people and a workable separation from traditional deities.[25]

The mythology surrounding Huitzilopochtli served to free the Mexica from political subordination to the Culhua. An account explaining the motivation for founding Tenochtitlán begins with the total rejection of Culhuacán through an unmistakable act of disrespect ordered by Huitzilopochtli. After the Mexica obtained one of the daughters of the ruler of Culhuacán to confirm their blood ties, they sacrificed and skinned her. A priest danced around, draped in her skin, in front of the outraged father.[26] It was a reckless act, suggesting that some factions may have been unsure of the wisdom of alienating the Culhua. Whatever the veracity of the account, the rejection of the relationship of the two cultures and the Culhua chief's anger made the departure of the Mexica prudent. For protection, they fled to an island in the lake, likely surviving marginally but over time creating their own tribute empire—eventually with sufficient resources to found Tenochtitlán in 1325, destined to become the geopolitical heart of what subsequently became the Aztec empire and the modern capital of the Mexican Republic.

An Imperial Capital

The city of Tenochtitlán lay at the heart of an urban-rural community based on real or perceived ethnic affinity of long standing. An ethnically based political entity, the *altepetl* consequently had both a territorial and a cultural aspect. Tenochtitlán grew into an imperial capital physically covering approximately ten square miles crisscrossed by a grid of wide streets and canals and tied to the lakeshore by three causeways. Tenochtitlán was one of the world's largest cities, with a population of 150,000 and perhaps as high as 200,000. As a consequence of the power and wealth gathered in one location, subordinate groups migrated to the center, challenging the tribal-specific foundations of the system. The difficulty of incorporating migrants into a still tribal-clan-based community led to their segregation in special districts. They may have had certain occupational tasks that set them apart from the main tribal group. Their economic contribution might be recognized, but that would not result in full inclusion within the dominant tribe.[27] Nevertheless the city's population provided a ready pool of warriors for expansion of the Mexica's tribute empire.

The city divided into four urban quarters, the *nauhcampa*, meaning the four directions of the wind, marked by broad streets that separated the four quarters, meeting at the exact center in front of the sacred compound. Narrow strips of cultivated land ran between the various units. A large civic-religious district located at the exact center axis of the city contained the palace and a multitude of temples that surrounded a massive pyramid, the Templo Mayor. The first pyramid was constructed in 1325 with the founding of the city and subsequently enlarged over the years to a height of forty-five meters, requiring over a hundred steps to reach the top, with its the two temples, one dedicated to Huitzilopochtli (the patron of the Mexica and the god of war) and the other to the rain god Tlaloc.[28] Houses of the nobility, sometimes two stories high, were located in the city center behind the sacred compound. The dwellings of the common people were one story, less grand, and well removed from the center of divine and secular administration of an impressive city.[29]

Each of the separate administrative bodies was further subdivided into *calpullis* (districts) that duplicated the same layout on a lesser scale in what has been described as a neighborhood community center, with all that implies.[30] The sociopolitical model borrowed from Azcapotzalco, after the Mexica succeeded in overthrowing it, was likely the standard in most of Indo-Mexico. Each of the calpulli functioned more or less independently, subject to the overarching needs of the chieftaincy. At the bottom of the administrative structure, the *calpulltecs* administered the districts (calpulli) of the capital. Just how many districts is not clear, and the territorial size appears to have varied. At least six calpulli consisted of descendants of the original Mexica; the *pochteca* (merchants) had seven, and the *amanteca* (fine crafts workers or artisans) had one, although subdivided by craft specialty, whereas the rest consisted of different groups that had been attracted by imperial power and prosperity.[31] The calpulli maintained a census of communal land with the name glyph of the cultivators used by the calpulltec for tax purposes as well as for labor drafts for public projects.[32] The office of calpulltec had tribal origins; in theory, he was elected from among the elders, although a noble could also occupy the position. Over time, a family came to occupy the office and likely attained noble status. The calpulltec assigned land held in common to heads of households. In the case of the pochteca, land distributions would not have been an issue; if they possessed land, it would have been worked by resident *mayeques*.

Under normal conditions, calpulli officials governed, disciplined, and kept track of their charges.[33] Punishment appears to have been reasonable and measured, although disrespect of authority was not tolerated and merited a harsh response. Everyday social violations might well result in temporary slavery as a means of community compensation. Habitual consumption of *pulque* (alcohol) appears to have been discouraged, although the elderly were permitted to indulge. Under certain circumstances, public alcoholics might have their head bashed in, a task that likely fell to the calpulltec.

The Aztec Confederation

The Mexica claim to imperial legitimacy rested on blood lines through intermarriage with more established chieftaincies that previously had asserted their right to the Toltec mantle. The triple alliance of Tenochtitlán, Texcoco, and Tlacopán assumed those claims and, with them, a self-imposed obligation to restore the greatness of earlier empires. As the Aztec empire expanded beyond the central valleys and its mainly Nahuatl-speaking cities, it incorporated a variety of peoples with different languages and traditions. Their shared patrimonies were the memory of Teotihuacán and Toltec civilizations and Quetzalcóatl. Indo-Mexicans functioned as a historical people, much as the Europeans who grounded themselves in the imperial Roman past and Roman Catholicism.

Itzcoatl (Obsidian Serpent), the paramount chief of the Mexica (1428–1440), successfully destroyed Azcapotzalco and assumed control of its tributaries. He took advantage of political factionalism among the Tepaneca cities to forge a triple alliance revolving around the cities of Tenochtitlán, Texcoco, and Tlacopán (Tacuba), formerly a Tepaneca city. The imperial partners followed the lead of Tenochtitlán, particularly in war.[34] The alliance created a strong predatory force able to extract tribute from more tribal groups than previously possible.[35]

Moctezuma I (ca. 1440–1469) went beyond the imperial core to bring most of central Mexico under Aztec control. His successor, Axayacatl (1469–1481), subdued Toluca and incorporated the market city of Tlatelolco into Tenochtitlán. After the 1440s, expansion was to the east and south among tribes and different language groups more prone to revolt.[36] In a geopolitical sense, the timing seemed propitious. Although strong chieftaincies existed, no empire along the lines of that of the Toltecs had emerged. The original arrangement between the business partners of the Aztec confederation called for four-fifths of tribute to go to the two larger cities and one-fifth to Tlacopán. The alliance soon brought the Nahuatl-speaking city of Cholula in the neighboring Valley of Puebla into a tributary arrangement. In 1473, Tenochtitlán's amalgamation with the nearby merchant city of Tlatelolco appears to have been an economic decision in order to make better commercial use of the tribute of the expanded empire.

Religious Cultures

Religious invention provided the superstructure necessary to explain the cosmos, human origins, the natural world, and the fragile nature of life. In Indo-Mexico, no group could claim to be original, aware that they depended on a common pool of explanatory myths and legends. As is common in many religions, theologians must imagine the basic physical elements before situating humans within them. The drama of life and death took place in the Indo-Mexican universe on two planes, the horizontal and the vertical. The Earth as disk surrounded by water occupied the horizontal plane, whereas the vertical provided the divine structure.[37] Indo-Mexico lived in a layered universe, as did Christianity. Theologically, it was structurally more extensive but, at the same time, not as fully elaborated as European beliefs. The Earth was sandwiched between the domains of the supreme deity with thirteen layers down to Earth and another nine levels down to that of Mictlan (the realm of the dead), an icy, cold place.[38] On the Earth, deemed to be female, humans interacted with an animated world of animals, plants, and the physical landscape; everything on Earth was alive and had to be accommodated as animated spirits. Humans functioned within a dynamic web of interaction with nonhuman forces, including gods, spirits, and animals.[39] Their everyday dealings with such forces could be treacherous and unpredictable.

By contrast, the nine subterranean layers appeared to be emotionally barren, nocturnal, and frigid. Consequently, the number nine was considered evil, associated with the black arts and sorcery. At the opposite end, the heavenly thirteen represented an auspicious number. The Lord of the Dead and his consort presided over Mictlan but had no active functions in the absence of a cosmology that required punishment for earthly sins. As with the upper layers, Mictlan as a concept of hell or the underworld remained philosophically underdeveloped. Gods, linked together, each with different functions and a generous number of avatars, provided the active structure. The gods that interacted with humans had no interest in their well-being. Although they demanded human sacrifice, they offered little dependable compensatory support in return. Humans cajoled their gods rather than loved them: an element perhaps true of many religions. Indo-Mexico appeared to exaggerate the negatives while downplaying positive elements, as in the case of Quetzalcóatl, discussed shortly. Rather than balancing negatives with virtue and goodness in a duality common in some religions, Indo-Mexicans devised gods that appeared to be more harmful than useful.[40]

The incomprehensible and often frightening whims of the deities required a priestly class charged with managing events and presiding over uncertain propitiatory rituals. Such important functions carried status and responsibilities. The priesthood functioned as an important social force that served, as well as controlled, believers in conjunction with, but subordinated to, the paramount chieftaincy. The most important functional link between the political and the religious levels involved human sacrifice. Blood fueled war, justified plunder and imperial expansion, strengthened social control, and kept the gods alive, but not at bay.

Indo-Mexicans' openness to the theological explanations of others took the form of incorporating newly encountered gods in their pantheon at a subordinate level. Such gods served as political hostages. Religious complexity engendered many contradictions that the high priesthood struggled with, often by employing avatars to resolve those contradictions. Inevitably, some avatar manifestations appeared to be contrary to the existing basic functions of a particular god. The black Tezcatlipoca's avatar, the red Tezcatlipoca, a milder version of the original, functioned as the Tlaxcalan deity Camaxtli and represented daylight. The use of the red version suggested an edging away from the dire activities of the black Tezcatlipoca. A certain amount of modification appeared possible; for example, the priests slowly shifted more importance to Huitzilopochtli at the expense of Tezcatlipoca. Ancient aspects inherited from pretribal days could also be trimmed, although they likely continued to exist in the realm of popular religion. Contradictory beliefs could be held unchallenged and not integrated into a coherent system, explained as the whims of unpredictable gods. Nevertheless, contradictions were part of a process that remolded a deity, suggesting intellectual slippage that retained the name but slowly changed the functions. Suddenly abandoning an outmoded explanatory deity or creating a new one is difficult once the pantheon is established.[41] Consequently, auxiliary gods are easier to add through the device of avatars. The use of avatars indicated that a religious structure had reached the limit of how many gods could be intellectually accommodated. Avatars can be created as necessary or allowed to fade away. That Indo-Mexicans did not endow their gods with inner logic may have been a major reason for the intellectual chaos they tolerated. In contrast, Christianity, with its roots in Greek and Roman logic, represented a different way of thinking from that underpinning Indo-Mexican theology. Because of the impossibility of Indo-Mexicans rationally reinterpreting their gods, they struggled, unable to do much more than make some modifications that seemingly could not keep pace with necessity[42]— perhaps an explanation of why human sacrifice took on a desperate extravagance that matched their unarticulated frustrations, eventually mounting to unsustainable levels on the eve of the European arrival.

The creation and the end of the world constituted the two pillars of belief in both Indo-Mexican and Christian theology. Those beliefs bracketed everything else. Principal deities, their innumerable avatars, lesser gods capable of undergoing explanatory transfigurations, demons, spirits, and an array of sacred and demonic sites all functioned within these two primary poles. Indo-Mexicans embraced several variations of the beginning and the rebirth of life (at least five times) before the definitive end of life.

In the beginning, a dual godhead existed combining male-female (Ometecuhtli-Omecihuatl). This godhead was referred to as the Lord of Sustenance, who ordered the creation of everything but did not demand human sacrifices, temples, or other earthly recognition. A thirteen-step heaven led to Ometecuhtli-Omecihuatl, who lived at the highest level of Omeyocan. Just what to expect at each step upward and when Omeyocan was reached is unknown.

The Lord of Sustenance delegated the actual creation of the Earth to his many sons, who, in turn, gave the task over to two of them, Tezcatlipoca and Quetzalcóatl, the former representing darkness and the latter light and physical elements such as the wind. What is of interest here is that the creation of the Earth resulted from a decision by one supreme God. Nevertheless, Indo-Mexican theologians struggled with the mystery of the initial creation. They felt comfortable explicating only the actions of the subordinate gods that undertook to make the Lord of Sustenance's decision a reality.

In common with many religions, including Christianity, fluid explanations began one level down from the divine pinnacle, sidestepping the question of God's creation. Nezahualcoatl, the intellectual ruler of Texcoco, constructed a temple dedicated to the concept of an all-powerful divine force, with its top level of painted stars on a black background but without physical representations of the supreme deity, who represented the ultimate unknowable beyond theological explanations. Eduardo Matos Moctezuma notes that the priests of the Great Temple of Tenochtitlán laid out their entire cosmology in "ceremonial and spatial order," stopping short of demonstrating the rationale behind the creation, as did Christianity.[43]

The physical construction of the world bypassed theology and settled for description. Existing matter formed the Earth, as the myth of Cipactli as a giant alligator or shark swimming in a primordial sea made clear. Set upon by Quetzalcóatl and Tezcatlipoca in the form of sea serpents, Cipactli is squeezed into two parts, with one section becoming the sky and the other the Earth. From the body parts, the gods made trees and other earthly matter, as well as molded the geological features of the Earth. Another creation story outlined the role of humans in the scheme and justified a religious culture revolving around continuous human sacrifice. This explanation also involved a couple but expanded the role of the female Citalinicue, the Star Skirt, the great mother of all the stars (also born as gods), who presided from the Milky Way and communicated by dispatching hawks. Quetzalcóatl and Tezcatlipoca figured prominently among her offspring. Her male consort, Citlallatonac starlight, appeared secondary. She gave birth to the first material object, the divine *tecpatl,* the flint knife used to open the chest cavity of sacrificial victims.[44] According to the religious myth, the tecpatl fell out of the midnight sky at the ancestral location of the Nahuas in the north and, in turn, gave birth to more gods. The stranded deities sent a hawk to the great mother to ask for people to service their needs, to provide the necessary respect and the blood required to maintain the strength of the gods. Star Skirt instructed them to retrieve the bones of an ancient people from the Lord of the Dead and revive them with their own blood offerings. Quetzalcóatl accomplished this task but not without mishap, dropping the bones, fracturing his sacred horde into fragments. Grinding the pieces into a paste with blood drawn from the genitals of the gods resulted in a male human child followed by a female, both suckled on the milk of the maguey.[45]

The human genesis began with sacrifice; the universe functioned but only if supported by the gods, who, in turn, depended on human sacrifices. In the absence of blood, the entire system would disappear along with the gods, with disastrous consequences for human beings. The duty of humans to feed and strengthen the gods with blood sacrifices represented a never-ending task, one that did not result in accumulating divine favors that could be exchanged at some point. Yet for all that people did for the gods, a static situation remained the best they could hope for—and even that could not be assured. Life had been extinguished several times before, and theologians believed that it would be again—a notion that may not be so far-fetched.[46]

Human beings progressed in bursts of time, with each stage ending violently and exterminating humans along with most of their gods. In the first stage, that of the Jaguar, the Earth's sun (personified by Tezcatlipoca, the smoking mirror) only dimly illuminated the world as humans subsisted on acorns and pine nuts until a race of giants killed them, only, in turn, to be devoured by jaguars and to have the half-lit sun ripped from the sky. Tezcatlipoca, however, survived to pass through all subsequent eons and occupy a principal position in the pantheon of Indo-Mexico.

Quetzalcóatl became the sun in the second stage. Humans survived on mesquite seeds until a series of hurricanes ended the eon and blew humans into the forests, where the survivors became monkeys. Tlaloc, the god of rain, brought about the third sun, an eon marked by the domestication of an early form of maize that concluded with massive volcanic activity that rained down fire and cinders as people fled, transformed into birds. Chalchiuhtlicue, the goddess of the waters, became the fourth sun, enabling human beings to live on acicintli seeds. Inevitably, destruction came as water gushed up from the Earth and the sky fell into the sea, causing a surge of water to wash over the land and humans to become fish.

The fifth eon had special significance, as it represented the last and final one in which the Mexica-Nahua lived. The god Nanahuatl had sacrificed himself to provide the fifth and last sun. Fire had been harnessed, culture bloomed, maize took its modern form, *octli* (brewed alcohol) developed, and a new people emerged who laid the foundations for successor groups as the fifth sun made its way to its inevitable end.[47] The five suns captured the evolutionary movement from prehistoric existence through a series of difficult eons to the fifth sun, but each step required the destruction of existing people and the willingness of a god to become the sun. Also recorded were the disasters that ended each eon, including the falling of the sky into the sea (perhaps the meteor that hit off the Yucatan coast, which may have played a role in the extinction of the dinosaurs) and a flood that was also recorded in Judeo-Christian-Muslim and Tupi Guarani Indian lore in the Amazon.[48] The fifth sun, destined to end in earthquakes that would shake the stars from the sky, would not be followed by another eon. An exhausted Earth and terminally spent sun would vaporize.[49]

The centrality of the sun and fire in the five eons, as well as related qualities of light, warmth, and earthly vitality combined in the form of the god Tonatiuh (he who goes forth blazing), drew on sun-fire cults with universal roots in ancient times. Fire as it climbed into the sky became the sun. Each arc as it moved to its zenith had its avatars, including Xochipilli, the morning sun venerated by palace officials, and the young sun Piltzinteuctli, and then declined until it returned to the underworld. The sun could not be taken for granted and might cease providing fire, light, and warmth. At midnight, resting in the underworld, the sun struggled to regain its strength. Until the dawn broke, one could not be certain that it had revived sufficiently to go about its trek from east to west. Uncertainty attended every sunrise.

The anticipation of nothingness after the fifth sun ended had an interim dress rehearsal every fifty-two years, the equivalent of a European century. Fear and foreboding agitated the multigenerational population, uncertain whether they faced disaster or would be given a reprieve. As the old fire died, no god or priest could offer assurances that a new one would be provided. The Mexica experienced at least four new fires before they arrived in the central valley and three such events after the establishment of Tenochtitlán. The new fire in 1507 was the last such ceremony before the arrival of the Europeans, although the Spaniards already had a presence in the Antilles, within striking distance of Indo-Mexico. Although the ceremony had ritual aspects, the Mexica understood they potentially faced disaster as the fifty-two-year cycle ended. As night fell, preparations for the possibility that the sun would not rise involved the entire society. All fires would be extinguished, as priests took up hillside stations from which to signal the end of the sun or its welcome reappearance. Pregnant women would be confined under guard and masked in agave leaves, as would infants. If the sun failed to rise, women would be changed into beasts attacking and consuming the men, while the children would become mice.[50]

In Tenochtitlán, the summit of the hill Uixachtecatl (prickly bush) became the doomsday focal point. An apprehensive priest placed the fire drill stick on the breast of a victim selected from those with sufficient status to be acceptable to Tonatiuh (the new rising sun). As the spark caught, the priest opened the breast cavity, extracted the heart, and threw it into the fire. As it became evident that the sun would continue, a dutiful population squeezed their cut ears, spraying blood in the direction of the successful ceremony. Relieved priests, arrayed as various deities, carried the new flame to relight the brazier in the temple of Huitzilopochtli that was associated with Tonatiuh, then on down the social structure to the general population. The people's survival did not negate the belief in the inevitable destruction of human beings as the fifth era moved relentlessly to its unknown final moment and apocalyptic conclusion.

Christianity embraced the notion of destruction also, but not of the faithful, who when resurrected would enjoy God's kingdom on Earth. Nevertheless, in the Christian notion, the struggle between good and evil intensified as the inevitable trajectory neared its apocalyptic conclusion. Evil would sweep all before it until God intervened. Thus, the fall of Jerusalem in 1224 to Muslim forces became an episode as the inevitable end of the world relentlessly approached. In the imaginary of what lay ahead, the Book of Revelation foretold disaster and the triumph of the Antichrist, followed by the end of the known world and the establishment of God's kingdom on Earth. The Indo-Mexican time table was more exact, although the end result appeared to be the same, with the exception of believers.

Conflicting Notions of Evil

The definition of evil in civilized societies is grounded in human ambivalence concerning their activities, often but not always including sexual conduct, interpersonal relations, and presumed responsibilities within the community. Definitions of what is acceptable are not static and evolve over time and vary across cultures. A ladder of sorts is created by punishment, broadly running from death to social disapproval. In Indo-Mexico, unacceptable conduct appeared to be more along the lines of civic rule breaking or political violations, punishable by enslavement or death but not requiring a moral code independent of the political authorities. The gods were interested neither in good conduct nor in reward or punishment tied to a particular act or person. In contrast, Christianity elevated evil to a major concern of God, the church, and the state, requiring an underpinning moral code. Christianity made a direct connection between evil and reward and punishment, albeit in the next world, except when it served an exemplary function such as being burned at the stake, wearing the San Benito, or being publicly flogged. The European definition that the thought and the deed, separately or combined, could be evil and offended an all-seeing God differed from the Indo-Mexican notion of evil as a personal failing, not a religious or political issue except for acts that violated tribal discipline. Indo-Mexico functioned as a well-ordered society but not as a moral society, as did Europe. Early Indo-Mexican converts could not grasp such a concept, much to the frustration of the missionary friars, and likely interpreted Christianity's moral philosophy as rules rather than principles.[51] The assignment of fallen warriors and childbirth victims to accompany the sun had nothing to do with the demands of that planet; consequently, a reward could hardly be expected.

The concept of sin appeared in nascent form as Tezcatlipoca and Tlazolteotl (the goddess of sexual passions) enticed people to do unacceptable deeds.[52] Nevertheless, society required that individuals assume responsibility for serious lapses in social, not moral, discipline. In cases of adultery, both parties were killed for an act that violated rules. At the lesser level, both Christianity and Indo-Mexico reacted in a similar fashion to a personal sense of guilt. The demand for ritual cleansing indicated that human beings desired to be cleansed. In the Indo-Mexican pictographs, a miscreant is pictured consuming his own excrement. As an example of a type of original sin passed from one generation to the next, when the midwife washed the newborn, she posed a ritual question: "What filth, what evil of the mother, of the father, does the baby come laden with?"[53] The cleansing water provided the newborn with a clean slate.

The rite of confession by individuals plagued by illness or deeply disturbed by some personal act required the services of the *tlapouhqui,* who tallied up a lifetime of unacceptable acts. On a propitious day, one arrived with a new reed mat, symbolizing a fresh beginning. Sitting completely naked on the mat, the contrite confessionary promised to reveal all without exception in the presence of Tezcatlipoca, who already knew everything as the god responsible for enticing hapless humans. At the conclusion of the recitation, the interlocutor set an appropriate penalty. The important role of confession or other compensatory acts indicated individual acceptance of blame and the hope to clear one's conscience. A mass collective display of contrition occurred during the festival of Xochiquetzal, the goddess of love and flowers, when individuals publicly confessed their guilt without being specific or providing details as to any particular act. Mass participation in the festival suggested a general acknowledgment of human frailty. To emphasize a new beginning, the entire community engaged in a cleansing bathing ritual at dawn.[54]

Discipline in the form of self-denial underpinned many of the rules taught to students in the *calmecac,* the school reserved for children of the nobility. Fasting and the piercing of ears and the body with thorns to offer one's private blood offerings likely gave some personal satisfaction, in a manner similar to rigorous monastic practices in Spain. The extremely pious drew blood from their testicles and threaded a knotted string through the wound. Bathing in ice-cold water in the mountains at midnight provided an individual cleansing. An established reputation for piety was useful for those individuals intent on a priestly career.[55] Self-sacrifice as a form of individual compensation for the creation of the Earth by the gods acknowledged the importance of personal offerings, in contrast to the institutionalized mass sacrifice of captives that sustained the gods. Nevertheless, it appears to have been penitence without reward. Compensation after death as a reward for piety or punishment for some act did not exist. Nevertheless, Indo-Mexican theology recognized different levels between the Earth and the supreme deity and between the underworld and the Earth. Just what each level represented is unclear; however, they provided a structure similar to Christianity's multiple tiers, in ascending order from hell to purgatory to heaven, all somewhere out of the existing world and all with established rewards or punishments for cause. Indigenous theology was seemingly moving toward a similar differential model for each level. Meanwhile, as likely was the case with primitive Eurasian religions, much of the sacred occurred in a cave, a sacred valley, inside a mountain, or as in the case of Quetzalcóatl, on a raft at sea. Evidently, Indo-Mexico had just begun to create an imagined world of belief suitably detached from the physical world. Only Mictlan, the world of the unfleshed, had some very limited underworld complexity.

The dead, with exceptions, journeyed to Mictlan, passing through nine different levels until entering the presence of Mictlanteuctli (the Lord of the Underworld, the Lord of the Dead). A dog depicted as yellow or blue served to guide them to the lowest level. Stripped totally naked, they disappeared into nothingness. What happened on the way to Mictlan did not constitute punishment; it provided a barely adequate explanation for what happened physically to the body after death. The Lord of the Dead and his consort had no connection with evil, as was the case in Christianity; in essence, the couple filled the need to have someone in charge. Christianity, however, also included an aspect of a journey after death. The Catholic last rites provided *viaticum*—food for the journey.[56]

The concept of an eternity reserved for all believers regardless of status, which made Christianity unending and promised perpetual heavenly rewards, had no direct Mesoamerican counterpart. The absence of punishment for cause meant that a heavenly reward for virtue and piety could not be envisioned. Nevertheless, the vagueness and ambivalence concerning an afterlife suggests an indication that the missing element would eventually be provided.

A glimmer of an afterlife appears in some accounts. Acclaimed rulers went to Mount Xicco, where they slept until being recalled to restore the greatness of their people. A ruler's household, from concubines to attendants to entertainers, was sacrificed to attend to his needs in a putative next world. Just as Iberian Celtic chiefs were buried at the center of a circle with the outer ring composed of warriors, the ritual presupposed afterlife needs. Cremation was reserved for those who were entitled to ascend skyward in the flames, such as warriors and deceased paramount chiefs. Their ashes were then buried along with the bodies of their attendants and jewels and supplies for the journey to the underworld. This suggests a protosoul that departed to accompany the sun, while the physical body presumably went in the opposite direction to the underworld. The peasants, however, were buried in unmarked graves and then began their journey to the underworld, without the pretense of ceremony and with just a few modest burial goods, perhaps slipped in by family members.

The concept of a soul existed in embryonic form as a life force (*teyolia*). Coupled with the rudimentary notions of a soul, an afterlife of sorts had been worked out. Fallen warriors and women who died in childbirth (the source of warriors or perhaps to recognize the physical trauma of birth) accompanied the sun. Fallen warriors escorted the sun in its ascent—a task that continued until they returned in the form of clouds, butterflies, or hummingbirds. Women who did not survive childbirth accompanied the sun as it descended in the west.[57]

Several other Earth-bound protoheavens had emerged also. Tlaloc, the rain god, lived shrouded in the mist in a high mountainous location called Tlalocan. Rain and moisture created a fertile green paradise filled with flowers and fruit trees, along the lines of the Garden of Eden, although it functioned as an infirmary. Those who were considered Tlaloc's chosen, such as individuals struck by lightning or drowned, dropsy victims, and those with running sores that accompanied their death, lived there. Another protoheaven was reserved for stillborn children and those who died in infancy. Its central feature was a many-branched tree where the children suckled breast milk, until they were returned to a living womb and another chance at life[58]—theologically suggestive of life recycled.

Indo-Mexico had not developed its theology sufficiently to accommodate and reward the virtuous in general. A life-after-death extension required a much more optimistic interpretation than indigenous theologians had developed up to that point. The missing element, the possibility of redemption and life after death in an afterworld open to the broadly deserving, required defining evil as an offense to God, or to the gods, and equating sin with punishment and its opposite with moral virtue and reward. The failure to offer hope and comfort to the living constituted a major philosophical-theological lapse but one that appeared to be moving slowly toward a positive theological resolution. It required elaborating a more complete notion of the underworld (Mictlan) and the role for Mictlanteuctli in extracting punishment—perhaps a construct similar to the European theological formulation of a hell ruled by Satan and a heaven presided over by God. To do so, of course, required significant theological modifications—a task that required time, if it could be done at all, or perhaps a new religion.

Both indigenous and Christian notions agreed that the gods were shape shifters. For Christians, the destructive shape shifter was the devil and his hellish minions. An Indo-Mexican description of the Lord of the Underworld seems not far removed from the European image. As envisioned, the ruler of Mictlan had shining mirrors in place of human eyes, with a large, hideous mouth, mirrored masks at the elbows and scattered around the body, and two horns. He could look everywhere all the time; nevertheless, just what his assigned task was had not been completely worked out.

The Imperial Chieftaincy

The office of paramount chief, with several interchangeable titles, including the *Huey Tlatoani* (the supreme leader) and the *Tlatoani* (he who speaks), was not quite a hereditary position, although it appeared to be moving in that direction. The elevation of a Tlatoani required acceptance and an election by those who were at the secondary governing level, much as in Europe. Personality, kinship, and other intangibles came into play until a consensus emerged, a process that likely began well before the death of the incumbent. Military leaders had to be assured that the supreme leader had sufficient skills to lead as well as to gain the respect of the army.[59] The Tlatoani was not a king, although the institution had the potential of evolving into one.[60]

Once selected, the new paramount chief sought acknowledgment by major tributaries and traditional enemies. At important moments, such as installation or death of a supreme Tlatoani, other paramount chiefs gathered as a ruling caste to bear witness. All were expected to make extensive comments and to present and receive gifts. Secrecy proved particularly important during major events, when long-standing enemies, such as Tlaxcala, would be invited to attend. They approached under cover of darkness and entered the palace through a special entrance and left the same way, without the general population being aware of their presence. Tlaxcala's paramount chief attended most elevations of Aztec rulers, and the Tlaxcalans, in turn, invited enemy rulers to their events under the same conditions. Not all invitees accepted; some rejected the invitations rudely. Nevertheless, a significant number did accept, attending in person or sending high-status representatives. One obvious purpose of the exchange of invitations was to make the legitimate ruler widely known. That, however, does not explain the need for secrecy.

Certainly, keeping peasants from wondering why they risked their lives warring on their enemies while the ruler invited those same enemies to participate in important events seems a worthy reason for the secrecy. Philosophically, the presence of enemies reaffirmed the legitimacy of a ruling structure they all had a stake in preserving as an important element in a shared cosmic worldview. The need to conceal the contact between enemies from the population, in general, suggests an awareness of the contradictions inherent in constant warfare to feed the gods and for imperial expansion and tribute and the need to maintain a ruling caste at the expense of the peasantry. It also suggests the partial ritualizing of violence—perhaps a step toward its control. Beyond that, some sort of league of paramount chiefs may have been emerging that eventually might have led to territorial and political cooperation. Meanwhile, clearly the palace functioned differently from any other element of a chieftaincy.

Investing the candidate to the chieftaincy involved a ceremony filled with symbolic acts. As he made his way to the sacred compound, the crowd remained totally silent, heightening the solemnity of the momentous occasion that would impact their lives. Two important nobles assisted him as he mounted the steps of the pyramid. They steadied him as he ascended, perhaps a suggestive reminder that he had reached the summit of power but not without the support of others. At the top, he was greeted by one of the high priests, who invested him with the appropriate insignia, dressing him in two mantles, one blue and one black, decorated with the symbol of death as a reminder of his inevitable fate. At that point, the priest delivered a homily to the effect that the ruler must act as a mother and father, guide and correct his people, keep order, and pay attention to the need for the sacrifices demanded by the gods. After the ruler humbly thanked the priest for his advice, the attending Aztec nobles swore fidelity to their new ruler. More than likely, this involved kissing his hand, a traditional gesture, although Alonso de Zorita does not mention it. This would be the last time the Tlatoani would be humbled by human beings.[61]

The paramount chief functioned as the first among equals of a council of five; the four other great ones commanded the armed contingents drawn from the four quarters of the city. By tradition, at least one of the great ones had risen from the common ranks of the army. The great ones might have kinship ties with the ruler. Their status, wealth, attire, and living standard rivaled that of the paramount chief. Often a successor came from the four or from the deceased leader's family. Theoretically, the god Tezcatlipoca chose the paramount chief, who then spoke for the deity under certain conditions. Consequently, he ruled by godly selection and could invoke the will of Tezcatlipoca. A designated Tlatoani selected a personal patron god who had a presumptive special connection with the ruler—a political as well as a divine patron. The choice of the sponsoring god set the tone and signaled the nature of the chieftaincy.

The selection of chiefs of any of the three cities that made up the Aztec Confederation required acceptance by all three, perhaps to assure the stability of the existing political balance and to avoid palace coups. When seven-year-old Nezahualpilli was selected by his father to become the next Huey Tlatoani of Texcoco, his older siblings plotted to depose him. The Mexica chief spirited him away to Tenochtitlán, where the confederation members confirmed the selection, putting an end to the plotting.[62]

A Tlatoani had extensive private land holdings and received a share of tribute considered his personal property. He had control over general tribute receipts divided between the three cities that made up the Aztec Confederation. In theory, the Tlatoani disposed of resources as he wished. In reality, tribute supported set communal demands that the chieftaincy had to fund. Lavish gifts exchanged with visiting dignitaries underpinned diplomatic initiatives as well as demonstrated the success and wealth of the confederation. All types of expenditures were protective politically.

Awareness of ambitious potential successors may have motivated Moctezuma I to restore the tribal title of *Cihuacoatl* (woman-serpent), a name that implied continuity of life. The origins of the goddess Cihuacoatl can be traced back at least as far as the Toltecs. Culhuacán and Xochimilco were devoted to her before the Aztecs appropriated the cult. In the ceremonial calendar, she appears more than any other goddess. Most importantly, she gave birth to Huitzilopochtli, the Aztec god of war. Consequently, her temple in Tenochtitlán adjoined that of her son. The goddess was envisioned as a shape shifter, able to take any form, including that of a serpent. On certain occasions, the individual chosen by the Tlatoani as the woman-serpent served as the chief administrator and the close adviser to the ruler, appearing in women's clothing. The symbolism is not clear, perhaps suggestive of a family integrated into the Aztec organizational structure with attention to the duality of male-female and the two different worlds of bureaucratic responsibly and leadership.

When the paramount chief took direct command of the army and left the city, the Cihuacoatl functioned in his place. Only the Cihuacoatl could enter the paramount ruler's presence without removing his sandals.[63] His distinctive black-and-white cloak made his legitimacy known well in advance of necessity. While the supreme Tlatoani functioned at the center of a political system, his ability to dictate was not absolute. Personality and acquired reputation played a role, as did the attitude of the other members of the council of five. Nevertheless, the inner circle avoided open displays of ambition or opposition and observed all the required formalities.

When the paramount ruler died (decided by Tezcatlipoca), a four-day ritual began during which the deceased theoretically still ruled, allowing time for political maneuvering over the succession until a new paramount chief was announced in the name of Tezcatlipoca. Selected members of the late Tlatoani's personal retinue were sacrificed in order to serve him in death, making room for a new palace clique, in essence, a change of administration but without excessively disrupting the sociopolitical structure.[64]

The Tlatoani's implied accountability to Tezcatlipoca indicated his semidivine status. Nevertheless, if a paramount chief proved inept or lost the confidence of the council and the army, he could be removed from office by a high priest, who was, in theory, obedient to the wishes of Tezcatlipoca. The procedure maintained legitimacy, although a palace coup had, in fact, taken place. Removal, however, could be politically disruptive, and more obscure ways may have been employed to speed up what appeared to be a natural death. Chimalpopoca (1414–1428), perhaps because of his timidity in dealing with the Tepanecas, was a likely victim. A hapless Chimalpopoca died either because of a murder made to look like suicide or because he was provoked into taking his own life or was held under water and drowned.[65] The ambitious Itzcoatl (1428–1440) succeeded him and broke the power of the Tepanecas. The selection of Tizoc (1479–1486), at the time still a child, turned out to be a mistake. He ruled only briefly, showed little initiative, preferred seclusion, and projected disinterest in the empire. One suspects that he was a victim of a palace faction. A concerned palace staff may have poisoned his food, perhaps directed to do so by the administrator. Nevertheless, his funeral in 1486 was conducted in the traditional manner, obviously for political reasons. In another case, an extremely aggressive, successful, and popular paramount chief, Ahuitzotl (1486–1502), fell ill after returning from war with the province of Xoconochco (now called Soconusco). A young man, seemingly in excellent health and good spirits, Ahuitzotl in effect wasted away, having been reduced to skin and bones when he died. Medical experts could not determine the cause but suggested he may have been poisoned.[66] If so, just who did it is an intriguing question; even at war, access to the ruler was controlled.[67]

Court intrigue tended to flourish in privileged isolation, fueled by gossip, rumor, and suspicion. Moctezuma II (1503–1520) had a habit of slipping into Tenochtitlán in disguise to see if his orders had been followed exactly. He did not fully trust his Cihuacoatl; on one occasion, during a campaign, Moctezuma II dispatched him back to the city with orders to behead all the tutors of Moctezuma's children, as well as the women who attended to his wives. One can imagine that the Cihua-coatl may have been somewhat shocked at the orders issued without explanation. Moctezuma then sent spies to verify whether his orders had been obeyed—in fact, they had been carried out to the letter.[68] Secrecy, at times a necessary tool at the top political levels, intensified negative behavior among the palace population.

All officials had appropriate judicial functions conforming to their office, indicating the acceptance by the chieftaincy of the ultimate responsibility to dispense justice and punishment. Local courts dealt with relatively minor cases, household or crop theft, usually imposing restitution or temporary slavery. Serious cases went to regional courts (tecalli). Crimes involving high-ranking administrators could be heard by the Cihuacoatl, with an appeal subsequently considered by the ruler. A superior tribunal reviewed cases every eighty days, examining the records and questioning officials and discussing decisions. Equality of laws and punishment could not be expected, and punishment tended to be more severe at the upper levels, where misconduct injured legitimacy. Restitution, temporary enslavement, or death, rather than imprisonment, accomplished the goal of justice.

The ruler had direct responsibility for the security of the city, a task that implied his basic responsibility for the well-being of all who lived within its boundaries. His agents could expect the paramount chief to inspect security arrangements personally at any time of the day or night. The fear was a surprise attack. Directly associated with security, the paramount chief oversaw attention to the gods. Priestly duties required around-the-clock attention. Attendants constituted night watchmen. Neglected gods could make nasty things happen. When sacrilege or a serious lapse in priestly duties occurred, corrective and public action had to be taken. Moctezuma I, for example, combining his security and religious responsibilities, dealt harshly with the priests in charge of the shrine of Toci (our grandmother), who failed to alert authorities rapidly enough to avoid its destruction during a surprise night attack. The hapless priests, forced into small cages set with sharp obsidian protrusions that could not be avoided, were kept alive as long as possible with minuscule amounts of food until they died from loss of blood and starvation.[69] Under normal conditions, priests functioned without direct interference. Priests explained and interpreted the parallel spiritual world that regulated the individual and collective life of the population, but they did not participate directly in governing the people. Nevertheless, religion located the people, institutions, and events within the sacred cosmos.[70] In a functional sense, priests served as the caretakers of the cosmos with implied rather than actual political authority—much as in Spain.

In the fifteenth century, Indo-Mexican society underwent social changes that suggested increased stratification: a movement toward hereditary lines of succession. Itzcoatl created new offices for his relatives, such as the *Mexicaltecutli* (chief of the Mexicans), the *tlacochcalcatl* (chief of the spear house), and many others that seem to have been more honorary than functional; nevertheless, such titles carried status that set them apart. Moctezuma I issued sixteen edicts governing the status of various sociopolitical groups. It may have been in response to the loosening of traditional behavior or confusion around status. Each edict carried the threat of death. The majority of them focused on status, with the intent of drawing rigid lines between the three basic levels. The status difference between the Tlatoani and the nobility widened but was mitigated by privileges designed to maintain sociopolitical loyalty to the paramount chief. Harsher measures separated the lower strata from the superior levels.

Moctezuma I decreed that a paramount chief should never be seen in public except under the most unusual circumstance, as befitting the representative of gods; only the Tlatoani could wear a golden diadem, although distinguished warriors could do so, along with wearing his insignia, when they directed soldiers (since they represented and executed the paramount chief's instructions) but at no other time. In effect, the Tlatoani claimed the army deployed for battle as his personal instrument. Meeting rooms in the palace designated for nobles and commoners could not be entered under pain of death by those who were not entitled to do so. Moreover, only the Tlatoani and the woman-serpent could wear sandals in the palace; this included any visiting paramount chiefs. Gold bands, chains, golden ankle bracelets, bells, and ear and nose plugs could be worn only by paramount chiefs, although the great noble could display precious nose and ear plugs and valiant warriors could wear plugs, but of bone or other nonprecious material. Nobles could wear gilded fine sandals in the city, but not the common people, except a person who had demonstrated great valor, and even then the sandals had be unadorned and of lower quality than that permitted the nobility. Fine cotton mantles could be worn as specified by the Tlatoani. Common soldiers were restricted to wearing only a simple mantel and a breechcloth and waistband without special adornments that might set them apart from others. They could not use cotton, only maguey fiber material. Their mantel had to extend to just cover their knees, no longer.[71] Only great nobles and notable warriors were permitted to build a two-story dwelling; no one was to build peaked roofs or some other device on their flat roof on pain of death, perhaps an indication that some were, in fact, doing so.[72] It is obvious that Moctezuma I intended to use sumptuary restrictions to redefine class and to exercise social control as the paramount chieftaincy hovered on the verge of a protomonarchy.[73]

Moctezuma II dispensed with the last remnants of tribal equality. He decreed that only the sons of nobles could wait on him personally. He directed them to perform all the mundane domestic tasks needed to keep the palace in order. In doing so, he delivered a pointed message that the status of the nobility was far below him, as well dependent on him. Some accounts indicate that he had the servants who had not been sacrificed on the death of his predecessor killed. The prohibition of commoners from viewing the Tlatoani specified the execution of offenders. When Moctezuma II appeared in public, they prostrated themselves in fear. That he viewed himself as divine, but not yet a deity, seems evident. Politically imposed social stratification posed the same dangers that destabilized Inca Peru.[74] Whether such restrictions had some connection with the poor performance of the Aztec army under Moctezuma II seems a possibility.

The Nobility

What once were favorites in earlier tribal times became nobles with their own demands and interests. To claim noble (tecuhtli) status, a prerequisite for office, individuals had to trace their ancestry through a male or female line to Acamapichtli (1375–1395), the first Mexica Tlatoani; some 25 percent of the population did so. In effect, nobles traced their ancestry back to the moment that a political structure emerged to replace the relative equality of a tribal conclave.[75] Such a requirement excluded those groups that had been absorbed by the Mexica as they went from a tribal group to a chieftaincy. A tecuhtli's position could be ascertained at a glance by his distinct attire and ornamentation. The upper political levels appeared richly adorned, bejeweled with distinctive feathered cloaks and insignia reserved for those in certain positions. They derived sociopolitical status from their office. In Tenochtitlán, an officeeholding nobility made the city function, collected taxes, assigned duties, and saw to proper sanitation—a challenge as the population increased.[76] A sizable force directed by nobles did the many tasks that kept a complex city working. Those who directed others had not yet become a select political subgroup, but their ties with the paramount chief separated them from nonofficeholding nobles, who had independent interests.

Nobles, in general, shared in tribute wealth, receiving income from land set aside and worked by the local peasantry or in a similar fashion in other parts of the empire. Nobles inherited or owned land and might found a chiefly house (*teccalli*) with retainers, the *tetecutin*, who were often relatives. A noble estate with its attached dependents, including those who worked the land, functioned as a socioeconomic subunit with its own resources.[77] The nobles, as in Spain, claimed exemption from taxation and had other privileges that set them apart. The sons of the nobility attended the calmecac. The children of nobles might be selected for office, but officeholding or its absence did not change the noble's status, although an office added sociopolitical prestige. Nobles constituted a pool of educated individuals easily integrated into the administrative or clerical structure, as needed perhaps, as official messengers or attendants to the paramount chief. A commoner in the family tree did not damage noble status and provided across-class connections but required recognized virtue, a process likely dependent on exceptional military feats.

As in most organized societies, socialization depended on education, with separate schools for nobles and those who were entitled to noble privileges. At the lower level, a school for commoners assimilated them into their designated role within the social structure. The six calpulli housing those who were considered Mexica but unable to claim ancestry back to Acamapichtli selected fifty young people to attend a calmecac. The parents of those selected did not have to go through the elaborate gift-giving ritual to place their offspring in one of the seven calmecacs. The school attached to the palace carried the best career possibilities and required lavish gifts and promises to assure admission. Instruction included the theological relationship of humans to the gods, the role of nobles and other social elements, the distribution of authority within the political structure, use of weapons, tactics, and the ceremonies and rituals reserved for distinct occasions. The nobility's place, privileges, status, and deportment were internalized through education, as is the case of all sociopolitical elites then and now.

The majority of Tenochtitlán's inhabitants were commoners; the *macehualtin,* near the bottom of the social hierarchy, nevertheless retained some residual tribal privileges. Each calpulli had a school, the *telpochcalli* (young men's house), that trained rather than educated the male children of commoners. It is likely that the same subject matter taught the children of the nobility constituted the curriculum of the telpochcalli, but with appropriate knowledge, status, and reward differentials appropriate for commoners. Civic revolts could not be imagined in the absence of the concept of the ruler's obligation to his subjects; nevertheless, the paramount chief had an obligation to preserve the chieftaincy and expand its reach as well as to preserve the cultural stability that his subjects expected. Legitimacy even in a stratified society can never be entirely assured. As noted, only disguised palace coups could be contemplated but not by people at the sociopolitical bottom.

Distribution of resources and privileges clearly favored the educated elite. Yet social advancement was possible. Individuals of exceptional valor who were able to capture four warriors on the battlefield entered the top levels of the army as members of various military orders such as the Eagle, the Jaguar, or the Otomí knights. In a similar fashion, a talent for piety and theology might have opened up a priestly career. Intermarriage also occurred on occasion. The exceptional route to noble status served to mitigate tension to some degree between the top and the bottom as well as to co-opt potential leaders.

The importance of birth dates *(tonalli)* in fixing one's life destiny provided a check on unrealistic expectations and, in certain cases, an explanation of social failure or success.[78] Individuals who were born under the sign of Ometochtli would become drunkards willing to do anything for a drink, selling their clothes and living in abject poverty. A drunkard would sleep with married women and entice young girls to engage in merry making as well as indulge in petty theft to support his addiction.[79] Those who were born under the eighteenth sign might become swindlers, shape shifters, wizards, or house robbers.[80] The need to delay a baby's naming ceremony until a more favorable sign occurred seems obvious, however; in case it turned out badly, the explanation was at hand. The descriptions recorded by Sahagún suggest a less orderly society on the social margins than one might expect. The differences among laws, customs, enforcement, and reality suggest the existence of tolerated fringe groups, perhaps excused by their birth sign but certainly not approved. In a city as large as Tenochtitlán, it is hard to imagine that ideal conduct was universal. The notion of the ideal Indian likely was a clerical construct.

The macehualtin constituted the functional socioeconomic backbone, whereas others provided the direction and reaped the advantage. At the lower level, one's social position appeared more neutral than either positive or negative, although imposed restrictions suggested a downward social trajectory. The European arrival disrupted the process and effectively undermined the sociopolitical structure by appointing macehualtin to positions that had previously been bestowed only on the nobility.[81]

Diego Durán related a mythical account of how the social structure came about. According to the story, when the Mexica overthrew Azcapotzalco in a no-quarter battle; killed the men, women, and children; burned the city to the ground; and ended their vassalage, they risked everything. Prior to the uncertain victory, the Mexica macehualtin, fearful of Azcapotzalco's military strength, pleaded with the nobles not to revolt, but, if they succeeded, the macehualtin pledged to recognize them as lords, to serve them, and to follow their orders in all matters. This part of the account appears to be a myth designed to legitimize the end of tribal equality.[82]

Supporting the nobility posed a growing burden for the economy throughout Indo-Mexico. The privilege of multiple wives (polygamy), restricted to the nobility while denied the macehualtin, assured an unbalanced demographic socioeconomic pyramid. With the nobility at 25 percent of the population, it might be manageable, at least after the formation of the Aztec Confederation, thanks to the flow of tribute from the empire. A similar sociopolitical pyramid may have characterized Indo-Mexico in general. The rate of noble births outpaced that of the peasantry. The poet-ruler of Texcoco was reputed to have had 2,000

wives and to have produced 117 children, a ratio that suggests some restraint. His son and successor fathered 114 children. Collectively, noble
births posed a problem.

At a certain point, the number of families claiming noble status became an economic burden. Economic distortions caused by inheritance
of both land and attached labor and other forms of wealth in the hands
of the nobility might require adjustment at the top or serfdom at the
bottom—a situation that heightened the risk of social revolt. A partial
solution divided the nobility into classes, with the high nobility, the
Tlatoque, at the top, followed by the lesser nobles *(Tetequhtin)* at the lower
ranks of the nobility.[83] Such a reallocation of status did not change the
reality that the upper levels extracted excessive wealth from those at
the bottom. A general reworking of the social structure seemed inevitable, perhaps by allocating status on the basis of individual economic
contributions instead of birth, similar to the general economic process
in Europe.

The Military

Violence, and the threat of its use, was endemic in Indo-Mexico. No
group could ignore the reality and expect to survive as an independent
entity. The psychological aspects of fear and uncertainty were evident
in material ways. Hilltop forts, laid out to give the defenders the high-
ground advantage, provided some reassurance but not against a large
and determined enemy. The Zapotecs, Chinantecs, and others chose
mountain peaks, which were much more difficult to attack successfully.
Both hilltop forts and mountain redoubts could not survive a prolonged
siege, however. Walls offered more protection, but only if supported
by an effective military force. Tlaxcala built high, thick walls that protected much of the modern state with entry points with even thicker
walls and zigzag passageways; they repulsed Aztec armies on many occasions and were never conquered. Nevertheless, walls constructed of
adobe reinforced with stone and wood might be very thick but could
be attacked with *coas,* digging sticks, at the base, and ladders could be
employed to go over the top. In some cities, concentric circles of walls
offered fallback options, such as the series of five walls protecting the
inner center of the city of Quetzalpec (on the Pacific coast). Although

the city fell to the Aztecs and their allies, it required some time to break through. The Tarascan, who fortified the cities of Ajucitla, Zitacuaro, and Teloloapan, succeeded in fending off the Aztecs. Surrounded by lakes, Tenochtitlán was easily defendable under normal circumstances, as was the city the Lancandon, which was built in the center of a lake.[84] Use of rough bridges and rafts constructed on the spot, much as Roman legions did in a different time and a continent away, were standard military tactics.[85] Dispersed rural groups, such as those of the Maya, could not be so easily reduced.[86]

The Tlatoani, in his capacity as the "Lord of Men," exercised broad military authority to determine when, how, and where to make war, although he consulted with the four great ones and sought the opinions of the distinguished warriors assembled for that purpose. Such a procedure resulted in spreading credit or blame for the outcome. The paramount chief issued orders to subject tribes and allies to join the effort. Each auxiliary contingent fought as a separate unit, although under the direction of the Aztec officials in charge. Nevertheless, in the event of an utter disaster, the supreme Tlatoani could not escape reputational damage; a series of defeats indicated a loss of the favor of Huitzilopochtli. War retained strong aspects of raiding, with immediate booty in mind but also a share of the tribute imposed, although minor contributors would have to be satisfied with booty. Captives for sacrificial purposes were divided among participating groups.

Although the military, in conjunction with the priesthood, provided the functional foundations of the chieftaincy, both were subordinate institutions. As the gatherer of sacrificial victims needed to feed the gods, the army served as the instrument, whereas the priesthood legitimized violence through its sacrificial functions. Only the paramount chief united both institutions in his very person. While the army and the priesthood had a degree of influence, they did not have direct political roles.

Nevertheless, great efforts were made to invest the ruler with warrior virtues and religious piety. A successful campaign that he led personally in order to gather sacrificial victims for his formal elevation likely required careful planning to avoid any unhappy surprises. On returning, he was careful to credit Huitzilopochtli for his success, appearing before the war god and ritualistically eating dirt. Normally, a reputation for presiding over military success was more important than leading armies personally, although the paramount chief could and did take to the field.

The army had three basic tasks, apart from supplying captives for sacrifices: preserving the existing tribute flow; suppressing revolts, both to intimidate and to discourage others who might be tempted to do the same; and imperial expansion, representing a new stream of tribute. Reliance on force made it difficult to peacefully consolidate the empire. Politically, expansion demonstrated power and had to be actively pursued. On the surface, an Aztec army appeared hegemonic and irresistibly powerful. Elaborate ceremonies demonstrated the army's importance. Honored veterans stood in front, followed by captors of one prisoner, then military skills instructors (called *elder brothers*), and finally students from the various schools. All generations from current to past to future shared in public and official esteem of the army. A cadre of well-trained warriors skilled at rapidly reconstituting an Aztec army managed the general call to arms. A draft drew all able-bodied men into the lower ranks; in effect, those of military age formed a militia, drawing on the tribal notion that all male members functioned as warriors, and in case of an emergency, young boys and older men might be utilized. Under normal conditions, well-organized units subdivided into 20-man squads, gathered into 400-man battalions, and functioned under the command of a Jaguar, an Eagle, or a member of another order of knights. Society had not been militarized totally, although men's instruction in the use of weaponry in the schools and an understanding of their military obligation prepared them for service when that moment came.

The return of a victorious army was greeted with shrieks, beating of drums, playing of flutes, blowing of conch shells, and dancing amid clouds of copal incense. Speeches, praising the men's valor and success, ended as the warriors went to the sacred compound to engage in the ritual eating of dirt before the image of Huitzilopochtli, after which the commanders reported to the paramount chief with the expectation of a distribution of honors and praise from the highest level. Returning victorious was a joyful occasion, except for the mothers and widows who had lost a son or a husband. A military leader visited each family to inform them of their loss, beginning an eighty-day period of mourning filled with various ceremonies that had the virtue of keeping the bereaved busy; otherwise, they had only "recourse to the Lord of

created things, of the day and night, of fire and wind."[87] A warrior's
death in the family required the household to fashion a cornstalk frame
draped with the cloak and breechcloth of the fallen, with his arms and
shield at the foot. A dead hummingbird attached to the frame, indicating afterlife activity, and white heron feathers, the sign of a warrior,
completed the ritual observance.[88] Widows of childbearing age were
encouraged to remarry and replenish the stock of warriors.

In contrast, defeat had bitter consequences. Perhaps an extreme example was the reaction of an angry Moctezuma II (ironically, the name
means "angry god") after a battle with Tlaxcala in which the army performed poorly. Moctezuma publically humiliated the army, ordering
that the returning warriors be ignored. He stripped the commanders
of status, seizing their previous battle decorations, ordered them to cut
off their hair tails (in effect, indicating their lack of military skills), and
ordered them to wear peasant clothing. A year later, Moctezuma began
another war with Tlaxcala but did not direct individuals to take up arms,
giving them the choice to stay at home or not. All understood that this
represented a chance to regain honor, and willing warriors flocked to
engage the enemy. This time both sides preformed with valor, prompting
Moctezuma to relent and restore their status and the honors he had previously stripped away.[89]

Army commanders drawn from the nobility and distinguished warriors functioned as a separate caste. Their membership in the Eagle,
the Jaguar, and other military orders encouraged association loyalty
apart from that of class and the population in general. Exceptional warriors could be elevated in rank, rewarded materially, and offered special recognition by the paramount chief alone. Moctezuma I, perhaps
under pressure, created a new status level of *Quauuhpilli*, conferred on
distinguished soldiers, that gave them some but not all of the privileges
of the nobility; his successor, Moctezuma II, abolished this minor breech
of status. Exemplary warriors wore padded cotton helmets in the shape
of the heads of wild beasts in order to distinguish themselves on the
battlefield. Excessive emphasis on individual valor, even reckless acts
of bravado, assured that ambitious military commanders seldom lived
long enough to enjoy their material reward.

While the flow of tribute depended on the army, economics did not
play a central or direct role in the philosophical matrix that motivated
warriors. The objective of warriors was to preserve honor by achieving

victory but, if not, to fight and die with honor and dignity. Fearful hesitation in the face of the enemy could not be excused. In contrast, the paramount chief and his administration took care of the material and economic benefits of victory, setting the tribute, or in the event of defeat, dealing with the consequences. Meanwhile, warriors functioned as economic instruments, but they ran the risk that they, too, would die, if not in battle, then as a sacrificial offering in the same fashion as those whom they captured. Indications exist that suggest they did not believe that their potential sacrifice would be rewarded sufficiently by religion's promise of allowing them to accompany the sun in its ascent. Of course, they could anticipate gifts from the paramount chief, but the cost-reward ratio may have seemed unbalanced to some war-weary veterans. A touchingly beautiful poetic lament, one of many, captures their sadness as well as a sense of military caste unity:

> If indeed I keep on weeping
> Plunged in the despair of not knowing—
> If indeed my heart repels the terrible thought—
> Then perhaps I shall not descend into the Mysterious Land.
> Our hearts here on earth cry out together,
> "Let it be that we never die, O my comrades!"[90]

Every paramount chief had to deal with tributary revolts, some more than others. But once a formerly independent chieftaincy had become a part of the tribute empire, it could not be permitted to escape. Some Aztec rulers reduced tribute under certain circumstances such as crop failure, but not Moctezuma II, who made a practice of never doing so, preferring the expense of putting down revolts. On occasion, economic tensions could not be contained. Moctezuma I conquered Cotaxtla, a Totonac trading center close to modern Veracruz, in 1459. After the amount of tribute had been agreed on, the army withdrew. Almost immediately, the reluctant tributaries killed the resident tax collector and allied themselves with the Tlaxcalans. Moctezuma I sent envoys to discuss the possible consequence of revolt, but they were killed, stuffed, and mocked with exaggerated respect at a make-believe banquet. An enraged Moctezuma then gathered his army and reconquered Cotaxtla, imposing an additional heavy tribute. Nevertheless, when Moctezuma I died, the tributaries revolted again, forcing another series of campaigns against Totonac cities.

On a cost-benefit basis, some parts of the empire may have not been worth it, a consideration that must have been a factor when planning future expansion.[91] On the other hand, to demonstrate weakness could be dangerous. The need for a large number of ceremonial blood offerings on certain occasions required military action—a political decision framed as a religious requirement but without any intention of incorporating the regions into the already overextended tribute empire.

As the army took to the field, elements of the clergy accompanied it. An elite group of high-ranking warrior priests, the sun's men, served as chaplains in the ritual preparation for battle as well as in the sacred burning of the dead in its aftermath. These priest-warriors adjudicated disputes over who received credit for prisoners, an important task because the number of captives determined military status and material rewards, but the priests also participated in combat. The special priestly corps, the *Chachalmecas,* undertook the task of the ritual sacrifice of prisoners.

Captives obviously represented a type of capital. Sharing of human sacrificial assets was important to all, from the peasant soldiery to those who extracted a larger share of wealth and privilege in Indo-Mexico. It meant survival of their world.

In 1487, the great temple, ordered constructed by an earlier paramount chief, was inaugurated by Ahuitzotl in an orgy of blood. Suitably adorned sacrificial victims formed into four lines; they numbered in the thousands and required days to dispatch in the prescribed ritual manner.[92]

Ritualized Violence: The Flower Wars

The fundamental belief that the gods sacrificed themselves to create the Earth and continued to do so to sustain it locked the gods and humans into a circular dependency—a relationship characterized by fearful respect coupled with regulated violence. Violence represented a collective tribal response to the needs of the gods and, hence, the people's own survival. On an individual basis, ritual blood touched every household and determined the ceremonial life of rulers, nobles, priests, and commoners. The flower wars did not impose tribute on opponents, who were considered enemies of the house. They engaged each other on a set battle site, at a set time, without the intention of upsetting the power balance, although the combatants would assess each other's military skills.

The flower wars represented a less disruptive method of feeding the gods than war but not without costs. The so-called enemies of the house, who had their own needs for blood sacrifices, agreed to a staged but deadly contest. High dignitaries from both sides watched the battle from behind a flower screen, hence the misleadingly benign name of *flower wars*. These staged conflicts, held at designated locations and at a set time, did not change the political balance between the contesting parties, as the gods feasted on the blood of warriors of both sides.[93] Nevertheless, they demonstrated the fighting prowess of the contestants, and any weakness would be noted. Contrived battles indicated maturing empires that preferred to avoid the uncertainty and expense of distant campaigns but were still in need of sacrificial victims.

Only the tecuhtli took part in the flower wars; common soldiers did not participate—honor as a preserve of the directive class drew in sufficient participants. While the battles were theoretically voluntary, those who took part must have been under social pressure to do so. The flower wars pitted the bravest and most accomplished warriors on both sides of the contest against each other, with the stated task of feeding the gods with blood, often the warriors' own. It had aspects of a game in that officials on both sides sent in reinforcements as they deemed necessary, but it also permitted personal contests as two renowned warriors faced each other. Anyone overpowered and dragged off the field of battle became a prisoner and eventually a sacrificial victim. The number killed and captured was reported to the paramount chiefs of both sides. Just how many died on the battlefield or subsequently at the hands of a priest is hard to determine. That no one party could allow its veteran force to be depleted without grave political consequences seems obvious. Flower wars suggested that Indo-Mexican warfare had moved toward rules governing wars, as had occurred in Eurasia. Less positively, it indicated that warfare, so closely entwined with religious needs, whether contrived or real, remained an activity that expressed the important values of the Indo-Mexican worldview.[94] The concept of arranged duels suggests a generalized desire to control and limit violence, while still obtaining satisfaction by inflicting sacrificial deaths.[95]

Internal political considerations may have played a role also; the difficulty of finding an alternative use for a professional military cadre should not be underestimated. In the event of an actual battlefield defeat, participation in a flower war might restore a degree of confidence.

Following the Aztec defeat and rout by the Tarascans, an important dedication of a stone representation of the sun required the sacrifice of warriors captured on the battlefield. Understandably reluctant to engage in an uncontrolled war before they had recovered from such a defeat, they turned to one of the "enemies of the house," the city of Tliliuhquitepec to the east of Tenochtitlán. That both sides fought with the objective of taking captives did not make the battle any less bloody. In the end, the Aztecs had 700 captives and the other side 420. The battle concluded when the Tliliuhquitepec leaders came to the Aztec leaders and spoke of their sadness at the loss of such valiant warriors. In response, the Aztec commander thanked them and departed until, in the account of Durán, "the gods might again summon them to another encounter."[96]

The religious beliefs that motivated the flower wars had an important temporal sociopolitical function also, whether intended or not. They demonstrated the subordination of the army to the political level of the paramount chief, as well as illustrated the important legitimizing but subordinate role of the clergy in what, in effect, amounted to a sacrificial culling of the officer corps. Significantly, although the priesthood might report the perceived need for blood, the decision whether to act on it lay with the paramount chief and his top advisers. In some cases, the political level regularly scheduled flower wars, as did Texcoco, which fought Huexotzinco and Tlaxcala alternately every other month.[97]

Flower wars required a high degree of trust and cooperation between erstwhile enemies. The arrangement between the Aztec Confederation and Tlaxcala is particularly interesting considering the latter's subsequent cooperation with the invading Europeans.

Tezcatlipoca and Quetzalcóatl

Indo-Mexico had yet to move theologically from gods in grotesque nonhuman forms to gods in human form. Consequently, the idea of an eventual fusion of the earthly and heavenly kingdom—the hope held out by Christianity—was difficult to imagine. Europe had long ago banished its monster gods to hell and gave them the task of dealing with punishment in an appropriately appointed underworld.[98] A possible explanation for the acceptance of hideously depicted gods in Indo-Mexico may be found in the use of sacred drugs. Imagination coupled with justified fears and hallucinogenic drugs can lead to vision of vivid nightmarish scenes.[99] The use of hallucinogens in Mesoamerica is well established, perhaps a result of the experience of early food gatherers with various plants, among them *nanacatl* (mushrooms); *peyotl* (peyote); several species of *Datura,* including morning glory seeds; and other substances. Hallucinogens broke the barrier between the earthly realm and that of the gods and brought individuals face-to-face and alone with particular gods, depending on the substance ingested. Music and dance intensified and facilitated the encounter. Personally confronting such gods took an act of courage.[100]

Tezcatlipoca represented the dark, dangerous, and unpredictable spheres of life. His elevation to the top divine level indicated the great fear that permeated Indo-Mexican theology. Tezcatlipoca presented a fearful image: a dreadful physical representation of black limbs, with a face painted gold with three black lines and either barely perceptible circles or sometimes black lines painted on all parts of the body. Perhaps even more chilling, he was left-handed, with one foot replaced by a mirror that provided a frightening glimpse into the occult; scenes of disaster shrouded in roiling smoke appeared on the face of Tezcatlipoca's mirror. The efforts of indigenous priests to placate Tezcatlipoca did not assure his favor. In a similar manner, rulers and governors traced their authority to him but understood that their position remained tenuous. As the source of putative state authority, Tezcatlipoca also served as its destroyer. The god acted without gratitude, logic, procedure, or predictability, suddenly replacing the mighty, delighting in sowing discord to the extent that he served as "the enemy of both sides."[101] Slaves, said to be his favorites, represented Tezcatlipoca's power to reduce all to that degraded status, including rulers.

In common with many other gods, Tezcatlipoca could take different forms, but to a much greater degree than most. As a coyote, he became the totem of the Otomí, but he could also appear as a skunk. In the form of a jaguar, he represented an ill omen. One of the Tezcatlipoca's most frightening apparitions, the night axe, a headless figure with a gaping chest wound that opened and shut with a thud, appeared to those who were unlucky to be caught at a crossroads at midnight. As a shape shifter and seer able to foresee impending disaster, his origins appear grounded in ancient shamanism. As a representative of disaster, Tezcatlipoca would snatch the sun from the sky when the world ended. Tezcatlipoca demanded to be fed with the blood of sacrificial victims but did not feel it necessary to protect or favor those who performed the sacrifices and, indeed, might visit an unexpected disaster on them. Disease constituted one of his unwelcome impositions. He played with a fearful people, helplessly forced to accept the back of his hand. Tezcatlipoca represented the harshness and uncertainty of life.

Sahagún believed that Tezcatlipoca represented the presence of Lucifer. It appears that the usually reliable friar adapted the Christian notion of the expulsion of Satan from heaven for attempting to supplant God to Tezcatlipoca's expulsion from heaven for arousing sexual desire. The victim was Quetzalcóatl, the plumed serpent.

Quetzalcóatl only partially balanced Tezcatlipoca, in that he evinced some concern for humans and their welfare. Identified as the wind in both its positive and destructive modes and as the wind before the rain, he shared control of water with Tlaloc, the ancient rain god. His association with the life-giving water and his representation as a plumed serpent (a fertility symbol) made him into a positive deity. The plumed serpent's image appeared on even the most modest pyramids, usually in rows, perhaps indicating a desire for a more positive theology.

Quetzalcóatl's origins may be traced back to the Huaxtec on the Gulf Coast, in particular, to a coastal settlement to the east of Panuco. The myth indicates that he landed at that location to begin the peopling of Indo-Mexico.[102] At the beginning of the last eon, the fifth sun, Quetzalcóatl (in another myth) and Tezcatlipoca share the task of creating the first man and woman. Somewhere along the way, the myth fused with a real person. The Teotihuacán culture passed it to the Toltecs, who made their own modifications before bequeathing the Quetzalcóatl cult to others, including the Mexica and the Mayans.

Quetzalcóatl had human origins in Topiltzin, a priest theologian opposed to the cult of Tezcatlipoca. Topiltzin advocated sacrifices of snakes, butterflies, and birds and symbolic individual bloodletting. He apparently attracted a significant group of priests and a sufficiently large following among the people to make his removal difficult. His opposition to human sacrifice challenged powerful interest groups, warriors, and priests associated with the cult of Tezcatlipoca. If Topiltzin succeeded in ending human sacrifice, the worldview of Indo-Mexico would have radically changed, and the existing basis of political authority would have collapsed. Those who were desperate to preserve the status quo formed a conspiracy to discredit Topiltzin's priestly reputation and end the threat. Tricked and intoxicated, shamed by a sexual encounter with his sister, a disgraced Topiltzin fled Tula to the east coast, where he likely died.

The myth goes on beyond historical indications to relate that Topiltzin departed across the sea on a raft of serpents, vowing to return on the same date as his fall—the year *Ce Acatl* (One Reed), roughly equivalent to 1519, the year that Cortés landed on the shores of Indo-Mexico. The myth of his return implied the inevitable destruction of the opposition and of state power based on war and human sacrifice. Meanwhile, the plumed serpent resided in Tlapallan, some sort of mythical Eden. Some scholars believe that Tlapallan had a physical location, perhaps the abandoned Toltec city of Chichén Itza.

In spite of the opposition to Quetzalcóatl's presumed efforts to end human sacrifice, the two high priests who presided over human sacrifices became Quetzalcoatls, indicating their extreme holiness. When they cut open the chests of their victims, they assumed temporarily the name of the god to whom the sacrifices had been dedicated. The Toltecs before them and the Mexica, also in a departure from logic, made Quetzalcóatl into a patron of warriors and war. Mexica warriors envisioned the plumed serpent floating above advancing armies, much as Spaniards believed that Santiago hovered protectively over them as they engaged the enemy. In a subtle acknowledgment of Quetzalcóatl's radicalism, the calmecacs, the schools reserved for the directive classes, considered him their patron. Such theological contradictions would eventually have to be sorted out, likely in Quetzalcóatl's favor.

A more positive use of Quetzalcóatl had already occurred in the important city of Cholula in the Puebla Valley. Cholula transformed itself into a merchant center under the protective patronage of Quetzalcóatl. Regional traders considered his avatar, the Lord of the Van (a commercial designation), as their patron. Cholula became a pilgrimage center, effectively demonstrating and, perhaps, sanctifying the utility of trade. The great pyramid constructed in honor of Quetzalcóatl, called the "Mountain Made by Man," was built in stages, beginning at the time that Teotihuacán dominated that city. The circulation of contradictory myths and the actual patronage of Quetzalcóatl appear to have been the initial stage of a theological struggle whose implications for religious structure and beliefs were at least equivalent to those of early Christianity. Widespread acceptance of the plumed serpent and his mythical rejection of human sacrifice suggested a potentially positive unifying belief and a radically different theology in the offing, given sufficient time.[103]

Priests, Sorcerers, and Magicians

The formal and informal spiritual community served the chieftaincy by attending to the gods, ordering the everyday religious rhythm and lives of the community, and directing the ritual activities of the people. The priesthood constituted a formal religious bureaucracy, but as in Spain, the priests, in spite of their usefulness, did not have the same status as political administrative officials or the high nobility. Novices and those who attended gods and their temples enjoyed personal esteem but not significant political status, with the exception of several high priests (*tlenamacac*) at the top of the priestly hierarchy. Two co-equal supreme clerics claimed a status level that required the paramount chief to go to them rather than the reverse, pro forma acts of respect not all that different from that of European monarchs in their relationship with the pope. The tlenamacac participated in the elevation of the paramount chief and advised officials on a variety of spiritual issues.

Priests maintained an elaborate religious regime that demanded constant compliance, daily private and public ritual practices often made solemn by human sacrifices, fasting, and abstention from sexual intercourse. The training that the clergy offered in the schools fused education with spiritual elements. Resident students of the calmecac served as temporary assistants to the priests, learning discipline, self-sacrifice, the use of the calendars, and how to read the painted books. The focus on piety required constant auto-sacrifices, piercing of the body with maguey spines to draw blood, and nocturnal visits to isolated shrines. Priests driven to display their piety exaggerated humans' ambivalence about sexual activity to the extent of mutilating their genitalia. Major temples might have forty or so priestly attendants; all had prescribed rites that occupied their time throughout the day and night in several shifts.

Priests dramatized the spiritual world by making the gods come alive and walk among the people. The process of semihumanizing deities, while strengthening beliefs, involved bringing the gods face-to-face with those who fed them. An individual purchased from the slave market or selected from prisoners awaiting sacrifice would be dressed as a deity, masked, and instructed to act accordingly. A suitable entourage accompanied him or her in public and made sure that no escape occurred. The representation (*ixiptla*) of a deity, considered to be the actual god or goddess, brought the two worlds together for twenty to forty days, although the representations of Huitzilopochtli, Titlacahuan (an avatar of Tezcatlipoca), and Nappateuctli served for the year, until sacrificed and replaced by new victims. An ixiptla circulated among the population, receiving all the respect and homage due the god that he or she represented until sacrificed, at which time the ixiptla fused with the actual deity. Possibly every god in the pantheon had an ixiptla once in the calendar year, with the exception of those that were being phased out or that had become abstractions. Another word for a priest, *tlamacazquii* (he who gives), recognized the rule-making function of religion, whereas the *teopixque* (keeper of the gods) placed a clerical layer between the gods and the people. Presiding over human sacrifices constituted an important function; the priests sanctified the warrior's blood gift to the gods. Of paramount importance, the priesthood coordinated an Indo-Mexican worldview with little room for religious deviance or experimentation.[104] Formal rigidity in what constituted a state religion set boundaries.

Nahuallis (sorcerers) claimed access to supernatural knowledge, fueled by intelligent imagination or experience that served to give imagined substance to events. Mysterious or unexpected events, if left unattached to some creditable reality, undermined political legitimacy. The leadership turned to diviners and sorcerers to paper over explanatory gaps in a manner that did not require significant modification of the belief structure but suggested a suitable explanation. Omens, usually physical phenomena that suddenly appeared, could not be left unaddressed but quickly disappeared in any event. Diviners presented the ruling elite with an explanation and a reason to take or suspend action. In certain cases, ex post facto omens were used to shift responsibility away from rulers, although the failure to read omens accurately would seem to be a lapse.[105] A consistent failure to do so might be fatal, professionally or physically. Although Moctezuma II desperately consulted nahualli after 1519, his late contemporary, Isabel, Queen of Castile (died 1504), did the same, although without the same sense of panic.[106] Nahuallis attached to the official retinue of the paramount chief assisted in determining the implications of events. Nahuallis, while not considered priests, had semiofficial recognition, combined magic with soothsaying, and had some of the same abilities as the deities. They could change shapes, becoming animals or birds, and belonged to the category of an *atlaca* (nonhuman), with access to the underworld as well as to the dwelling places of the gods. A nahualli could also become a life force such as fire or blood. Esteemed sorcerers formed part of the paramount ruler's inner circle. They responded to the need for tactical measures such as spells but also looked into the immediate future.

A subcategory of magicians endowed with more limited talents served individuals, including the many personal needs of the peasantry. Magicians viewed the world as made up of forces they could redirect for set purposes. Some specialized in rainmaking, protecting crops, or vengeance. One could call on them to destroy personal enemies by burning an image, magically poisoning, or mysteriously and perhaps gleefully plucking out various vital organs of the target, among other practices. Magicians could not circumvent the will of the gods but could suggest mitigating steps; a magician provided one of the few ways that individuals could have a degree of control.[107]

Women had a unique connection with religious matters. Of all the pillars of the chieftaincy, only the priesthood allotted important roles to women. For females, knowledge transfer occurred within the religious structure. Female gods required attendants and priestesses to perform religious rites. Mothers could dedicate young girls to a religious life. At a certain age, such girls lived in the temple and over time might become priestesses. A woman's religious commitment, however, did not have to be permanent. Women accepted and applied approved sociocultural values within the family and with others in everyday interactions. In effect, women served to balance the religious and the secular. For their own family needs, women turned to *curanderos*—sorcerers, soothsayers, and simple diviners.[108] The curanderos, a designation that included midwives, although not considered priests, often had sufficient education to be able to read pictographs and count the time needed to determine the propitious moment to initiate treatment or stimulate a birth. To divine the seriousness of an illness, the curandero arrived after dark, placed a white cloak on the ground next to the patient along with a small image of Quetzalcóatl, and threw twenty kernels of corn on the cloth (the number of days in a month, according to the Mexica calendar); the way the kernels displayed determined if the patient could be expected to recover.

The steam bath (*temazcalli*) had both symbolic and curative uses. One crawled through a small opening into a darkened room symbolizing the womb. Entering represented a return to nonexistence, whereas reemerging signified a reborn life. The Mexica associated illness with darkness, as many societies did and continue to do today. The mother goddess Yohualticitl served as the goddess of the steam bath, and her male companion, Yohualteuctl, represented the spirit of the dark night. Both these deities did not appear on the ritual calendar but appear to be creations of popular religion.

The Reallocation of Resources

Indo-Mexico's economic foundations rested on tributaries, with trade being secondary. The Aztecs' tribute network collectively contributed more resources than could be produced internally. Some tributaries had subtributaries; thus, the system constituted an economic network that channeled resources to a centralized location. Nevertheless, the cost of acquiring and maintaining a tribute empire far exceeded that of voluntary trade. On occasion, intimidating and threatening first rather than launching an attack might be worthwhile. Once a potential tributary had been identified, often because of some attractive resource, an emissary would be dispatched to request supplies. Acquiescence signaled the acceptance of tributary status; or if the request was rejected, negotiations began with the recalcitrant city. Only after efforts to reach an agreement failed did hostilities begin. Nevertheless, trade had a long history in the region and could be accomplished without the expense of an army. The growing importance of trade is suggested by the reaction to the breaking of previous trade relations without any explanation. Breaking an agreement was viewed as a provocative act with negative material consequences justifying war. Trade could not meet all imperial demands. Only war expanded or lost an empire.

For all the savagery accompanying war and defeat—including killing, looting, enslavement, sacrifice of warriors, reassignment of land, and in some cases, total destruction of a city—a certain formality was involved in the declaration of war. An envoy would be dispatched with unguent and chalk to anoint the paramount chief of the side declared against, followed by an exchange of weapons. If a potential enemy refused to respond, he was subject to the indignity of having his messengers forced to dress as women and dispatched back to their ruler.[109]

Nevertheless, warfare for the purpose of expansion became less feasible as the empire exceeded its optimal size. Consequently, sacrificial victims, required for religious needs, could not be as readily acquired. The gods' demand for warriors taken in battle rather than everyday human beings proved problematic. The overriding importance of ritual human sacrifice posed an imperial dilemma; the religious core of the Mexica worldview depended on such sacrifice. The skull rack (*Tzompanco*) provided a semipermanent record, a visual reminder of the power of the imperial chieftaincy, but at the same time, war required going farther afield, eventually beyond military means.[110]

The economic impact of war was negative across Indo-Mexico but in a scattered pattern. Those who held large numbers of tributaries, such as the Tarascans and the triple alliance headed by Tenochtitlán, may have had an advantage, but a far-flung empire became more difficult and expensive to control. Maintaining a creditable threat was crucial; thus, the extravagant displays of wealth and presentation of gifts for visiting dignitaries suggested that the powerful could well afford any required campaign. The propaganda of the gift, just as in Europe, had both a protective and a seductive function, one suggesting that respect and intergroup alliances had their rewards. Few, if any, of Indo-Mexico's rulers accepted the notion of disinterested generosity.

One has the impression that a ruler either created an empire or became part of another: remaining independent was possible only if no larger power coveted another's resources or if distance offered some protective isolation. The expense of constant wars could be balanced by the tribute paid every eighty days. The initial looting of the defeated city represented an immediate infusion of wealth. Looting and robbing individuals presumed to be enemies was, in fact, the only pay soldiers received, a privilege they defended aggressively and one that the Romans, El Cid, and all medieval European commanders understood. When the defenders of Xilotepec surrendered to the Aztec ruler Ahuitzotl, they begged him to stop the looting of their city. He ordered commanders to stop the men from looting, only to have the soldiers complain that the chance for plunder was the reason they fought, not just to die. Ahuitzotl sent his officers street by street to haul them out physically. In cases in which victory was a foregone conclusion, a military commander had difficulty holding his force together, as the men raced to be among the first to grab choice items. A commander ordering his men to instantly kill anyone attempting to leave camp without permission seemed to have worked, at least on one occasion. Honor was an attribute of the noble officers, but the soldiers responded pragmatically.[111]

Commercial Activity

Mesoamerica adopted the well-established pochteca trade system whose origins have been traced to the Gulf (of Mexico) Coast long before the Aztecs rose to power. These large-scale merchants formed guilds in at least twelve cities in the central valleys; the membership of the guilds set codes of conduct and regulations and formed a corporate group able to represent their interests to the political authorities.[112] The pochteca linked regional exchange networks into a broader Indo-Mexican context, indicated by the widespread use of shared pottery motifs across Mesoamerica.[113] Interdependency required shared procedures approaching those of commercial law. The merchants adjudicated their own commercial disputes and, in serious situations, imposed the death penalty. Their judicial authority represented a rare departure from tradition that placed enforcement and capital penalties in the hands of a judiciary, with the paramount chief as the final authority. Merchants shared the same religious explanations provided by the priesthood and ordered their lives by the same calendar, although they had some unique ceremonial events. The pochteca had their own divine patron, Yacatecuhtli (long-nosed god), as did other distinct occupational and calpulli groups.

The pochteca functioned as a merchant caste with a separate status ladder based on professional achievement. Sons followed their fathers, and families intermarried, lived in their own separate districts, and generally remained apart from others. Their degree of social isolation suggests that they originally may have been outsiders with different tribal roots, allowed to function because of their usefulness and trading skills. The pochteca occupied an ambivalent position halfway between the nobles (tecuhtli) and the craft workers. Privileges long reserved for the tecuhtli had been encroached on by these large-scale merchants. They could own land, sacrifice slaves, wear insignia, and send their children to the calmecac. Although the army brought cities into the tribute empire, only the pochteca had the ability to manage external trade. They sought out opportunities within the empire and beyond. Wary trading partners with justification viewed them as advance scouts of an expanding empire. Demand for some sort of scarce product reported by the pochteca might precipitate a Mexica attack and the imposition of tribute.

Pochteca columns, heavily armed against attack, represented the aggressive spread of commerce and trade across Indo-Mexico. When it became necessary to fight, merchants dressed in full combat regalia—an indication that they had received military training and could claim a degree of the social respect lavished on warriors. When a pochteca died during a trading expedition, his body would be tied to a wooden frame left on a hilltop and dried by the sun, in effect claiming the same connection with the sun as warriors and those who were cremated.

When pochteca returned from exhausting treks across Mexico with precious and often exotic goods, they received the attention of the paramount ruler and those tecuhtli who had entrusted trade goods to their care. Indications that the tecuhtli and the pochteca had profitable contact suggests the extent of status flux. That the paramount chief consigned goods to the pochteca to trade on his account suggests that mercantilism had taken root. Theoretically, tribal traditions called for items received in tribute to be distributed to tribal members. Under the chieftaincy, the process of converting tribute into private property was well advanced, as was a shift from administrative nobility to a simple hereditary one not involved in governing.

Nevertheless, wealth became a problem for a society in which personal advancement theoretically followed from state service rather than as a function of capital accumulation or a good deal by sharp traders.

Political control in a chieftaincy rested, in large part, on restricting the achievement of status; in effect, the protostate decided who received esteem and under what conditions. The concessions to merchants show that the system had begun to evolve. Indications of social and economic contacts with the tecuhtli suggest that the pochteca's influence could not be resisted much longer.

The wealth of the pochteca created a fourth pole of power indirectly tied to the basic three divisions of administrative, military, and religious institutions. Accumulating wealth posed less of a problem than circumventing restrictions on its display. Public displays of wealth and socializing with the nobility were not allowed, although the prohibition was evidently not enforced. When permitted, gift giving by individual merchants demonstrated their status and success, which rivaled or exceeded that of the nobility. The pochteca lived frugally but yearned to spend lavishly and did so during the annual festival of Panquetzaliztli.[114] Structurally, society could not concede status based on wealth in nonnoble hands or allow the purchase of a noble lifestyle, as permitted in Europe. Nevertheless, such restrictions appear to have been increasingly unsustainable.

Variations in status existed within the pochteca, with privileges for the best traders or for those who had undertaken highly successful diplomatic missions. Although they had the right to send their children to the calmecac along with the children of nobles, they would not be called on for civic or military service. In addition, they acquired land on the same basis as the tecuhtli, as discussed previously. In the 1400s, Mesoamerica experienced a period of sharply increased interregional trade that elevated the importance of merchants. The implication of the boom in commerce for the socioeconomic and political structure, as well as for long-term interdependence, was not immediately apparent. That the pochteca posed a threat to the rigid distribution of status, as had European merchant-traders, seems obvious.

Another occupational group out of sync with the putative sociopolitical structure was the highly skilled craft workers. Skilled artisans who worked gold and other precious material and those with trade skills added value to the raw material that entered the city as tribute. Those with refined talents, referred to as Toltecs, thrived with the demand for the distinctive feather work that indicated an official function and jewelry restricted to certain groups as a sign of honor or special favor.

Use of precious metals and gems in religious displays, masks of the principal deities worn for sacred purposes, and gifts for a variety of uses by officials and others kept them busy. They expected to be well paid for their skills and were not disappointed. Sculptors of a statue of Moctezuma I received an advance of clothing, ten loads of squash, ten loads of beans, and two loads each of cotton, cacao, and chilies, as well as a load of maize and other items—by any standard, they were well paid.[115] Nevertheless, on completion, they also received two slaves each and more loads of various materials; they likely used factors, bartered, or sold the items they did not intend to use. Publicly respecting the contributions of skilled producers would become necessary at some point.

As a hereditary occupational group, artisans may, at one time, have been a separate tribe or a contingent that splintered off, perhaps as a result of war or famine. They lived in a district referred to as Amantlan. A sacred hymn provides a clue to their possible origins, recording that the Mexica conquered the men from Amantlan. Local lore asserted that workers of precious gems descended from the people of Xochimilco. Workers of precious metals appeared to have connections with the Yopi, who occupied the arid land across mountains. In general, the Toltecs received much of the credit for refined artisan techniques. Similar to the pochteca, these useful outsiders occupied an ambiguous position.

Another skilled and likely hereditary occupational group was the painters of hieroglyphic codices. Their skills had much in common with European medieval scribes, in that several forms of recording had to be mastered. They understood how to render the spoken word into sounds as well as how to deal with important details in each glyph. That the early Spanish friars marveled at how quickly they learned Latin should not have been a surprise. The status predicament of what may be described as a complex knowledge industry had less pressing reflections among those who were involved in more modest forms of commercial or skilled activity.

Among the less exalted craft workers, an undetermined number of foreign workers, attracted to the wealth of empire, plied their skills. These individuals made pots, reed mats, and other everyday items. They, in fact, competed with rural home production. Disdainfully referred to as *Chichimecas,* they enjoyed little respect. Nevertheless, semiskilled artisans set up stalls in markets, indicating that the demand was sufficient to support manufacturing industries and distributors as well as at least modestly to compensate those who produced them. Those who cultivated communal land might be subject also to unpaid labor in various city projects and, in return, receive gifts and food in exchange for their labor. Just how the vast number of porters and others involved in the transportation of goods were compensated likely was a mixture of agreed term, slave labor, and tribute in service of the community. In a similar fashion, cultivators who worked communal land disposed of at least a part of their crop on their own account, as the bustling activity in large central markets indicates. Profit, petty or otherwise, infused all levels. The existence of voluntary slavery, as discussed earlier, indicated some sort of family financial planning.

Tenochtitlán, as the directive heart of the Aztec empire, at the macrolevel functioned as a collection depot for much of Mesoamerica's resources. Tribute, drained by force from a wide region, sustained the city and a population that had grown far beyond its own resources. War, coercive intimidation, and unwilling tribute restrained the development of voluntary trade—a reality that inhibited the economic momentum that springs from active trading based on mutual advantage and broad-based demand. An economy based on extracting at the imperial level, on the one hand, and producing goods to meet market demands, on the other, is not very sophisticated in spite of the complexity noted at the level of the retail marketplace. From the mixture of profit and corvée labor the Spaniards chose unpaid labor under the guise of a community obligation.

Goods drawn in from many different regions made value-added manufacturing possible, including embroidered cloaks, religious images and masks, fine and lower-quality jewelry, feather work, and copper items that yielded a profit. Tenochtitlán absorbed tribute, in part, by becoming a manufacturing center using raw material received to add value and export it to others. Tribute provided a subsidy, at the expense of the tributaries, for manufacturing activities. Rules governing dress and ornamentation hindered the development of a mass market for expensive goods, as they do in any consumer society. Inexpensive items to meet everyday demand depended on agriculturists and part-time production of woven cotton items, clay pots, and storage baskets. A group of internal merchant-traders functioned as wholesale distributors, providing allotments to retailers. One-day neighborhood markets moved from one location to another throughout the city. Economic activity created capital in varying amounts at multiple levels in society, which conflicted with a political and social system that found it difficult to channel wealth and readily reallocate status based on individual commercial achievement.

Mesoamerica in the late fifteenth century verged on a commercial revolution along the lines of medieval Europe in 1000–1300. As is usually the case with macromovements, regions exhibited concurrent stages, from a protomarket to a nearly fully integrated market stage by the sixteenth century.[116] Two parallel commercial systems functioned: tribute and trade, often dealing with the same commodities. Nevertheless, the Aztecs decided on what items they wanted as tribute, indicating economic planning. Decisions made in Tenochtitlán could distort availability, however, and injured sending economies. The many regions that formed the empire spread such distortions across Mesoamerica. The extensive trade in feathers for cloaks and other uses depended on birds found only in the tropical lowlands, as did the trade in cacao, cotton, and animal skins. Copper from newly incorporated Oaxaca, valued on par with gold, may have been the most important reason the Aztec empire expanded into that distant region. Other high-valued tribute items included amber and turquoise, which were important in the crafting of religious masks as well as jewelry. Gold mixed with base metals depended on tribute as well as trade. Military supplies in the form of uniforms and headdresses, padded armor, shields, and obsidian for weapons came from a number of regions.

A few examples give some indication of the burdensome volume of imperial tribute on individual cities. From Xilotepec came 800 loads of women's wear, 800 loads of loincloths, over 3,000 loads of cotton textiles, and many other mundane items in equally large quantities.[117] Cuauhnahuac sent 8,000 packets of paper annually, some 33 percent of demand—an indication of the number of codices manufactured and used to record information. Tochpan delivered almost 7,000 loads of cloaks, 60 sacks of feathers, paper, and much more. Other members of the Aztec Confederation also had their tributaries. Texcoco demanded 40 loads of cloaks, 20 loads of fine-colored shirts, 400 sacks of cochineal, 400 loads of women's tunics and shirts, gold items, and several live eagles from Tochtepec and their tributaries. Tribute payments might be required every three months, annually, or on an agreed-on schedule.[118] The combined volume of tribute strained the productive capacity of many parts of the empire and semi-impoverished subject cities, as their people labored to meet tribute obligations.[119] Tribute worked against trade, but tributaries could trade with others for goods that would be dispatched to Tenochtitlán. While trade fostered voluntary interdependence, tribute acted to beggar others and maintained resentments that dated back to the forced subordination of the tributary. A mixed tribute-trade empire provided access to resources and underpinned expansion; political rationalization lagged far behind.

Consumer demands and the production required to satisfy perceived needs as well as basic necessities (food, clothing, medicines, and so on) in a large and growing city could be brought together only in a centralized, well-organized marketplace. In the Mexica capital, as trade and tribute flows grew, it became necessary to incorporate forcefully (in 1473) the adjacent merchant city of Tlatelolco, with its energetic merchants and its well-established marketplace. Turnover of inventory can only be estimated. Meeting demands of some 20,000 consumers a week (80,000 a month) required a vast network of suppliers and a large numbers of *tamemes* (porters) to keep the Tlatelolco market stocked. Well organized with sections for each type of merchandise and with judges drawn from the pochteca to set prices, settle disputes, and enforce the rules that required sellers to set values in terms of the equivalent value in cotton cloaks (for large purchases) and for other items such as cacao beans (for small items) serving as protocurrency, the market compared well to similar international markets such as that of Medina del Campo in Spain.[120]

The Tlatelolco market was not unique. Hernán Cortés reported on the marketplace of Tlaxcala in similarly glowing terms. He estimated that some 30,000 buyers and sellers utilized the Tlaxcala marketplace every day, more or less the same as the Tlatelolco market. Cortés noted that an array of medicinal herbs, clothing, foodstuffs, and other necessities could be obtained. In addition, he observed barbershops that offered shaves and washed hair, suggesting the existence of a service economy that complemented commerce in goods.[121] Such markets functioned as powerful engines of exchange.

The nature of tribute items, some perishable and others subject to disintegration over time, required the imperial center to engage in trade in order to dispose of unwanted surplus items. Pricing tribute presented a problem, as the actual cost of production was unknown. Aztec merchants who engaged in the secondary trade had an immediate price advantage, subsidized by distant tribute payers. The initial trade in a circumscribed trading zone was only the beginning of a much larger trading network, accounting for the discovery of trade goods by archeologists at great distances from their point of origin.

For Tenochtitlán, the profit margin must have been excessive, but only if the cost of military enforcement was laid aside. Obviously, the value of commerce in the central valleys, considering not only the two markets just noted but also that of the merchant center of Cholula and a host of secondary markets, must have been very significant. A host of smaller buyers and sellers and street vendors made up the bottom of what appears to have been a buzzing commercial scene equivalent to that of Castile and perhaps more.

The missing element was an efficient way to store value. In the absence of actual money, multiple exchanges of the same goods became expensive in terms of labor. Barter involved the physical transportation of goods, a costly transfer depending on distances, although the expense would be forced onto tributaries. The cost of goods increased with each step taken by a porter carrying a load on his back, until bulk items became prohibitively expensive beyond a certain radius.

A system of protomonetary value in the form of the determined cost of cloaks, quills filled with gold dust, cacao beans, and other small but scarce items such as small copper axes indicated how close Indo-Mexico had come to modern monitory exchange. Many but not all items had intrinsic value based on practical material uses, a reality that contributed to stable prices. Money requires that its backing, in terms of valuable content, be low enough to be too expensive to melt down or divert to other uses but in sufficient demand that it remains in circulation.[122] The problem with cacao beans and copper axes is they could be diverted to other uses, and in the case of cacao, beans lost value as they deteriorated. The use of the Pacific coast oyster shell, however, came close to being a perfect monetary item.[123]

It should be kept in mind that barter requires a grasp of the value of what is being offered and of the items presented in exchange. That Indo-Mexico verged on modernizing exchange seems obvious. Nevertheless, forced tribute in kind and plunder clearly posed significant obstacles to economic advancement. That commerce had evolved far ahead of the sociopolitical structure seems clear. Over the long run, the balance between trade and tribute favored trade, but that, in turn, required sociopolitical modifications across Mesoamerica. In Indo-Mexico, only labor remained without a developed market of some kind to establish the actual cost—a prerequisite for the creation of a wage system. As will be discussed next, the absence of a wage system led to abuse of Indian labor in the early Indo-Spanish period.

Feeding the Population

The question of whether Indo-Mexico consumed human flesh out of necessity, as well as whether food supplies were sufficient to support the population of central Mexico, needs to be examined. Most scholars agree that limited cannibalism was not a response to inadequate food resources. Some very primitive tribal groups in the north who depended on hunting and gathering may have had little choice but to resort to human flesh.[124] The heart and blood belonged to the gods, but the warrior who had taken a prisoner in battle claimed the body, retrieving the corpse as it rolled down the pyramid steps and inviting his friends to the feast. Just how much of the body would be consumed is in doubt. Consumption may have been restricted to certain parts. To share the body may have been a way of establishing positive communion with the gods.[125] An adult male has more or less the same percentage of protein as pork or beef: about 16 percent if fully utilized for food. In spite of the massive number of sacrificial victims, when divided by the population, they would not be a significant source of protein.[126] Had human flesh been a necessity, access would likely not have been restricted by ritual. In addition, had hordes of hungry cannibals consumed the human seed corn, it is difficult to imagine how impressive civilizations could have emerged. On the other hand, the justification for human sacrifice, to feed the gods and buy time for the Earth itself, appeared to be worthwhile, objectives that the population could accept as such. Had cannibalism been a major feature of life in Indo-Mexico, the Europeans would have made full use of it to justify their presence.[127] They did not and could not do so.

Population growth in Indo-Mexico and its concentration in cities shaped both the production and distribution of foodstuffs. Supply pressures required continuous agricultural expansion wherever possible, as well as drawing in supplies from other regions through trade and tribute. Not surprisingly, the paramount ruler of the Aztec empire dined in abundance, making simultaneously a political and gastronomic statement. A typical palace menu might include corn cakes, wild game, and fish and fowl of every conceivable variety prepared in over 300 dishes. The ruler selected what appealed to him and, on occasion, favored an individual with a dish he particularly enjoyed. Usually he ate alone behind a screen that shielded him from view, his chosen meal placed on a white tablecloth and attended by several women. Permission to eat in the presence of the ruler was a sign of high esteem. At the conclusion of the meal, the ruler ordered that all visiting dignitaries be served, followed by the palace retinue. Some 1,000 dishes had to be prepared daily to feed the palace staff, visitors, and messengers who arrived at all hours. Who could doubt the prosperity and power of the Mexica? The paramount chief and his retainers and nobles (some 25 percent of the population) ate well, but the population in general enjoyed a reasonable diet.

The macehualtin supplied the labor for agriculture and the exploitation of other food resources. At first glance, judging by a Eurocentric diet, the macehualtin did not consume sufficient protein. The daily recommended amount of protein for a male between the ages of nineteen and thirty is 56 grams a day, and for females in the same age bracket, it is 46 grams a day but jumps to 71 grams with pregnancy. Corn or maize, the foundation of the Indo-Mexican diet, has less than 4 grams of protein if it is eaten alone, disregarding the way humans often combine different foods. Corn gruel *(atolli)* and tamales could be reinforced with fish, seeds of various types, fruit, and honey. Tortillas, then as now, were eaten with beans, chilies, and tomatoes. Beans provide 7.5 grams of protein per 100 grams, but combined with available animal protein such as iguana meat (with 24.4 percent protein), supplies 112 calories of energy. Armadillos have 29 percent and rabbits 20.4 percent, all respectable amounts of protein from locally abundant animals.

The way food is prepared also impacts nutritional value and caloric content. Preparing corn by using alkaline cooking with lime and heat and then washing and cooling before grounding into dough *(masa)* to make tortillas dramatically increases the calcium content. *Pozolli (pozole)*, boiled corn ground into masa and then mixed with water and flavored (may be fermented or not), has more quality protein and other essential nutrients than unprocessed corn. *Agave* (century plants) and nopal cactus can be cultivated but grow in the wild also. *Octli (pulque),* derived from cultivated agave, has substantial food value, whether fermented or fresh. A serving of pulque provides 26 percent of the daily requirement for calcium, 12 percent of vitamin C, and 2 percent of iron; the nutritional value of pulque is likely the reason that the elderly had permission to consume the drink without restrictions.[128] Insects such as dried red maguey worms have 71 percent protein; grasshoppers at the low end have 30.9 percent, with many other species in between. Insects varied in their availability, whereas some such as axayacatl (*corisella texcocana*—a species of aquatic insects called water boatman) with 68.7 percent protein could be harvested year round. In addition, insect protein supplies essential amino acids. Other foodstuffs collected from the wild provide high-quality protein, such as mesquite pods and seeds, with an energy value of 294 calories, more than European beef. *Tecuitlatl* (spirulina), the green scum collected from lakes with high saltwater content, was sold in the market to be eaten with chilies and tomatoes and has been shown to be a modern wonder food.[129] The variety of the pre-Columbian diet, only briefly presented here, offset deficiencies in any one staple or domestic animal.

Agricultural techniques were also quite impressive. Planting corn, beans, squash, and amaranth *(huauhtli, amaranthus)* together fixes nitrogen in the soil, reduces pest damage, preserves moisture, and increase yields by 50 percent. Amaranth (planted above the corn seed) provided weekly edible greens rich in vitamin A, among other nutrients, without any impact on the germination of corn. Amaranth is a very efficient protein producer that grows year-round at lower tropical elevations. Amaranth's abundant seeds can be stored for a considerable period and eaten when desired. Chia (*salvia hispanica,* a species of mint) produces a high-energy seed that slows the process of carbohydrates turning into sugar. Aquaculture in the form of *chinampas* (floating agricultural platforms) loaded with bottom mud planted with vegetables, when fixed in place, provided up to seven crops a year. Indo-Mexicans combined hunter-gatherer resources with sophisticated agriculture and processes that enriched the nutritional value of what they consumed. It is not at all obvious that the lower classes in Indo-Mexico lived with a negative protein balance and presumably a bodily craving for protein.[130]

Nevertheless, the absence in Indo-Mexico of large domestic animals able to provide protein in amounts equivalent to that of European animals could not be compensated for by smaller domesticated creatures, including dogs, turkeys, and ducks. European domestic animals, for example, beef, with 18.7 percent protein, supplied 244 calories of energy; and pork, with 17.5 percent, supplied 194 calories. Although a significant amount of this protein was in the form of fat, these animals were convenient sources of substantial amounts of protein. Perhaps the most successful European introduction came in the form of chickens, a low-cost producer of eggs and meat. Chickens multiplied rapidly in the new setting, and their care mirrored that of turkeys.[131]

The issue of how many people could be supported in a sustainable way in the Valley of Mexico remains in dispute, although it appears that under normal conditions, the population had sufficient food. At the elevation of Tenochtitlán, corn produced one crop a season, but the planting, growing, and harvesting of corn depended on a narrow window of opportunity, which, if deviated from, could impact the crop. A delay in the rainy season (May–September) could be disastrous, as could an early frost in the fall. At lower elevations, two crops could be harvested, dependent on rain but without the worry of frost. Consequently, in Tenochtitlán, supply stability rested on tributaries. Corn as a tribute item made up the bulk of food imports, but amaranth and chia constituted a lesser yet important percentage of such transfers. Corn, a bulky item, came from considerable distances, in at least some cases requiring a trek of eight to ten days. The number of people who could be supported for a year by the tribute in staples has been estimated between 40,000 and 150,000.[132] Whether all the tribute in grains was consumed in Tenochtitlán or whether it entered the market as surplus cannot be determined. Nevertheless, under normal conditions, the carrying capacity of the central valleys and most of Indo-Mexico appeared adequate. The ability to survive widespread climatic cycles was another matter.

The growth in nonagricultural occupations, political and military personnel, and the priesthood placed demands on Indo-Mexico's ability to sustain the people materially. In addition, a growing industrial-craft sector, processors of cotton cloth, feather workers, and many other handmade specialties made Tenochtitlán an important industrial center as well as a market for food. The large number of porters who constituted the transportation sector in the absence of draft animals and wheeled carts required high-energy protein. The sustainability of those who were involved in nonagricultural pursuits, vital to advance Indo-Mexican civilization, under normal conditions rested on sufficient food supplies, although abnormal weather conditions led to famine.

Shortages at the imperial center spread the misery across the empire as subject groups came under pressure to deliver more foodstuffs as tribute. Chalco supplied large amounts of grain to Tenochtitlán, but that too depended on the harvest. Spreading scarcity heightened the possibility of revolts that threatened sociopolitical control. Dealing with rebellious tributaries, however, required the mustering of a physically weakened military force that had to be supported in the field, making further demands on food while not resolving the problem of its scarcity. Supplies just before the harvest could be expensive and in limited quantity. Once the harvest appeared certain, the Tlatoani, in honor of Xilonen, patron of sprouted maize plants and an avatar of Chicome-coatl (seven serpent, the goddess of maize), distributed tamales to the people for a period of seven days, followed after an interval by green corn tortillas, indicating an imminent harvest.

Stored grains offered some relief until supplies ran out, but prolonged disasters such as the drought noted by Durán in the Valley of Mexico that began in 1454 and lasted three years led to widespread suffering and out-migration. The storehouse of the Aztec chieftaincy provided minimum rations for a year before it too ran out. Starving individuals sold their children to people from regions not impacted by the drought so they had a chance of surviving.[133]

Crop failures could not be offset effectively by other sources of food, although different climatic zones might be able to offer limited supplies. Hunting animals attracted to the marshes that ringed the lakes supplemented food supplies during normal weather conditions; but their numbers declined during droughts, as did stocks of fish, frogs, waterborne insects, worms, and surface organic growth. Plant roots also could be resorted to; but harvesting the roots destroyed the plants, and the lack of rain made regeneration unlikely. Chinampas, a usually reliable source, failed as lake levels dropped and receded from the shoreline and water quality fell.

The paramount chief Ahuitzotl, alarmed at the level of salinity in the lake water, turned to the springs of Coyoacan some six miles away with the idea of channeling water into the lake. In spite of advice that controlling the flow would be difficult and could result in flooding, the project proceeded and ended badly, as predicted. Nevertheless, Ahuitzotl understood the importance of agricultural engineering in the provisioning of the city. He ordered the construction of a dike to control lake-water levels and salinity, as well canals to channel water to the fields. Chinampa cultivation was expanded significantly as the improvements made it possible.

The introduction of large domestic animals from Europe (and the Antilles, where they had been introduced earlier) modified, but did not replace, the basic Indo-Mexican diet. European cereals such as wheat added bread, but the indigenous population remained ambivalent about wheat. European food-animal imports provided more resources; however, the primary purpose was not always nourishment but manufacturing inputs, hides and wool, or transportation.

Socioeconomic Realignment

Resource concentration in Tenochtitlán and other large markets that recycled trade and the tribute extracted from other empires created concentrated abundance. Accumulated capital, as indicated by the pressure on the system exerted by the pochteca, needed an outlet beyond what the current system offered. The absence of a mechanism for absorbing and distributing wealth posed a crucial problem in a sociopolitical structure that conferred status and gift rewards on the basis of an individual's political and military functions in support of the chieftaincy rather than economic success.

Redefining status in socioeconomic terms as well as modernizing economic exchange required reorganizing virtually everything else. Craft workers, small-scale traders, and retailers may not have had the same opportunity to acquire wealth as did the pochteca, but they were on the same upward trajectory and faced the same frustrations. Those without such skills, however, suffered with little hope of relief. The obvious solution—a better distribution of wealth—conflicted with centralization of power as the chieftaincy moved toward a protomonarchy. The chieftaincy and the nobles absorbed a larger share of tribute. The widening socioeconomic gap between the nobles and the peasants who produced basic necessities, filled the ranks of the army, attended to the infrastructure of the city, made up the bulk of sacrificial victims, supported religious festivals, and paid in-kind taxes could not be sustained indefinitely without slipping into a feudal arrangement. Although theoretically the lower classes were still tribal members with certain rights, in reality, the socioeconomic balance had shifted in favor of the nobility and the protostate. The implied social compact of a tribal society had all but vanished on the eve of the arrival of the European intruders.

Along with specialized service tasks performed by merchants, a significant group was constituted by porters, market vendors of all types, midwives, astrologers, engineers, architects, and those who performed many similar activities necessary to sustain urban populations. Labor, land, marketing, consumption, and individual wealth were linked together in Indo-Mexico. This explains the increasing interaction between the pochteca, anxious for status, and the tecuhtli, anxious for a return on their resources. Along with the activities of the entrepreneurial nobles, the volume of tribute encouraged the paramount chief to dabble in trade. Chieftaincy lifestyle restrictions acceptable in earlier times and those decreed by Moctezuma I and Moctezuma II ignored the pressure generated by wealth.

Land and labor was the key to rationalizing the socioeconomic structure, as the Europeans understood immediately. A certain amount of ad hoc rationalization had, in fact, already occurred. Land had been dedicated to support the officeholding elite and had been allocated to individuals, especially the land of tributaries. A checkered pattern of landholding resulted in a type of absentee landlord. In theory, land remained communal; only the use of the land had been alienated. In fact, land use transferred to the succeeding generation even when heirs had no state functions that warranted support. Such estates, called *pillalli,* functioned as private property. Land without labor, however, cannot generate capital. The missing element, a permanent labor force tied to the land, began to emerge. A step below the macehualtin was a category of landless peasants who were technically free; the *tlalmaitl,* nevertheless, did not have rights enjoyed by the macehualtin. They had no claim to tribal privileges, did not receive an allotment of land from the calpulli, and worked land awarded to a tecuhtli. As labor bound to the land, they accompanied the land as it transferred, somewhat in the

manner of a European serf. They owed a share of the crop to the beneficial owner or negotiated an amount in return for the right to farm a set
portion of land. In the absence of tribal rights, they neither paid taxes
nor supplied corvée labor. Nevertheless, chieftaincy law governed
them, and they had the same military obligations as the macehualtin.

How many people fell into this category is open to speculation, perhaps 20 percent. The origins of the tlalmaitl are unknown. They may
have belonged to different tribes and become detached by war, drought,
famine, or other natural disasters. Indo-Mexico had little room for unattached people, leaving few options other than tlalmaitl status. Demand for such arrangements indicated a movement toward self-generated
wealth unconnected to state service or tribute—in short, nobles supported by labor bound to their landed estates.[134] Confiscatory transfer
without compensation constituted an additional source of wealth for
the Aztecs. Consequently, Aztec nobles had holdings scattered around
the empire. Nobles likely traded land in order to consolidate property.
Although transfers by inheritance and marriage occurred, land was, in
fact, a fairly static asset. Land with an assignment of labor further impoverished those who were forced to supply both inputs. Movement
toward slavery created a more fluid labor market.

Two types of slavery existed: slaves *(tlatlacotin)* who entered slavery
voluntarily and those who were captured and enslaved. The two had
quite different prospects. In the first category, individuals and families unable to pay their debts or interested in contracting new ones had
the option of selling their labor by agreement; four witnesses had to
attest to the arrangement. Debt slavery could be passed on to an individual's son or widow in case of death, an indication of the importance
of contractual agreements. The value of a slave was equivalent to enough
goods to sustain a person for one year, or twenty *quachtli* (simple
cloaks).[135] An individual who failed to pay taxes could be sold in the
marketplace for the amount owed. Voluntary slavery, not necessarily
permanent or considered shameful but with some impact on status,
functioned as an open-ended institution, providing a variety of ways
to rejoin the free population. A slave owner purchased labor but not
ownership of a slave's body. Separating entitlement to labor from a particular individual had logical consequences. A revolving substitution
of individuals could meet the obligation. At times, a family or group
of families combined to sell a worker's labor and then all took turns

assigning an individual to fulfill the agreement. In another variation, a child might be a slave until reaching marriageable age, when another child would take up the position. In this respect, it appeared to be similar to a European apprenticeship in the best of circumstances or an indentured servant in the worst.

Children could not be born into slavery but might inherit the debt. Slaves could marry a free person, hold personal property, have a slave, and regain the right to dispose of their labor by returning the original price. The commodity in all cases remained labor. Treatment of slaves appears to have been relatively benign, and one suspects that some slaves considered it advantageous to work in a prestigious household. Incidences of slaves marrying into tecuhtli families are recorded. In a celebrated case, a slave woman gave birth to the distinguished paramount chief Itzcoatl. Freeing slaves of their labor obligation by decree appears to have been a frequent occurrence, indicating that political leaders viewed slavery as a consequence of disaster or a poverty-driven expedient. In addition, a grateful patron might relinquish his right to labor on his death. Reforms in the early 1500s canceled debt if a slave died while providing labor. A free person responsible for a slave's death in childbirth had to provide compensation, provide a replacement, or take her place. Urban slavery in the household of a noble or merchant seems to have been the most frequent.

Another category of slaves had much grimmer prospects. Prisoners taken in war might be spared and used as slaves until their final service had to be rendered. Within the empire, providing a set number of slaves as part of the tribute encouraged slaving parties to go beyond the empire to seize victims. These unfortunates would eventually be sacrificial offerings. They had none of the protection offered voluntary slaves. In general, the institution of slavery did not make a significant economic contribution, but it had the potential to do so. Its existence encouraged the conquistadors and early settlers to contemplate indigenous slavery as a possible labor system. The Crown, aware of the possibility, believed that it would jeopardize the papal conveyance and prohibited it.

Moreover, by the latter decades of the fifteenth century, the limits of tribute empires had been reached and exceeded. Trade and the broadening of consumption made force, the threat of violence, and tribute less useful, but they could not be abandoned easily. Tribute engendered prosperity for certain groups, requiring a different stratification model and movement away from a chieftaincy toward a protomonarchy.[136] Tribalism, with its sense of equality and social unity grounded in shared fortune and misfortune, had long since reached the end of its usefulness. The tecuhtli governed over a macrosociopolitical structure that the economic system had made archaic. In major social categories, status lagged behind economic reality. Increasingly, irrational distortions created an untenable situation.

Deification

Semideification of leaders began in 1486 when Ahuitzotl, the paramount chief of the Mexica, proclaimed himself Huitzilopochtli's high priest, laying claim to being the god's principal agent. Moctezuma II cultivated a reputation as a devoted adherent of Huitzilopochtli, maintaining a private chapel in the sacred enclosure of that god. He reputedly felt close to Quetzalcóatl also, following one of many myths that the god had served as the first paramount chief of the Mexica and that all successors occupied his original position. That Quetzalcóatl promised to return made every occupant a temporary stand-in until the god could reclaim his rightful place. The unpredictable Tezcatlipoca would be nudged aside cautiously.

Moctezuma II, on his assumption of directive power in 1503, faced problems that threatened to unravel the empire and with it the military, economic, social, and political foundations. At the start of the sixteenth century, it appeared possible that Tenochtitlán would meet the same fate that other earlier cities had previously: an Indo-Mexican cycle of grandeur followed by decline, destruction, and dispersal. To make matters grimmer, a series of omens were interpreted negatively by worried soothsayers as the year of Quetzalcóatl's return approached. Victory or defeat in war served as a sign of favor or disfavor. Moctezuma's selection as paramount chief required him to demonstrate military prowess. Descending on the hapless cities of Nopallin and Ixpatepec, he returned with some 5,000 prisoners destined to sustain the gods. Moctezuma's elevation occasioned the most elaborate ritual and public acclaim in the history of the empire. Prisoners mounted the pyramid's steps to the sacrificial altar, where priests cut open the chests of their victims, removed the still-quivering heart, and tilted the body off the sacrificial stone over the side and down the steps. Blood, the food of the gods, dripped down and pooled on the steps as the celebratory orgy of death and political elevation continued.[137]

An Overextended Empire

The center of imperial domination shifted decisively, but not immediately, to the Valley of Mexico with the creation of the Aztec Confederation. The valley's assortment of lesser chieftaincies could not resist. The Otomí maintained a foothold in the Valley of Mexico to the north, whereas in the northeast, Huaxtecs, Totonacs, and Mazatecs soon fell within the empire. In the south, Mixtecs and Zapotecs had been incorporated, as had some Maya speakers. Tlappanecs, Cuitlatecs, Coixcas in the southwest and, farther west, Mazahuas and Matlaltzincas rounded out a diverse empire. Under the leadership of Ahuitzotl, aggressive military campaigns created a bicoastal empire that, on the Pacific coast, stretched from north of Zacatula to south of the Isthmus of Tehuantepec and, on the Atlantic side, from Tuxpán in the north to what is now the Guatemalan border to the south. Not all went well for Ahuitzotl, as his defeat at the hands of the Tarascans, discussed shortly, demonstrates. He overextended the empire, leaving his ill-fated successor, Moctezuma II, the task of hastily consolidating control over conquered tributaries and filling in some of the gaps. Nevertheless, time had run out.

Normally, the only imperial officials that tributary subjects came in contact with resided in their midst for the sole purpose of monitoring the economy and supervising the collection and dispatching of tribute to Tenochtitlán. The *calpixqui* (tribute collector) and a small staff provided up-to-date information on the resources of subject cities and potentially troubling attitudes. Violent defiance could not be tolerated. Ahuitzotl descended on Oztoma and Alahuiztla on the Tarascan frontier, slaughtered the entire population, and replaced them with 2,000 settlers. The settlers had little to work with after the killing of every man, woman, child, dog, and bird and the uprooting of trees in a no-holds-barred assault in retaliation for killing Aztec envoys and throwing their bodies to the vultures. Not surprisingly, neighboring Mixtec and

Zapotec cities immediately offered to become tributaries.[138] Moctezuma I subsequently dispatched 600 married couples and their families along with another 120 people from the other members of the triple alliance to Oaxaca to repopulate the well-situated city of Guaxaca. Subsequently, the colony served as a base for further expansion.[139]

The usual pattern was not so harsh. After a defeat, suitably submissive chiefs were treated with respect and allowed to retain any tributaries they might have, although the negotiated tribute amount included such assets. The Aztecs permitted cities and towns and their surrounding countryside to function under traditional rulers with administrative autonomy. While this arrangement relieved the Aztecs of the expense of administration, it heightened the possibility of a rebellion. No attempt was made to assimilate tributaries into an overarching territorial entity with a common destiny and integrated administration. A more robust imperial presence might be required on frontier posts, with even a garrison if necessary. Limited colonization in frontier regions occurred but not as a general policy, perhaps because of internal resistance to such relocations.

The Aztec empire, well entrenched in the south center, with a bicoastal presence, had reached its geopolitical limits by the early sixteenth century. Further expansion of the empire would be structurally difficult. Soconusco, today on the Pacific-coast border of Mexico and Guatemala, perhaps the farthest western reach of the Aztec empire, required an approximately 1,000-mile trek over narrow mountainous pathways from Tenochtitlán. Lesser but still arduous distances existed throughout the Aztec empire.

In spite of the difficulties and the expense, to ignore distant revolts encouraged a political unraveling on the imperial fringes with the potential of spreading to core regions, eventually bringing down what, in reality, constituted a fragile imperial arrangement. Such campaigns consumed time and resources. Putting down the Soconusco revolt required at least sixty days to reach the battle site, a calculation based on Roman legionnaires' known ability to march twenty miles a day loaded down by seventy pounds of equipment and supplies. The Aztecs did not build all-weather roads, as did Rome, but traveled on trails able to accommodate several warriors abreast.[140] Nor could they use water (rivers and seacoast) transportation to establish resupply depots in useful proximity to the army. Each soldier consumed two pounds of maize and half

MAP 1. The Mexica-Aztec Empire, 1519

a gallon of water a day; a self-sufficient army could carry food for about eight days. Consequently, Aztec armies lived on a chain of tributaries, likely leaving severe food shortages and resentment behind.[141]

In view of logistical and political problems posed by vast distances, further expansion logically required the creation of subimperial-affiliated political bodies to manage a far-flung empire—an arrangement that required the decentralization of tribute and a federated, rather than confederated, political structure. The empire risked fragmentation if the subparts became too powerful or acquired a separate chain of supporting tributaries. The general distrust of others and the absence of widely recognized and legitimate blood ties able to create interlocking family dynasties resulted in a fragile and uncertain geopolitical balance throughout most of Indo-Mexico. Force or the threat of it remained the most effective guarantor of imperial unity. Rather than decentralization, the trend was toward centralization as Tenochtitlán's partners in the confederation became more subservient.

In the absence of the concept of a unified state, the empire remained a collection of urban points under subordinate chieftaincies of doubtful loyalties. Their only clear obligations involved tribute, as well as supplying soldiers on demand. If, as occasionally happened, a subject city killed the tax collector and his staff and refused its tribute payment, an avenging military force soon appeared to extract a heavy penalty.

The imperial center had no positive responsibilities in return for tribute. Nevertheless, the reality was that the Aztecs claimed that a city's tribute meant that others had to refrain from conquest or face retaliation by a formidable army. The imperial center created a monopoly on the use of force within the empire, which provided the unintended benefits of a *pax Azteca* but at great expense to the imperial parts.

The Aztec empire faced competition to the west from the Tarascan empire, centered in the modern Mexican state of Michoacán and from Tlaxcala to the northeast. In a manner similar to Tenochtitlán's empire, the Tarascans incorporated diverse tributary groups, including Nahuatl and Otomí speakers. The Tarascan empire posed the most formidable barrier to Aztec expansion in the west. To the east, Tlaxcala directed a confederacy of four Nahuatl-speaking cities in close proximity to Tenochtitlán but did not pose a serious threat to Aztec expansion to the southeast. Nevertheless, there were natural limits to Aztec expansion. The Tarascans, like the Mexica, had arrived in the region fairly recently and followed much the same trajectory, including establishing an imperial confederation of three cities around the rim of Lake Patzcuaro.[142]

In 1478, the Aztecs seized Xiquipilco on the Tarascan empire's eastern border before striking deeper into the territory of its rival, only to experience a crushing and politically decisive defeat. The Tarascans assembled some 40,000 warriors and fought on their home territory, with shorter supply lines and ease of communications. The Aztecs fielded 24,000 warriors, including tributaries, of which only some 200 of the Mexica contingent survived the give-no-quarter Tarascan response. Aztec remnants retreated in utter disarray to the rugged terrain around

Toluca.[143] The Aztecs' leader, Ahuitzotl, had grossly underestimated Tarascan strength; they dared not repeat an invasion but settled for a hostile western frontier. Had the Tarascans followed up their victory with a counterinvasion, they could well have toppled the Aztec empire.

An Imperial Model Exhausted

The Aztec empire had been extended in a haphazard manner, leaving hostile groups encapsulated among tributaries and ambitious competing empires on its borders. The most obvious challenge came from the Tlaxcalans and the Tarascans. However, unconquered pockets that had been bypassed in favor of richer and more enticing sources of tribute constituted a frontier problem. Tribal groups with few resources but protected by a difficult terrain made it expensive and profitless to bring them to heel but dangerous to ignore. In what is now the modern state of Guerrero, primitive mountain tribes required almost constant punitive expeditions to bring them under control, but as soon as Aztec forces withdrew, they rose up again. Maintaining access to distant Soconusco, an important source of cacao, required fighting hostile tribes that hovered along the route and the possible revolt of an important part of the tribute empire. The constant gnawing on the periphery indicated that the expansionist days of empire had ended, and much of what had been gained previously now required resources to defend. Plunder, seemingly inexhaustible in the early years, no longer provided an infusion of easy wealth; further expansion was not a viable option but nevertheless would be attempted, with disastrous results. The larger enclaves, including Metztitlán and Tototepec in the northeast, close to the Tarascan border; Tlaxcala, within striking distance of the Aztec capital; Teotitlan, almost directly south of Tlaxcala; and the Pacific-coast enclaves of Yopitzingo and the Mixtec confederation of Tototepec (not to be confused with the northeastern one of the same name) attracted the attention of Moctezuma II. That these enclaves had survived so long presaged the difficulty of now reducing them and appropriating their wealth. Moctezuma chose to attack Tlaxcala to the east and the Mixtec Pacific-coast enclave of Tototepec in a series of fruitless campaigns that demonstrated Aztec weakness. News of each setback encouraged revolts as tributaries sought to escape from long-resented obligations.

Aztec armies, accustomed to victories, suffered demoralizing defeats. When they returned to Tenochtitlán, Moctezuma II further humiliated them by forbidding any display of relief that they had survived or public gratitude for their efforts. On more than one occasion, he refused to receive defeated warrior leaders. Where to turn for new tributaries and sacrificial victims was not clear. To the north, the arid lands made expansion pointless, and to the west, the Tarascan empire and mountainous terrain blocked the Aztecs. Penetration into highland Guatemala would require a major long-distance effort and probably a permanent garrison engaged in a perpetual campaign waged in territory that favored the native population. Moving against the lowland Maya had little obvious economic value, and an easy victory could not be taken for granted. Victory had a positive psychological effect in the early stages, until defeat portended a disastrous end. Semideification of the ruler may have been an attempt to ensure control over society as the expansion stalled. Just what a divine ruler would mean for the tribute empire remained to be determined, but it suggested political consolidation.[144] The uncertain implications of deification posed a danger, but so did maintaining the status quo. An Indo-Mexico in a state of uncertainty would be ill prepared to fend off transatlantic intruders.

Internal restructuring to shore up control at the top seemed necessary; this soon evolved into rigid stratification. Moctezuma II, following the trend established by Moctezuma I, concentrated power in his hands by reducing advisers who had formerly exercised independent authority to mere administrators responsive to him. In 1515, he ended any pretense of shared direction of the triple alliance by imposing his choice of chief on Texcoco. Acting to undercut deification, a series of natural and man-made disasters occurred. Crops failed in 1505, 1506, and 1507, resulting in widespread hunger: emergency stores were soon depleted. Tribute could not be squeezed out of tributaries or taxes from the starving macehualtin. A listless population responded to demands without enthusiasm. With little choice, the chieftaincy had to suspend tribute, with immediate consequences for the already weakened imperial economy.[145] Enforcing collection of overdue tribute was a fruitless endeavor. Even provisioning an army in the field became problematic. Indo-Mexico worried more about starvation than about Aztec armies. Uncertainty led to a feeling of helplessness and confusion about where to turn. The better-watered lowland offered little prospects for relief.[146] Those institutions that had formerly seemed so stable now seemed fragile: their worldview no longer functioned as it had in the past. Unaddressed religious vulnerabilities and the destructive myth of the avenging Quetzalcóatl played a role in the pessimism that gripped Indo-Mexico. The belief in the end of the world as the fifth sun died; the failure to create sympathetic, caring gods; a minimal notion of an afterlife; absence of a rescuing salvation—in short, a negative set of beliefs made it difficult to regain confidence even after the string of crop failures ended in 1508.

The worldview of the Aztecs began to unravel. Central parts of their spiritual cosmos that previously provided support now led to despair. Blood remained the energizing force for war and expansion, but the gods had withdrawn their support, as indicated by Aztecs' defeats at the hands of their enemies. Their war god and tribal patron Huitzilopochtli, selfishly insistent on blood sacrifices, seemed disinclined to help. Tezcatlipoca, one of the traditional sources of the legitimacy of the chieftaincy, had apparently exercised his well-known fickleness to humble the Mexica.[147] Predictably, negatively interpreted omens confirmed the worst.

Nezahualpilli, the paramount chief of Texcoco with a reputation as a powerful diviner, related to Moctezuma a series of nightmares that prophesied the end of the empire, the destruction of cities, and the humbling of the people. He stated, "We, meaning the leaders and our children, will be killed"; Moctezuma lived to witness the disaster. As proof of the omen's veracity, Aztec armies experienced a string of military defeats with bitter losses.[148] A dying Nezahualpilli may have extrapolated the decline of the confederation to its obvious end in violence. Subsequently, Tlaxcala defeated the army, with massive losses, further shaking Moctezuma's confidence.

The appearance of a comet in 1517, visible from midnight to daybreak in the eastern sky, was taken as an ill omen, even though Nezahualpilli, more knowledgeable about astronomy, pointed out that its presence was ancient. It seemed to bleed fire as it crossed the sky—surely something so impressive had meaning, but soothsayers, priests, and diviners provided little comfort. Once the search for ill omens began, they could be found in abundance: the spontaneous combustion of Huitzilopochtli's temple in a fire that raged unchecked in spite of efforts to extinguish the blaze; apparently hit by an unseen and unheard bolt of lightning, another temple burned to the ground; comets in twos and threes crossed the sky from west to east (perhaps a meteoroid shower). Lake Mexico, with no apparent cause, rose rapidly, flooding part of the city and undermining houses. Several other rumored omens indicated generalized hysteria: a disembodied voice of a weeping woman in the night, sobbing uncontrollably and calling out, "o my sons, . . . we are lost . . . o my sons where can I hide you?" A fisherman caught a magnificent bird with a diadem in the form of a mirror. When Moctezuma looked in the creature's mirror, he saw a large number of warriors coming toward him. Suddenly, the bird disappeared, but the message had been delivered. Two-headed men and men with one head and two bodies, appropriately called *tlacantzolli* (men squeezed together), appeared, but when they were taken to Moctezuma, they also disappeared. One may assume that the more fantastic omens circulated among the people rather than in the palace, although natural phenomena would have been visible to all. In Tlaxcala, another set of omens disturbed the population and its leaders, suggesting that the hysteria had become regional. The Tlaxcalan fantasy involved a radiance that appeared before daybreak as a large, brilliant white cloud. Even more unsettling, a large dust whirlwind that occurred in the same place many times over the course of the year suggested a massive descent of the gods to Earth.[149] Omens spread fear but offered no explanation of why they had been visited on the hapless humans of Indo-Mexico.

To add to the distress, strange rumors circulated throughout Indio-Mexico about the arrival on the eastern seacoast of floating towers or mountains. Pale creatures in human form, dressed unlike anything seen before, emerged and disappeared into the bowels of floating monstrosities. On land, they rode large, deer-like creatures and directed fire sticks at those whom they attacked. The return of Quetzalcóatl became an imminent possibility. Perhaps he had returned to reclaim his rightful empire. If so, what would happen to Moctezuma II? A confused and apprehensive population experienced a crisis of confidence. Their worldview appeared incapable of placing events, real or imagined, in a useful explanatory context.

2

THE FORMATION OF
EURO-SPANISH CULTURE
Iberia Enters History

W E KNOW MORE about Euro-Spanish history simply because more of its records survive, often by sheer accident, as in case of the preservation of Greek thought, but also because more of it was recorded at the time. What we know supports the notion of similarities across time and space, but it is important to note that while Europe's basic trajectory followed a similar path to that of Indo-Mexico, it had evolved at a different rate with significant variations. The civilization that contemplated Indo-Mexico in the early sixteenth century had experienced waves of migrating barbarians, tribalism, plunder, slavery, trade, the intellectual force of Roman law and organization, the replacement of paganism, the elaboration of Christianity, the collapse of empires, and in the case of Spain, the Muslim invasion and the prolonged battle to retake the peninsula. As the imperial power, Spain could impose its will, though to a certain extent, but not completely, held in check philosophically by Roman law and the Christian notions of political benevolence as well as by Indo-Mexican cultural resistance. Nevertheless, Spain's cultural legacy became the instrument that reoriented Indo-Mexico toward European culture.

From a topographical standpoint, Spain had much in common with Mesoamerica. The Iberian Peninsula, with a landmass approximately twice the size of Italy, has many different climatic zones, extremes of elevation, varying rainfall, and differing soil conditions that made life difficult or relatively manageable. A high central table land *(meseta),* bordered on three sides by mountains, lies at its center. The seas that wash the peninsula are also different, reasonably placid in the Mediterranean and anything but on the Atlantic side. In antiquity, forests of pine and oak covered most of the peninsula. Ideal conditions for ranching existed in Extremadura, and the good soils in Castile produced abundant wheat, along with olives and grapes. The rich soils of Andalusia made for a reasonably bountiful agrarian economy. Moreover, mineral resources, particularly gold and silver, made the peninsula the richest region in the Roman Empire, an assessment recorded by Pliny.[1] Much of what we know about early Spain is from Roman sources that tend to concentrate on its economic potential.

The peninsula's contact over land with the greater European landmass was restricted by the high mountains of the Pyrenees on the northern border; in winter, heavy snows blocked the mountain passes, virtually sealing off the peninsula until the spring thaw. In sharp contrast, Africa lay within arm's reach—some eight miles away across the Straits of Gibraltar. The shallow waters of the straits provided easy access in both directions. Modern civilization as it arrived came by sea, as it did in the Western Hemisphere in 1492.

Spain's movement through history seems like a passage through all stages of human evolution. In prehistory, it experienced a continuous stream of Indo-European tribes that passed through. The Liguria, the first known inhabitants of the Iberian Peninsula, left scant clues to their origins, society, and religious beliefs. Around 900 BC, the first wave of Nordic Celts entered Iberia, settling north of the Ebro River. The Iberians, who followed around 650, possibly coming from Africa, are known equally dimly. There was another influx of Celts around 600 into the central tableland. When more Iberians arrived, this time from across the northern mountains, they mingled with the Celts, forming the Celt-Iberians. Nevertheless, not all Celts were amalgamated with the Iberians. The exact origins of the Celts and Iberians as yet cannot be determined. Movement into the peninsula appears to have been a semimigratory one, with different tribes functioning contemporaneously in set geographical locations rather than a series of successive invasions, forced amalgamations, displacements, or worse. Doubtless, tensions existed between the various groups, along with intertribal warfare that had local consequences to be sure, but such elements were not the defining feature. Roman sources offer some information on indigenous tribal organization that suggests a degree of uniformity across the peninsula. Each tribe controlled a distinct geographical space that it recognized as its territory, including a number of fixed, semiurban settlements, each with a defensive hilltop fort. On occasion, tribes might join together against a common enemy. Their warriors elected a war leader, an individual of proven valor and battlefield success. A nobility existed, possibly hereditary and likely made up the cavalry. A different phase, contemporaneous with Celtic movements, began with the arrival (ca. 1200 BC) in the Iberian Peninsula of the Phoenicians, who explored the trading possibilities of the peninsula, going through the Pillars of Hercules to establish a trading post at Gades (Cádiz) and then traveling north to the mouth of the Tagus River. As seaborne Bronze Age traders, they sought copper and tin but also traded in wool. Trading colonies of the Phoenicians and Greeks introduced their civilizing influence in the south. Subsequently, the Carthaginians moved across the Mediterranean and established Carthago Novo (Cartagena) in 228 BC on the southeast coast, directly across the Mediterranean from Carthage, becoming the conduit of Carthaginian influence in the peninsula. Carthago Novo, as the site of rich silver mines, financed trade as well as operations against local tribes and functioned as a capital of a Carthaginian province. As the Phoenicians withdrew, the Carthaginian assumed control of their settlements and expanded to the west. Greek refugees from Phocaea fleeing Persian invaders may have been the first true colonist-settlers, rather than transient merchant-traders and miners. Just how much the succession of merchant-traders influenced the Iberians is hard to determine. What is well established, however, is that imperial Rome and Roman Christianity overrode the peninsula's past, becoming a lasting formative experience, one that was transmitted to the Western Hemisphere in 1492.

Rome Enters History

Rome entered history (ca. 753 BC) with a founding myth that emphasized the centrality of warriors. The wolf that nursed Romulus and Remus, the legendary human founders, captured a calculated determination that was evident as Rome expanded across much of the Eurasian world. According to legend, the two twins descended from Alba Longa's ruling dynasty. The early history of Rome is known only dimly;

nevertheless, archeologists have pieced together a speculative outline. Rome began as an insignificant village in the Latium region of what is now central Italy. Latium, by the Bronze Age, a settled agricultural region with small, autonomous cities, was threatened by Etruscan expansion on the other side of the Tiber River. A Latin confederation, composed of some thirty settlements and led by Alba Longa, was formed to ward off the Etruscans. Leadership changed violently. After destroying Alba Longa in the middle of the seventh century, Rome became the dominant regional force.

By the middle of the third century, Rome had conquered all of Italy below the Po River, ousted the Greeks of Magna Graecia in the south, and was positioned for a wider empire. Plunder, tribute, and slaves provided the motivation. At what point Rome made the transition from a tribe to a chieftaincy to a broader political structure is unknown. As the dominant power in Italy, Rome's language displaced others as it advanced in both directions. Roman civilization, while built on that of the Greeks, was organizationally and administratively more innovative. The Roman Empire eventually extended from the Atlantic to the Rhine, the Danube and Black Sea in the south, the Sahara in Africa, and the Syrian Desert and the Euphrates River delta in the east. The Persians posed the only imperial competition after the destruction of Carthage, until the Muslim challenge emerged.

As a slave-based agricultural economy supplemented by plunder and trade, Rome required land, labor, and capital. War, followed by enslavement, represented a transfer of productivity from one group to the victors. In addition, opportunistic plunder acted as an immediate economic stimulus. Not all conquered people were enslaved. Although initially plundered, those who capitulated negotiated a tributary arrangement that over time evolved into taxation as provinces became culturally and politically tied to the concept of empire.

Rome's class structure, politics, economic well-being, and political stability, as well as its civilization, depended on war and the treasure and slaves that it provided. Rome was not unique in its economic dependency on violence; the civilized Mediterranean world relied on force, as did the barbarians who preyed on the empire. The claim that Rome was the most violent force in the ancient Mediterranean world is not without merit.[2] Empires cannot be created or kept intact without varying degrees of force. In the case of Rome, its positive gifts of civilization, law, enforced peace, and security obscured the role of force and the predatory behavior that characterized its expansion. The world viewed from Rome consisted of empires and barbarians, a division also made in Indo-Mexico between the civilized on one side and the Chichimecas on the other.

Conquest made political reputations as well as provided wealth. Pompey the Great and Julius Caesar both campaigned in Spain and became rich as well as politically important. War made, as well as restored, the fortunes of many Roman families. Funding a war fell on the military commanders, with the expectation that they would be amply compensated, along with the staff and legion soldiers, and importantly would repay borrowed funds. An essential contribution from the Roman Senate on behalf of the government added an element of state capitalism. For investors, conquest was a business proposition, and for the Roman state, war added new provinces and taxes. Those who advanced money for expeditions expected a handsome return; they functioned as a combination of both venture and booty capitalists. The reputation of a commander served as a form of collateral. Raising legions in the period of expansion depended on the confidence of prospective recruits that the experience would be materially rewarding. Roman generals often faced the temporary disintegration of their forces as frenzied soldiers searched for booty. Pompey's initial foray into Celtic-Iberian Spain got off to a confused start when a scouting party found a buried cache of gold, prompting the rest of the army to spend several days digging for more, while ignoring orders.[3] Caesar, on more than one occasion, withdrew his legionnaires away from surrendered towns before darkness to avoid the possibility that some might disobey and sack them.

A military campaign depended on a high degree of planning, organization, logistics, and discipline. A commander might be in the field for several years, maintaining contact with Rome through frequent dispatches. A horde of camp followers accompanied the army, providing auxiliary services. They traveled behind the battle-deployed legionnaires and stripped the fallen of anything of value. Slave contractors also accompanied the troops, ever ready to advance funds pending the sale and distribution of newly created slaves. Julius Caesar during the conquest of Gaul enslaved an entire town of 30,000 men, women, and children in retaliation for their resisting. When an excessive number of slaves flooded the market, the victors slaughtered all but those who could be ransomed. The sack of Jerusalem in 70 BC flooded Syria with slaves and gold, forcing the price of both commodities to fall.

The anticipation of plunder, one of several motivations to risk one's life, had economic consequences for both sides. On the losing side, sacked towns could not easily recover; disrupted trade contacts might never be reestablished, and populations, enslaved and dispersed across the Mediterranean world, would never return. Even those towns that surrendered rather than resisted lost a significant amount of their capital, with immediate consequences for trade and commerce. Nevertheless, a timely alliance with the Romans could restore a town's fortunes at the expense of others. Capital flowed to Rome and its provinces. Armies, plunderers, slave dealers, and battlefield scavengers in effect redistributed capital and culture. More positively, legions served as economic multipliers by consuming and concentrating capital; their use of money doubled the value of assets, with the buyer holding purchased commodities and the seller coin.[4]

Emperor Augustus supported a standing army that along with auxiliary soldiers (locally recruited in the provinces) numbered 300,000 men by the third century AD. Its main function was to secure the northern and eastern borders against the tribes moving west. Containing the tribes required stationing forces on the Rhine and Danube Rivers. All frontiers serve as acculturation zones where elements of different cultures intermingle. On the Rhine and the Danube, the tribes adopted Roman practices and might be allotted land within the empire. Nevertheless, the empire could not absorb the number of tribes that sought land, nor could it stop opportunistic raiding. The threat inevitably engendered harsh assessments of barbarians. As the physician Galen, who served the army on the eastern frontier, amusingly observed, whether he intended to amuse or not, "I am no more in favor of Germans [meaning barbarians] than of wolves and bears."[5]

The economic benefits of war and conquest did not remain static. Rome's dependence on expansion became costly. Conquered people were initially plundered, then forced to supply tribute, a responsibility that over time evolved into taxation as provinces became culturally and politically tied to the concept of empire. Provinces expected to receive imperial benefits, including peace, protection, access to trade, and political predictability in return for loyalty. Roman citizenship was extended to favored elites and absorbed them into the governing class, while it acted to deprive a subject population of leadership—certainly a useful tool but again one not without expenses. As parts of the empire matured, costs increased in many ways both obvious and less so, such as the forgiving of taxes owed by provincial oligarchs.

The cost of wealth extraction through war inflated as one went farther afield to identify suitable targets. At a certain point, expansion of Rome's western empire made little economic sense. Even peace was expensive and required the stationing of legions to repel interlopers. Consequently, the focus shifted eastward with the founding of Constantinople and the dividing of the empire into two separate parts. While joined by family ties, history, and some shared interests, the parts functioned independently. From a business standpoint, the division appears similar to the spin-off of an underperforming asset. In order to cut expenses and deal with barbarians crossing the Danube River to loot and destroy productive villages and farms, western emperors turned to employing tribes, bringing them into the military structure to fend off others intent on penetration. Over time, barbarian units became indistinguishable from actual Roman legions in dress and battlefield tactics. Nevertheless, the empire could not accommodate all the tribes anxious to cross into its domains or employ them as soldiers or allow them to settle in Roman provinces. The Huns were an interesting exception in that they remained north of the Danube, although they pushed others to seek shelter in Roman territory as well as raided in Italy. The Huns sacked Rome twice; however, they appeared to prefer the great Hungarian plain. Defending the integrity of the western empire posed an increasingly difficult problem. The pressure from tribal groups in search of food, bounty, and land became intense, and in the end, it was impossible to hold the frontier.[6]

Breaking the Tribes: Acculturation in Roman Iberia

Competition between two imperial powers that were ever anxious to expand and the lure of underexploited natural resources changed the economic focus from available and opportunistic trade to direct exploitation. The Iberian Peninsula became an economic geopolitical pawn between Carthage and Rome. The three Punic Wars (264–146 BC), particularly the second Punic War (218–202 BC), changed the historic and political trajectory of Spain and indeed of Western civilization. The Carthaginian defeat at Metaurus (207 BC) ended Hannibal's attempt to destroy Rome. The year before that decisive battle, Romanization in Hispania had been reinforced along the southern coastal regions, but only weakly in the interior and in the north. The fall of Carthago Nova in 209 BC to General Scipio Africanus, followed by the slaughter of all men, women, children, and animals, including dogs, cats, and birds, enabled the Romans to attract awestruck and apprehensive tribal allies eager to be on the winning side.[7]

Leadership among the Celts and Celtic-Iberians before the arrival of the Romans depended on recognized bravery and battlefield success. Politically, the warrior elite functioned within a nonhereditary chieftaincy based in small, fortified towns and villages that were placed at defensive locations; semisubsistence agriculture and herding limited the population of tribal towns. The inhabitants were likely made up of related clans. Interior towns served more for protection than for commerce, indicating a fear of raiders and general insecurity. The existence of paramount chiefs and a nobility is suggested by the large number of cavalry that could be mobilized and directed against Roman legions, at times with devastating success.

Rome brutally suppressed tribes that hesitated to become allies; nevertheless, the tribes remained restless, and a series of revolts came close to reversing the Romanization of the peninsula. Rome resorted to massacres, peace agreements soon broken, and double dealing. In the bloody and protracted war with the Numantines (Celt-Iberians on the Ebro) that ended in 133 BC, the Roman commander built a wall around the Numantines' fortress and starved the defenders into submission, but not before they resorted to cannibalism and mass suicides. Those who remained alive were sold into slavery, and the fortress was razed to the ground. Frontier wars against the Celts and Celt-Iberians had both economic and political aspects. Caesar resorted to raids whose purpose was to raise money and pay off debts. In the end, the hard-pressed tribes had to adjust to the new political, administrative, economic, and religious reality.[8] A heterogeneous, hybrid culture existed, one initially weighted toward that of the Celts and Celt-Iberians and then slowly absorbing imperial elements until Romanization laid down a lasting foundation. In the end, legions and diplomacy brought the Iberian tribes under control. In Spain, only one legion (composed of 6,000 men) appeared sufficient to assure control, testifying to the acculturation of the Iberian tribes.

As an established imperial power, Rome preferred to negotiate (using force as a last resort) but when scorned could be merciless. In most cases, treaties allowed the local elite to remain in place, although hostages might be required to guarantee submission. Roman infrastructure, in the form of roads, bridges, aqueducts, and other engineering projects, changed the economic and social structure of the interior, further strengthening dependency. The location of economically viable resources determined what settlements would be Romanized initially, although in general the pace of cultural change was not forced. Corduba (Córdoba), the capital of the Roman province of Baetica, established at the highest navigable stretch of the Guadalquivir River, relied on the silver and copper mines of the Sierra Morena. Its population of Romanized immigrants and indigenous peoples lived in their own districts separated by walls.

Small villages with pre-Roman names continued to exist in isolated regions only lightly touched by Rome. In general, those in the west and northwest had minimal contact with the conquerors. Nevertheless, the Celt and Celt-Iberian indigenous elite had little choice but to adopt elements of Roman culture if they wished to preserve their status and serve as effective political go-betweens with the conquerors and their subjects. They served as indirect but subordinate agent-rulers. Officials in population centers that had municipal status (municipium), a select group, automatically received Roman citizenship, a distinction that sociopolitically separated them from those whom they administered.

Use of Latin, associated with Romanization, was not mandatory, although it had obvious advantages. Prior to the Roman period, the natives had arrived at the preliterate stage in the process of haltingly developing a usable alphabet. That it would become immaterial in the face of the highly developed Roman alphabet is not surprising, although it lasted for some time on the periphery, often as a mixture of characters. Roman authorities established (ca. 97 BC) a school for the sons of the indigenous elites at Osca (modern Huesca in the Ebro Valley), teaching all the subjects that separated the Roman elite from the lower classes. Basic instruction in Latin for children was available in a number of villages and towns, and a secondary education could be pursued in larger centers.[9] Advanced education required studying in Rome. Romanization carried with it a rich intellectual legacy that produced Seneca, Martial, Quintilian, and Lucan—all Hispania born. Four Roman emperors, including the justly revered Trajan and Hadrian, came from Hispania.

The lower classes in the cities, towns, and countryside had little incentive to abandon their culture. Roman polytheism could coexist with Celt and Celt-Iberian polytheistic notions, with minimal confusion and with similar explanatory needs.[10] The number of indigenous gods may have far outnumbered those of Rome's more disciplined core pantheon. The three major indigenous cultures in Iberia—Celt, Celt-Iberian, and Basque—had their own deities and sacred subsystems. Each tribe had local deities as well as shared gods and innumerable spirits. Nevertheless, the multiple functions of each god could be roughly matched with the newly introduced counterparts; consequently, indigenous gods survived, dressed more or less as Romans. Animism ran through indigenous beliefs and practices to a much larger extent than those of Rome. The bull cult as a symbol of potency and strength cut across ritual beliefs. The Celt horse cult carried the dead upward, rather than to an underworld. Caves functioned as devotional sanctuaries along with sacred groves, forests, and mountaintops, as they had from primitive times.

Adopting the religion of the conquerors—a prudent action by the native elites, although not forced on them by pagan Rome—effectively deprived the conquered people of independent spiritual leadership. From the perspective of the elite, publicly accepting Roman beliefs minimized to a certain extent their sociopolitical subordination, but it did not mean that the old beliefs disappeared. The lower classes, with fewer incentives to embrace the new beliefs, separated themselves culturally from the indigenous elite. Celt, Celt-Iberian, and Basque beliefs became folk religions. The Romanized culture of the Iberian elite coexisted with tribal notions, which barely imbued with those of the imperial power.

The decentralized authority inherent in polytheism did not pose a temporal threat to the emperor; it was enough to be slipped into the pantheon. Linking the emperor's earthly power to that of the gods, an understood means of flattery, created linkages in both directions. The semidivinity of the imperial head had Greek roots; it included an emperor in the religious explanatory system, as an anointed (*divus*) personage but not a god (*deus*). Consequently, the image of an emperor was included in religious compounds with an accompanying altar. Subsequently, Spanish monarchs enjoyed the same status, although without an altar.

The imperial cult had local importance as a reminder of imperial order and offered a setting for ritual acts of loyalty and respect by a population that would in most cases never actually see an emperor. Permission from the emperor to build a separate temple to house his image had to be solicited, presenting a unique opportunity to call attention to his loyal subjects. Some act of benevolence might be expected in return. Parades in honor or the emperor involved an entire community. An altar set up in front of a resident's house provided an opportunity to make an offering as the parade passed by. More formal animal sacrifices, usually of a bull, before the image of a ruler were standard procedure.[11]

The imperial cult in Spain may have been more sincere, in that it fused with pre-Roman practice. Nevertheless, when the municipality of Tarraco (Tarragona) informed Emperor Augustus that it had dedicated an altar to him and that a palm tree had grown out of it, the amused emperor observed that the residents must not have performed many ceremonial altar fires.[12]

The Destruction of Polytheism

While all change is transitional, at certain times it is psychologically and intellectually important or even revolutionary; monotheism proved to be all three. Well before the birth of Constantine (ca. AD 274), Rome's decline in the west had become apparent, the loss of imperial momentum in part explainable by the limited economic potential of the western empire. The city of Rome became a ceremonial center with residual political importance. Emperors no longer resided there, a reality that acknowledged the absence of an imperial focus. Rome's legions in the west served to defend already achieved gains and to prevent westward-moving barbarians from crossing the border into the empire. When expansion stalled in the west, the empire moved to the Greek-speaking east, where expansionary prospects were more promising. The establishment of Constantinople as the eastern capital was a rational economic and hence political decision as well a defensive one. Coinciding with the shift eastward was the unexpected rise of Christianity, which overturned sociopolitical values and recast the culture of both the western and eastern empires.

Roman polytheism had served the empire well: Greek Hellenism, part of Rome's intellectual legacy, allowed for a diverse number of gods. An inclusive pantheon permitted those who depended on particular gods to do so, secure in the recognition of the validity of their cult locally or regionally. Adding gods from various regions (including those of conquered people) to the pantheon allowed for a reassuring spiritual universalism. Not all gods were equal; some had more acceptance and authority—a hierarchy existed, one that Christianity retained but deeply trimmed to exclusionary proportions. Polytheism came under scrutiny, but it remained the dominant model. Whether it would be vanquished by monotheism was not at all clear. Monotheism required a more straightforward objectification of God to separate the godhead from the prior beliefs—a difficult but not impossible task.

Mani (AD 216–276), a member of a Christian sect in Mesopotamia, claimed to be the final messenger of God, the direct recipient of revelations.[13] Manichaeism avoided identification with any earthily region or empire as well as stepped out of history. Claiming to be Christian, Manichaeism absorbed local gods but restricted them to their supporting myths, thereby philosophically separating and isolating them from Manichaeism's core beliefs.[14] Mani followed in the footsteps of Buddha and the Persian Zaraduston on one level and Jesus on another, a strategy that avoided a direct confrontation by recognizing a circumscribed polytheism.

Mani and his followers drew on the Apostle Paul's example and aggressively proselytized following the well-trodden path of civilization from the western empire to the Fertile Crescent and farther east to India and China. Manichaeist texts appeared in many languages, allowing literate "hearers" to reflect on, as well as to pass on, important aspects. These texts assured that Manichaeism continued to live, at least philosophically, even after it failed to become a universal religion. The special place of merchant-traders in Manichaeism may have accounted for its rapid spread. That it was not associated with an empire accounted for its momentum, while its limited political usefulness explains its failure. Rome eventually persecuted Mani's followers.[15] Roman Christianity fared much better, but it too could have failed.

Before Constantine's Edict of Milan of 313 declared toleration, Roman Christianity functioned as an inward-looking cult, one that did not engage society publicly by openly preaching, although eventually evangelizing became the energizing force of Christianity. Only after the emperor acted did Christians come into the open and aggressively, and in many cases excessively, engage in evangelization. Not satisfied with toleration, Christianity developed a hostile approach, to the point of advocating the destruction of representations of polytheistic gods and their temples. Constantine's intentions and role are unclear. Nevertheless, he decided to use Christianity, taking care to maintain control of what he appeared to view as an instrument. Constantine remained the Pontifex Maximus (head of state religions and imperial cults) until his death in 337. Constantine publicly worshipped the sun and issued coins the obverse of which bore the image of the emperor and the reverse, the sun. He also issued coins with representations of the god Mars and the Christogram (Chi-Rho). He appeared to deal with a problematic reality by employing the approach of Manichaeism, perhaps to be on the safe side.

Most significantly, Constantine did not attempt to Christianize the army. Christianity existed side by side with polytheistic beliefs, until Constantine's patronage began to tip the balance in favor of Christianity. Material favors such as assignment of state revenues to build Christian basilicas and generous endowments of land to support them and their activities, the exemption of Christian priests from taxation, and allowing preachers to use imperial transportation all indicated official preference. That the emperor allowed Christian leaders to use the imperial palace as their headquarters as well as to dine with the emperor combined material privilege with psychological support to give them confidence and influence far beyond their actual numbers.[16]

Emperor Constantine assumed the de facto role of an archbishop—God's will became Constantine's duty.[17] Whether the emperor's will coincided with God's (or the reverse) is impossible to determine. This represented the transformation of what previously had been an earthly imperial power into one based on supradivine authority channeled through the emperor. Another factor that must be considered is the emperor's difficult, harsh, and angry personality. Did he look for a fight and thus set the stage accordingly, perhaps with results he did not anticipate or perhaps in a deliberate attempt to delegitimize polytheism?

Beginning in 331, temples were stripped of their treasures, enabling Constantine to issue gold coinage. Nevertheless, he accepted baptism from the Arian Bishop Eusebius of Nicomedia, but only as he lay dying. Christianity's association with Constantine provided the momentum for it to become viable, but success was not assured. Polytheism had been dealt a blow yet lived on.[18]

Emperor Julian (Flavius Claudius Julianus, ca. 331–363), an impulsive, well-educated individual, spent a large part of his life as a crypto-polytheist, while biding his time until he became emperor in 361. When his moment came, he reopened temples and championed the old rituals and sacrifices. While he declared toleration, he favored polytheism and urged Christians and others to convert. Violence against Christians went unpunished in spite of tolerant words. An edict on the qualifications of teachers and instructions of what they should teach excluded Christians. Julian's career myth asserted that Zeus had instructed the sun god Helos to guide him. In Julian's treatise *Contra Galilaeos,* he suggested that polytheism unified men with their gods; moreover, for all the obvious diversity of cults, in general they traced human origins to a common father and supreme ruler. Julian's rethinking of polytheism emphasized its universal potential.

Nevertheless, Julian insisted on his brand of religion, condemning the philosophy of the Cynics as unnecessarily dividing what should be one. In order to strengthen his universal brand, Julian used the sun cult in the form of the Persian god Mithras, which appealed to soldiers and officials. It posited a seven-level hierarchy of believers and made claims to superiority over others' gods. Julian's attraction to the sun god drew on the deep pools of Greco-Roman polytheism that accorded the sun a privileged position. Mithras gained universal momentum to the extent that it might have blunted Christianity's appeal. It remained a pro-touniversalist cult, however, burdened by excessive polytheistic diversity and restricted gender attraction. Julian was the last of the non-Christian emperors. He died campaigning against the Sassanid Empire, ironically the last pre-Muslim regime of Persia. Had he defeated the Persians, his efforts to reverse the decline of polytheism might have had more success, although it seems that the trend toward monotheism (not necessarily Christian) had become unstoppable. Nevertheless, had he avoided defeat and death at Maranga, the rise of Christianity might have been more problematic.[19]

The Social and Political Shock of Monotheism

The question, of course, is why the state supported monotheism. On the face of it, paganism served society well, but did it serve the state? A well-stocked pantheon had something for everyone. Major festivals such as the Olympics, held in honor of Hercules every four years at Daphne (Antioch), brought the entire community together and attracted visitors. Polytheism engendered toleration of the gods of distant lands, often trading partners, although such acceptance did not rule out violent competition with other empires, such as that with the Persians. At the same time, it offered believers a sense of confidence that they had access to higher authority and power; in effect, the gods functioned within a decentralized spiritual world and within a de facto federated spiritual empire.[20] Nevertheless, the strengths of polytheism from another standpoint constituted its weakness. As a way of countering decentralized religious loyalty, the imperial cult of a semideified emperor served as a unifying civic cult, but as the empire evolved, it was not sufficient.

The practice of seizing other people's gods and carrying them off implied cultural captivity and the transference of the gods' protective role to the victor. It addressed the problem of political balance. Some gods might develop broad appeal in certain regions, which could create an inconvenient political focal point. Emperor Aurelian (270–275) seized Palmyra (272–273) and promptly carried off images of the Sun and Bel to grace his temple of the sun, without the thought that he had embraced Syrian gods. Constantine in a similar fashion removed the obelisk from the temple of Amun in Thebes with the intention of sending it to Rome, the "temple of the whole world."[21] Roman polytheism encouraged a degree of toleration that did not require belief or punish disbelief. Toleration embraced a multitude of divine manifestations, leaving the choice to the individual, perhaps influenced by the popularity of a god. Consequently, the imperial capital became a holy city long before Christianity and the Roman Catholic curia.

Monotheism offered uniform control of minds as an important complement to the control of territory. Constantine declared himself to be the servant and minister of the supreme king, and God responded allegedly by making him ruler and sovereign. The objective, as stated by Eusebius in his *Vita Constantini,* was "one God, one empire, one emperor." When the emperor encountered obstacles, he reached out to God, who then gave him a special cross (the Constantine Cross) with instructions "to conquer with this."[22] An ambitious emperor's Christian mythology underpinned his drive to create a universal Christian empire.

Polytheists became progressively more silent as the process continued and as they realized that the trend was irreversible. At a certain point, conversion could not be avoided, but they attempted with some success to hold on to as much of their old rituals as possible. Consequently, regional forms of Christianity could not be eliminated, and some had to be allowed to coexist as acceptable rites.

Semipolytheistic modifications as well as surviving entrenched practices, inevitably nurtured by the least instructed elements, in semisecret locations could not be controlled.[23] The psychological need to directly protect oneself from evil explained the continued reliance on witchcraft, magic and omens, charms and maledictions. A sense of proactive personal empowerment in the face of potential calamities spilled over into Christian rituals through an exaggerated focus on certain aspects of Christian beliefs, thus distorting the approved balance, while practitioners still could claim to be devout believers. The church, pressed by religious survivals, struggled to maintain its theoretical monopoly on the power to mediate between good and evil. It succeeded to a greater extent at the macrolevel than at the local and lower social level, an outcome that characterized Indo-Mexico also and for similar reasons.

Deference and Privilege under Attack

From an imperial point of view, an elite is necessary, as is a sense of caste cohesion among those who rule. Stability and political continuity depend on the level of satisfaction of the existing ruling generation, projected onto the next by the proper formation of the children who will replace their parents. A ruling generation ensures that its children are inducted into the elite. An empire of many large provinces, cities, and trade routes required an extensive managerial elite and the cultivation of bonds that tied them together as well as justified their functions.

In the Roman Empire, one's "devotion to the muses" (learning) signaled membership in the governing caste. An empire-wide literary culture bound members of this caste together. Those in every province of the empire who made up the ruling families hired professional grammarians and rhetoricians in order to guide their charges through an intellectually demanding course of study. Virgil, Cicero, Homer, and Demosthenes and the thoughts and commentaries of many others provided the intellectual material to construct a common foundation for the governing elite, one shared with their counterparts across the empire. Acquiring high culture, particularly if one resided in remote provinces, was expensive and might necessitate traveling to several different centers of learning. Once acquired, *Paideia* (high culture) had to be displayed in rigid conventions, a certain manner of speech and gestures so that observers understood immediately the superior status of their interlocutor and by implication their power and authority. When nobles encountered others of their caste from any part of the empire, they instantly recognized their shared status, common bonds, and social expectations; in short, they "knew rules of the game," all of which engendered a sense of superiority and privileged entitlement.[24]

Individuals of acknowledged culture served as *consuls* (governors) and in other important positions; consequently, they had political constituencies and sought to accommodate the powerful. As large landholders with peasants paying rent as well as subject to taxes, they used their position to avoid taxes—in effect shifting the burden down to the bottom by trading on the dependency of the emperor on their skills and regional political importance. When they received notification of the taxes to be levied, they collected them from the peasants, while delaying collecting them from the rich and influential. Eventually, the emperor, in a display of imperial favor (*beneficia*), could be counted on to wipe the slate clean; he had little choice.

Christianity Becomes the State

Pompey the Great plundered Jerusalem in 63 BC. Palestine remained an imperial province until the revolt of AD 66, when the people drove out the Romans. Four years later, the Romans returned; after a brief siege, they breached the city's walls and killed everyone in their path.

A punitive massacre slaughtered another ten thousand. The chained survivors marched out of the ruined city as the temple, set on fire by Romans, burned down. A Jewish revolutionary nationalist, Jesus of Nazareth, was crucified for sedition.[25]

The death of paganism was not sudden or complete. Christianity was not inevitable. There were other possibilities. Christianity, as reworked by the Romans, represented an intellectual advance, in that it offered an after-death life in the flesh, a focus on one God, and equality in the faith, if not in actual life. Christianity challenged social and political rules.[26] It shifted an enhanced degree of sociopolitical legitimacy to the poor, to be exercised by their divine, if often self-appointed, representatives: preachers, holy men, and mystics.

The seeds of class disdain for the upper class were not hard to find.[27] The Stoics, with their high moral principles, along with the Cynics, those marketplace preachers with long, unwashed hair and dirty rags to cover unclean bodies who harangued their often-captive audiences to correct their moral faults and to confront their failures, provided a template. Moreover, those believers who received revelations became important by that reason alone, rather than through learning. Christianity dismissed the importance of class, learning, officeholding, and status. Thus, the patriarch of Alexandria Athanasius's *Life of Saint Anthony* portrayed the saint as a peasant without education or refinement but taught by God. Augustine drew the inescapable conclusion that the "uneducated rise up and take heaven by storm," while his learning counted for little.[28] That he went from a pagan teacher of Latin rhetoric to Christian convert (387) to bishop to sainthood reflected wise career decisions that others would make, perhaps for similar reasons. The elevation of the poor and humble formed a constituency and forced Christian rulers to adopt sincere, or at least pro forma, concern for the lower classes.[29]

That the lower strata of society would be the most likely to hold on to elements of polytheism meant little because the displacement of the ruling elite was the unstated objective.[30] The ill-clad, untrained Christian monk fresh from a cave or the desert—sometimes barely but usually not literate—possessed what the notables did not: wisdom that only God could teach. Christianity drew on material as well as psychological (spiritual) inequality: the absence of respect, those elements that had been denied the lower classes in the past, provided the political and spiritual momentum. Consequently, to regain the moral high ground, the notables had to function behind a façade (whether sincere or not) of humility, sacrifice, service to, and love of the poor. Christianity chose the revolt of Jesus as its centerpiece. He died on the cross for sedition, not for blasphemy, in an attempt to overthrow Roman rule in what became the Holy Land. A reworking of events several decades later turned the revolutionary into a compassionate defender of people without respect. Church councils set about determining what constituted the New Testament.[31]

Christian discourse acquired its own formalisms, terms, and mannerisms that were seemingly the reverse of paideia but able to demand deference.[32] Christianity, as a constructed religion, condemned those who clung to a polytheistic past, refocused authority, and made the emperor a direct agent of God, changing the spiritual matrix and consequently the worldview. Miracles, healing, and good fortune, however, in the same fashion as in the past, remained the means by which people determined who had been chosen to be favored. But now the list was narrowed down to one God and his son, Jesus, although a sizable number of saintly patrons might play a role.

The triumph of the impoverished and poorly educated constituted a socioeconomic and political revolution that altered the Roman system, but not entirely. Subsequently, the educated classes joined the movement, as it became evident that it could not be resisted. The basic Roman framework was taken over by the nascent Roman Church, including its attachment to order and bureaucracy. The church's institutional leadership fell to those who had performed the same task under the empire. The pope assumed the office of the Pontifex Maximus; priests were put in place, and various councils began the task of deciding on orthodoxy, with the hope that their authority would be sufficient to gain compliance. Just what beliefs constituted Christianity had to be determined—a difficult process, fluid and somewhat arbitrary and consequently subject to dispute. The period of doctrinal anarchy based on evolving notions of what represented acceptable beliefs did not end with the imposition of a hierarchy. An ongoing but muted struggle for control pitted the clergy against the laity on a number of issues. The meaning of death is perhaps the best example. It became a contested area between the formal church and those who experienced it in their families. The disputed meaning of death represented an unrecognized psychological revolt against the theological separation of heaven from Earth. Awaiting resurrection of the body could not be so easily accepted by those who were still alive and without formal religious functions that connected them with the next world. A compromise could be found in holy relics that in effect bridged the two spheres. The transformation of the burial place of saints into a location where the presence of the saint is assumed acted to unite both heaven and Earth, but under the supervision of the bishop, who had the ability to enlist the dead in support of a clerical agenda. Both the church and the state were served by controlled ritual. The state redirected clerical theological institutions when useful, often with the cooperation of the papacy. The devotion in Spain to Saint James, the cult of Santiago de Compostela, supported a warrior cult and functioned as a quasi-state instrument in Spain during the Reconquista and in conquest America.[33] As an unintended result of saintly cults, recipients of favors gained socioreligious esteem apart from the formal structure. A balance of sorts involved feasting at gravesites and ceremonial visits that included the dead in the active community, but under the direction of the family, not the church. It seems obvious that certain elements that might well fall under the church were reserved by the laity as part of the foundation of popular religion.

While achieving an acceptable level of orthodoxy was crucial to control, contradictions, both in material ways (lifestyle) and in theological (intellectual) formulations, opened the opportunity for others to determine what constituted certain supporting aspects of Christianity. Tension between the priesthood and the theology perceived by the laity opened the way for local variations in spite of established orthodoxy.

The Destruction of Tolerance

Paganism by its nature is tolerant of other gods and beliefs. Various pantheons existed around the empire, including gods of Egypt with dog and animal heads. The notion that every religious community should be allowed to practice its beliefs did not mean approval or disapproval but did indicate respect. Visiting emperors might make a cult offering to the local gods, as did Hadrian and others. Diocletian honored the major gods as well as regional ones, demonstrating the importance of the overall unifying pantheon as well as imperial recognition of secondary and tertiary levels.[34] Perhaps to gain regional status, local gods often received Roman and Greek names. Only two groups practiced exclusion: Jews and Christians. Rome nevertheless tolerated the Jews and exempted them from conscription and various legal actions on the Sabbath. Even after the Jewish revolt was put down harshly, persecutions remained restrained. As their numbers and confidence increased, Christians became more intolerant thus creating a greater problem for the Roman rulers.

Christians' lack of respect for the Roman gods led to demands that they be thrown to the lions when the public felt the need to appease their deities. The spread of Christianity provided a useful explanation for military defeats and disasters such as famine. Concerned about events, Emperor Decius decreed (250) that all citizens make sacrifices to the gods and obtain a certificate of compliance. His successor, Valerian, seized churches (257) and prohibited private worship. Valerian's son (Galliano) reversed the policy. Christianity subsequently made halting advances.[35]

Belief in one God required rejection of all others.[36] The old gods might survive but were demoted to devils, demons, and moral tricksters. The concept of Satan as the reverse of God provided a home for all the discards of polytheism, now driven into the underworld. Destruction of temples and idols and the prohibition of rituals followed. In the 380s, physical destruction accelerated as Christian momentum became unstoppable.

In Egypt, the praetorian prefect Cynegius, in a brief visit, left behind a notorious reputation for breaking idols and demolishing shrines. In Syria, Bishop Marcellus of Apamea (near Hama), frustrated at the slow pace of conversion, employed the army to destroy temples. While watching with evident satisfaction the destruction of Zeus's temple compound, the bishop was recognized, seized, and burned alive by the angry mob; he was not the only bishop to be martyred.

Such fury was rooted in Christianity's lack of respect for polytheistic spirituality, apart from the economic and social impact caused by demolition (temple compounds served as commercial markets among other things) and the loss of an established community center. In Alexandria, the bishop requested Emperor Theodosius to transfer the temple of Dionysus to him, with plans to transform it into a Christian church; he then proceeded to claim all the city's temples. Widespread mocking of polytheistic icons as they were paraded through the streets led to mass rioting, as well as the torturing and crucifixion of Christian captives. The army put down the disturbances and, along with pious monks, finished destroying the city's temples.

Alert to the balance tipping in favor of Christianity, many people decided that resistance would be fruitless: conversion, whether sincere or not, offered a physical refuge. Sincerity had never been important in polytheism; one chose the gods that appealed, those that delivered what one expected, and if they did not, one proceeded to select others. Such an attitude made conversion to Christianity, in the face of coercion or hope for preferment or the desire to be part of a powerful group, a pragmatic matter. Bishops understood that many commitments remained in doubt but decided sagely to let God make the final judgment.[37]

Christianity's momentum depended initially on imperial preferment and subsequently on state force. The imperial state moved slowly, even deliberately, until the late fourth century. The final steps appear predicable. Emperor Gratian (378–383) renounced his official position of Pontifex Maximus and ordered the removal of the Victory Altar from the Senate chamber. Moreover, he withdrew the traditional privileges of the old priests but did not attempt to suppress polytheism. In Spain, the praetorian prefect received instructions to destroy temples if it could be done without causing civil disturbances.[38] Finally, Emperor Theodosius, a native of Spain, recognized Christianity as the state religion and in 392 decreed the suppression of blood sacrifices and polytheistic rituals. A long line of Theodosius's successors felt it necessary, to the point of it becoming pro forma, to prohibit former practices, indicating that these practices continued in spite of the physical destruction of the spiritual environment and the withdrawal of political support.

Complete suppression, in view of the reality that the Christian church existed in a preliminary organizational stage and faced the task of determining orthodoxy, could not be expected. Bishops came from different cultural-ethnic backgrounds, from varied historical experiences and different languages. Although Latin and Greek served as the languages of the church, bishops interpreted issues differently. That they retained unacknowledged vestiges of old beliefs seems obvious. Bishops gathered in church councils, in an unending number of meetings, to hammer out differences, to establish a degree of uniformity, and to decide on what should be considered orthodox or heresy; approval or disapproval came down to a consensus, though not necessarily a complete one. What strand of Christianity would become the accepted version could not be determined with certainty. The religious marketplace continued to produce various elaborations that had the potential of becoming an orthodox version; when they failed, they were dismissed as cults or schismatic notions.

Christianity in Roman Spain

Around 250, Roman soldiers, traders, and travelers brought Christianity to Iberia as part of their mental baggage. The new religion soon established a toehold in the towns along the Mediterranean but did not penetrate deeply into the countryside. Social and ethnic barriers retarded the spread of Christianity, and the *rustici* (peasantry), at least through the fourth century, found polytheism more congenial and useful.[39] The Christian Council of Elliberis (Elvira), now an abandoned city close to present-day Granada, was the first council (ca. 302) to be held in Roman Spain. Nineteen bishops drawn from all the provinces attended to address the problem of a flock that wavered between the old gods and an ill-understood, even unwelcome monotheism. Folk religious beliefs associated the gods with physical and geographical features: mountains, forests, rivers, and springs, among other aspects of the landscape. Deva, the Celtic goddess of waters, remains personified by the turbulent River Deva that flows through Cantabria and Asturias. Sacred pagan sites, often unmarked or with modest shrines, drew little attention. The altar to Erudinus on the Cantabrian mountain peak of Dobra in Santander, dedicated in 399, received sufficient notice to be recorded. Constructing a Christian church on a site dedicated to the Celtic god Endovellicus in the vicinity of Evora sanctified the site, while seemingly co-opting the ancient god's mystical powers, a practice employed by Spanish friars in Mexico that transformed sacred land into Christian sites without totally eliminating the prior religious association. The tactic diluted pagan beliefs but encouraged the melding of religious notions.

In a similar fashion, replacing gods with Christian saints fused the two in the minds of the faithful, as did celebrating Christian holy days on the old festive calendar. These accommodations represented a tacit abandonment of the attempt to replace fully the gods with one God and the failure to convince the people that one deity could do the work of numerous specialized gods. The prohibition of the practice of Christian matrons lending adornments, including dresses, to street processions of the old gods testified to the coexistence of the old and new beliefs, as did the need to forbid the sacrifice of animals in churches. Other practices that had deep roots in pre-Christian Roman Spain, such as feasting among the graves of deceased relatives and maintaining home altars, preoccupied the members of the Council of Elvira, worried about what they interpreted as the shallowness of Iberian Christianity.[40] In fact, both graveside feasting and the use of home altars were common practices among many groups and remain so particularly among lower-class Mexican households in our own time. Private worship, including household chapels maintained by the wealthy, facilitated personal religious deviations and avoided priestly supervision.

A serious challenge to orthodoxy emerged in the form of Priscillianism, which preoccupied Catholic bishops for at least two hundred years. It began as a secret cult society founded by Priscillian, a rich and learned noble, around 370. Priscillian served as bishop of Avila (381–385). Alleged to have been involved with magic in his early days, Priscillian fell under the influence of an Egyptian follower of Mani and adopted Manichaeism's mix of Zoroastrian and Christian doctrines along with regional polytheism. Augustine, bishop of Hippo, toyed with Priscillianism briefly before rejecting it, as did other bishops.[41]

In Spain, diversity of practices created regional forms of Christianity. Compounding the confusion, the use of simplified sermons written at a level judged suitable for the rustici created Christians unable to connect form with its appropriate theological foundation. As a result, ritual forms of everyday Christianity practiced by believers had little philosophical substance and differed minimally from previous practices. A frustrated Saint Augustine (354–430) expressed his anger with the mind-set that made it possible to claim to be a Christian while still honoring pagan gods. The tactical response of Christianizing pagan holidays, matching ritual for ritual, and the use of saints submerged as well as validated the influence of paganism on Iberian Christianity. Sacred relics that attached magical properties to such objects became the focus of cults. Objectification of belief, a characteristic of pagan religions, passed through into Christianity, the successor faith. The minimally instructed and the theologically trained functioned on distinctly different levels of belief.

Martin de Braga's sermon *De castigatione rusticorum* (ca. 574) provides a picture of the continuous struggle against religious folklore. Braga addressed propitiatory rites rendered at a crossroads and other occasions that required beseeching immediate personal protection. Convincing those who were new to the faith to substitute Christian incantation such as the Lord's Prayer and the sign of the cross for pagan ones in effect relocated such superstitions from a pagan into a Christian context. In a similar fashion, Christian homilies drew on folk religion to make simplified examples understandable to a semipagan audience. While the objective was spiritual edification, it reinforced the folk mind-set. Sermons avoided problematic issues in order to strengthen the morale of believers as they faced evil. Truth and justice could be represented allegorically, while evil required personification in the form of the devil and his activities.

Gregory the Great (540–604), one of the most influential early Catholic theologians, understood the need to teach the laity. In many respects, he was a hands-on pope, not a profound thinker. His style is perhaps symbolized by the introduction of the *Stations of the Cross,* which actively imparted a lesson to believers. Gregory wrote homilies, laced with quotations from the scriptures, that demonstrated simple lessons. Many of his homilies dealt with behavioral issues such as greed or gluttony. Some of his sermons are amusing, although it is unclear if Gregory intended to amuse. The use of anecdotes humanized homilies and influenced the presentations of medieval popular preachers as well as objectified theological elements. Homilies dealt with temptation, sinful acts, and their sad end result. Stories from the four books of the *Dialogues* constituted a treasury of subjects, demonstrated by the story of a bishop and a Jew. As the story goes, a Jew sleeping in the ruins of an abandoned temple to Apollo overhears a demon reporting to the devil about his success in tempting a bishop to pat a young nun's bottom. When the Jew is discovered by the demons, he makes the sign of the cross, protecting him from harm, and escapes. Meeting the bishop, he reveals this knowledge and how he obtained it. All ends well: the lustful bishop is repentant and dismisses all females in his employ, and the Jew becomes a Christian. The lessons to be drawn are multiple: that all are tempted but can repent and take action to avoid evil; as a practical reminder, that the sign of the cross protects even nonbelievers against demons; and that pagan ruins attract satanic agents and should be avoided.

Confusion accompanied early Christianity in spite of Gregory's attempt to exert control.[42] The church had yet to settle on important theological issues. Some bishops employed triple immersion following the Arian practice, rather than single immersion. This suggested a division of the divinity into the three parts of the Holy Trinity rather than its unitary character in Catholic theology. The Fourth Council of Toledo (633) called for standard prayers and ritual practices, without immediate results. The Council of Toledo required individual priests, when they traveled to the seat of the bishopric, to report how they celebrated Mass and conducted baptisms.[43]

Complicating the situation, seventh-century bishops created a complex liturgy that could not be philosophically understood at lay levels. Different layers of religious sophistication created various degrees of Christianity, a situation repeated after 1492 in the New World. Meanwhile, the Eleventh Council of Toledo (681) continued to deal with the problem of folk religious practices, with their ill-disguised pagan rites.

Religious folklore revolved around evil and the activities of creatures that tempted the weak and on occasion destroyed them. While the devil had a primary role, he was a composite of several entities, including Lucifer and the Antichrist. He could appear as he wished in whatever gender and age he chose: perhaps as a priest, a nun, a learned man, a beautiful young girl, an old hag, or whatever he deemed most useful. Demons abounded, and over the centuries, learned scholars calculated just how many went about their evil duties. Monsters, giants, were-animals, demons, elves, sprites, ghosts, trolls, dragons, mares, and an assortment of little creatures existed also, but not necessarily as followers of the devil. In many cases, they represented pre-Christian entities and pagan gods, no longer in their original sense but as morally ambivalent models in the context of Christianity. Thus, the Celtic god Cernunnos, the horned god of the wilderness who served as the lord of fertility and the hunt, master of the underworld, moved totally to the dark side, losing all positive aspects but nevertheless surviving and continuing to receive attention.[44]

At a practical level, religious folklore filled in the explanatory gaps that formal religion did not. Religious folklore determined how the people conducted themselves throughout the day and into the night. It provided an explanation of everyday bad luck, the death of a farm animal, minor accidents in the fields, and the unexpected sudden disasters that befell individuals. Dealing with strangers could be tricky because of the devil's ability to assume different shapes. Black, the devil's favorite color, followed by red, a preference shared by Tezcatlipoca, provided clues to the devil's presence, as did the stench that he left behind.

Moreover, religious folklore offered some control of one's personal landscape. Avoiding crossroads at noon and midnight because of the concentration of other unworldly creatures, attracted by the hour and place, seemed prudent. Being cautious of caves, holes, and odd geological formations that could be used for occult purposes or serve as entry points to hell seemed natural. Keeping these in mind allowed the prudent to proceed in reasonable safety. Duality gave each side a place, such as conceding the left side of a church's exterior structure as the devil's side. Even directions had symbolic importance, with north the direction of hell. Cold and ice in a European context stood for misery, although general agreement placed hell in the central core of the Earth, presumably with more than sufficient heat to torture evildoers and ward off the cold.

The forces of darkness did their utmost to encourage sinners to indulge their passions and then seized the moment to carry them off to hell, demonstrating demonic perversity.[45] The desire for a little more predictability in devil-human relationships may have inspired the myth of certain individuals who had made formal contracts with the devil, theoretically permitting both sides to obtain what they wanted. In the thirteenth century, pacts with the devil became a popular topic in plays and literature, and several purported pacts would be reproduced. Rumors of the Roman curia's cooperating with the devil circulated, perhaps indicating a mild but potentially damaging, antiauthoritarian reaction by the laity.

Possession of knowledge could easily be construed as sorcery. Pope Sylvester II (999–1003), who studied at the Universities of Barcelona, Córdoba, and Seville with Arabic teachers, became suspect for introducing Arabic knowledge of astronomy and mathematics to Europe. Rumors circulated that he had studied at Al Karaquine University in Morocco and was a Sephardic Jew. Supposedly he stole a book of spells from an Arab philosopher during his studies in Spain. That he rose to the papacy in spite of such suspicions appeared to be explainable to many people as because of a pact with the devil. He became the archbishop of Rheims, then the first French pope.[46] The legend transmuted knowledge into sorcery by linking Sylvester II to suspect Arabic teachings. Such tales subjected the powerful to the same degree of religious surveillance, constant stress, and temptation as the laity.

Prophesies extracted from the Old Testament and the New Testament's Book of Revelations to John (the Apocalypse) played a central role in activating believers and made religion dynamic, moving toward a climactic moment. Much of the forward-looking material came from the Book of Revelations. As a series of dreams or visions, it lent itself to a variety of doomsday interpretations. Revelations engendered a fearful urgency that enthralled, as well as horrified, believers.[47] Fear underlay riveting sermons by the Catholic clergy, including the Franciscans, the Dominicans, and the other mendicant orders. A Mozarab (Arabized Christians and Jews) refugee priest who had fled from Muslim territory wrote the *Prophetic Chronicles* at the court of Alfonso III of Asturias-León. Drawing on the Old Testament books of Daniel and Ezekiel, he identified Al-Andalus as the land of the giants Gog and Magog, who governed as the last judgment neared. Alfonso III was given an important role by the self-serving author of the *Prophetic Chronicles,* as the king who would overturn the evil rule of the giants and take control just before the end of the earthly world.

Evil appeared to be an anomaly explainable and understandable to the laity by personifying it as the devil, providing him with a separate kingdom (the underworld), and providing him with a family history. The devil's wife was a shrew. His grandmother Lillas, or Lilith, derived from the goddess Cybele, or Holda, the magna mater of the gods who ruled the wild beasts and the world in its primeval state, must have been equally as unpleasant. The nature of the devil's family suggests self-flagellation. As a shape shifter, the prince of darkness appeared in many forms. Predictably for Mozarabes, Muhammad represented one of his apparitions. The church's Council of Toledo (447), attempting to provide an actual portrayal of the devil in his basic form, described him as a large, black, monstrous apparition with horns on his head, cloven hooves, ass's ears, claws, fiery eyes, gnashing teeth, and a huge penis; his presence could be detected by the distinct smell of sulfur.[48] All the aspects of evil personified that were embedded in Europe's religious mentality appeared to have counterparts in Indo-Mexico, although definitions of evil differed. The continued existence of evil suggested a failure of sorts, a crucial battle not yet won by the church. Nevertheless, the devil and evil justified the continued spiritual struggle.

A more reasoned approach to the nature and causes of evil by Saint Thomas Aquinas (1225–1274) dealt with evil as both an intellectual and a spiritual problem. Evil to Aquinas meant the privation of something that the individual should have by nature but did not have in reality. Evil by itself could not exist without its opposite: good. In effect, this was definition by opposites, but real and superior good remained vulnerable. Evil could spring only from the desire for good poorly understood. The task of teaching was crucial when people were confronted by evil. Bishops and Christian monarchs through their agents bore overall responsibility for the task of instruction. While Aquinas presumed positive intent in human behavior, he did not dispense with the need for forceful guidance: a directive responsibility with spiritual well-being in mind. Establishing the proper instructional circumstances might require force, a notion that legitimized coercion under certain circumstances, by rulers and their agents. Evil's existence, not necessarily its origins, depended on ignorance. Thus, the clergy's failure to properly instruct the Christian community opened the door to evil. Aquinas's template became functional in Indo-Mexico in the sixteenth century, although it also failed because of lapses in instruction. Cults, self-constructed spiritual notions, and religious folklore could not be eradicated. The impoverished and isolated mountainous border region of southern France and northern Spain nurtured a series of cults.

The Basque peasantry had a reputation for backwardness and folk religions that preserved significant ancient Celtic and Celt-Iberian survivals mixed with Catholic elements. In Vizcaya, numerous cults proliferated, generically grouped together as the *fraticelli*. On the eve of the contact with America, the Franciscan friar Alonso de Mello sought to create a theocratic state in the regional capital of Durángo on the basis of Saint Francis's extreme notions. Royal officials responded harshly, arresting hundreds and sentencing thirteen ringleaders to be burned alive for heresy. Less politically charged but still scandalous events included the activities of the transborder witch Hendo, who attracted a number of young women apprentices. This event challenged the authority of the priests and the state. Friar Juan de Zumárraga headed the investigation and trial of the Biscayan witches until, in the midst of his judicial duties, he was named the first bishop of Mexico.[49] It is likely that the closed Basque community in Indo-Mexico dabbled in minor forms of heresy.

Labor, Land, and Cities in Roman Spain

The indigenous tribal population of Roman Spain consumed a limited amount of modestly priced trade goods imported from Italy and elsewhere, but commercial exchange could not have been that extensive. Their actual economic contribution likely consisted of labor rather than commerce. The structure of Rome's economy was dependent on both free and slave labor and the wars that made enslavement possible. Slaves labored in obscurity, largely unrecorded by history. Roman law did not recognize slaves as legal persons, although if freed, they gained or regained legal standing. For most slaves, it was likely a permanent condition under difficult circumstances, although they were entitled to a modest cash *(peculio)* allowance. Just how much the economy depended on slaves is difficult to determine, as is the number; a certain percentage of slaves would have been shipped to Italy. With the end of the wars of conquest, the supply of indigenous slaves declined. Spain may have been a net importer of slaves in order to meet its needs, particularly in the mines.

In agriculturally favored regions, the relationship between the urban center and the surrounding rural resources followed the Roman model: an urban villa as the elite property owner's principal residence. Nevertheless, agricultural properties, the main source of elite wealth, were working assets with functional farm buildings and a resident labor force. Small farms were interspersed among larger units. Both large and small units supplied urban markets, while the large estates also exported their production and manufactured the clay vessels needed to ship olive oils, fish paste, and wines. Not surprisingly, regions with good agricultural land became Romanized to a much greater extent and more rapidly than did economically marginal areas. In general, Rome's culture spread from coastal areas into the interior, following the peninsula's natural resources.

Southeastern and eastern coastal settlements first occupied by the Phoenicians, Greeks, and Carthaginians were the sites of the first Roman cities. Gades (Cádiz), founded by the Phoenicians (ca. 1100 BC), was a natural commercial crossroads that attracted merchants from across the known world. When granted Roman citizenship by Caesar in 49 BC, Gades had a large number of citizens who were worth at least 400,000 sesterces and had a mint. As a cosmopolitan city, Gades had all the amenities demanded by Romans, including baths, a forum filled with shops, and streets overflowing with strange-looking people selling all sorts merchandise from many parts of the empire, as well as local production. A journey from Rome to Gades required a short week's sea voyage, while a journey by ship to Alexandria at the other end of Rome's North African empire consumed a month.

As one moved inland, more rustic conditions could be observed, eventually giving way to frontier sparseness in the northwest. Finally, in AD 19, Emperor Augustus established Roman rule virtually throughout the peninsula. The campaign to subdue the mountainous north, while never completely successful, was conducted personally by Augustus. The Via Augustus, one of the great highways that ran from the north to Gades in the south, served as an imperial symbol of the end of an era. The protracted Roman conquest was analyzed by Livy, who explained it as a consequence of the difficult terrain that favored tribal warfare, as well as the nature of the people, who resisted an external imperial force.[50] Rome used military force in its relations with such tribes but functioned more importantly as an organizing agent, establishing the concept of geographical unity captured by the name *Hispania* and establishing various provinces that suggested more control than likely was possible.

In the new economic environment, the indigenous population was at a disadvantage. Land and minerals were transferred to the conquering power at the expense of the tribes. Large stretches of ancestral land would be reassigned to legions for cultivation and pasture as well as for imperial estates. Transferring land to modern cultivators likely was a state imperative. As the conquering power, Rome decided on how property would be distributed; indigenous claims based on custom and possession might be respected but could not be demanded. Roman surveyors apparently did not reconfigure well-established indigenous urban spaces, but the surrounding countryside was organized along

Roman lines. Unfortunately, documentation focusing on property rights in the early period is scarce. Prior to the 199 imperial rulings that set property ownership conditions in what amounted to frontier home-steading terms, we can assume a confusing, perhaps ad hoc transfer of land. The 199 formula allowed private ownership after ten years' residence or twenty years' absentee possession, presumably under active cultivation, to accommodate the diverse holdings of wealthy agriculturists.[51]

Spain supplied food crops, livestock, and highly prized horses, but of most importance, its silver mines and gold deposits underpinned a significant portion of the imperial economy and supported some of the empire's wealthiest citizens. Spain's economy had a number of economic drivers: consumption, as villages became towns and then cities; trade demands that could no longer be met by coastal production alone; taxes that required native subsistence farmers to increase production to meet state demands; the financing of production with debt that in turn generated capital; the monetary stimulation of legions and auxiliary forces stationed in Hispania that contracted for supplies of all sorts, as well as the money spent by individual soldiers for various personal services; and the impact of Italian colonists, along with their skills.

The agrarian trading economy, supplemented by mining and internal consumption, supported a society in the process of accelerating complexity. Cities functioned as cultural crucibles where wealth, status, and Roman culture all converged to transform the indigenous population. Romanized indigenous elites created a Hispano-Roman society; they sent their sons to Rome to be educated, decorated their residences with expensive mosaics, dressed in the approved style, and displayed their learning, at times traveling between Rome and Spain.

Acculturation spread across every economically viable region. Rome did not force the adoption of its culture and ways; the utility of that culture appealed to many people in Iberia's commercially advanced south and eastern coast but was only lightly adopted elsewhere. The Basques and Cantabrians in the northwest remained virtually untouched. Romanization of the lower classes took considerably longer, even then not complete at the time the Visigoths entered Spain in 406. Incomplete acculturation permitted the reemergence of elements of the old culture, although much modified.[52]

Urban Psychology, Wealth, Politics, and Patronage

Cities brought together the complementary functions of religion, law, and social control, as well as trade, agriculture, and artisan production. They existed within a network of similar hubs throughout the Roman Empire. The sparsely populated countryside, beyond the country villas and agricultural estates, had little attraction for the Romanized elite. Travel by land could be time consuming, uncomfortable, and boring. Small villages and towns offered little in the way of diversion. Moreover, the divide between rural and urban cultures was too great to inspire mutual appreciation.[53] The use of native languages isolated both sides and made interaction difficult and at best awkward. It must have been a relief to reach a city and Romanized culture. Nevertheless, the growth of cities led to the intensification of agriculture to meet urban demands. The need to pay taxes made it necessary to monetize production. Food processing in the form of a large-scale salted-fish operation exported a percentage of the region's production in the form of fish paste. Olive oil and cereals, in steady demand across the Mediterranean world, also served to create everyday trade links, while Iberia's mineral deposit attracted Italian gold and silver miners. The emergence of villas accompanied the growth of viticulture and mixed production.[54]

Concentration of wealth could only be accomplished in cities. Close contact with partners, investors, traders, mineral exporters, and other clients was necessary. Beyond pragmatic considerations, wealth also determined who ruled. Spain's cities were well ordered socially in the Roman manner, dependent on a multitiered elite, separated by degrees of wealth, who occupied the upper levels. The senatorial level required property worth at least a million sesterces; the *equites* (knights) had to have assets of 400,000 sesterces and the local gentry 100,000, although it varied regionally. The senators, should they have the desire and perceived aptitude, could serve in high political office or as military leaders. The equites might be appointed as governors and assume military positions, also rising to senatorial status as they accumulated wealth. Acculturated regions, such as the eastern coast and the Iberian provinces of Baetica and Citerior, understandably had a larger number of senators and knights than did the interior. At the lower elite level, a provincial elite of municipal councilors, magistrates, and priests ordered city life. Successful men automatically entered the Roman nobility. The combination of wealth, politics, and learning created an imperial elite across the empire. The equality of cities ended in the fourth century as the reformed empire closed local mints and established a hierarchy of cities.[55] A designated metropolis dominated the other cities in the province, an organizational model introduced in Indo-Mexico in the sixteenth century.

Interaction between the urban classes functioned as a semiformalized patron-client system in an institution unique to Spain: the *hospitium*. As often is the case in societies with an unequal distribution of wealth and respect, the community expected the economically powerful to demonstrate benevolent patronage. Clients could be a town or city, with the patron as a public benefactor financing public entertainment or perhaps the distribution of food or sponsoring a monument or perhaps a public bathhouse or some needed infrastructure project; in return, patrons had the right to expect respect, support, and assistance from their clients. Politicians as patrons could turn out supporters to demonstrate their personal popularity. The patron-client relationship served to tie the social classes into a network of mutual, if unequal, dependency. Even people of relative modest resources, such as centurions, might have clients, suggesting subordinate circles within overarching ones. The more clients a patron had, the higher the level of social status. Freed slaves automatically became clients. The relationship tended to pass from one generation to the next.[56]

Cities had access to the corvée labor of the peasantry and the extracted wealth of empire, providing the funds to create civic grandeur and pride of place. Urban notables vied with each other to beautify cities and to elevate their personal status. With distance from the center of authority came autonomy, to the extent that a commonwealth of cities functioned. Rebellion as a possibility was restrained by the existence in Rome's arsenal of punitive massacres and executions. The Jewish revolt of AD 66–70, followed by a punitive massacre and destruction of the Second Temple, is perhaps the most remembered example today.[57]

The Philosophical Foundation of a Neoempire

In the early fifth century, the Visigoths retreated into Spain after being defeated by the Franks.[58] They found a political semivacuum but not a cultural one. Roman imperial contraction forced the Visigoths to progressively establish an independent existence as successors to Rome in the Iberian Peninsula. Roman rule, finally terminated by Euric, the Visigoth king (466–484), along the eastern coast and the Ebro Valley, lingered on culturally. Imperial symbols of authority continued to be used, and Rome's justification of the state became part of the Visigoths' worldview. Nevertheless, traditional Visigoth notions of an elected kingship, along with the need to convoke an assembly of notables to deal with important issues, following the pattern of Germanic assemblies, survived. Some 300 or more tribal clans would have to be dealt with, as would the hostility of the Basques and Cantabrians, who defied Visigoth attempts to bring them under control. Nevertheless, the Visigoths, still semitribal and only partially Romanized, viewed themselves as agents of Rome, a perception that provided legitimacy for what became an occupation with some minor aspects of a conquest. The fusion of Germanic tribal notions with Roman law created one of the foundations of the yet-to-be-imagined American empire, subsequently modified by the frontier culture that resulted from the Reconquista.

Just how many Visigoths entered Spain is not known, nor is the actual composition of the successor regime, which may have picked up smaller and different tribal groups as it wandered across the empire; perhaps no more than 20,000 Visigoths ruled over some one million Hispano-Romans along the coastal fringes.[59] If such population estimates are correct—and they seem reasonable—any redistribution of landed wealth would not have been economically or politically disruptive, while the size of the ruling population would have been sufficient to develop a warrior aristocracy. More problematic, Visigoth leaders professed the Arian version of Christianity; consequently, a seamless religious fusion of Hispano-Romans, mainly Catholics, and Gothic Arians could not be expected. The Visigoth ruler's support of Hispano-Roman Catholics remained in doubt. Towns and cities had competing churches and a divided Christian flock.[60] Hostility between Catholics and Arians posed political difficulties as well as the potential for civil war.

Rome's fragmentation forced the Visigoths to develop a creditable monarchy, moving beyond what in effect was an elected chieftaincy. The political notion of a population of subjects under a directive state did not exist in the Germanic tribal tradition. The Visigoth king Leovigildo (569–585) harmonized to a workable degree Germanic and Roman governing traditions, borrowing practices from the Byzantine emperor Justinian. Leovigildo in 580 convened a series of church councils at Toledo to work out reforms, astutely combining religion and politics. The king acted as the nominal head of church councils, a structural detail that permitted political intervention when necessary.

Leovigildo understood the importance of image and was the first Visigoth ruler to dress accordingly. He presided in rich silk robes and used a crown and a throne, in imitation of the popular image of God's heavenly kingdom. He issued coins with his image, using the natural circulation of currency to publicize his authority, and established Toledo as the imperial capital. The use of imperial titles on documents suggested his importance and their emanation from a centralized, legitimate entity. The Visigoth monarch harmonized slowly Arian religious beliefs and practices with those of the Roman Church. The official Visigoth conversion to Catholic doctrine in 589 completed the late Leovigildo's reform agenda.

Subsequently, the Visigoth monarchy permitted the Fourth Council of Toledo (633), made up of the kingdom's bishops along with the high nobility, to validate the elective succession. Validation by the church council signaled to Christian society, and more importantly to the aristocracy, that the issue of who would rule had been settled. To avoid any confusion, the Fifth Council of Toledo (636) declared that kingly eligibility was restricted to members of the high nobility. In reality, the king remained weak in relation to the combined nobility. When the Moors arrived, they understood the actual distribution of power and referred to powerful nobles as viceroys.[61]

The need for a unifying legal code was met by the *Fuero Juzgo* (654), also known as the *Liber Ludiciorum,* which had the immediate political goal of merging the Hispano-Roman population with the ruling Visigoths. It represented recognition of fusion between them, not an imposition. The document acknowledged the power of God, followed by the authority of the king. It remained in force until the much-more-complex *Fuero Real.*[62] The *Fuero Real* (1255) reflected the Platonic ideal of an organically layered society, with each level assigned a legitimate role under a wise ruler, as well as the Stoic notion of a universal commonwealth. Each social layer and those within it had to be permitted to follow their calling in order to preserve harmony and order. The

Fuero Real did not seek to override custom and local and regional *fueros* but sought to establish the guiding role of the "wise" king. The impulse clearly originated with the monarch, who, "aware that the people have suffered, decide to grant them this fuero"; the monarch did so *"en el nombre de Dios."* The *Fuero Real* advanced the notion of a divinely regulated political hierarchy. As explained in its opening rationale, "God created His court placed Himself at its head, organized archangels and angels in supporting positions, then extended the structure into the temporal world with a monarch at the head of a court supported by the nobility."[63]

A political structure as orderly as its divine model complemented that of the inclusive *ecclesia,* the corporate unity of all believers, but without subordination to papal authority. It strengthened the already evident reality that the church had become a useful political tool honored by, but increasingly a political captive of, the monarchy, following the path laid out in the *Fuero Juzgo.* That it strengthened the authority of the monarchy seems obvious, but it did not necessarily strengthen the monarchy's power to impose or intervene in all aspects of human conduct that fell under Natural Law. As a political concept, Natural Law inserted a legitimate layer above that of the king that was entitled to function separately, independently, and harmoniously; in short, the monarch could not violate Natural Law, which functioned to order human affairs at a level untouchable by kings or popes. The emerging modern state sought to absorb and subordinate Natural Law under a monarch by stressing his direct connection with the deity.

The "Siete Partidas" of Alfonso X (El Sabio), one of the most important medieval codes, went further and posited a dependency on divine benevolence as conveyed through the monarch as the political agent of God on Earth. Royal authority came directly from God, not the church or the people. It separated favors into two distinct spheres: private grants *(fueda)* and the bestowal (not a grant) by the king of an official office that could be withdrawn at the monarch's pleasure. The seven purposes of law defined in the "Partidas" were, in the order listed, to inspire confidence, to regulate, to command, to unify, to reward, to forbid, and to punish. The order of purpose went from the positive to the negative, implying regulation and considered divine judgment. Such powers were eternal, passed through inheritance. The "people" consisted of all men together—the superior, middle, and inferior ranks—a definition that recognized the existing social hierarchy while putting everyone under a royal umbrella, overriding any limitations inherent in Natural Law. The "Partidas" sought acceptance of a divine monarchy, with benevolence (in the eye of the royal beholder) as the sole limiting objective.[64] The Crown succeeded in blunting the reach of Natural Law in Indo-Mexico and clearing the way for a relatively unobstructed, albeit underfunded, evangelization effort in its American empire. The early missionary friars employed Natural Law in defense of the Indians.

Curbing Arbitrary Power

Education accompanied the growth of medieval towns and cities across western Europe. The more intricate commercial, political, and social networks in urban centers encouraged the study of previously unexamined processes. Latin, the language of scholars throughout Europe, facilitated the rapid dissemination of intellectual advances. The demand for knowledge outstripped the ability of monastic schools to instruct larger numbers in an increasingly complex society, including priests, lawyers, notaries, city officials, merchants, and a diverse group of managers that made society function. Urban schools broke the Benedictine Order's hold on education and high culture, conveyed to select students in a monastic setting. Friars, free to circulate in secular society, assumed virtual intellectual control of the schools as teachers and students. Such schools became fruitful recruiting grounds for the Franciscans and the Dominicans and played a crucial role in the formation of the Dominican intellectual tradition and the transformation of the Franciscans into a highly educated, academically oriented order. The curriculum, mainly theology and law, allowed instructors to apply analytical tools to written sources and to draw interpretations, in sharp contrast to the memorization characteristic of a monastic education.

Dominican and Franciscan intellectuals addressed seemingly conflicting elements within Christianity, providing interpretive solutions. In the process, the friars dealt with economic and political issues such as money, lending for interest, just price, profits, private property, business partnerships, just war, imposed conversion, rights of pagans, idolatry, and unnatural sins, as well as under what condition God, the monarch, or the pope had jurisdiction. Of paramount importance, clerical intellectuals introduced intent as an interpretive tool in the study of law. Law studied separately from religion appears to have been the key to change, which then spilled over into areas of more religious sensitivity. A focus on the intention of texts, sacred or legal, allowed for competing interpretations, while the text remained unchanged and valid. The expansion of texts stimulated further critical examination of issues.[65] In the end, different views had to be contemplated, resulting in a further intellectual refinement.

Aristotle's compositions and his emphasis on common good became part of the mix in the twelfth century, by way of the caliphate of Córdoba. Aristotelian radicalism viewed the community as an end in itself, unlike Christianity, which projected an afterlife and an interactive relationship between earthly kingdoms and the kingdom of heaven. A ruler's activities could be justified only on the grounds of the common good, moral as well as physical, with benevolent intent (*beneficium*).[66] Saint Thomas Aquinas adapted such notions to fit the needs of a Christian community, using the term *just* (implying divine judgment by a godly ruler) as a condition of common good. Consequently, common good functioned as both a temporal and a divine principle, but not necessarily linked together, as the possibility of an unjust ruler existed. Aquinas, however, asserted that by conveying authority to a ruler, the community alienated it rather than delegated it. In a similar fashion, power and authority constituted separate elements. Francisco de Vitoria, following the Scot John Mair (1487–1550), then of the Paris School, neatly divided the two concepts, with power coming from God and authority bestowed on a ruler by the community. Subsequently, Francisco Suárez asserted that authority came from the people as individual members of a community, an important distinction that made the conveying of authority even more complex. Domingo de Soto went further to assert that individuals had full control over their rights, suggesting that those rights could be reclaimed. More radical, Fernando de Vásquez de Menchaca (1512–1569) posited the notion that changes in rulers could occur as circumstances required, and the people's authority could be withdrawn. Vásquez de Menchaca elevated the law over the monarch, who should submit to it.[67] The validity of a ruler's decrees depended on whether they addressed the "public good." The question of who would judge a monarch's compliance with the law and the validity of royal decrees became crucial. The schoolmen accepted the challenge but only through examination of prior notions, arriving at an opinion but not an outright judgment. In their university lectures, they dealt openly with issues that discomforted monarchs as well as popes. The public lecture, the *relectio* that followed the end of a university course, provided a summary of the scholars' reasoned opinions before a larger audience. Their published works, pointedly dedicated or addressed to the powerful, applied pressure as well as provided guidance. Politically, the debate process protected a ruler from charges of acting arbitrarily and without due deliberation and made the case to other monarchs as well to the educated classes across Europe. On a functional level, the schoolmen restricted the monarch's actions. Disregard for the public good and arbitrary behavior, in effect, was not acceptable.

Pandemics: Transformative Disasters

The psychological, historical, and intellectual legacy of Europe included the impact of a series of epidemics and pandemics that swept the known world well before the New World became part of the global disease community. The pandemic that struck Indo-Mexico in the early sixteenth century is often separated from its European antecedents in spite of having been an extension of the same disease. The implication is that the Spaniards deliberately introduced smallpox as a weapon during the destruction of Tenochtitlán. The death rate on both sides of the Atlantic was horrible and transformative.

Thucydides recorded a 430 BC epidemic in Athens; others that were unrecorded likely occurred. Between AD 169 and 194, the Roman Empire experienced epidemics that claimed the life of Emperor Marcus Aurelius. Emperor Claudius Gothicus died in a pandemic that lasted for twenty years on and off between 250 and 270. Smallpox, measles, and typhus are believed to have caused early epidemics.[68] Just what diseases became epidemic is often difficult to determine. Descriptions left by observers, many quite graphic, are not exact enough to pinpoint the disease, quite apart from mutations that might have occurred.

As the civilized world knitted together, pandemics, in particular those caused by the plague, became common. Greek and Roman scholars knew about the existence of plague before it became a pandemic. They referenced cases in Egypt, Libya, and Syria and described its symptoms, morbidity, and mortality. Nevertheless, certainty that the *yersinia pestis* (the plague organism present among rodent colonies) caused the pandemic is not possible, in spite of the description of contemporary observers who reported swelling in the groin and neck and other symptoms consistent with the disease. Others have suggested anthrax or an ebola-like hemorrhagic plague, as well as a combination of several diseases, including typhus. Eventually, we will know with more certainty, as microbiologists search mass burial sites to extract material from the skeletal remains, including noneruptive teeth, which appear to be one of the last refuges of the pathogens.

The role of famine in prolonging suffering by weakening resistance to disease may be assumed, but to what degree remains a question. That some pandemics involved animals as well as humans is another variable. The actual number of victims is impossible to determine. While the written sources have diagnostic limitations, they do provide useful information on the political, economic, and social impacts of pandemics that form part of the historical memory.

The impact and response to such massive mortality exposed the latent tensions between popular causal notions of disease and suffering and religion's formal explanatory claims. Many people questioned the legitimacy of their suffering and its sources: if it was punishment, then which God or gods inflicted it on them and why? Some believed that by abandoning paganism and the state cult (a ritual acknowledgment of the protective function) they had lost protection; however such views could not be accepted fully. Mortality that impacted so many people, regardless of class, generation, social functions, and piety or the lack of it, shocked and stunned the fearful but as yet still living; the arbitrary nature of the plague pushed many to the edge of insanity.[69] The religious explanation lumped all together as sinners in need of repentance and, consequently, experiencing appropriate punishment. The Black Death weakened respect for both clerical and political authority, leading to open reversions to polytheism in some cases, while many others practiced paganism in semisecrecy.

The church, unable to insist on orderly ritual obligations, particularly funeral rites, struggled to regain control. Parading of icons and penitential processions to holy sites created an aura of spiritual activism. Pope Gregory I (the Great) organized a series of such processions as early as 590. Subsequently, Jacobus de Voragine's *The Golden Legend* (1275) recast a legend about King David to fortify Gregory the Great's claim to a successful intercession to end the plague. According to Jacobus, Pope Gregory viewed the Archangel Michael standing on top of Hadrian's tomb, wiping blood from his sword, and sheathing it, signaling God's decision to end the plague.[70]

A major plague pandemic began in Central Asia in the 1330s, reached the Crimea in 1346 and the Roman eastern capital of Constantinople in 1347, and then spread to the Mediterranean world, arriving in Spain in 1348. Castile bounced back but not the kingdoms of Aragón and Catalonia. The population in Aragón went from just under 500,000 in 1348 to about 220,000 100 years later. Barcelona had only 28,000 inhabitants in 1497. Population decline could be attributed also to migration to Valencia, Mallorca, Murcia, Sardinia, and Sicily and movement to southern cities, as well as to the reorientation of trade to the Atlantic. The plague reached east to Arabia and north to Scandinavia and crossed the channel to England. Recurring bouts lasted for over a century and a half, eventually becoming less regular and disappearing from much of Europe in the late eighteenth century.

The plague drastically reduced the labor supply and competition for workers. Decreased demand for land unbalanced the distribution of wealth as large estates. Attempts to decree the rollback to preplague wage levels could not be sustained. Emperor Justinian, in response to the outbreak of 541 in Constantinople—a pandemic that came to be known as "Justinian's plague" because it occurred during the emperor's rule—"announced in 544 the end of the pestilence and ordered that current prices and wages be set back to their pre-plague levels."[71] Subsequently, the English ordinances of 1349 and 1351 attempted to defy market realities. The latter ordinance instructed sheriffs to detain laborers who moved from their home county chasing higher wages and to return them, which was likely unenforceable. Some 50 percent of the European workforce consisted of serfs, and many took advantage of scarcity to become free-wage workers. Mobility with no questions asked indicated the impending collapse of the institution. Slave labor responded to economic opportunity in a similar manner. Predictably, the authorities sought to tighten control. After the first pandemic in Spain in the mid-sixth century, the Visigoth slave code provided punishment for assisting a runaway or failing to cooperate in the apprehension of fugitives. Other attempts to control runaways occupied much of the time of royal agents by 700.

To what extent demographic decline and its inevitable economic contractions opened the way for the conquest of the Iberian Peninsula must be considered. Pandemics established a downward population trend that was difficult to reverse. An outbreak of plague in Basra (Iraq) in 706, intriguingly referred to as the "Plague of the Maidens," acknowledged the reality of generational disruption.[72] We know that Roman military strength in Constantinople suffered from manpower shortages for at least a century after the first pandemic. A second pandemic's vast territorial reach depleted possible sources of recruits even more. Devastation in the Balkans appears to have attracted Slav migrants. Power vacuums left by the plague encouraged Arab movements into Syria. In Italy, the pandemic and the devastation caused by an attempted Byzantine Reconquista allowed the Lombards to settle.[73] Visigoth Spain, as part of the Mediterranean world, suffered from the first and second pandemics, a contributing factor in the Moors' arrival and their swift advance into France, which demoralized the badly bruised Christians.

The long, drawn-out Christian campaign to retake the peninsula, which ended in 1492, the year of contact with the New World, resulted in part from slow population recovery. As the final battle to take the last Moorish stronghold of Granada raged, so did the plague on both sides. Subsequently, Seville, the port of entry and departure for the Americas, served as a two-way disease transfer point to the Western Hemisphere and back, in spite of quarantines and other public health measures. The port city experienced innumerable plague epidemics, including one that killed 8,000 of its inhabitants in 1568, the same year that deaths from disease in New Spain may have peaked. Woodrow Borah and Shelburne Cooke's 1963 estimate of Indo-Mexico's population before the European arrival of twenty-five million, at the time believed to be too high because of the carrying capacity, now seems reasonable. It fell to one million at the beginning of the sixteenth century.[74]

3

MOORS AND CHRISTIANS
A Fateful Encounter

S PAIN'S HISTORICAL TRAJECTORY deviated from that of Europe to an important degree beginning in the 700s. Roman influences and Christianity remained important but were modified as a result of direct hostile and prolonged contact with Islam. No other European country experienced occupation and the creation of a militarized frontier that lasted almost eight centuries. Spanish Christianity faced extinction. The bitter struggle ended in 1492, the year of the initial contact with the Western Hemisphere and just short of two decades before Cortés landed on the shores of Indo-Mexico in 1519. The religious contest and the slow pushing back of the frontier had a long-lasting impact on the Spanish character and society and on the nature of its Catholicism. These elements, combined with prior historical experiences, had a role in Spain's reaction to the Moorish conquest and subsequently Castile's reorganization of Indo-Mexico.

Around the 630s, the Arabian tribes began to move northward. Just what motivated them is unclear, although religious unity played a role. The timing was propitious; decades of war between the Byzantine and Sassanian empires ended in 628. Both empires had fought each other to the point of exhaustion. The Sassanians had taken Jerusalem in 614 and two years later a large part of Egypt, an important source of Byzantine grain. Adding to the pressure, the Balkans became unstable. A twenty-six-year war drained the treasuries of both empires, wore down the soldiery, and made it impossible to reinforce and hold Byzantine enclaves in Spain. The successor to the prophet Muhammad, Caliph

Abu Bakr (632–634), began a series of raids on the Eastern Roman Empire and the Sassanian (Persian) Empire. Muslim raiders likely uncovered some surprising vulnerabilities that led to more ambitious plans far beyond occasional raiding forays.

The defeat of the Byzantine army at Yarmuk in 635 made it impossible for the Eastern Roman Empire to hold on to Syria. The surrender of Alexandria to an Arab army in 642 provided the Arabs maritime resources, skills, and a significant fleet. From that point on, Arab armies went from isolated by desert sands regions to other civilized enclaves along the narrow coastal strip all the way to Ceuta (taken in 706) on the Tangier promontory, within eyesight of the coast of Visigoth Spain. Along the way, the Berbers allied themselves with the Arab conquerors. After reaching the barrier of the Atlantic Ocean, Muslim expansion had little option but to turn north into Spain. It should not have been a surprise; what may have been surprising, however, was how quickly the Visigoth monarchy collapsed. In retrospect, its collapse seems to have been inevitable.

Spain's slow but steady socioeconomic decline undermined its institutions. Large unproductive landholders, an impoverished peasantry, and an all-but-destroyed middle class struggled to survive, while roving bands of robbers and slaves infested the countryside. In desperation, the hunt for scapegoats had turned on the substantial Jewish community in 616, further damaging an already weakened economy and precipitating a revolt. The Visigoth monarchy, in an advanced state of disintegration, could do little to cope with the existing situation, let alone reverse it. In many respects, the disintegration mirrored the same process that made it possible for the Visigoths to supplant Rome's hold on the peninsula. Visigoth political factionalism and struggles over succession produced many ambitious candidates in search of power. Factions vying for dominance invited external forces to intervene on their behalf. Byzantine and Frankish interventions preceded that of the Moors, but the Moorish arrival proved the most fateful and enduring.

Political factions, possibly ambitious individuals, or more likely accurate intelligence may well have encouraged the arrival of the Berbers. The Berber chief, Tarif, launched a raiding party across the straits in 710, and the following year, Tariq, a Berber freedman (of Musa, the North African governor), led a force of 7,000 men into the peninsula. Collaboration with disgruntled Christian elements may have occurred.

Subsequently, in 712, Governor Musa led 10,000 Arab and Berber soldiers into Spain, seizing the cities of Seville and Merida.[1] In the face of back-to-back assaults, the Visigoth state collapsed like a house of cards, as most of the peninsula fell to the forces of Islam by 718. After the invaders consolidated their gains, they subsequently crossed the Pyrenees, to be defeated by the Franks at Poitier in 732, and crucially, failed to hold on to the key city of Narbonne. Nevertheless, in the short space of twenty-two years, the Moors went from raiders to conquerors and governors. Arab armies combined warfare with a dynamic religion as they moved northward. The shock and the decisive collapse forced the Visigoth remnants to huddle in the northwestern mountains and rally around Christianity, virtually the only thing they had left. Survival could not be taken for granted. Subsequent Muslim waves from North Africa, Asia Minor, and as far east as Yemen and Syria represented the last east–west cultural flow in medieval times.

The long, drawn-out struggle against Islam was largely dependent on what remained of Christian Spain, with little help from coreligionists. To the immediate north, the Carolingian Empire (750–900) sought to resurrect the Roman Empire but with middling success. In reality, the Roman Empire had fragmented into protonational states. The Carolingians could not restore the urban settlement pattern or the economy that had characterized the Roman Empire. Large parts of the Carolingian Empire survived in rural isolation, dependent on local lords who were theoretically charged by the emperor to administer the law and protect the peasantry. The Carolingians succeeded, at least for a time, in consolidating a feudal empire, with former Roman Gaul at its center. The Carolingian Empire extended across the Pyrenees only to the Ebro River, a natural barrier that delineated the southern frontier of Catalonia, excluding much of the Iberian Peninsula. It had few resources available to confront Arab-Berber power. The bedraggled elements on the Iberian side of the northern mountains could not offer much help or hope.

From an economic and cultural standpoint, the Arab-Berber seizure of Visigoth Spain represented an overdue reinvigoration, something that the exhausted Christian regime could not have accomplished. The invaders introduced dry-land agricultural techniques, along with new crops such as cotton, citrus fruits, sugarcane, and rice, along with reforms in land tenure—all of which revitalized agriculture and increased food supplies and exports. Manufacturing of leather goods, paper (introduced by Arabs), textiles, carpets, weapons, pottery, mining, and new construction projects underpinned a healthy economy. An active import and export trade that flourished, made possible by an extensive merchant fleet, drew in North Africa, particularly Egypt, and even Constantinople into a mutually profitable economic relationship. Byzantine traders transshipped goods produced in Muslim Spain to the east as far as India. The exchange of goods and capital through a linked trade network created a vibrant trading economy, initially with limited participation from the Christian community, which was uncertain about its survival.

The most important consequence of 711 was the replacement of a dysfunctional and discredited Visigoth elite. The Arab trade network and the intangibles of aesthetics all constituted revolutionary change. Of great consequence for Europe and Western civilization in general, Muslim scholars reintroduced Greek learning, which had survived somewhat miraculously in Arabic translations. The city of Toledo served as the point of cultural transmission after its recapture in 1085 by Christian forces. Many Muslim scholars remained in the city, soon to be joined by Jewish refugees fleeing intolerant Almonhades rule. During the time of King Alfonso El Sabio (the wise), 1252–1284, the monarch of Castile and Leon, multilingual translators worked with scholars from across Europe to make available to Latin readers the extant works of Aristotle, Euclid, Galen, and Hippocrates, as well as learned commentaries by Muslim scholars on Greek thought. Studying with Arabic scholars became a sought-after experience but one that caused some negative suspicions.

Less positively, the invaders brought with them internal divisions that made for political complexity and periodic turmoil. Tensions surfaced almost at the moment Muslim forces entered the peninsula. Berber tribesmen made up the bulk of the soldiery, while Arabs occupied the directive levels and absorbed much of the fruits of the conquest. Most Berbers did not speak or read Arabic and deeply resented their inferior position relative to their Arab leaders. Moreover, their superficial conversion to Islam had not swept aside ancient beliefs but rather created a Muslim façade behind which they venerated local saints and worshipped at small shrines, in much the same manner as the nominal Christians who so concerned St. Augustine and a succession of church councils.

Demographically, the semidisaffected Berbers outnumbered Arabs by a wide margin. Berber resentment eventually coalesced around Kharijism, a form of Islam formed in reaction to Arab dominance. In 740, a massive rebellion in the Maghreb spread across the Straits of Gibraltar as the mainly rural Berber population attacked urban-dwelling Arabs. Only the arrival of 7,000 Syrian cavalry saved the day. Arabs' preference for Jewish and Christian administrators reflected their doubts about the loyalty of their Berber coreligionists. Arab rulers appeared to have more confidence in openly Christian and Jewish subjects, using them extensively in their administration, even sending bishops on important diplomatic missions. For Jews and Christians, such positions provided a positive connection, if not an actual social alliance, with the Muslim community. Jews and Christians fell in the category of *dhimmiyeen*—protected by their monotheism and other aspects they shared with Islam that made them partially acceptable, although they paid a higher tax than Muslims.

In the 750s, crop failures and the endemic border wars forced the Berbers to abandon the Duero valley and to move south. Demographic realignment also took place among the Mozarabes (Arabized Christians and Jews) as taxes and economic pressures on non-Muslims mounted. Many moved northward, increasing the population of what remained of the old regime. Not all fled. In urban areas, many well-established and prosperous Christians remained, pragmatically adopting Arabic names. The attractions of trade through Muslim channels prompted opportunistic conversions. In the late eighth century, an increasing number of Mozarabes converted to Islam. Conversion to Islam of non-Arabs did not lead to total integration; their descendants were referred to as *Muwallad,* meaning "having adopted the faith," a term that set them apart from other believers, creating a religious subcategory that took a Christian form with the divisive distinction between New Christians (suspected of being crypto-Jews or Muslims) and Old Christians (above suspicions), a prejudicial notion that passed to the New World after 1492.

The Christians who remained under Muslim rule became acculturated to the extent of speaking, reading, and writing in Arabic, wearing Arab clothing, and living a lifestyle scarcely different from their host culture. The archbishop of Seville felt it necessary to translate and annotate the Bible in Arabic for the use of his own coreligionists; probably the archbishop also referred to the Arabic translation for his own

MAP 2. Al-Andalus, 711–1031

use.[2] Nevertheless, in spite of assimilation over several generations, converts found it difficult to penetrate the Arab elite.

The establishment of the Umayyad Emirate (kingdom) after 755 provided a political center for Al-Andalus. Nevertheless, it was not politically effective until 912, when Abd-al-Rahman III established a caliphate, in effect an empire but also a political designation that proclaimed him to be a legitimate successor to the prophet Muhammad. Such a designation put him on the same philosophical and hence political level as other caliphates and freed him from the theoretical supervision of Baghdad and a newly formed caliphate in Egypt.

During the caliphate, Al-Andalus reached the height of administrative effectiveness as well as cultural influence.[3] Agricultural prosperity underpinned its splendor; the golden revival of Al-Andalus was followed by gradual decline and contraction. Between 1008 and 1031, the caliphate shattered into some thirty small kingdoms *(taifas)*. Fragmentation of Muslim power increased the security of Christian microkingdoms and opened the door to military and economic alliances, between them and ambitious taifas rulers. Nevertheless, the small Christian kingdoms competed with each other for tribute and opportunistic territorial expansion. Muslims who allied with Christians against Muslims and the reverse indicated that economic and political interests trumped religious differences.

Energizing Myths

Northern Spain, with its poor soil and rocky, almost inaccessible terrain, sheltered remnants from the southern and mountain tribes that were isolated from the Christian kingdoms on the other side of the mountain range by Basque tribes that controlled the mountain passes. As a fringe area, it could expect to be absorbed over time into the general culture of the peninsula. The unwillingness of Moorish rulers to devote their resources to subdue such a region is understandable; nevertheless, it proved to be a mistake. Moorish political control on the peninsula spread like water pooling on an uneven stone floor. That it pooled in the fertile spots may be explained by topography and the demands of agriculture. Meanwhile, the Christian population in the north scratched a living from the rocky soil. The north preserved and nourished Christian militancy along the frontier in the form of opportunistic raiders and eventually daring settlers who formed small kingdoms over time. The process engendered myth making and, when combined with Christianity, provided emotional momentum.

Those who remained in the south negotiated a degree of security with rulers who readily accepted tributary arrangements. A negotiated capitulation avoided destruction on one side and the necessity of employing force on the other. It involved a transfer of suzerainty and payment of the *jizya,* an annual poll tax, and the *kharaj,* a land tax. All else remained the same, including property rights, religious practices, existing governing structures, and laws—a pragmatic accommodation that ensured religious complexity, as well as established a patchwork of political control with a high degree of interaction between the suzerain and his Christian tributaries.[4] In regions directly controlled by Muslim rulers, Christians lived under a policy of official toleration, subject to additional taxes. Religious toleration resulted in a Mozarab Christian community, one influenced by Muslim culture and practices, to the extent that Mozarab Christian rites competed with the Latin rites endorsed by Rome.

The relationship between Christianity and Islam remained uncertain and still in flux. That both sides did not fit into the dismissive category of paganism seemed obvious. A significant number of Spanish medieval philosophers regarded Islam as a heretical form of Christianity—a level of confusion reflected also in the Moorish notion of Christians and Jews as "People of the Book." At the lower social levels, a nominally Christian population (still semipagan) likely assumed that Christianity and Islam constituted variants of the same religion.[5] Meanwhile, the northern mountains served as a refuge for a badly mangled Visigoth-Christian culture—a place for some, but by no means all, Christians to regroup and begin to nibble at the fringes of Moorish power. Regaining confidence in the aftermath of defeat required drawing distinctions between Islam and Christianity and rejecting the Mozarabic accommodation that could only lead to assimilation.

A reinforcing myth emerged in its basic form in 731, even before the decisive battle that turned back Muslim expansion north of the Pyrenees. Pelayo, the designated initiator of the Reconquista, was a protonationalist creation, an effort to set a start date on a continuum that ended in 1492 with the fall of Granada. The known facts hardly support the role assigned to the engagement at Covadonga. The story goes that when the Moors reached the northern mountains, they encountered the hostility of the mountain people, led by the Asturian chief Pelayo. Exactly what happened is unclear, as were Pelayo's intentions. That something sufficient to be noted in a Moorish report occurred provides corroboration and the following account of how it ended. Pelayo survived holed up in a cave with a stubborn group of followers, and the Moorish attackers soon departed to resume their march into Europe (732). That they decided not to waste any more time dealing with a handful of tribesmen huddled in a cave seemed a sensible decision. That the Moors' aborted thrust north ended with a retreat back into the Iberian Peninsula had little to do with Pelayo and his cave. Nevertheless, the momentous defeat ended the notion of Moorish invincibility. Consequently, the minor incident at Covadonga on the Iberian side was identified as the moment the Christian Reconquista began, an interpretation of events that grossly magnified the importance of what happened but nevertheless served as a badly needed morale booster.

While Pelayo marked the designated beginning of the adventure, Christians found their motivational force in the cult of Santiago (Saint James), one of the twelve apostles. James supposedly preached the faith for six years in Spain. He then returned to Jerusalem, only to be beheaded by King Herod. Allegedly, his devoted followers brought his body to Spain for burial. During the time of Roman persecution of Christians, the burial site was forgotten. Fortunately, in 813, a hermit reported mysterious music and a bright star shining on an oak tree. The bishop, on examining the site, found an altar and three bodies but only two heads. An inscription indicated that Saint James was one of the bodies. A church was built to mark the location, and Pope Leo III spread the word to the Catholic world. Santiago de Compostela became a popular pilgrimage site and an energizing cult. The discovered Santiago, presumably reunited with his head, subsequently hovered above Hernán Cortés as he advanced on Tenochtitlán in 1521.

South of the Ebro (beyond the southernmost extension of the Carolingian Empire), Christian remnants absorbed refugees from Muslim areas in the south, settling them on land depopulated by Christian thrusts southward. Over time, the mountain valleys housed a significant population that was relatively secure from Muslim raiders. The Christian kingdoms expanded as the Muslim frontier moved south, away from the mountainous north. Raiding the border should not be understood as an organized or a protonationalistic reaction: who could have envisioned the outcome of the almost 800-year Reconquista? Asturias, Pelayo's land, was the first kingdom to emerge in 791, followed by Galicia and León, which subsequently became the Kingdom of León. At the time, what is now Asturias and Galicia remained primitively Visigothic, barely touched by Roman urban culture. It must have been a shock to those Romanized southerners who fled northward. One can speculate that this may have been one reason not to abandon the cities in the south for the wilds of the Christian fringes in the north. Castile, initially an extension of the Kingdom of León, became an independent kingdom during the time of Fernando III.

The Moorish withdrawal to the south was a rational economic decision, not a retreat. An extensive swath of the northern peninsula had poor soils, and it made little sense to devote energy to squeezing minimal production out of its unforgiving land. The withdrawal created a political vacuum, however, that allowed the Christians to expand their territory. Nevertheless, the small Christian kingdoms periodically dealt with random military assaults until the early eleventh century. Caliph Al Mansur (978–1002) directed some fifty assaults against the northern kingdoms. In 985, he plundered Barcelona and massacred its inhabitants, and in 997, his army sacked Santiago de Compostela. After 1031, Moorish power weakened to the extent that deep raiding expeditions could not be mounted. Consequently, the Christian counterthrust met little opposition except what nature provided. Isolated and marginal Christian kingdoms, perhaps with memories of the fertile south, had an incentive to probe southward.

Pope Gregory VII (1073–1085), deeply concerned that the Moorish threat endangered the shrine of Saint James de Compostela, organized efforts to defend the site, setting the stage for the crusades that followed his papacy. Gregory offered land to those who went to Spain if they succeeded in wresting it back from the Muslims, although such grants would remain under papal suzerainty. The timing was propitious, as established landholders adopted primogeniture to protect family wealth and status, leaving younger sons at loose ends, land hungry, and willing to fight for status and resources. While the initial struggle between the Moors and the Christians was over plunder and territory, both sides rapidly adopted the concept of a Holy War.[6] Popes Alexander II (1062–1073) and Gregory VII internationalized the Reconquista by calling on French knights to go to Spain in return for remission of penance for their sins. After a forty-day siege, in the latter months of 1064, Barbastro fell to the Christians, followed by the brutalization of the hapless population. Within a year, it was retaken by the Moors.[7]

The fully elaborated notion of a crusade followed under the guidance of Pope Urban II. At the Council of Clermont (1095), he stressed the need to avoid the sad spectacle of intrareligious conflicts, ironically, a lament shared by Islam. By directing force against unbelievers, the church functioned as both a spiritual and a secular unifying force. Pope

Urban established a theoretical protective community of believers, while redirecting soldiers, resources, and violence against unbelievers in competition with kings. Channeling organized violence led to the creation of military orders, a contradictory mixture of aggression and pursuit of a peaceful Christian world, believed achievable through conquest. The military orders combined monastic practices with a knightly code of honor. These warrior monks represented the first disciplined and autonomous military organizations to emerge in the post-Roman era. Beyond their activities in Palestine, they inspired the founding of other military orders, most notably in Spain.[8]

The Templars and Hospitallers were the first orders to have a presence in Spain. The indigenous Order of Calatrava ironically was formed in the aftermath of its dogged defense of Cáceres, to which the Templars had declined to commit their forces. The Order of Santiago emerged with the Christian conquest of Cáceres in 1170. All such orders theoretically were universal and required papal recognition. Less prestigious defensive organizations were the *hermanidades,* the local brotherhoods of resident knights formed to defend cities. Militant Christianity merged the tasks of defense and expansion of Christianity with the seizure of territory, a combination that subsequently played itself out in Indo-America as the church became subordinated to the monarch. The idea that to be a subject of the Crown one had to be a Christian emerged as a political tool during the crusades, a notion solidified in the final stages of the Reconquista into a subdefinition that to be Spaniard one had to be a Christian with a long line of Christian ancestors and, subsequently, with the Reformation, a Catholic Christian.[9]

Social mobility depended on plunder and military participation on a contested frontier. In the lower Ebro valley, the bishops of Tortosa and the Hospitallers in the early 1300s offered privileges in an attempt to repopulate the land, as did Alfonso VII in 1339 in the case of Colmenar de Oreja; all worried that a population vacuum might lead to a reoccupation by the Moors. In some respects, these worries mirrored those of Cortés in Indo-Mexico, and the exemptions and rights appeared much like those that were granted to those who were willing to homestead the North American frontier centuries later. Formally in a written document, Alfonso exempted settlers from taxes if they remained for a year. Settlers had complete control over their property, with the right to dispose of it as they pleased. Moreover, they did not have to share the fruits of raiding except with the lord of Oreja. A colonist's past brushes with the law would be overlooked, as would informal sexual arrangements—certainly an attractive package, though it may have not been enough. The northern kingdoms thought in terms of settled territory, while migrants hoped for the plunder as well as the social mobility that only a frontier could offer. As El Cid advised, "He who stays in one spot will see his fortunes diminish."[10]

The pursuit of plunder resulted in labor scarcity; thus, preserving the existing Moorish peasantry on the land was important. Large expanses of almost uninhabited land behind the actual frontier created favorable conditions for sheep and cattle herding, much less labor intensive than agriculture, as the Reconquista moved into the southern grasslands of La Mancha and Extremadura. The military orders that were heavily committed to the frontier had large flocks; in one case, two orders disputed claims to 42,000 head of sheep in the Tagus Valley. Others had equally as impressive flocks; nevertheless, a class of small stockmen coexisted with the large-scale herders.

Merino sheep produced high-quality wool, which was in demand in the Low Countries, France, and Italy, as well as for domestic production in southern cities such as Cordoba, Cuenca, and others. The need to settle disputes over ownership of animals as well as to maintain access to winter and summer grazing land led to the establishment in the 1270s of Real Concejo de la Mesta, an association of ranchers.[11] The economic contribution of wool exports legally elevated herding above agriculture.

Social flexibility accompanied the shifting frontier. As the need for both mounted knights and foot soldiers increased, the extent of the privileges offered to colonists became more generous, and with these privileges came social mobility. Feudalism, which as noted earlier was characteristic of Europe north of the mountains, never took hold in the south except in parts of Catalonia, although semifeudal arrangements of various types in exchange for defensive support were common. The opening of new land and the presence of a significant number of Moorish peasants (some 30 to 35 percent of the population in Aragón and parts of Catalonia) created uncertainty about whether the frontier could be held. Consequently, Christians remained organized for warfare, with "a curious mixture of 'democratic' and noble [meaning warrior] characteristics."[12]

Sociopolitical Impact of the Moving Frontier

The economic importance of peasants, combined with their contribution as infantry soldiers in terrain unsuitable for large-scale cavalry, could not be ignored or unrewarded. In tenth-century Castile, free Christian peasants made up most of the population. New frontier settlements functioned under *cartas pueblos* (charters) with self-governing, autonomous councils. Castilian peasants met in open village meetings to make important decisions. Associations of peasant villages gave way to associations of towns to deal with common problems, including allocation of land, division of herds, and use of the commons. In other areas such as southern León, Christian migrants established freeholds based on land occupation. In the thirteenth century, all remaining serfs received the status of *colonos,* with freedom of movement and legal standing. Free peasants without land worked as salaried labor, and in certain regions, *yunqueros,* owners of cattle or oxen with limited or no land, grazed their animals on the commons. The attraction of the frontier remained.

The warrior mentality of the shifting frontier made transient settlers impatient with social and economic restrictions and fees imposed by monasteries and traditional nobles. Respect for authority was more than balanced by a strong sense of self-worth, engendered by personal success. The Reconquista fashioned a resourceful people but not one that could be governed easily. In many respects, they exhibited the social equality that characterized earlier tribal groups and collectively functioned as a de facto political force that few challenged. The territorial extent of the frontier as well as its protracted existence molded the people's political relationship with power and authority.

The success of newly created frontier nobles as well as the expectations of the peasant soldiers who accompanied them challenged kings, and would-be kings, who were well aware that they did not have a monopoly on organized violence, nor could they rely on a deep sense of loyalty to the monarch. The shifting militarized frontier and the economic importance of plunder kept all sides in a state of insecurity, broken occasionally by alliances between Muslims and Christians as their interests coincided. The unsettled contest over territory offered opportunity as well as danger. A status transformation could be abrupt, either positive or negative. While it was unlikely that a frontier warrior would become one of the great magnates who served as the king's advisers, individuals of recognized valor and luck assumed noble lineage. On a basic level, a horse, armor, and the ability to maintain them, coupled with military success, made a noble. Clearly, the frontier blurred all the levels of the social structure to the advantage of those who were at the bottom. Noble status was a fluid concept and remained so, as the New World became a transatlantic extension of the Iberian frontier.

Just how many individuals earned or fraudulently claimed noble status cannot be determined, but on the frontier, it mattered little; all Spaniards as they stepped ashore in Indo-Mexico did so as *hidalgos* (lower level nobles). That noble status exempted one from taxation was a benefit that went from one generation to the next and served as royal validation. The conquest of Valencia by El Cid was glorified in the *Cantar de Mío Cid,* which noted with little exaggeration that those who entered the city as foot soldiers left as rich *caballeros* (gentlemen).[13] The *infanzones* and caballeros and the socially confusing *caballeros villanos* (common or lesser knights) concentrated in cities protected by municipal rights. The frontier continued to exist in a physical sense until the fall of Granada in 1492.

The Reconquista became part of Spanish culture as frontier notions fused with the leveling and unifying elements of Christianity. Moreover, philosophical interpretations of kingly authority by the schoolmen formed a formidable counterbalance to the emerging protomodern state. Carlos I (Emperor Carlos V), the first Austrian Habsburg, marked a break in historical continuity between the monarchy as an institution and those who ruled. Organizing what constituted a Spanish American frontier fell to the Habsburgs, but history could not be swept aside. A well-entrenched group of traditional advisers modified Carlos V plans, although not without resistance. In Indo-Mexico, the organizational structure (to be discussed shortly) drew on traditional political elements, but carefully modified to minimize as much as possible the political challenges to royal authority that were present in Spain.

Markets, Monarchs, and Constitutionalism

In common with most of medieval Europe, Spain functioned economically as a collection of microeconomies. Agriculture at the time represented around 80 percent of all economic activity. Ranching and mining made up the rest. Distance and topography dictated the maximum territorial extension of both market and political units. In 1490, the average radius of a political unit was fifty miles, encompassing two microeconomies.[14] Markets had to be within ten or twenty-five miles at the most from the point of production; poor roads and difficult terrain compounded the obstacles, resulting in a string of market towns at the center of a productive circle of no more than a twenty-five-mile radius in all directions. Only economies with access to rivers or on seacoasts and inexpensive barge- and ship-borne transportation enjoyed a highly profitable trade in agricultural commodities. For foreign traders, a combination of money sales of luxury goods from the east and bulk commodities on the return trip maximized profits. Money mitigated the problem of distance, although poor, expensive transportation remained an obstacle. Nobles generally appropriated local agricultural production directly under semifeudal arrangements, with little need for the exchange of money. How much they could demand was set by custom and the threat of violent action if violated. Those who received commodities either had to use them or had to convert them to money is some fashion.

In the north, Aragón and Catalonia initially used Carolingian coinage, but the frontier kingdoms of Castilian León were economically oriented toward the Muslim south. Fernando I (1035–1065) minted the first Castilian coin. The Almoravids' gold *morabitín*, however, dominated the frontier region in the early twelfth century, and its use moved northward. Alfonso VIII of Castile (1155–1214) in 1172 minted the *maravedí*, borrowing elements from the Almoravids, including Arabic lettering, presumably to facilitate exchange with the Moors. After the decisive battle of Las Navas de Tolosa in 1212, the maravedí was no longer minted but continued in circulation. It may only be a slight exaggeration to observe that money, mints, and economically viable monarchies went together.

What initially had been a war of attrition with little royal participation pushed back the Moorish frontier. Small northern monarchies had little choice but to extend their authority into the vacuum. With few resources available, they devised ways to assert their authority and at the same time encourage continued advances. The introduction of the encomienda placed Moorish peasants under an individual strong enough to protect them from others and to allow them to continue their productive activities. It also effectively established permanent outposts to hold the frontier, permitting further forays into Moorish territory. As the frontier contracted into more heavily populated regions with cities, the various kingdoms had to shoulder more responsibilities and expense. After the decisive battle of Las Navas de Tolosa, the military advantage passed to Christian forces, although the struggle continued until 1492. Castile and Aragón, the two most powerful kingdoms, eventually had full responsibility for pressing the Reconquista to its successful conclusion. The monarchs bore much of the expense of taking fortified cities; rarely did plunder cover costs. A siege could last months and in some cases well over a year; the siege of Seville required seventeen months. A financially exhausted Fernando III had to appeal to Castilian towns in order to successfully complete the siege. In the struggle to gain the support of towns and the nobility, the monarch had to offer inducements. Convening a Cortes (parliament) to obtain consent to raise new taxes involved bargaining with nobles and representatives of cities; in blunt terms, it came down to money in exchange for rights and privileges. Constitutionalism flourished in large part because of the drawn-out Moorish resistance to the advancing Christians. The existence of a patchwork of *fueros* (localized rights and privileges), supported as customary rights, served as the immediate source of authority, with the monarch restricted to the theoretical overarching level.

Nevertheless, only kings had the ability to organize an army and to direct the Reconquista in its latter stages. In the campaign and subsequent victory of Las Navas de Tolosa that turned the tide permanently in favor of the Christians, Alfonso VIII gathered his forces, worked with several other kings, executed the battle plan, and prepared for financial and material contingencies—tasks beyond the organizational ability of most nobles and soldier peasants. Nevertheless, he also drew on the frontier nobility and those who aspired to social mobility or at least a share of the plunder.

Politically, the Las Navas de Tolosa victory relied on the sociopolitical unity that had emerged out of necessity during the Christian Reconquista.[15] The accepted idea that the relationship between the monarch and the people had originally been a contractual one drawn up in mythical times required a monarch to be respectful of demands and privileges. In the Kingdom of Aragón, a more formal arrangement than that in Castile required that prior agreements had to be reaffirmed and refreshed with each royal succession. This constituted a restatement of the rules of sociopolitical engagement. A monarch swore to uphold all the rights and privileges of the nobility in each of the three political units joined together as the Kingdom of Aragón, consisting of the County of Catalonia, governed by a count (the king held the title of the Count of Barcelona), Aragón, and Valencia—each one with its own unique structures and laws. The conditional nature of the arrangement between the monarch and Aragón was bluntly stated. The oath is well known but bears repeating: "We who are as good as you and together are more powerful than you, make you our king and lord, provided you observe our privileges [*fueros*] and liberties, if not, not."[16]

At the lower levels, charters and privileges conceded to cities served also as a counterbalance to the high nobility. The urban caballeros, confronted by aggressive nobles who dominated the countryside, manipulated the Crown to counter the power of the nobility. The monarch, unable to tax the nobility and the clergy, had a financial interest in the well-being of cities. By the time that frontier expansion slowed in the thirteenth century, the basic trend as well as the sociopolitical balance already had been set. Subsequently, in the late 1400s, Queen Isabel consolidated a degree of directive authority over the cities. Nevertheless, municipal authority in close contact with its urban constituency remained intact. That municipalities were the first institutions to be put in place in the New World testified to their foundational importance.

The End of Toleration in Spain

By the middle of the thirteenth century, the Iberian Christian kingdoms gained what turned out to be permanent military superiority. As the Reconquista gathered momentum, Castile became the dominant Iberian monarchy with responsibility to engage the enemy. Territorial expansion became state policy, passed from ruler to ruler. While not all rulers lived up to such expectations, those who failed to mount attacks on the shrinking Moorish domains came under criticism. The confidence that came with the kingdoms' strong military position turned attention to the internal reordering of their conquests. The former policy of discriminatory toleration that was practiced by both Muslim and Christian rulers, allowing nonbelievers to remain in place but subject to taxation and exclusion from certain activities and bureaucratic positions, progressively became more restrictive. Non-Christian minorities, the Moors and Jews who had previously been tolerated, now were perceived to pose a problem, but each in a different manner.

As Moorish territory fell into Christian hands, Castile incorporated a sizable Muslim population. As it took Moorish cities, Castile expelled the Muslim ruling elite but not the Jews and left the urban population and the surrounding rural peasantry in place. Official toleration, based on the need to keep productive Moorish labor in place, lasted until the Morocco Merinid Caliphate seized the southern tip of the Iberian Peninsula. The apparent attempt to reverse the Christian advance emboldened the large Mudéjar population (Muslim converts to Christianity) in the southern regions of Castile to throw off their Christian overlords.[17] The revolt of 1263 almost succeeded.[18] Consequently, following the failed attempt, the Muslim and Mudéjar population was driven south to Moorish Granada and North Africa.[19] Powerful landholders protected their Moorish labor from expulsion until the general removal in the early sixteenth century.

The Jewish population, in contrast, had a positive, if complex, relationship with both Muslim and Christian rulers. Educated Jews had a long history of service to both caliphs and kings. In addition, noble families often employed Jewish physicians as part of their households. While most Jews labored as artisans, traders, and small shopkeepers, a small but important number of well-educated Jews served in key positions in society and appeared to be favored by rulers and noble patrons; it was assumed that they had excessive influence over policy. Kings relied on them as tax farmers (a result of Christianity's ambivalence concerning wealth); consequently, as tax collectors they came in negative contact with a wide swath of the lower classes, who resented their activities. It should be kept in mind that nobles and the clergy were exempt from taxation, although both provided funds in less public ways. Jews also became important at the municipal level; their admin-

istrative talents led to a perceived monopoly on such positions, leading
to friction.

The notion of collective Jewish responsibility for the crucifixion of
Jesus made Jews into popular scapegoats, particularly during difficult
times such as food shortage or tax collection. Folk myths often focused
on imaginary evils, such as the notion that Jews ritually sacrificed kid-
napped Christian babies, a myth widely believed among the peasantry.
The authorities did little to address the situation, perhaps relieved not
to be the focus of such attention. A pogrom beginning in Seville in 1391
spread quickly; within weeks, it reached Barcelona in the north. Widespread fear in the Jewish community led to a wave of quick conversions, with only minimal religious instruction. Becoming a Christian
(a *converso*) theoretically removed the obstacles that limited opportunities, offering protection but exposing conversos to the charge of
heresy.

Assimilation of converso families and intermarriage of rich converso
families with the nobility led to conspiratorial notions that they had
infiltrated all levels of society and a general suspicion that conversos
remained crypto-Jews who used their conversion for political and economic advantage. The pogrom in Toledo in 1449 resulted from a royal
tax collected by Alonso Cota, a converso. Chronic urban unrest resulted
in yet more anti-Semitic violence, leading up to another pogrom in 1473.

In addition, the nobility became concerned that the urban population in general had grown too powerful and threatened to weaken the
influence of the Old Christian warrior class. The urban population constituted an increasingly prosperous and important commercial middle
class. Out of a combined Castilian-Aragón population of some nine million, the middle class numbered perhaps around half a million.[20] Just
how many were Jews is impossible to determine; nevertheless, Jews appeared to the archetypal urban dwellers. Political fears, resentments,
and economic considerations were transformed into collective religious
hysteria directed at the Jews. Religious zealotry, fused with paranoia,
became a highly destructive force that touched on every aspect of life.
That many people profited from it seems obvious; at the lower levels, a
sense of powerlessness played a role, as did simplified religious beliefs.
Envy and angry resentment became deadly emotions.

After the final assault on the last Moorish stronghold of Granada in
1492, Queen Isabel faced the immediate problem of a large Muslim

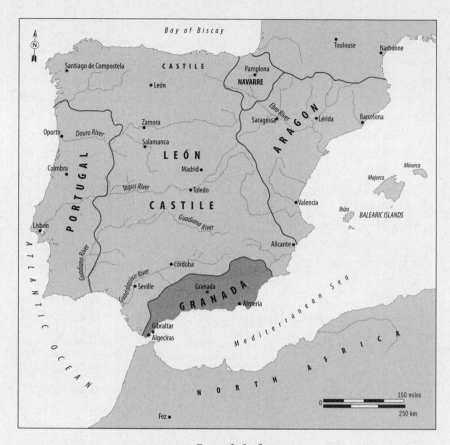

MAP 3. Granada before 1492

population now under Castilian rule. Forced conversion violated canon law, but an aggressive evangelization might yield results or at least encourage the recalcitrant to move to North Africa. Isabel realized that the Catholic clergy in its current state of laxness would be unable to execute such a large-scale evangelization. Ill-trained clerics could hardly be trusted to impart orthodox doctrine and to separate Muslim theology from that of the church. Moreover, clerical morality concerned the queen, who was well aware that vows of chastity seemed to be honored only when convenient. A significant number of the lower clergy openly lived with their unsanctioned wives and children, untroubled by their transgressions or by their bishops. Reform of the Castilian clergy would have to be undertaken if the evangelization process had any chance of success. Consequently, Isabel petitioned the pope to allow her to select clerics for the evangelization of Granada.

Reform, Paranoia, and Expulsion

The Reconquista as it moved to its conclusion was intellectually perceived on both sides as more of a religious issue. Important economic and territorial aspects that had preoccupied monarchs earlier tended to be brushed aside. Thus, the fall of the last Moorish kingdom in 1492 represented a Christian triumph. The Catholic monarchs, Isabel I (1474–1504) and her consort and coruler Fernando V, anticipating the end of the last Moorish stronghold of Granada, contemplated a Spain completely under Christian political and military control. The imposition of religious unity over a then multifaith population appeared to be the only way to assure loyalty. For Isabel and her consort, Christianization meant security; they would soon change their views. Queen Isabel reformed the Spanish church, strengthening its moral foundations as well as those of the monarchy. A lax Catholic clergy and a confused laity had to be turned into an effective unifying instrument, and orthodoxy had to be restored. Clerical reform was part of a larger process of institutional restructuring, but one in which Isabel took a personal interest. The pope permitted the Franciscan provincial Francisco Jiménez de Cisneros (subsequently the archbishop of Toledo, the primate of the Spanish church) to begin a general reform of the clergy.[21] That the priesthood needed reform was obvious, that they wanted it less so. Clerical reform began in the 1480s with the regular orders. Cisneros energetically brought the order up to his high standards, but not without defections. Some 400 Franciscan friars departed for Morocco with their wives and children and converted to Islam. Jiménez de Cisneros was successful with the regular clergy (the orders) but achieved mixed results with the secular priesthood (the parish priests). The reformed orders, although small in numbers, demonstrated their zeal in the New World after 1492.

Catholicism under Isabel became uniquely intense and insular in comparison with other European kingdoms. Political loyalty became a matter of adherence to the true faith. With the reluctant permission of the pope, the monarch established an Inquisition. As discussed shortly, the Inquisition came close to destroying the social fabric in Spain and left a bitter legacy. Subsequently, in Mexico, it had the potential of sparking a rebellion before being reined in by Emperor Carlos V.

The Criminalization of Belief

The establishment of the Inquisition came about for complex reasons, including the growth of cities and a commercial culture that threatened the role of the nobility. The monarchy, however, envisioned the institution as a way of providing religiopolitical unity and security as well as resolving the suspicions that surrounded the conversos, including doubts about their conversion, cultural assimilation, and political loyalty.[22] Pope Sixtus IV had to be convinced that a state-directed institution, by its very nature a political instrument rather than one focused on evangelicalism and controlled by Rome, should be established. Reluctantly, the pope authorized a Castilian Inquisition in 1478. By 1484, the Crown extended its authority to Aragón and in 1487 to Catalonia; at the time, some 150,000 conversos and an equal number of Jews constituted a small minority but were enough to fuel paranoia.

Seville, with a small but significant number of conversos, became the first target. Denunciations, imprisonment, investigations, and presumption of guilt set the pattern. Those who were arrested and imprisoned by the Inquisition were held indefinitely until an investigation was completed. Meanwhile, they had no contact with the outside world and did not know who had denounced them. The fate of a smaller number was execution, followed by burning. The criminalization of belief cast a wide net that entangled a terrified population. Confiscation of property impoverished families, disrupted economic relations, and rewarded opportunists. Greed and envy and institutional support explains much of the activities of the officials. Rich conversos were more likely to be investigated than poor ones. Conversos also served as officials of the Inquisition and as informers; some may have been sincere zealots or hoped that by demonstrating Christian zeal they might escape suspicion or worse. The Inquisitor General, Tomás de Torquemada, not a compassionate individual, had converso roots. With the assault on conversos under way, attention to the Jewish population that had refused conversion followed.

Expulsion of the Jews from several regions had been decreed earlier but not enforced. A decree of 1492 ordered the expulsion of those Jews who refused to accept Christianity, a second wave of victims in Queen Isabel's drive for religious unity. Nevertheless, the Moorish population of newly conquered Granada posed the major obstacle to religious uniformity. The agreed-on terms of capitulation allowed them to retain their religion, the use of mosques and other religious institutions, their language, and Muslim laws and customs, in exchange for accepting Castilian rule and allowing the introduction of a Christian clerical hierarchy as well as the newly created archbishopric of Granada. The choice of Hernando de Talavera as archbishop (1493–1499) appeared to be a fortunate one. A converso and a University of Salamanca graduate in theology, he adhered to canon law governing conversion. He did not favor forced conversion and was critical of the Inquisition. He saw his task as a missionary one: to educate and provide a Christian example, a slow process.

His replacement, the Cardinal Archbishop Francisco Jiménez Cisneros, proved to be much less patient, organizing mass conversions and the burning of Arabic religious texts. Jiménez de Cisneros's harshness fueled a revolt that dragged on in the Alpujarras mountains until 1501. The revolt nullified the terms of Granada's capitulation, resulting in an ultimatum to accept Christianity or leave. In 1502, an estimated 200,000 migrated. Emperor Carlos V (Carlos I of Spain) continued the pressure on the Moriscos (Muslims forced to convert to Christianity), but restrictions could not be enforced uniformly. Influential nobles, well aware of the economic importance of Morisco agricultural labor, protected their workers, while others saw a chance to seize their property. Bribing officials added a degree of temporary security.

A series of decrees posed the same choice in Navarre in 1515 and in Aragón in 1525. Most of those who were threatened had little choice but to comply, but they did so superficially: they retained their dress, spoke Arabic, and lived more or less as they had in the past. The sheer number posed an enforcement challenge. In Castile, Moriscos made up 10 percent of the population, some 500,000, half of those in Granada. Moreover, the birth rate alarmed Christians, who observed that "all Moors marry."[23]

Felipe II (1556–1598), took a more aggressive approach to a problem made ever more unsettling by the reality that the Mediterranean in the

1550s had become a Muslim lake. An edict of 1567 attacked Moorish culture; it required Moriscos to adopt Castilian dress and to abandon their traditional customs—obviously an attempt to break the cultural cohesion of Granada, the only remaining concentrated Moorish enclave in Spain. The 1567 edict encountered passive resistance at a worrisome moment. Rumors (at the time plausible) about an Ottoman maritime offensive by Selim II, including an attack on Spain coordinated with a rebellion by Granada's Moriscos, alarmed the Crown. Moreover, Morisco corsairs based at Algiers, Cherchell (Roman Caesarea), and Salé could be expected to plunder the Spanish coast.

The rumored Ottoman-Morisco attack never materialized, but at the very end of 1568, the Moriscos revolted in response to the edict of 1567. A completely unprepared monarchy, already overextended dealing with the revolt in the Netherlands, struggled to gather additional military forces. A bitter conflict resulted in 60,000 Morisco deaths. Some 50,000 fled to North Africa, and several thousand were enslaved. The revolt lingered on until 1571, the same year as the decisive naval battle of Lepanto that stopped Ottoman expansion into the western Mediterranean. The final expulsion of Moriscos occurred in the early 1600s.

Meanwhile, an unknown but significant number of Jews, Moors, and Moriscos had been absorbed in the general population, raising the possibility of heresy. Fear rather than reality underpinned the ritual of the auto-de-fé (act of faith). The ritual suggested that it had more to do with the Inquisitors than with their hapless victims. Even more divisive and widespread was public humiliation. The Inquisition maintained records of those whom it punished, as did the parish. Individuals sentenced to wear the San Benito, a long-hooded robe of rough, brown cloth, ran from a minimum of a year up to an entire lifetime. The public indication of one's supposed lapse into heresy damaged the entire family, while the victim became a pariah, unable to live a normal life. At the end of one's sentence, the parish church displayed the penitential garb in the church as an object lesson. The San Benito remained on display, much to the family's shame, until the fabric disintegrated and memories faded.

Ironically, many people found it necessary to prove that they did not have a Jewish or Moorish background. The *limpieza de sangre* (purity of blood) certification, beginning in the 1400s, carried the notion of tainted blood forward to successive generations. It remained in use until 1865 (although by then restricted to only a few occupational categories), serving as an item of direct social, and indirectly religious, discrimination.[24]

1492 in the European Context

On the Iberian Peninsula by the middle of the century, Castile could look forward to victory over the Moors: the Christians may not have an easy time of it, but the trend favored them and appeared irreversible. In the wider Mediterranean world, one could not be so sanguine. The decade of the 1450s appeared to represent an acceleration of the biblical clock. That year, Mahomet II succeeded his father as the Ottoman sultan. The Turks conquered much of the Balkans, as the aptly named terror of Europe squeezed the remnants of Rome's eastern empire, and in 1453, the unthinkable occurred as Constantinople fell into Ottoman hands. The shock stunned the Christian world, which viewed the bastion city as able to withstand any siege. Aeneas Silvus Piccolomini (Pope Pius II) viewed the calamity as the "second death of Homer and a second destruction of Plato." The humanists worried that western Europe would be thrown back into the dark ages.[25] The westward advance of Islam caused near panic—whether Rome would be next became a question, if not as yet a certainty. In the face of the threat, Pope Pius II (1458–1464) in 1461 proposed what amounted to a policy option to consider the religious inclusion of Mahomet II. As a lure, the pope suggested that such a conversion would make Mahomet the greatest man of his time as well as the emperor of the Greeks and the east. Pius went on to list the things that Islam and Christianity had in common, mainly one God, agreement on the centrality of faith, an afterlife of reward or punishment, immortality of the soul, and the acceptance of the Old and New Testaments. With more than a touch of desperation, Pius appealed to reason in support of his view that the prohibition of theological discussion under Muslim law itself violated reason.[26] What is interesting here is the idea that a fusion and creation of an Ottoman–Eastern Orthodox rite might be possible (at least in the mind of Pope Pius). It is not clear that the letter formally reached the sultan, although Ottoman spies might have reported its existence. Mahomet II in any case would have had little reason to entertain the idea as the victorious onslaught continued.

The unraveling of security and the realization that most of the world to the east posed a danger to Christianity made a seaborne escape into the Atlantic crucial as a way of circumventing the psychological and actual Muslim barrier that followed the fall of eastern Christendom. The Portuguese led the way as they inched down the coast of Africa hoping to break the Arab monopoly on the spice trade by a daring run around blocked land routes. Their plan included making contact with a semimythical Prester John, reputed to be the monarch of an isolated Christian kingdom somewhere in eastern Africa. Rumors of the existence of the Coptic kingdom filtered through Muslim sources. Columbus's idea of sailing west to India fitted in with the grand scheme.

Meanwhile, the wider struggle to stop and reverse militant Islam did not favor Christian kingdoms. An endangered Hungary soon faced defeat at the Battle of Mohács in 1529, and Vienna came under siege. Almost inevitably, the Ottomans brought down the Hungarian Christian kingdom in 1542. A hostile presence on the Adriatic, as well as the Ottoman thrust into North Africa, threatened European commerce in the Mediterranean until the decisive sea battle of Lepanto in 1571 stopped Islam's advance and stabilized religious boundary lines in Europe.

Meanwhile, Spain had taken possession of the Antilles, and subsequently Cortés inserted Indo-Mexico into European consciousness. The apparent disintegration of Christendom, coupled with making contact with the New World and what seemed to be the last of the pagans, signaled the possible beginning of the end of the earthly world. That the friars in Mexico almost immediately introduced the religious play *Moros y Cristianos* in order to enlist their charges in the struggle against Islam is not a surprise.

4
CREATING MESTIZO MEXICO
The Philosophical Challenge of America

T HE INCLUSION of the Western Hemisphere in the known
world virtually completed global society; had Columbus actually reached India (his stated objective), the impact of his voyage
would have been quite different, perhaps opening up a new crusade
route and pressuring the Ottomans, but it would not have been transformative.[1] As the first "New World," the hemisphere had to be philosophically integrated into the Christian world, a Eurocentric imaginative process that initially disoriented both European and indigenous
populations.[2] Much of the process had to do with displacing indigenous political authority as well as understanding mentally and physically what each population confronted.

The Antilles Experiment

In the last decade of the fifteenth century, no one could imagine the
Western Hemisphere's territorial extent. The small, even tiny islands
reported by Columbus; his notion that he had arrived off the coast of
the Asian landmass; observations concerning the nature of the then-
designated Indians—all combined to create wildly inaccurate perceptions of the discovery.[3] That Spain fell back on its own historical experiences and its institutions to provide some manageable context is not
surprising. The Antilles, although no one could have anticipated it at
the time, served to prepare Europeans for the unexpected and the

encounter with advanced civilizations on the landmass.[4] Meanwhile, the situation in the known world presented a grim scenario for the Christian world.

Ottoman power in Eurasia had become increasingly worrisome for Rome and Christian monarchies. Having conceded the issue of the church's temporal power in favor of Christian monarchies, it made sense to allow the Castilian monarch to deal with the new discoveries, which were still perceived to be a collection of islands with small, primitive, pagan populations—exotic to be sure but of uncertain importance. The issue of their humanity had to be decided by the pope, who subsequently declared them to be worthy of receiving Christianity. Not so easily decided was their civilized standing, an issue that had previously confronted the ancient Greeks. Aristotle, well aware of the variations of civilization, posited the notion that those who had the capacity to reason, to create orderly cities, to establish laws, and to live in civic harmony were free by nature, while those who lacked such abilities were slaves (meaning servants) by nature and best suited to be directed by their rational superiors. Ptolemy of Lucca, the author of the final section of Saint Thomas Aquinas's work *The Rules of Princes,* maintained that some parts of the world appeared more suited to servitude than freedom. The influential intellectual John Mair in Paris directly addressed the new discoveries in the Antilles, sweepingly declaring that the people lived as beasts and that therefore the conquerors justly ruled over them.[5] A consensus on the nature of the indigenous population did not exist.

Nevertheless, the native population in the Antilles met the basic philosophical criteria as understood in Europe of an orderly, organized people. They sustained themselves as distinct groups by hunting, gathering, and cultivating roots and had tribal institutions. On the other hand, the Europeans had a much more complex and organized society, philosophically beyond the comprehension of the island's indigenous population. Consequently, the population in the Antilles could not defend themselves, although impassioned clerical defenders argued their case, and they became philosophical wards of the state. The idea of native inferiority lay just below the surface in the minds of many of those who defended the indigenous population.[6]

Natural Law, Just War, and Legitimacy

Closely connected with the central issue of political legitimacy was the use of force. Without legitimacy, the use of force became an act of violence. Justifying attacking another organized and legitimate entity preoccupied the Greeks, as well as the Romans. While human ability to rationalize inevitably supplied a reason for war, Christianity required a more formal legalist and moral justification. Jesus charged the apostles to take the word to all parts of the world, and this became a mandatory obligation for the organized church. The accommodation with secular authority, symbolized by the notion of the two swords, implied a shared unity between a Christian monarch and the pope. Consequently, Pope Alexander VI, aware of scarce resources, conveyed the task of organizing the church in the Indies to the Castilian monarchy, already present in the Antilles, along with the right to collect the tithe to finance the project.[7] The church in effect removed itself from all directive aspects of the Christianization effort in the New World. By accepting the papal concessions, the state became directly responsible for the evangelization of Indo-America even before comprehending the territorial extent and the millions of Indians involved, as well as the difficulty of the task. It meant that the Castilian monarch assumed responsibility for the material and spiritual well-being of his new subjects, who theoretically were entitled to the same protection and benevolence as other subjects of the king. Rome did not appreciate fully the inability of the indigenous population to uphold their end of a mutual process of demand and response that characterizes a positive and functioning political arrangement. The mismatch proved disastrous for the island Indians and in the end only met the needs of the Europeans.

To what extent the charge conveyed possession remained unclear, as did whether it was permissible to require the Indians to accommodate European religious, cultural, and socioeconomic needs. Those who favored force reached back to Aristotle's notion of a natural hierarchy of man and Saint Paul's judgment that human beings have an inner light, but if they refuse to follow it, they are guilty of ignoring God's gift. Even more sweeping, Saint Augustine dismissed pagan virtues as merely vices in disguise and argued that nature if left alone is incapable of any good, suggesting the need for intervention. Opponents of force labored under the handicap that settlers had already introduced forced labor in the form of the encomienda system and initially slavery, both softened marginally by pro forma religious obligations.

A number of clerics in the Antilles denounced the situation in terms that suggested that the abuse of the population amounted to contravening all laws: civil, canon, moral, and theological, as well as the will of God. Both Fathers Miguel Salamanca and Antonio de Montesinos were well aware that the issue of legitimacy had not been totally settled, in spite of the papal conveyance. The Dominicans dispatched Montesinos to Spain to lay the matter before the monarch, while a Franciscan represented the other side. The Crown appointed a panel to determine the matter. Matiás de Paz, OP, a professor of theology at the University of Valladolid, one of the appointees, placed the moral issue in its political and economic context in his work *De dominio de los reyes de España sobre los Indios* (1512), declaring that the overarching religious goal justified a political and hence economic presence. Juan López de Palacio Rubio, a chaired professor of canon law, also at the University of Valladolid, and a member of the Council of Castile, predictably upheld legitimacy based on the papal grant and the task of Christianization. The following year (1513), he wrote a document, the *Requerimiento*, to be read to Indians explaining why they should submit to Spanish rule. Copies of the document were distributed to the leaders of expeditions to the islands before they were allowed to sail.

The *Requerimiento* began at creation with a review of Christian theology, asserting that God created heaven and Earth along with a man and a woman from which all are descended; but when the human population reached a certain level, it spilt into groups, some 5,000 years after the world had been created.[8] The implication was that all were part of God's created family who had drifted apart. Saint Peter had been commanded to govern the world from Rome, encompassing Christians, Moors, Jews, Gentiles, and all other sects. Saint Peter's jurisdiction was universal and passed down to his papal successors, one of whom had assigned the new discoveries to the monarch of Castile. Consequently, all indigenous people should submit to their appointed lord without resistance and immediately, once they have been informed of the facts and understood what was required. They must allow the preaching of Christianity but must convert of their own free will. If they refused to comply, then they would be subjected to a no-holds-barred conquest, followed by the enslavement of all men, women, and children and the loss of their goods. The *Requerimiento* referred to forcibly entering the indigenous people's country, a tacit admission of aboriginal political legitimacy. Once the document was read to tribal groups, certified by a notary, and signed by witnesses, it constituted a contract. That the document reflected the legalistic thought of learned academics seems obvious.[9]

Those who confronted hostile Indians reacted with some amusement, trading stories of reading the document from behind trees, in the middle of the night, and without an interpreter. Even the document's principal author, López de Palacios Rubio, understood its amusing incongruities; nevertheless, he believed the document met Spanish legal needs. Bartolomé de las Casas, after reading the *Requerimiento,* claimed he did not know whether to laugh or cry. Less amusingly, the document provided a basis for justifying the pillaging of hapless populations. Such legal niceties, while deemed useful, represented philosophical skirmishing, with European needs and objectives in mind and with the indigenous population as nonparticipating objects.

The Crown, with little accurate information concerning the nature of the indigenous population in the islands, assumed that the inhabitants had at least some of the same self-protective attitudes and reactions as those present in Spain.[10] The first clarification of the royal position on Indian-Spanish relations was based on the perceived situation in the Antilles, but with the Spanish background in mind. The Laws of Burgos (1512, amended 1513) preceded contact with Indo-Mexico, and it set the basic template across the empire for the next thirty years. As was customary, its thirty-five articles reflected the problem-specific nature of royal legislations.[11] Its instructions centered on the treatment of Indian workers. Thus, article 24 called for respect, no whipping or calling them dogs, and punishment decided on by independent officials *(visitadores);* not all of these were enforceable. Pro forma articles about the importance of evangelization did little except to validate the Spanish presence. Article 25 ordered that at least one-third of Indians held in encomiendas be assigned to the gold mines (gold washings) and more if the holder wished. The article noted, "many persons who have Indians . . . serve us poorly by using them to sow and cultivate."[12] The functional institution was the encomienda, an arrangement that had performed effectively but differently in Spain.

The encomienda as an institution that evolved from the *behetria,* an association of *infanzones* (minor nobles) and insecure urban settlements that jointly and voluntarily commended themselves to a powerful noble for protection in return for tribute. The Crown, unable or unwilling to extend its protection, could grant an encomienda to a powerful noble, who collected tribute in return for administrative and protective tasks.[13] In some cases, the arrangement and its tribute became hereditary, and in others, those who were commended reserved the right to change protectors. This constituted a semifeudal layer that worked well under frontier conditions and helped to stabilize the frontier and incorporate productive Moorish peasants. A reasonable economic and sociopolitical balance between all the elements of the institution as it existed and performed in Spain explained its success. No such balance was possible in the Antilles or subsequently in Indo-Mexico.

The Burgos enactment amended the encomienda to include an explicit religious and cultural apprenticeship that it did not have in Spain. It limited the number of Indians held by one person in an encomienda to no more than 150 and not less than 40 (art. 35). In return, the holders functioned as lay missionaries, instructing their charges in basic Christianity. Movement from one master to another was not allowed; in effect, the Indians were bound to a person, not a particular piece of land, a condition that allowed the holder flexibility to select the type of economic activity he preferred. In addition, Indians were to be congregated in new settlements for the purpose of evangelization. The Crown ordered that the former villages be burned to the ground so that the displaced inhabitants would not be tempted to return. Relocation in reality meant laboring in gold washings and cultivation of food crops under harsh conditions.

What both the Crown and the papacy failed to appreciate was the absence in the Antilles of counterbalancing interests (such as those present in Spain) able to react effectively to violations or unacceptable treatment. In the Antilles, the monarchy's inability to protect Indians' property and their status as free persons and its failure to honor existing social and political organizations legitimized by Natural Law were disastrous. From a political standpoint, the situation discredited the Spanish monarchy and laid the basis for the Black Legend, a discourse difficult to refute after Las Casas's exaggerated portrayal, which is still emotionally alive in our own time. Subsequently, in Indo-Mexico, the intent of the Laws of Burgos remained, but it conflicted with the reality that the encomienda had become a central institution, although modified and regulated, albeit with difficulty, as discussed shortly.

An Expanded Philosophical Construct

Queen Isabel, anticipating the imminent fall of Granada, contemplated a difficult evangelizing campaign. She understood that a lax clergy likely would be unable to evangelize effectively and consequently petitioned Rome to expand her fragmented authority over the church to allow her to select competent missionaries. The Bull of Granada (1486) allowed Queen Isabel virtually complete control over the clergy in Granada. The Granadine concessions and subsequently the *Real Patronato de Indias* must be placed in the context of the fall of Constantinople in 1453 and the Lutheran religious rebellion that flared up in 1517. Both events frightened the papacy, which was uncertain whether Christianity could survive or verged on unraveling uncontrollably. An alarmed curia sought to enlist state support, offering more direct control over the clergy. Consequently, Rome allowed the Castilian monarch to deal with both the introduction of Catholicism and the clerical organization in Granada and the Antilles. The *Real Patronato de Indias* followed the same model as the Bull of Granada, although it was somewhat expanded and subject to additions over time. It allowed the Crown to effectively direct the church in its new setting as well as to absorb or redirect church revenues as the monarch decided.

Castile had long nourished imperial objectives, but they had been formulated without the Western Hemisphere in mind. Spain envisioned a further elaboration of Aragón's Mediterranean expansion, perhaps a move into North Africa and Italy to counter the Ottomans' westward thrust, just as the Antilles entered European history in 1492. The existence of inhabited islands was not particularly exciting or unique, although gold washings had some immediate attraction.

With the landing on the mainland in 1519, Castile began to understand the magnitude of the Western Hemisphere. To make sense of events, the Bible had to be consulted and a far grander scheme devised that incorporated a New World.[14] A Christian crusade, with aspects of a limited war of salvation, would have to be launched against a significantly larger pagan population. Of most importance, events indicated the coming of the apocalypse, which was prophesied to occur when the world had been exposed to Christianity, followed by the conversion of the Jews.

Of immediate importance to Spain was its proprietary claim to the New World. The issue, seemingly settled in the Antilles, could not be applied to the densely populated mainland. The monarchy needed the confidence that came from an acceptable title, beyond that conceded by Rome on the basis of underpopulated islands. The pope's conveyance had to be strengthened in the face of European criticism. The issue of Spain's legitimate presence in the New World required rummaging through Europe's philosophical foundations. The process of examination and debate by university intellectuals, undertaken with the Crown's expectations of a supportive decision, nevertheless produced ambiguity but with sufficient support to allow the monarch to proceed more or less only marginally hindered.

Proprietary rights could not be easily dealt with because they were both economically useful and politically limiting. In Europe, the issue had become somewhat settled. Both Roman and Visigoth law separated the state from private property, but the line between them could not be drawn unambiguously because actual possession was required to alienate property. Did the Crown actually possess? A monarch's proprietary claim resulted from conquest (possession by force), but did this allow legal alienation of land in the hands of others? In the New World, straightforward conquest was muddled by the papal charge to introduce Christianity, not war or plunder.

The advanced civilizations on the mainland obviously possessed independent sovereignty and laws. A solution had to be found to legitimize the situation. The right of conquest, appropriate to legalize the seizure of Moorish wealth and territory during the Reconquista in Spain, could not be easily applied in Indo-Mexico. The plundering of the conquistadors did not establish a legal foundation for proprietary rights in Indo-Mexico or elsewhere in the New World.[15] The subtle distinction between ownership (the right to convey) and political possession acquired by conquest presented a difficult problem. Jean Gerson (1363–1429), a scholar and chancellor of the University of Paris, defined possession as the right to dispose of freely, as did Francisco Suárez, who observed that indigenous property could not be forfeited to the Crown except under certain well-defined judicial conditions. Juan de Mariana went further, asserting that a monarch could not claim proprietary rights without permission. Jean Bodin (1529/1530–1596), a professor of law at the University of Toulouse, separated authority from actual ownership, providing a partial solution by creating a form of political usufruct that existed along with property rights, a modern idea. Francisco de Vitoria placed the issue in an international context of relations between different legitimate groups within a "Republic of the Entire World."[16]

The tug-of-war over property rights was confusing enough, with a sufficient selection of concepts to be workable but never completely convincing. Other powers might grumble—as allegedly did the French king, who supposedly questioned the existence of Adam's will conveying the New World to Spain—but all reluctantly accepted the reality. Spain held on to the New World virtually unopposed until the seventeenth century, when it lost a few islands. It warily noted English and French coastal settlements in North America, but its mainland empire remained secure until the independence era in the early 1800s.

European control over indigenous subjects drew on vague elements, such as demonstrated benevolence, the spread and defense of Christianity, restraint in imposing punishment, and concern for their general well-being. The one important material concession by Rome, authorizing the Crown to collect the tithe and to use it to spread the faith, soon became a major source of revenue that functioned as a tax. The papacy's conveyance of the New World's population for the purpose of evangelization and organization of the church became more of a religiophilosophical matter as the initial occupation made the transition to an imperial dependency. Spain's title to the Indies remained philosophically problematic but politically functional. Prior to Christianity, the ancient right of conquest established legitimate possessions. When Rome officially converted, the papal charge authorized possession.

The Conquest of Mexico

The intrusion of medieval irregular soldiers in the Indo-Mexican world occurred at the moment that medieval Europe gave way to the Renaissance. What was soon to become archaic in Europe was new in

Indo-Mexico; consequently, medieval ideas and actions constituted the foundations of much of the replacement worldview. European intruders began to destroy Indo-Mexico's long-standing worldview almost at the moment of contact. The battle to wrest control from Indo-Mexico's chieftaincies may have been one of the last medieval campaigns and was certainly one of the most fateful in the newly created transatlantic world.

Hernán Cortés's landing on the mainland in 1519 represented Europe's breakthrough into the continental Western Hemisphere. It coincided with the technological game changers of gunpowder, cannon, shipbuilding, horses, war dogs, and wheels that revolutionized how Europeans waged war and conducted trade.[17] The development of the bronze-cast, slender-tube cannon, able to propel heavy wrought-iron balls, was enhanced further by its being placed in a small, maneuverable carriage that was able to redirect fire as appeared most useful.

King Charles VIII of France provided a preview of the technological advances that were soon to shock Indo-Mexico. Charles battered his way down the Italian peninsula, conquering Florence and then reducing the Naples fortress of San Giovanni in eight hours (1495). The fortress had previously withstood a seven-year siege. Spain embraced the new technology. Cannon played a decisive role in Queen Isabel's campaign to conquer Granada. In the battles of Cerignola (1503) and Bicocca (1522), numerically superior French and Swiss forces fell to Spanish gunners. Cannon altered tactics, strategy, and outcomes. All understood that the old notions of a high-wall defense as the preferred method had given way to one of cannon-assisted defense in completely redesigned forts and ships.[18] Mobile defense and offense appeared more effective than fixed positions. The new cannons were placed on galleys that could be effective in shallow coastal waters as an auxiliary to land forces, but the galleys' length and keel made them unsuited for the high seas. Larger oceangoing sailing ships, redesigned to carry the weight of heavy guns and more-than-adequate supplies, offered an excellent platform. The Portuguese used their floating platforms to gain control of the Straits of Ormus in 1507 and to establish trading ports on the Indian coast. The gunpowder revolution made possible firearms, the harquebus, and subsequently, the much-improved musket. In 1508, the trading city of Venice replaced crossbows with firearms. The technological revolution could not be ignored. Cortés's generation came of age with gunpowder and consequently had a different grasp of military strategy.[19] Technology made any attempt to reverse the Mexican conquest after 1521 unlikely to succeed.

The conquest of Indo-Mexico coincided with political instability in Spain: the confusion and resentment attending mismanaged dynastic changes following Isabel la Católica's death in 1504. A revolt had been simmering for seventeen years in the chaotic aftermath of Isabel's death. At issue was what was perceived to be poor administration and, subsequently, the expensive ambitions of Carlos I, soon to be Emperor Carlos V of the Holy Roman Empire. Isabel's will conveyed Castile to her daughter Juana, cruelly called Juana la Loca because of her mental incapacity. La Loca's Burgundian husband greedily took material advantage of the situation until her death. After a series of regents, the Crown passed to the Hapsburg Carlos I, who then embarked on a successful financial quest to buy the title of Emperor of the Holy Roman Empire, a goal he achieved in 1519, the year that Cortés landed on the coast of Indo-Mexico.

Castile's experience with a foreign monarch and his predatory advisers was painful and deeply resented. Carlos I's successful pursuit of the emperorship bankrupted Spain. He did so without the consent of the nineteen cities that were entitled to meet as a Cortes to consider such transformative matters, an omission that constituted a violation of established tradition. A price would have to be paid. The 1520–1521 Revolt of the Comuneros' charge of poor administration was supported by a long list of grievances as well as proposed solutions that amounted to the constitutional subordination of the monarch and his administration to the Cortes, all bluntly laid out in the petition. It provided for representatives (*procuradores*) elected by the Cortes cities who would meet every three years, with or without the presence of the monarch or the need to be convened by the king, in order to attend to the commonweal of the realms. The revolt constituted a constitutional insurrection, one that spread to Segovia, Zamora, Madrid, Burgos, Guadalajara, and Tordesillas. A junta in Tordesillas attempted to assume the authority of the king's *Consejo Real* (royal council). The Comuneros' demand that in the event the monarch left the kingdom he would be required to appoint a regent who must be a native of the Kingdom of Castile and León suggested the possibility of a breakaway revolt. With some justification, the Revolt of the Comuneros has been referred to as the first modern revolution.[20] The issue was forcefully decided in favor of the monarch at the Battle of Villalar in 1521. The revolt explains the Crown's suspicions about Cortés's intentions after the fall of the Aztec capital that same year and the shabby treatment of him that followed—only partly made up for by a title of nobility and material rewards. Virtually at the same time as the Crown's victory at Villalar (April 23, 1521), Cortés reduced Tenochtitlán to ruins (August 13, 1521). It is unlikely that anyone fully realized that several historical events and their resultant cultures had collided in both Europe and Indo-Mexico.

Prior to Cortés's arrival, Indo-Mexico appeared to be in the midst a transition that would eliminate the last vestiges of tribal equality. The increasing burden of supporting the nobility fell on the peasantry, which had so recently been stripped of any remaining tribal respect by both Moctezuma I and Moctezuma II. To further undermine stability, the probing of the eastern coast by the Europeans had shaken Indo-Mexico, creating uncertainty and fear. Two attempts to establish a Spanish presence on the mainland failed but resulted in information that Cortés's expedition made use of in 1519.

Mainland inhabitants were reported to be well organized, warlike, and able to repel intruders. Information, while sketchy, influenced the expedition's planning. Cortés, an experienced soldier, understood the value of intelligence; consequently, his first objective was to locate and free a Spaniard who was being held as a slave by an aboriginal group on the Indo-Mexican coast. Information about the political structure, economy, religious beliefs, and customs of the indigenous people and how to approach their leaders could only come from an informant who understood their language. To a remarkable extent, Cortés's planning paid off. The rapidity with which Cortés made language contact with Tenochtitlán, even before his arrival in the Valley of Mexico, enabled him to piece together a workable notion of what he faced, to recruit Indian allies, and to lay the initial foundations of a permanent Castilian presence at the heart of Indo-Mexico.

Cortés proceeded along the coast, landing at what is now the city of Veracruz. Before moving inland, Cortés received a Mexica delegation that had been alerted to his arrival and bore the ritual regalia of Quetzalcóatl, Tezcatlipoca, and Tlaloc. Had Cortés understood the game and indicated some connection with Quetzalcóatl, his entry into Tenochtitlán might well have ended the Aztec regime without a fight. Of course, the Spaniards thought the regalia gifts. Nevertheless, Cortés used the occasion to fire the ship's great cannon to intimidate the delegation.[21] Meanwhile, Moctezuma remained paralyzed with foreboding, confused and indecisive, still unsure of whether he dealt with men or gods. He contemplated fleeing and hiding in a cave. Cortés became a military force on the coast. After a victory over the Potonchán of Tabasco, as was customary, the defeated offered gifts, food, and women and prepared to negotiate tribute payments. Gifts of women represented a hoped-for biological alliance with these powerful intruders. While the Spaniards may have missed that point, Cortés quickly singled out a woman who spoke both Mayan and Nahuatl, known as Malinche. She provided Cortés with Nahuatl language contact through the rescued Mayan speaking Spaniard. Renamed Doña Marina, she became the conquistador's mistress and adviser, playing a crucial role in his understanding of subsequent events. Cortés, advised not to approach Tenochtitlán by way of Tlaxcala, disregarded such advice, probably advised by Doña Marina of the Tlaxcalans' deep hostility to Aztec power. His initial use of diplomacy did not work well; messages of peace and friendship were seen as a sign of weakness. Moreover, Cortés, accompanied by Aztec tributaries as guides, porters, and warriors to reinforce his own men, made it difficult for locals to determine whose side he favored. Tlaxcala's leaders took no chances and vigorously opposed the Europeans. Over several days and nights, the hard-pressed Cortés barely avoided being forced into a disorderly retreat. Cannon, carried up from the coast by Indian porters, made it possible to fight on. Cortés continued to send pleas for peace and friendship, releasing some prisoners as an indication of goodwill. From the Tlaxcalan standpoint, the armies had reached a stalemate; in reality, the Europeans could not have survived more than a day or two more.[22] At some point, Tlaxcalteca leaders decided that it made sense to accept the Europeans as allies. Indian prisoners captured by the Tlaxcalans probably provided clarification of Cortés's actual intent as well as information of his activities and behavior on the coast.

Cortés intended to go through Cholula as he advanced on Tenochtitlán, perhaps with the idea of securing the direct route to Veracruz and supplies of its stores of ammunitions and horses. The Tlaxcalans advised against this plan because Cholula had become a tributary of the

Aztecs; nevertheless, Cortés proceeded as planned, gaining access without a fight, although he had several thousand Tlaxcalan warriors with him just in case. At Cholula, Cortés—warned by the Tlaxcalans and assisted by Marina, who gathered details of a possible plan to kill the intruders—fell upon the Cholulans, slaughtering some 3,000 and sacking the city. It is possible that the Tlaxcalans provoked the massacre to make it impossible for Cortés to back out of their alliance. An equally plausible explanation is that Cortés sought to intimidate Moctezuma in advance of his arrival in Tenochtitlán.[23]

Cortés usually tarried for days in each city on his way to the Aztec capital, while sending messages to Moctezuma of how much he looked forward to meeting him. The subliminal message could not be missed: every day he advanced closer, he would soon arrive, and he expected to enter the city. When news of the costly massacre reached Moctezuma, he believed that he had no choice but to negotiate. Many of his advisers pressed for an all-out military effort to exterminate the Europeans and punish the Tlaxcalans. Meanwhile, a frightened Moctezuma contemplated going into hiding, dismissing those who urged an all-out attack on the intruders. Moctezuma temporized and prepared to negotiate, perhaps believing that both sides shared the Mesoamerican rules of war and defeat. The Mexica anticipated that tribute demands would be punishing and that the loss of their paramount role in the empire was likely. What they could not envision happened: the total destruction of Tenochtitlán and the Mexica army, followed by enslavement of survivors, including women and children, and the imposition of a new worldview that subordinated Indo-Mexican history to that of the intruders.[24]

Cortés approached the Valley of Mexico through the Chalca cities that had resisted the Aztecs for decades but had finally been reduced to tributaries in 1464. They deeply resented their semicaptivity. Obviously, during the seventeen days Cortés spent in Tlaxcala, he had been well briefed on geopolitical realities. Finally, on November 8, 1519, the Spaniards boldly, perhaps unwisely, found themselves in a precarious situation and crossed the causeway into Tenochtitlán, where Cortés and his men came face-to-face with Moctezuma. The Europeans were escorted to lodgings in the heart of the city. Cut off from most of the Tlaxcalan escort, which remained camped outside the city, they were placed in a dangerous situation. The next move appeared to be up to the Aztec leader. The notion that the Spaniards were gods had long since been discarded. Had Moctezuma taken the obvious step of killing them and deploying the army against the encamped Tlaxcalans outside the city, the outcome would have been very different. Did Moctezuma perhaps contemplate an alliance with Cortés that could expand the empire and unify Mesoamerica under the control of Tenochtitlán—in short, accelerating an already evident trend toward political consolidation? Such an alliance might break the stalemate that made it impossible to resume imperial expansion. One can only speculate.[25]

Cortés, an experienced soldier, must have had a plan in mind; otherwise, he had entered a trap. To complicate the situation, an Aztec force attacked a former Totonac tributary that had gone over to Cortés's side. The European Veracruz garrison came to the tributary's assistance, only to be defeated. Cortés faced the loss of control of Veracruz and his supply lines. Unsure of who had ordered the attack, he seized Moctezuma—in effect, a coup de main that allowed him to govern through the hapless paramount chief. Whether Cortés suddenly realized the danger or whether the seizure was as part of a previous plan is not clear. Cortés misunderstood how Indo-Mexican politics functioned—the paramount chief was all powerful but only if he met expectations and advanced the imperial agenda. It would only be a matter of time before the nobles, priests, and the lower classes realized that Moctezuma served as puppet.

Another incident indicated divisions among the Spaniards. The Cuban governor Diego Velasquez sent a well-equipped force to arrest Cortés and resume control of the expedition. An alarmed Cortés rushed down to Veracruz, possibly to negotiate with the leaders, but instead attacked them in the middle of the night. He then convinced the men to join him and returned to Tenochtitlán with a force of over 1,500 soldiers and more horses and cannons. Meanwhile, Pedro de Alvarado, left in charge of the garrison holding Moctezuma prisoner, made a disastrous tactical error. A large crowd, assembled for an important religious event, alarmed the uncomprehending Alvarado, who ordered the massacre of the unarmed celebrants. An outraged city laid siege to the European compound, lifting it only to allow the returning Cortés to reenter and join his trapped men. A discredited Moctezuma, forced onto a rooftop in an attempt to reverse the dire situation, was killed. It is not clear if he was struck down by a stone or killed by the Spaniards; by then, both sides had little use for him. Moctezuma's ignominious death and replacement by Cuitlahuac; the entrapment of the Spaniards in the heart of the city; their daring but costly flight out of the city, known as *la noche triste* (sad night; June 30, 1520), with only a third of Cortés's force surviving; and finally the bedraggled and wounded survivors regrouped on the mainland—it all seemed miraculous. One more obstacle remained: a force of Aztec soldiers, intent on exterminating the Europeans, blocked their route to Tlaxcala and safety. Even then, if they made it through to Tlaxcala, the continued support of their allies could not be taken for granted. The understandably vengeful Aztecs offered the Tlaxcalans every possible inducement to kill the Spaniards; they refused.

Subsequently, in the siege of Tenochtitlán, Cortés used platforms that were loaded with cannons and floated on the surrounding lake to destroy the fixed positions of the beleaguered Aztecs.[26] Cortés and his gunners knew the simple formula for making gunpowder and where to find the ingredients, including the necessary sulfur extracted from the volcanoes that ringed the Valley of Mexico. New technology ably deployed and a commander versed in tactics made possible by gunpowder made the difference, but Cortés was also willing to take calculated risks. Nevertheless, without Indian allies, the siege of Tenochtitlán could not have happened, and of wider importance, the rapid pacification of Mesoamerica would have been impossible. What followed must be seen as a major tragedy. Cortés—an educated man who had studied law, with mixed results, at the University of Salamanca, contemplated becoming a soldier in Italy, and subsequently fought at the battle of Algiers in 1542—had both intellectual and military interests. He likely read Desiderius Erasmus's *Manual of the Christian Soldier* (1503). He understood the implications of gunpowder and the new tactics that it engendered, including the use of shipboard cannon fire. That he chose to bring cannon with him as he departed Cuba bound for Indo-Mexico in 1519 is not surprising.

The Europeans' siege of the beleaguered Mexica by ships prudently constructed in Tlaxcala (out of reach of arsonists) and then reassembled on the lake, fitted with cannon, and launched turned the lake to their advantage.[27] The demoralized defenders hid over 40,000 bodies, stacked out of sight, and more littered in the ruins. The newly selected paramount chief, Cuitlahuac, died of smallpox. A pitiful but highly symbolic moment signaled the end. Cuauhtémoc (Cuitlahuac's successor), attempting to escape in a canoe, was spotted and chased down. He stood up with weapons in hand but slowly lowered his arms in recognition of the overwhelming futility of further resistance. The fall of Tenochtitlán marked the end of indigenous sovereignty in Indo-Mexico and the beginning of a new hybrid creation.

The Spaniards initially failed to grasp that a major transatlantic process was under way, preferring to see their victory in the simplified context of a Christian triumph.[28] It proved much more complex. The notion that a group of intrepid Spaniards and a few horses toppled an Indian empire ignored the onslaught of disease, famine, contaminated water, and three months of bombardment by waterborne cannon. Awed but uninformed, Europeans settled on a popular-history version of events, a heroic myth that at its heart rested on assumed European superiority and Indian incapacity.[29]

Confusion over Authority

The presumptive transfer of governing authority to the Europeans occurred based on conquest. The final assault on the Mexica stronghold of Tenochtitlán and its subsequent destruction left little doubt that the Europeans were militarily superior. The Crown, uneasy about toppling political entities in the New World, hoped to keep indigenous authority intact at all but the very highest level. The notion of rule by natural lords, an important philosophical concept in Spanish political thought, had an implied hierarchical ladder that could not be casually disregarded. Hereditary rulers posed a major problem for the Europeans because the Indo-Mexican political system appeared based on the same concept as in Europe. Prior to Cortés, some fifty Tlatoanis functioned in the Valley of Mexico, although many were subject to more powerful states as tributaries. They all could claim a long line of related rulers to justify their political pretentions; subsequently, they asserted the right to the status of a *cabecera* (regional political authority) with others under their control. The high indigenous nobility had traditionally provided paramount chiefs, just as Europe's high aristocracy supplied kings. The hereditary monarchy of Castile could not brush aside the importance

of lineage but at the same time could not count on the loyalty of a displaced ruling elite.

The problem of royal inheritance required buying off the children
of Moctezuma: his daughter Leonor received the encomienda (right to
tribute) of Ecatepec; his daughter Isabel obtained that of Tacuba; and
his son Pedro received the grant of Tula. All were perpetual and in-
heritable. Recognizing hereditary claims, but with a bias in favor of the
Castilian forms, shifted the social status of the remaining Aztec Indian
nobility, including relatives of Moctezuma, to the Spanish side of the
ledger. The indigenous nobility, still in a state of shock but anxious to
regain their footing, accepted Castilian titles of nobility and the transfer
of land to them as personal property with certain traditional rights over
their inhabitants, in addition to the assignments of encomiendas. In
doing so, they adopted basic elements of the Spanish worldview, publicly
acknowledged by their participation in Christian rituals, often performed in the presence of Cortés and before an indigenous audience.

The indigenous leadership's collaboration acted to deprive the Indian population of legitimate leadership. At the lower level, a disoriented population must have verged on withdrawal but soon chose to
view Cortés as a transtribal figure who was able to establish order and
win the cooperation of the nobility on down. Cortés's popularity among
the Indians may be explained as the transference to him of godlike protective qualities that assured that life went on.

Keeping the Indo-Mexican society functioning involved ending war
and plundering and adjusting the sociopolitical system to meet the needs
of both sides. Steps would be taken to merge European economic demands, particularly labor, with Indo-Mexico's institutions; Cortés operated a silver mine in Taxco and introduced sugar cultivation with indigenous labor. The conquistadores and early settlers negotiated the
immediate functional modification of indigenous societies to meet their
needs. They did so with Spanish norms in mind.

As frontier inhabitants intent on survival, the settlers did not necessarily accommodate the concerns of the monarchy. Royal officials,
worried about Spain's legitimate claims in the New World, in turn did
not appreciate the everyday difficulties of the settlers. The fact that royal
wishes could be ignored on the new Hispano-Indo frontier, particularly regarding labor issues, emboldened settlers at the same time that
it alarmed the monarchy. The struggle over the encomienda exempli-

fied the clash between pragmatic adjustments by the settlers and the theoretical and philosophical needs of the monarchy.

Post-1521: Tenochtitlán–Mexico City

Differing political concepts made governing awkward in the aftermath of the military success. The Castilians thought in term of territory, population, and political obligations, while Indo-Mexico thought of empire as based on obligations, with territory a secondary consideration.[30] Traditionally, tribute-paying rulers remained in authority as long as they met their obligations. The rapidity with which the tributaries of the Aztecs acknowledged Cortés perhaps can be traced to their assumption that they would be left alone as long as they met tribute obligations. They likely expected to strike a new arrangement with the Spaniards under the same political terms. Chieftaincies across Mesoamerica soon heard about the military strength of the newcomers and their alliance with Tlaxcala. While some rumors and accounts of recent events may have been disquieting, what had occurred seemingly followed the traditional Indo-Mexican political pattern of force followed by tribute. Nevertheless, Aztec tributaries and independent tribute empires could not be expected to automatically accept Cortés as the successor to Cuauhtémoc, the last Aztec ruler, and to subordinate themselves to what was now the intruder capital. A show of force would be needed and possibly more to establish Spanish control. Local leaders resisted internal interference but were willing to accept, perhaps reluctantly, Cortés's overarching authority. Those who had contested Aztec power before 1521, however, posed a problem that required active force to bring them under domination, but in the end, they could not hold out in the face of the mobilization of Indo-Mexican forces directed by Spaniards.[31]

A series of revolts in the 1540s, including the Mayans in 1546, tribal groups in Oaxaca in 1547, and the Zapotecs, Guachichiles, and Guamares in 1550, marked the end of potentially effective resistance. The Crown progressively imposed the Spanish municipal model on Indian communities bypassing traditional families which had held office in favor of newcomers, including some Mestizos who accepted the new order.[32] In doing so, it created agents who depended on the new order.

The Spaniards drew heavily on the Tlaxcalans and the defeated Aztec Confederation for thousands of warriors as well as porters to forcefully expand and control their empire. While Indians from central Mexico made up the core, Tarascans, Zapotecs, Mixtecs, Chiapanecs, Tzotzils, Tzeltals, Otomies, and others, as well as various Mayan groups, participated. Spanish armies mixed different groups together, although they continued to fight separately and under their own insignia. Logistics followed the established pattern of the pre-Spanish time, with food provided by cities that were willing to reassume tributary obligations. The passage of sizable armies quickly assured that tributaries laid aside notions of revolt and could be drawn on for additional armed men. The Europeans in effect reaffirmed the power of the city of Tenochtitlán rather than the Aztec Confederation. Assumption by the Spaniards of the role of frontier nobility charged with directing Indian allies drew on the traditional definition of European nobility. The ability to own a horse, armor, weapons, and sufficient resources to support a warrior lifestyle mirrored the requirements of the Castilian frontier. Nevertheless, an Indo-Mexican-frontier nobility did not emerge. The original conquistadores had quasi-noble standing, with the exception of Cortés, who was elevated to the nobility out of necessity, but a new class of functional nobles did not emerge—an early indication that the Castilian Crown intended to organize its American empire differently in order to avoid the political complexity that characterized Spain.

Labor

A moral and practical struggle began almost immediately over the issue of labor in the form of slavery and the encomienda. Spain's historical experience with slavery was of little help. Castile had encountered primitive natives in the Canary Islands some sixty miles off the coast of Africa around 1344. Guanche islanders provided slaves for the labor market of Seville without legal or philosophical complications. In a similar manner, the inhabitants of the Antilles became vulnerable to enslavement by the early European settlers in spite of the papal grant. To complicate matters, the Scots Dominican friar John Mair raised the issue in 1510 of whether the Indians fell into Aristotle's category of natural slaves (servants), as discussed earlier.

The situation on the mainland, however, was morally and politically more complex than in the islands, made so by sheer numbers and cultural variations from undeniably civilized to somewhat primitive tribes in the north. It became a divisive issue between the monarchy and those who toppled the Mexica, who expected that the Crown would respect the rules of war allowing enslavement of those who had resisted. The monarchy, however, understood that introducing Indian slavery conflicted with the intent of the papal conveyance of the New World for the purposes of introducing Christianity. While the Crown approached the issue of slavery as a moral one with political consequences, the settlers saw it as a simple question of access to labor. The purchase of individual slaves was less controversial, but as clerics noted, indigenous laws governing slavery were much less punitive than those of Europe.

The Dominican scholar Francisco de Vitoria in 1539 laid out the argument, concluding that the Indians functioned under their own rational laws and had a civic life. Their unacceptable practices did not alter that reality and could be blamed on lack of instruction, following the views of Saint Augustine. They lived not as natural slaves but as people capable of advanced reasoning if properly instructed. Consequently, the monarchy had an obligation to hold them in a state of tutelage until they became fully rational.[33] Vitoria supported the Crown's legal placement of Indians in a special protective category as religious and cultural apprentices but not as slaves.

Cortés, faced with no other options, settled on the encomienda. Ever the pragmatic moralist, he had witnessed the destructive impact of the encomienda system in the islands and had opposed it. When he contemplated the postconquest situation in Indo-Mexico, he changed his mind. Cortés's army consisted of unpaid freelancers drawn from the Antilles who had the expectation of collecting booty. As he described them in a letter to Emperor Carlos V (1524), defending his award of encomiendas, they were men of "low quality, violent and vicious."[34] The distribution of plunder, initially seemingly inexhaustible, was not enough to hold such booty capitalists in place. Cortés faced the prospect of roving bands of desperate soldiers, perhaps reinforced by another influx from the islands, all of whom with few exceptions would engage in predatory behavior. Just how much would be tolerated by the indigenous population before a reactionary revolt occurred was not clear.

Cortés understood that sustainable wealth, unlike finite booty, depended on land and labor. Both came together in the encomienda: the two separate but interrelated pillars of a stable socioeconomic situation that in turn made politics viable. Moreover, the need to keep Europeans from returning to Spain or pursuing their dreams of wealth and plunder as new discoveries attracted them was obvious. Cortés, with full appreciation of his worth, awarded himself some 23,000 Indians in his encomienda and much less to his men, but enough to suggest that they could live a privileged lifestyle re-creating what they imagined others enjoyed in Spain. "Their tastes . . . had been formed in Castile, Extremadura or Andalusia, and now that riches had come their way," they intended to enjoy their good fortune.[35]

Cortés, driven by what he believed to be necessity, clung to the encomienda at the moment the Crown had decided on its abolition because of its devastating impact in the islands. When the news that encomiendas had been granted in New Spain reached Europe, a greatly irritated monarch demanded that such grants be reversed and prohibited the use of the encomienda. Cortés, on the distant frontier of Indo-Mexico, ignored imperial orders. The Indians, unable to set the terms of commendations, had to accept those imposed by the intruders. Negotiations in the face of overwhelming pressure for labor from armed and threatening conquistadors with whom few could communicate effectively could not be expected. Cortés had explained all this to Carlos V, pointing out that without the encomenderos, the monarch would have to send paid royal troops to secure Mexico. Moreover, Cortés very astutely pointed out that because the Indian did not use coin, some device had to be used to transform in-kind wealth and labor into European money if the monarch expected tribute payments. While both Indians and Spaniards understood the notion of a right to tribute labor, the Europeans saw it as the socioeconomic foundation of a semifeudal creation. Cortés pressed the Crown to make grants hereditary, with mixed success, although his own holding would be made so by the recognition of the Marquesado del Valle and Cortés's elevation to the high nobility.

As frontier inhabitants intent on survival, the early settlers did not necessarily accommodate the concerns of the monarchy. The tendency of some encomenderos to abandon their grant for the lure of new discoveries presented another problem that troubled Cortés, as noted earlier.[36] Subsequently, Carlos V prohibited the awarding of a new encomienda to those who had abandoned one elsewhere and ordered holders to build a stone house within two years. A stone house might have anchored the footloose in Spain as the Reconquista ended, but not in frontier Mexico. In any event, such rules drawn up in Spain could not be enforced on the other side of the Atlantic. Royal officials, worried about Spain's legitimate claims in the New World, in turn did not appreciate the difficulties of the settlers. The fact that royal wishes could be ignored on the Hispano-Indo frontier, particularly regarding labor issues, emboldened settlers at the same time that it alarmed the monarch. The struggle over the encomienda exemplified the clash of pragmatic needs with the abstract philosophical underpinning of the monarchy.

Dispensing with the Conqueror

A reactionary Crown understood that a self-constructed seminobility had to be made subservient to royal authority, by royal largess in the form of honors, officeholding, or something tangible, but they could not be allowed to claim legitimate noble status. This required wresting the reward structure away from Cortés, who had the potential of becoming a latter-day El Cid. Meanwhile, Cortés acted with a free hand, rearranging indigenous elements as he believed most useful. The tone of his correspondence with Emperor Carlos V suggested an equality that must have been unsettling to the monarch and his advisers. His request for missionaries, seemingly innocent enough, impinged on policy matters.

The arrival of the early missionaries could not obscure the reality that they constituted an institutional counterbalance to Cortés and his men's freewheeling redistribution of resources. They were soon placed within the institutional structure in the form of bishops appointed by the king. Increasingly, Cortés became hemmed in; if he had any idea of establishing a Mexican kingship, time to do so was short. Whether it could have been done seems doubtful. A unified indigenous institutional foundation in Indo-Mexico did not exist. Cortés would have had to govern as paramount chief and rule by indigenous law and customs. At best, he would have become a political tool of a fragmented tribute kingdom: a man who would be king, perhaps with a predictably short life span. Moreover, a handful of Spaniards could not repulse the horde of European opportunists that would surely follow, had they tried to do so.

A suspicious Crown, with a fresh memory of the Revolt of the Comuneros, contemplated the possibility that Cortés might assume independent governing control of some sort. His obvious popularity with the Indian population suggested that he could draw on the indigenous population for support; the Crown rushed to head off such a possibility. What Cortés lacked—a well-established, legitimate institutional role—Spain's monarchy had, and it rapidly deployed its institutions. That the first institutions introduced were judicial ones indicated that the Crown anticipated a struggle over political legitimacy. The monarch appointed Beltrán Nuño de Guzmán, a ruthless, cruel individual but an experienced conquistador and, of some importance, a bitter enemy of Cortés, to be president of the first high court, the Audiencia, in 1528. The establishment of a judicial body suggests that officials in Spain believed that a power struggle with Cortés might be imminent. Nuño de Guzmán stripped Cortés of property, reassigned encomiendas to his followers, and circulated a rumor that Cortés had died on his expedition to Honduras. A pious Nuño de Guzmán attended the appropriate religious services for the putatively dead conqueror.

Cortés had departed for Honduras, taking Cuauhtémoc, the last Aztec paramount chief, with him, to forestall any possible attempt to restore Indian sovereignty. His purpose—to assure himself that the revolt of his disloyal lieutenant, Cristobel de Olid, had been put down—indicated the extent of his unease that his legitimacy by the right of conquest might be insufficient. He took with him a large force of Indians and Spaniards with the expectation that he faced a battle with ambitious fellow countrymen. While that did not occur, the episode demonstrated the violent nature of rule by conquistadors: Olid died of stab wounds; Cuauhtémoc was strangled, accused of having plotted a revolt; Nuño de Guzmán abused his royal commission and terrorized hapless Indians; and the Crown had been forced to connive to achieve its ends.

The second Audiencia (1530), headed by a professional jurist, succeeded. In less than a decade, the Audiencia became an important and respected extension of royal jurisdiction. Meanwhile, a disgruntled Cortés returned to Spain to be showered with honors but excluded from governing the land he had effectively brought under Spanish dominion. He was prohibited from returning to Mexico. When the Crown relented and allowed him to return to New Spain, officials in Mexico City had orders not to allow him to enter the city. A disgruntled conqueror again returned to Spain. With the perceived challenge of Cortés behind the monarchy, the imperial reorganization proceeded.

Christianity provided the structural context of Spanish imperialism in the New World. In its new setting, it differed psychologically and materially from how it functioned in Spain. The eight-centuries-long Reconquista of Christian Spain to push the Moors from the peninsula concluded in 1492 but left a legacy that explains in large part the intensity of Spanish Christianity and its impact. In Spain, the extermination of the competing belief systems of Islam and Judaism became the goal. Uncertainty in Europe, with the Muslim resurgence in the east and the discovery of the Antilles followed by Indo-Mexico, mixed fear and hope in equal measure. Spain confronted an unexpected, ambiguous religious situation. The papal conveyance recognized Castile's sovereignty in the New World but with the obligation to Christianize. The charge in the Americas, unlike that directed at the Jews and the Moors, was to convert Indo-American pagans, not to destroy them. Just how much political and social pressure could be applied to advance indigenous Christianization remained unclear, in spite of the church's theological stand against forced conversion. The European political-religious mission—crafted under unique historical circumstances but now dedicated to the destruction of a worldview grounded in a different experience—made for an epic but strangely muted psychological struggle. Spain's putative religious benevolence in realty sought to destroy and replace. It was not an even match, with the reality of conquest followed by epidemic disease. Subsequently, Christianity served as a physical, cultural, and psychological weapon employed in the interest of the Spaniards, though not completely.

The destruction of Tenochtitlán in 1521 discredited the indigenous gods but did not destroy them. Nevertheless, demolishing shrines, smashing sacred objects, disrupting ceremonies, and suppressing the Indians' ritual calendar, coupled with pressure on them to convert, indicated the powerlessness of their gods to protect them. On a political level, flogging indigenous leaders engaged in prohibited rituals and subjecting others to the Inquisition served to physically discipline offenders but did not address the confusion over what might be appropriate and under what circumstances. In the absence of predictability, the human response is to become passive and submissive when confronted by authority.

The initiative shifted to the destroyers and their cultural beliefs. Survival for Indo-Mexico depended on publicly accepting an alien religion and acknowledging the political reality that indigenous sovereignty had passed to the intruders. By the middle 1550s, Spanish rule appeared irreversible. Along with the superiority of European technology, political organization mixed with civic order and warfare combined to virtually eliminate covert indigenous resistance.

The religious imagination—the questions that human beings ask of their priests—are very similar across cultures. The elaboration of Christianity required centuries to approach settled orthodoxy, meaning a coherent, comprehensive belief system. In contrast, Indo-Mexico's beliefs were still only partially formulated. Important loose ends such as what happened after death, notions of heaven and hell, spiritual rewards for piety, and the formation of a benevolent supportive pantheon remained to be addressed, although nascent attempts to resolve such theological issues had been made before the Europeans arrived. Consequently, religious conversions initially launched by Cortés and given some substance by the missionary friars succeeded in getting across the macro elements of Catholic theology. Enthused missionaries talked to the crowds, preformed mass baptisms and Christian marriages, and introduced new rituals. They could take pride that mass human sacrifice had virtually ended, accomplished rapidly with an immediate decrease in war.[37]

That the Indians were avid learners was obvious; indeed, a few became exceptional Latinists and read European history and philosophy. Unfortunately, distrust and a preference for submissive disciples motivated missionaries to withhold from the Indians the means to advance to the same level as those who sought to instruct them. Church building, excessively indulged in during the early missionary years, seemed more appropriate, although it reflected the availability of enthusiastic, unpaid Indian labor. What seemed to be a promising start obscured indigenous inattention to Christianity's finer points and the reality that Spaniards had an insufficient grasp of Indo-Mexican theology, thus dismissing similarities as Satanic tricks. It was these similarities, preserved in the crevasses, nooks, and crannies of the historical mind, that allowed for survival of elements of Indo-Mexico's religious experience.

Moreover, the religious instruction provided by the friars condemned many Indians to the level of children in the faith, a lesser category that morphed into an inferior social position but also made it possible for them to hold on to pagan religious concepts. The notion that evil and heresy reflected a failure of instruction supported a degree of reluctant toleration but did not mandate learning. Religious practices that were tinged with pre-Cortésian aspects but with enough familiar content to be acceptable as Catholic notions seemed sufficient. In reality, poorly understood, even totally misunderstood, rituals provided a protective spiritual canopy for popular notions drawn from prior religious beliefs mixed with Catholic fragments. An everyday popular religion emerged that was impossible to root out.[38] On some level, the missionaries understood that insistence on orthodoxy risked losing all. They failed to capitalize on the initial excitement to generate religious momentum or to enlist an indigenous clergy to cement ties with believers who were anxious to participate at a respected level.

Nevertheless, missionary activity between 1524 and 1556, when the secular clergy began to replace the friars, succeeded in breaking Indo-Mexico's religiocultural integrity. On a collective and individual level, Indian understanding of the new religion remained rudimentary and mixed with traditional elements that distorted both belief systems. From a political standpoint, the breaking of religious integrity favored colonial authority. The bishops who led the mission misread the situation. Faced with what they perceived as backsliding, they employed Inquisitional powers to frighten the Indians into some semblance of Christianity, until the Crown, concerned with the political impact, restrained them.

Failed Evangelization

Cortés, from the moment he landed on the coast, understood the need to attack the enemy's cultural foundations. He destroyed idols as the Spaniards moved toward Tenochtitlán and continued to do so after the fall of the Aztec capital, thereby demonstrating that the European gods were more protective than and superior to those of Indo-Mexico.

Nevertheless, the uncoordinated activities of the few clerics who accompanied Cortés during the conquest and who engaged in sporadic evangelization met with minor success. Friar Bartolomé de Olmedo, best known for his attempts to restrain Cortés from too aggressively destroying Indian altars, resulting in his title of the "First Apostle of Mexico," reacted tactically. He failed to understand that during the military stage, Cortés's actions made sense and mirrored indigenous practices. The crucial first assault directed at the religious core of Indo-Mexico's worldview had already been made before the arrival of the first missionaries: the end of mass human sacrifice removed the keystone that supported the indigenous belief structure.

Nevertheless, soldiers were ill equipped to offer a replacement for the discredited religious core of the indigenous worldview. One of Cortés's first letters to the monarch requested the dispatch of missionaries to launch an organized pacification effort. The small number of friars dispatched by the Crown faced a gigantic task, one that could only be done in a superficial manner, as they were well aware. Their initial lightning strikes, much like a fast-moving raiding force, succeeded in disrupting indigenous beliefs in the crucial valleys of Mexico and Puebla as well as elsewhere, but they hardly resulted in many actual converts.

The initial evangelization efforts were crude; in the absence of the ability to communicate in indigenous languages, missionaries used common signs to convey their message. Even the most elementary theological notions could not be conveyed with any certainty. Any sign of acceptance by listeners could only have been political and tactical or the desire not to offend. Religious confusion rather than conversion served to semiparalyze Indian understanding well into the first century of Spanish rule. Nevertheless, the friars immediately began to study Indian languages and produce sermons in indigenous languages. Whether to use Spanish terms or indigenous words and names to explain Christian beliefs became a divisive issue. Use of the name of the Indian goddess Tonantzin for the Virgin Mary must have caused confusion. Employing Spanish and Latin terms avoided some of the difficulties, but in 1555, the first Mexican Synod ordered all sermons in indigenous languages to be withdrawn because of translation errors. Simplified replacement sermons offered understanding at the expense of theological depth. In 1565, the Provisional Synod prohibited the distribution of the scriptures, substituting an indigenous catechism translated by experts and approved by the hierarchy.[39] Missionary friars tended to concentrate on the now defunct Aztec empire and Nahuatl because most of the empire's former imperial tributaries spoke Nahuatl as a second language. Numerous small pockets of potential converts of other language groups had to be ignored in the early stages. A de facto division of missionary fields among the orders reflected language boundaries and likely led to variation of understanding on both sides. While some missionaries became accomplished linguists, it cannot be assumed that all had adequate language skills. The friars grappled with ten major languages including some dialects; the various orders learned only those languages spoken in their particular mission fields. The Franciscans, with the largest mission field, developed some competence in six of the major languages. Nevertheless, the friars understood that Nahuatl served as a lingua franca and advocated that other language groups be taught Nahuatl rather than Spanish, a position defended on the grounds that the structure of the Spanish language was totally different; in addition, many Indians were already bilingual. At a higher level, some missionaries sought to preserve Indian culture and not to Hispanicize their charges, hoping to re-create early Christian purity of thought and action in Indo-Mexico. While the monarchy did not reject the study and use of Indian languages, it ordered that Castilian Spanish be taught. The direct order of 1550 to the Dominicans and Augustinians indicated that officials believed that teaching Spanish would lead to acceptance of Spanish "social organization and good customs."[40] The orders feared that "bad" European customs might be the problem. Had the monarchy gone along with employing Nahuatl as the language of New Spain, it would have inserted a cultural layer and priestly class between the monarchy and its new subjects. The political ramifications would likely have been unacceptable.

The early small contingents of friars remained administratively tied to Spain. To what extent this inhibited tactics or their identification with the New Spain mission field is uncertain. The Franciscans functioned as part of the Spanish province of San Gabriel de Extremadura until 1535. The Dominicans were subordinated to the order's superior general and then to Santo Domingo until 1532, when they established a separate province. The Augustinians arrived in 1533, represented by only seven brothers. All three orders were soon reinforced by additional contingents from Spain, and in the 1540s, Creoles, Spaniards born in

Mexico, modestly increased their numbers. The Franciscans established convents in Texcoco and Churubusco, both in the Valley of Mexico, and planned a large complex in the rebuilt Mexico City. Both the Dominicans and the Augustinians founded convents in the Valley of Mexico that, like those of the Franciscans, served as strategic and tactical planning centers. Overbuilding of monastic structures soon came under criticism: some were pictured as barely utilized, with a handful of friars rattling around in an empty space. In general, the Franciscans moved northward, while the Dominicans advanced to the southeast. The Augustinians then filled in the gaps. Competition among them, with some scandalous exceptions, could be controlled.

An immediate issue, with important consequences, was what cultural expectations the orders entertained for Christianized Indians. Could they be elevated to European standards, or would they remain children in the faith and cultural apprentices? The initial positive reaction was exemplified by Pedro de Gante, who enthusiastically taught Latin, the language of scholars, to a promising group of students and insisted that intellectually they equaled Europeans. Gante's school provided the model for the secondary school of Santa Cruz de Tlatelolco. Avid students suggested that an indigenous elite, well grounded in Spanish culture, could be created in one generation. The political and social implications soon became evident. The usefulness of the political, social, and economic subordination of the defeated population was clear and was strengthened and justified by suspicion.

Once the danger had been sensed, proof could be found everywhere that the Indian religious worldview remained a potential threat. Those who rejected indigenous education, including most settlers, the Dominican order, nervous officials, and others, limited access to ideas. That the Indians had so quickly learned how to manipulate the legal system to defend their interests underscored the potential challenge to the new order. The notion of an indigenous Christian clergy appeared to be tantamount to entrusting neophytes in the faith with the task of instructing the superficially converted.

Political fears, hidden behind perceived indigenous moral weakness, relegated Indians to low-level positions in the evangelization process, such as interpreters and assistants. In 1539, they were allowed to take minor, revocable orders only. Pious indigenous women in a similar fashion had few religious possibilities that carried social respect. Some

200 years later, the Capuchin order established the first nunnery for Indian women, a long-overdue move in the direction of religious-cultural equality with European women.

The Church Synod of 1553 formally prohibited the ordination of Indians, Mestizos, and blacks. Race, a suspect category infused with concerns about loyalty, pushed the native population to the bottom of the social pyramid. Escape required becoming a Mestizo; when the church relented, Mestizos who were biologically or culturally allied with Spain were the first non-Europeans to be allowed into the priesthood.

The notion of the Indians as timid, child-like, cooperative, and mold-able made them vulnerable to social experimentation by well-intended missionaries.[41] In order for the missionaries to maximize their efforts, with the approval of the Crown, they relocated small villages and amal-gamated larger tribe groups, with little thought to the damaging con-sequences. The concept of a unified community of Christian believers, along the lines of that recently achieved in Spain with the expulsion of the Jews and Moors, was applied to amalgamate tribal groups. It is not clear if the Indians agreed to voluntary relocation or for that matter any such concentration or if they assumed that they could not refuse agents of the new dominant power. Relocation damaged tribal tradi-tional institutions and trading patterns and disrupted village industries reliant on locally available resources.

Friars Bartolomé de las Casas, Vasco de Quiroga, and others could not resist the temptation to experiment, while other, less prominent clerics indulged their transformative fantasies on a lesser scale. Las Casas, convinced that he understood the Indians, backed experiments that backfired. His plan to establish agricultural communities in Tierra Firme (Venezuela) with mixed Spanish and Indian settlers lasted two years before being destroyed by labor-hungry Europeans (1520–1522). His Vera Paz experiment in 1537, designed to demonstrate that his trea-tise *The Only Way (De Unico Modo)* would work to pacify hostile In-dians, also had a sad ending. He asserted quite correctly that kindness and consideration were natural human traits but ignored the powerful motivations of profit, the labor shortage, the perceived need for forced labor, and the brutality that accompanied coercion—in short, every-thing that he himself had declared the Europeans visited on the hap-less Indians, although he referred to them as un-Christian vices.[42] By ignoring his own rhetoric, he visited devastation of those whom he intended to help. The Vera Paz experiment—to subdue hostile Indians in the province of Tuzutlán, now part of Guatemala, who had repulsed at least three attempts to reduce them by force and who might have yielded to kindness and compassion, in short the *Only Way* in action, but in the end, the experiment visited death and destruction on both sides. In reality, the initial violent reaction of indigenous leaders may have been more effective as a negotiation tool to establish some type of protective autonomy.[43] Unfortunately, the labor shortage that hindered the commercialization of resources made for unrelenting pressure for the division of Indian labor among the European settlers. A ten-year struggle between the friars and the labor-hungry Europeans ended in a reactionary revolt in Vera Paz to restore the religious core of indigenous culture. The burning of churches, killing of missionaries, and collapse of the Vera Paz experiment, followed by war, devastated the region's indigenous population. In a letter dispatched to the king in 1556, the somewhat bewildered friars expressed the wish to clearly explain to the monarch, and perhaps to themselves, what happened.[44]

Las Casas after 1543 came to the equally unrealistic conclusion that forming the Indians politically into separate republics, joined together only in the person of the monarch, should be considered. In effect, he advocated basing a political structure on the Spanish concept of a República de Indios that posited the existence of an ethnic category distinct from the República de Españoles that would function within politically subordinated chieftaincies.[45] In reality, a partial restoration of pre-European chieftaincies ignored tribal and language divisions and the impact of Christianity, which sought to place all within a Christian universe. Deacculturation, already evident in central Mexico's cities by the early 1530s, made any autonomous restoration impossible.[46]

An experiment with a more positive outcome, one often referred to as an example of clerical benevolence, was one directed by Vasco de Quiroga. As the first bishop of Michoacán, Quiroga tested his notions on a grand scale: having read Sir Thomas More's *Utopia* (1516) and being impressed with what he saw as the simple virtues of his native charges, he sought to re-create what he believed to be the model of primitive Christian communities using the Indians as his subjects. In addition, Quiroga, concerned with the number of abandoned children—many of them biological Mestizos, some sheltered in monasteries, others in the streets—hoped to rescue them and acculturate them in organized towns established by relocating populations from isolated areas to readily accessible locations. The bishop gathered his charges into two communal centers and organized their daily lives to achieve what he believed to be a balance between spiritual and temporal needs. The bishop encouraged craft specialization by his communities, the fruits of which can still be seen and appreciated in our own time. The family lay at the organizational heart of his two Pueblo Hospitals: Santa Fe de Mexico in the vicinity of Mexico City and Santa Fe de la Laguna in Michoacán. He sought to re-create stable extended families based on lineage and intermarriage. His settlements were governed by Indians, except for a Spaniard who had overall jurisdiction as the *alcalde mayor* or *corregidor* appointed by the Audiencia in the king's name. The idea was to draw Indians into a controlled cultural environment following a semimonastic model, similar to that which had allowed monasteries in Spain to prosper. A six-hour workday left time for religious activities and instruction. Individuals faced expulsion if they set a poor example; committed a hideous or scandalous act; indulged in laziness, drunkenness, or unacceptable behavior; or ignored the common good.[47] Quiroga envisioned his Pueblo Hospitals as an organizational model that could be used throughout the Hispano-Indo empire. Quiroga's good intentions may be assumed, although his model presumed European superiority and Indian incapacity and employed relocation.[48] That Quiroga's model ran counter to the Crown's long-term economic needs and political aspirations did not trouble the kindly bishop, nor did it concern political authorities, well aware that they functioned on an experimental frontier.

Relocation changed the political relationships between other villages and towns. Huejotzingo, previously sited in an inconvenient mountainous region, was moved to a more accessible location. The population of 40,000 must have been traumatized or at the very least disorientated. The assumption of control by the friars displaced the local indigenous leaders. Decision making passed to the friars, as did responsibility. As self-appointed guardians, the missionaries had a proprietary interest in their charges. The missionary fathers became settlement planners, reconstituting villages and towns as they believed most useful for their purposes.

That the friars tended to re-create a Spanish urban environment is not surprising; nevertheless, as noted earlier, both societies were urban focused. From an architectural and political standpoint, they shared common urban elements. Both societies located important structures at the heart of villages, towns, and cities. A church replaced a pyramid, a municipal palace replaced the quarters of the tribal chief, and a central plaza provided an administrative focal point. In spite of architectural similarities, relocation of tribal groups destroyed their attachment to place. Rootlessness led in part to the decultured drift of Indo-Mexicans into impersonal cities as cultural Mestizos. Gathering together small tribal groups that had been devastated by epidemic disease made some sense, although it likely constituted a double trauma for the survivors.

To an admirable extent, the evangelization effort by the orders was individually heroic, but the actual project was not a massive Christian crusade. An inadequate number of religious personnel at all levels characterized the church in the first century of Spanish rule. The decision to exclude Indian converts from the priesthood, in retrospect a mistake, reflected Spain's deep suspicion of converts. Consequently, the number of missionaries (regular orders) or secular priests never came close to an army of the Lord, even as a demographic disaster overtook the indigenous population.

A Spiritual World Replaced

The conquerors succeeded in decapitating the Aztec empire's political leadership, but the secondary level remained intact. The transition from force to consensual governing remained problematic, complicated by pressure to redistribute wealth to the Europeans, a delicate task that might spark a rebellion and a host of minor but collectively important socioeconomic adjustments. In reality, the Castilians constituted a small, weak occupying force. Security depended on unbalancing the religious-based worldview of Indo-America and on its rapid replacement as much as possible by that of Spain. A number of elements worked in favor of the intruders, who exploited existing language and tribal divisions and long-standing resentments over tribute, warfare, and sacrificial victims.

The paramount chieftaincy and the indigenous priesthood (*nana-hualtin*), discredited and humiliated by defeat, and the high nobility, co-opted by the conquerors in the form of Castilian titles of nobility, land grants, and limited institutional jurisdictions (encomiendas), could not regain leadership. The lower officeholding Indian nobility, threatened by Europeanization, were the only possible challengers to the new worldview. They retained sufficient legitimacy and managerial functions to insert themselves between the Indian masses and the demands of the Castilians authorities, making themselves useful to both sides.[49] They in effect balanced demands and cultures, including efforts to preserve prior beliefs and the European counterthrusts, intentional or not, to destroy them. The imposition of Spanish requirements that elections should be held for all town offices ran counter to indigenous traditions. The process of identification of suitable officeholders came down to those who had occupied equivalent posts under the old regime. Challenging community tradition would be divisive, although it is unclear if or how often royal officials insisted on elections in the early post-conquest period. Enforcement was probably spotty at best.[50]

Preservation of the symbols of the indigenous worldview—idols, the explanatory codices, masks, and ritual items hidden from the intruders in caves, buried, or otherwise concealed—indicated the hope among the indigenous people for some sort of continuation of their beliefs. A strong oral tradition allowed for transmission of indigenous knowledge from the older generation to their children, a natural process beyond the control of European friars and subsequently the secular clergy. The discovery and destruction of sacred caches, referred to as *Huitzilopochtlis,* became an obsession of the missionary friars, aware that the earlier attacks on pagan idols had not been completely successful. The objectification of indigenous gods in the form of sacred idols made their destruction crucial. Although Christianity also permitted images, they appeared in human form as a devotional focal point. It is unlikely that the fine distinction between idols and images meant much to the converts The friars' reactionary and destructive zeal could not eliminate them all; fortunately, modern archeologists have unearthed a reasonable numbers of them. The energy poured into smashing idols may have stemmed from the missionaries' initial misreading of the openness of the population to Christianity as well as its willingness to give up ancient gods. Angry disappointment followed, with the realization they had misread the situation.[51] The conduct of the Spaniards posed another problem. Inquisitional powers, conveyed in the papal bull *Omnimoda,* that gave the friars episcopal obligations in the absence of bishops dealt mainly with European and stranded foreign (Protestant) sailors. The irregular soldiers who had defeated the Aztecs held few things sacred, providing a poor example for Indians being urged to adopt Christianity. Inquisitional powers delegated to friars in 1522 worked mainly to punish soldiers who were guilty of blasphemy. The following year, two edicts were targeted at Jews, perhaps a pro form response but apparently intended to curb the crude verbal behavior of the conquistadors. An auto-de-fé in 1528 resulted in two individuals, likely Spaniards, being burned as suspected Judaizantes (Judaizers). The difficulties of converting Spaniards into role models abated as many settled down as they aged and became agriculturists.[52]

The Franciscans had adopted mass baptism as an interim tactic rather than the preferred but time-consuming instruction in the faith before baptism. Critics of mass baptism justifiably focused on the superficiality of conversion.[53] From a political standpoint, quick baptism signified an alliance of sorts with the Spaniards as well as introduced contradicting loyalties that unsettled the indigenous worldview. Those who were baptized received a Christian name. While it would seem unlikely that the new name immediately displaced the indigenous one, it signified a personal connection with the Spaniards.[54] Juan de Zumárraga, as a Franciscan, supported baptism before complete instruction in the faith, but as archbishop, he sought unrealistically to use Inquisitional powers to enforce orthodoxy among indigenous converts, some 200,000 baptized Indians mainly in the central valleys. He ignored the reality that the Europeans were a tiny minority in an indigenous sea, perhaps under 10,000, with a very small number of missionary friars. Premature concerns with orthodoxy conflicted with the Crown's immediate objective of sociopolitical security. While the monarch may have been prepared in the short term to settle for pro form conversion as a political gesture, the missionaries now pressed for religious control over the baptized.

Nevertheless, the inability to individually deal with so many intended or unintended violations of the faith made exemplary punishment of the indigenous leadership the only option. Zumárraga as a bishop had apostolic Inquisitional powers, although he hoped to get the

Crown's agreement to establish an independent Holy Office of the Inquisition in Mexico City. While he was never successful, he proceeded
to act as if his wish had been granted, even allowing others to refer to
him as Inquisitor General. He became notorious for harsh punishment,
particularly in the case of Don Carlos Ometochtli, the paramount chief
of Texcoco, who was accused of heresy, investigated, tried, sentenced
in an *auto-de-fé*, and burned at the stake on December 1, 1539. While
this was a high-profile case, there are some indications that an internal
struggle among the Texcocan high nobility made Don Carlos vulnerable to the Inquisition. Zumárraga continued his exemplary campaign
until the Crown curtailed his apostolic Inquisitional powers and restrained his attacks on indigenous leaders. Nevertheless, overzealous
persecution of presumed backsliding converts reached a high level in
1561, when the Franciscan provincial of the southern province of Yucatán, Friar Diego de Landa, sought to discipline the Mayans. Crown
moderation eventually restored a measure of order.

In 1532, a little over a decade after the destruction of Tenochtitlán,
the authorities in Madrid instructed the governing Audiencia to study
the feasibility of dividing New Spain into dioceses, a step toward stan-
dardizing the clerical institutional structure across the transatlantic empire as well as bringing the friars under political control. Politically,
while the orders might be influenced, they functioned independently
of the direct supervision of kings, popes, and bishops. They viewed their
conversion efforts in the *doctrinas* (equivalent to a parish but administered by the friars) as dictated by charity, not the formal obligation imposed by a bishop on the secular clergy. The Council of Trent man-
dated, among other reforms, that the orders be made accountable to
the local bishops; a reform authorized by the papacy for the monarchy
to appoint New World bishops theoretically gave the monarch indirect control over the orders.[55] Nevertheless, the cooperation of the regulars in New Spain could not be taken for granted, as their threat to
withdraw from the doctrinas made clear. The struggle between the
bishops and the orders had a confusing history well before the *Ordenanza del Patronazgo* (1574). Many of the twenty-three articles of the
Ordenanza had been promulgated earlier, without much effect.[56] In 1565,
Pope Pius IV had revoked all privileges obtained by the orders that conflicted with the reforms put forward by the Council of Trent. Two years
later, his successor, Pius V (a Dominican), began to reverse those

restrictions, and within less than a decade, Pope Gregory XIII confusingly supported Trent but gave the Jesuits new privileges that violated the custom of treating all the orders the same. Nevertheless, the ordinance of 1574 had some immediate consequence in Mexico. Archbishop Pedro Moya de Contreras ordered that parish benefices be subject to competition between potential candidates. The Third Mexican Provincial Council (1585) attempted, largely unsuccessfully, to address long-standing issues in accord with the Council of Trent's mandate to standardize institutional procedures.[57]

The secular clergy structurally could not match the level of commitment of the regular clergy, who operated within a self-reinforcing religious community as evangelizing teams usually composed of three brothers.[58] In contrast, the parish priest operated alone, with the nominal supervision of his bishop, and was surrounded by his parishioners and subject to their concerns. The introduction of the secular clergy changed the relationship between the Indian population and Christianity. A parish priest functioned as part of the community, not as a director, although he was not without influence. As a community member, he had personal obligations to his flock and depended on them directly for food and material and social support. Consequently, competition for a reasonably prosperous parish meant that the secular clergy would underserve less desirable rural areas. The Third Mexican Provincial Council suggested that money from community funds and a uniform method of determining financial support for parish priests be implemented. The reality of scarce resources prompted clerics to become self-supporting businessmen as Indo-Mexico made the transition to a modified European economy. One needs to keep in mind that the secular clergy did not take vows of poverty and often inherited assets, managed family estates, and could decline a benefice and consequently devote all their time to commerce. Land, livestock, marketing of grains and other foodstuffs, mining partnerships, and a host of minor opportunities attracted the ambitious, including canons of the cathedral chapters.[59] In certain respects, the combination of religion and commercial activity was more realistic than the model offered by the orders, although the regulars clergy operated large estates. As noted by John Frederick Schwaller, the involvement of priests in the economic life of New Spain gave them a certain vitality that reflected reality.[60]

The regular clergy viewed the seculars with disdain as unlettered, undisciplined, avaricious, and sexually predatory. In reality, in the case of the latter, the number of cases of both the regular and secular clergy soliciting sex during confession in return for absolution does not appear to support the notion of an out-of-control secular clergy and a highly disciplined regular clergy. Withdrawal of the right to hear confession appears to have been more or less evenly split between them, although enforcement might be problematic in both instances. The modest status differential between secular priests and parishioners may have made both sides vulnerable to misconduct.[61]

Nevertheless, the inevitable fading of missionary zeal, marked by the introduction of the parish priests, spawned a degree of toleration toward the indigenous population. Bishop Pedro de Feria of Chiapas noted that the Indians were New Christians, not Old Christians, and thus could not be expected to comprehend the finer points. Feria reported that during a visitation in 1584, he encountered cryptopagans, idol worshippers, and Indians who confused Jesus with one of the local gods. Moreover, the ruin of an old temple was guarded, with the notion that when the missionaries departed, they would take Jesus with them, allowing the Indians to use it again.[62] Feria's experience was not unique. The Third Mexican Provincial Council accepted the tenuous grasp the Indian population had on basic elements and explained it as their lack of capacity to understand or even to remember from one lesson to the other what they had been taught.[63] The council's explanation, expressed in 1585 and approved in 1587, represented unintended acceptance of the survival of pre-Christian elements and a Mestizo religious mixture. On the ground, the parish priest understood the everyday strengths and weaknesses of his flock, sympathized, empathized, scolded, and in the end might ignore their lapses. Complex theology was of little use to the priests or to the villagers. Popular religion flourished in a lively parallel world of simplified orthodoxy. Remnants of Indo-Mexico's pre-Christian religion, debased and detached from its broader context as well as infused with Christian elements, functioned at the level of protective witchcraft, often with local variations. Priests, attuned to gossip, may have been aware of what went on in their absence that conflicted with Christian beliefs but were reluctant or powerless to intervene. In the rural countryside outside the central valley, Catholic orthodoxy crested and then drew back. The initial consolidation of the new religious mixture, although still in flux, took place in rural villages. Mexico City, Guadalajara, Puebla, and other cities became islands of recognizable Roman Catholic practices, although not without additional indigenous elements as Indians moved into cities.

While Indo-Mexican theology made humans responsible for the well-being of the gods, Christianity reversed the relationship between the gods and humans. Religious discipline, virtually absolute before the conquest, under Christian rule allowed greater latitude, in part because of the negative perception of Indian capacity. The Indians' loyalty to *their santo* (saint) exceeded their loyalty to the broader community. Every *barrio* (neighborhood) had its own image, and each had its saint's day, with appropriate public celebration that collectively reaffirmed a separate identity. The barrio financed the celebration, organized it, and established the symbols, both ancient and Christian, to be honored and the music to be played. Use of pulque and brandy created an emotional situation over which the authorities had little control. El Santo served as the foundation of a partially reconstructed indigenous worldview using Christian elements.[64] The use of saints and popular saints verged on a rival pantheon, but it was a localized one that did not reinforce religious unity across the kingdom. Home altars provided a more intense individual focus. Altars intermingled pre-European and Christian symbols and representations. Daily attention, new flowers, items of clothing, treats, and lighted candles created a personal cult controlled by the family.[65]

The tendency of the missionaries to build shrines on pagan sacred ground, noted during the Christianization of the Celts in Spain, also occurred in New Spain. Among other attractions, sacred sites supplied reusable building material. The Basilica of Our Lady of Guadalupe, one of the most important pilgrimage sites in the Catholic world, resulted from such a miscalculation. A Portuguese secular cleric, aware of a site dedicated to the goddess Tonantzin, constructed a shrine to Our Lady of the Apocalypse on the same spot. A small image of the Virgin was eventually replaced with an image painted by an Indian that many people compared to a similar one in Guadalupe, Spain, although the Mexican one incorporated indigenous symbols—hence the name Our Lady of Guadalupe. The cult became popular with the Indians and soon others. The appalled Franciscans believed that worshippers were involved in barely concealed idolatry and did their best to discourage the emerging cult. Viceroy Alonso de Montúfar, however, encouraged devotion to the image for that reason and as a means of disfavoring the Franciscans. Consequently, from the beginning, the image served as a cultural bridge as well as a political instrument. Subsequently, the myth of the Indian Virgin was further elaborated to include the Indian Juan Diego's meeting with the Virgin, the rose-covered hillside, and subsequently the erection of the pilgrimage site of the Basilica of Our Lady of Guadalupe on Tepeyac Hill. Pope John Paul II canonized Saint Juan Diego Cuauhtlatoatzin in 2002.[66]

Satan's Work

As the clergy became familiar with Mesoamerican theology, they discovered many similarities with Christianity and assumed that Satan had purposely fabricated them in order to confuse apprentices in the faith. Similarities made it difficult to draw lines between the two theologies. Key elements of indigenous belief were discredited but not necessarily destroyed; they were detached from the religious system that gave them validity and reattached to popular Christianity. Theological similarities between the two systems caused confusion that favored popular reinterpretations.

The notion of one God who had created the world but had not been created was the shared starting point of both systems. The end of life on Earth seemed similar also. The apocalypse and the burning out of the fifth sun posited the same thing, although the physics favored indigenous theology. The two theocracies differed on the nature of gods, their relationship with humans, the creation, and the survival of the world. Indo-Mexico believed that life had been extinguished several times and would be again, but just one more time. The notion of life ever after had barely been explored in Indo-Mexico but was fully developed in European religious beliefs. Indo-Mexico, perhaps as a consequence of the harshness of its experience, believed that while the gods had created the world and its inhabitants on the orders of one supreme deity, they had done so at the expense of themselves; consequently, they could only be sustained by human blood. Perhaps resentful, the gods had no interest in the well-being of those whom they created. The supreme deity, only dimly perceived, seemed disinterested also.

Indo-Mexico's spiritual world was hostile. Fear, rather that gratitude, served to unify believers. Consequently, elements of inclusive rewards for the faithful were missing in Indo-Mexico but could be supplied by Christianity.

Mass sacrifice, potentially the fate of all, was the linchpin that held the indigenous system together. As a social control device, the rigidity of fear worked for Indo-Mexico but restrained positive innovation.[67] The mass communal nature of religious ceremonies made deviations even less unlikely. Christianity shared many of these notions but added a positive ending. In both systems, sacrifice had to be acknowledged. In Christianity, sacrifice was restricted to one person, presented as a selfless act, while in Indo-Mexico, it took on an excessively violent form. Nevertheless, Christianity recognized the validity of Old Testament blood sacrifices and the violent death of Jesus. References to the body and blood of Christ are symbolic. In Indo-Mexican theology, mass sacrifice was both actual and symbolic.

As noted, both sides agreed on the existence of one supreme God; however, confusion over how the creator could create without being created impelled them to take their devotion down to a level that could offer a reasonable explanation of sorts. Both systems chose to make their devotional focus at least one step down: to Jesus, Huitzilopochtli, or Quetzalcóatl. The limited objectification of God allowed secondary entities to come close to overshadowing the supreme deity.

The Indo-Mexican creation of the gods occurred in a whirlwind of natural forces involving the sea, stars, and sacrifice, not always voluntary. Biological relationships among the gods, including births of sons and daughters, and the possibility of their death humanized as well as expanded the pantheon but did not provide attention to the needs of humans. In contrast, Christianity centered on the Son of God, suggesting a biologically complex relationship and tightly centralized distribution of celestial authority. The creation of saints as human exemplars offered multiple points of spiritual influence in addition to Jesus and the Virgin Mary.[68] The Virgin had the advantage of being able to manifest herself physically in different locations, with each apparition worshipped as a quasi-separate entity. Christianity had a well-developed sense of evil, sin, hell, Satan, and an afterlife, which added drama to everyday life. Duality, good versus bad, sharpened the intensity of belief, a characteristic of popular religion in both Spain and Mexico.[69]

Indo-Mexico understood the concept of sin and the concept of original sin at the moment of birth.

On a personal level, while indigenous and Christian beliefs and many rituals differed, often they did so in too subtle a manner to be kept apart by spiritual apprentices. Of central importance was the human need to devise an explanatory belief system. Poorly understood fragments of Christianity and embedded remnants of the Indian culture's discredited beliefs were relied on. In the process of amalgamation, differences were less troublesome than similarities for the earnest friars. For those apprentices in the faith, similarities must have been a relief.

The balance between reward and punishment in Indo-Mexican theology was undeveloped, but initial steps toward such a concept had been taken. Fallen Indian warriors and women who died in childbirth accompanied the sun, with the soldiers eventually becoming hummingbirds. In contrast, hell as a place of punishment was well developed psychologically in Christian theology. While the underworld existed in Indo-Mexico, the dead disappeared after the last journey. Nevertheless, for designated leaders, death served as a holding state, with the promise of a return to life when needed, almost a superhero notion. The second coming of Jesus suggested the same rescuing mission.

Christianity elevated poverty and contact with the divine in all its forms over sociopolitical position—whether king, paramount chief, or priest—and devalued formal learning as a spiritual guide for the laity. Missionary friars and others never tired of remarking on the humility of the indigenous population. Equality before God leveled all spiritually but not socially. Conversion did not place Spaniards and Indians on the same footing. Early successful efforts to educate Indian nobles did not enjoy much support among the missionary friars, with the exception of Pedro de Gante. A large percentage of the indigenous population had only superficial contact with the new religion. Theological confusion in the absence of effective evangelization eventually resulted in a mixed or Mestizo belief system, with elements of both religions chosen as individuals preferred.

The ideal, as envisioned by the papacy, of the incorporation of the New World into the Christian community had been based on the situation encountered in Indo-Mexico. The church assigned what at the time must have seemed to be sufficient resources to implement conversion. The tithe, dating back to the early days of Christianity and used for its institutional support in Spain, was extended to New Spain.[70] The king, as the patron of the church, received one-ninth of the tithe, although he generally transferred his share back to clerical coffers, until royal bankruptcy required its retention. The Crown in 1501 and again in 1512 defined the items that fell under the tax well before Indo-Mexico entered its calculations. Cortés collected the tithe in 1523–1524. The Indians were included in the tax base but only on items associated with Europeans: *las tres cosas* (the three things: wheat, cattle, and silk) that were established by Zumárraga and collected directly by the church. The *tres cosas* became royal policy in 1544. At a certain point, indicating cultural fusion, indigenous economic activity broadened out to include more items and industries, prompting the church to request that Indians pay the tithe on all items originally introduced from Europe. By the 1590s, this appears to have become settled policy.

In a significant departure from Spanish practices, nobles, who were exempt from the tithe in Spain, paid in New Spain, as did encomenderos, royal officials including the viceroy, and members of the military-religious orders. In spite of an expanded tax base in New Spain, tithe revenues did not cover fully the costs of secular priests, although the Crown offered some additional financial support. The church generally contracted tithe collection to private individuals who hoped to deliver the contracted amount and keep the surplus.[71]

In 1551, pressed by the church, which was anxious to train priests, and settlers, who hoped to provide a vocation for their sons, Carlos V authorized the founding of the Royal and Pontifical University in Mexico City, following the model of the University of Salamanca. With pontifical permission, the university conferred baccalaureate, licentiate, and doctoral degrees in the seven columns of knowledge: theology, scriptures, arts (logic, mathematics, metaphysics, and physics), canon law, decretals (papal decrees), rhetoric, and philosophy. Graduates usually entered the priesthood. Advancement within the church required the licentiate and doctoral degrees, and law required the study of Roman and canon law. The fledging university, dependent on part-time professors drawn from the vice-regal bureaucracy, eventually became an impressive institution in the seventeenth century.

Candidates for the priesthood had to demonstrate that they had sufficient funds to support themselves at a minimal level. Many had barely enough, a reality that invited abusive fees and exploitation of parishioners and made side businesses inevitable for many students and a full-time activity for some. While only individuals who were deemed of pure blood (absence of Jewish or Moorish background) theoretically could gain admission to the university and subsequently the priesthood, in reality, it was class and not race that served as the de facto social filter.

Meanwhile, indifferently trained priests lived with and depended on their parishioners, whose beliefs mixed European and Indo-Mexican notions. Imposing orthodoxy under such conditions could not be expected. Both sides cooperated to present a façade of spiritual unity. Looking the other way preserved harmony. Not surprisingly, Indo-Mexico's indigenous inner spirituality remained largely intact at the local level. In New Spain, the initial objective of exterminating one religion in order to make room for the other had to be abandoned. The actual number of parish priests, in a similar fashion to the undermanned orders, could not attend to the religious needs of rural New Spain. In reality, Indian believers determined the substance of their own religious needs. The accommodation between an overarching Christian theology and popular religion allowed for a less dramatic process of slow acculturation to a modified modernity. Christian orthodoxy became a matter of class; it was more often found in the cities and served as a social device, as it remains today.

The Land Regime

Adjusting the indigenous economy to meet European needs inevitably required transferring land to Europeans under acceptable title. Spain had been taken by surprise by the existence in Indo-Mexico of an organized and civilized population with its own established laws and land and labor regimes. Unavoidably, the inclusion of the Europeans in an already settled land regime required displacing indigenous cultivators in some legal fashion. The most straightforward method involved grants for meritorious service during the Aztec conquest, following Spanish practices that had been employed to populate land seized from the Moors. The municipal council of Mexico City between late 1525 and July 1528 made 23 major grants (*mercedes de tierras*) and many smaller ones. Viceroy Antonio Mendoza in 1542–1543 made some 218 grants, a task made easier with population decline, when Spanish law governing abandoned property could be used.[72] The difficulties of devising a new land regime were compounded by the Crown's recognition of various claims under existing indigenous law. The official division of the population into two legal republics (in the Socratic sense of distinctly organized peoples) took the form of the República de los Españoles, which covered Europeans, and the República de los Indios, applied to indigenous people. Theoretically, two parallel societies existed, with their own laws and joined in the person of the monarch.[73] In reality, a uniform legal regime across Indo-Mexico never existed, unlike in most of Spain. The Spanish Crown's recognition of Indian law was a legal fiction in spite of similarities in customary law among ethnic groups. Complicating matters, Cortés had preempted the Crown by adapting both to the needs of the conquerors and what he perceived to be those of the Indians without consultation. The slowness of officials in Spain to respond encouraged illegal and unscrupulous means to resolve the property dilemma by whatever means Spanish setters could devise.[74]

Several categories of land existed in Indo-Mexico: land dedicated to support of the religious establishment (teotlalli); land for the support of community houses (barrio governance); land of paramount chiefs (thaloque); noble landholdings (tetecuhtin); and land communally controlled by the calpulli and worked in common (calpullalli).[75] Assignment of communal land conveyed only its beneficial use, although its use passed from one generation to the next. As has been discussed, movement toward private ownership was already far advanced, but it was moving in the direction of a feudal system that benefited the nobility but not the peasantry, a trajectory much the same as that discernable earlier in Europe. Land that had been assigned to the Indian priesthood and the chieftaincies could be distributed by right of conquest, as the successor regime wished; nevertheless, it was a limited amount. Consequently, opportunists appropriated property under various pretexts. Ambitious indigenous peasants, aware of the attempts by Indian villagers to claim communal land, responded by converting beneficial usage into property, while European competitors with claims of service during the conquest pressed for immediate distribution. Cortés, anxious to hold Spaniards in Mexico, issued mercedes (grants) that conveyed property in the guise of a reward, but with the intent of anchoring the recipient in a still unconsolidated conquest. Agricultural land held as communal property represented the bulk of centrally located fertile bottom land, legally an awkward problem for land-hungry settlers. The European concept of private property, rooted in Roman law, recognized the right to dispose or retain, implying the existence of a reasonably fluid market; such a market did not exist in Indo-Mexico.

The converting of communal land into private property involved Europeans, the indigenous nobility (tecuhtli), and opportunistic peasants (macehualtin) who asserted that customary use conferred ownership. Doubtful claims in the post-1521 confusion might be affirmed after several recorded transfers made titles virtually unassailable. Attempts by the indigenous nobility to appropriate communal land on the basis of gifts by the conquistadors and in some case *mercedes* granted by Cortés faced challenges in Spanish courts from the Indian peasants, who understood that politically the best legal code was that of the conqueror. Litigants personally presented their case in Nahuatl in the presence of a Nahualato, a translator, and a European judge who had little or no knowledge of preconquest legal practices. The resort to lawsuits by indigenous claimants under Spanish law soon got the attention of the Crown, perhaps worried that the royal administration might be vulnerable. The New Laws of 1542 instructed judges to shield Indians from the machinations of malicious lawyers, perhaps wishful thinking.[76]

The Dysfunctional Encomienda

The Spaniards did not destroy preconquest economic relationships that appeared to be useful. This was particularly evident as applied to labor, with useful aspects being selected out from a complex civic-institutional framework. The distorted indigenous labor regime became exploitive and devoid of any communal utility. Tribute, a concept well understood both in Spain and in Indo-America, provided a preliminary solution to the problem of labor. In contrast, land ownership relied on displacement by any means necessary, until the series of pandemics left abandoned land in their wake. The encomienda and the *repartimiento* (compulsory labor draft) demonstrated the difficulty of balancing European economic needs against indigenous socioeconomic damage. Maintaining quasi-preconquest institutions, such as the *coatequitl* (assigned labor for community projects), which was designed to add communal value such as the construction of dikes, but modifying it to obtain labor to the benefit of Spanish settlers, assured a degree of acceptance by the Indians but at the same time distorted the institution to the disadvantage of the indigenous peasantry. On the positive side, the Crown managed to end indigenous slavery in large part because of the alternative labor supply available in the form of the encomienda and the repartimiento.

The introduction in the New World of the encomienda, however, conflicted with the monarchy's intention to establish direct political control. As a semifeudal institution, it had become archaic in Spain. In New Spain, it came back to life. The encomienda system as it functioned in its new setting allocated a set number of heads of households (on average 6,000) to the holder. The actual amount of labor tribute was not clearly specified, an omission that encouraged unbridled exploitation. An encomienda in theory carried the obligation to Christianize (meaning Hispanicize) the tributaries, to protect them from illegal extractions as new waves of Europeans followed in the conquerors' footsteps, and to maintain a body of armed retainers that could be mobilized in case of Indian rebellion. The theory, again drawing on the Spanish experience when armed Moors were just to the south, was that encomenderos would rally to defend their landholdings and labor.[77] In New Spain, insecurity apparently did not rise to that level, with the one exception noted shortly, and few holders, if any, had a sufficient number of retainers to make a difference. The focus on profitable agricultural enterprises made it obvious that an encomienda was almost purely a labor arrangement. Although it carried social prestige for the holder as a royal grantee and receiver of tribute, the romantic notions of a band of frontier defenders never quite made it across the Atlantic. Had the system worked as envisioned, the encomenderos would have been a true frontier aristocracy.

Although tribute could be paid in kind or in money, labor provided the best return. Labor costs, perhaps with a few gifts or bribes to Indian officials and minimal provisions, were virtually nonexistent.[78] Access to low-cost labor made even marginal economic activities profitable. Free tribute labor at times involved supplying material inputs. In 1548, the Marquez del Valle (Cortés) ordered Coyoacan tributaries to build a residence for an Audiencia judge and supplied the seventeen beams for the initial structure, likely furnished by his tributaries. As economists are aware, any item subsidized by others is not rationally utilized. This likely was the case with much of tribute labor.[79]

Confusion, whether claimed or real, about who was subject to tribute led to illegal levies, abuse, and fraud. In some cases, encomenderos made nobles, exempt under indigenous rules, paid tribute. A constant struggle over the actual head count of a village or town, with the encomendero almost always claiming that the town should pay additional tribute and the town insisting that the population had decreased as people moved, fled, or died, became a contentious issue. Judicial authorities were obliged to conduct head counts in an effort to settle the matter. Both sides engaged in deceptive practices such as bringing in outsiders willing to claim residency or hiding people to demonstrate the opposite.[80] Tribute in kind or in labor and personal service was a major burden for the peasantry; beside the demands of encomenderos, the former indigenous nobility also collected tribute in the form of personal service and food, on the basis of preconquest customs. What labor gained in return is difficult to determine: perhaps some familiarity with European ways and techniques, use of the Spanish plow, and if Alonso de Zorita and others are to be believed, Spanish vices.[81] Only a relatively small number of Indians were exempt as a reward for special services during the conquest, such as Tlaxcalans and those who engaged in the construction of Mexico City on the ruins of Tenochtitlán; they remained exempt until 1564.

The Mixton Rebellion

The military usefulness of the encomienda was soon tested by the one serious indigenous rebellion, the Mixton War in 1541–1543.[82] The rebellion had several causes: indigenous reaction to the encomienda system; the disinterested administration of several governors who were more interested in exploring the northern territories; and the rejection of Christianity by Chichimeca tribes in the Tepeque and Zacatecas mountains, in spite of the best efforts of the Franciscan friars. The Chichimecas advocated a millennium version of Indo-Mexican religion that promised sensual pleasures and immortality.[83] Finally, the failure to understand the seriousness of the situation before it had gained momentum indicated an out-of-touch administration and a false sense of confidence in Spanish military superiority. Suddenly the revolt swept across the weakly held western fringe in the vicinity of the newly established settlement of Guadalajara.

It is worth going into some detail about this rebellion because it provided a notion of what might have happened in central Mexico but somewhat miraculously did not. What started out as an attempt to arrest a few disloyal Indians ended bloodily. Another attempt at pacification led to a four-hour battle that forced the Europeans and their Indian allies into a disorderly retreat to Guadalajara, rescuing Spaniards as they fled for their lives. A further escalation led to the assembly of fifty mounted soldiers along with foot soldiers, Indian allies, and most importantly artillery and firearms. The objective, a large rocky outcropping, the Peñol of Mixton, appeared vulnerable to a frontal assault, an almost fatal error as the force found itself attacked from both the front and the rear. It came close to a rout. The survivors struggled to return to the now doubtful safety of Guadalajara. Other Indians joined what appeared to be a successful revolt against the intruders. An alarmed Viceroy Mendoza sent reinforcements to several garrisons, deterring an immediate attack on Guadalajara, and succeeded in stabilizing the situation.

Pedro de Alvarado, recalled just as he was about to sail on a new voyage of discovery, berated those who advised caution and set out with 100 mounted men, 100 infantry, and 5,000 Indians, without waiting for aid from Mexico City. He confronted the enemy at the Peñol of Nochistlán and launched a frontal assault, only to be thrown back with heavy losses. Finally, a mismanaged infantry charge resulted in disaster, and the army broke and ran. Fortunately, those who had advised caution had followed Alvarado's force in anticipation of problems and rescued those they could reach. Alvarado had dismounted and fought on foot before attempting to make his escape on horseback, only to be thrown into a ravine with his horse on top of him. Carried back to Guadalajara on a litter, he died of his wounds.

The series of defeats emboldened others to drop any pretense of loyalty to the Europeans. Indications that some Indian groups in Michoacán and near Mexico City were considering their options must have been alarming. Viceroy Mendoza, fully aware of what he faced, called on the encomenderos and gathered a force of 30,000 indigenous soldiers mainly from Texcoco and Tlaxcala and personally took command.[84] A desperate viceroy authorized the use of horses and firearms by Indian warriors, who up to that time had not been allowed to have access to these weapons of war. Not given to bravado, the viceroy gathered a large stock of ammunition and cannon and proceeded to attack the fringes before moving to the center of the revolt, beginning with the Peñol of Nochistlán, where Alvarado had been routed. A battle ensued that lasted eight hours but failed to penetrate the defenses. Consequently, the viceroy cut off the water supply and laid siege to the fortress, using artillery to reduce its defenses. Indian prisoners were executed or enslaved. The next objective, the Peñol of Mixton, lay at the center of the revolt. After three weeks under siege, some surrounding villagers defected to the Spaniards as artillery pounded the defenders. Deserters revealed a secret approach that made victory possible but not easy. The seizure of Ahuacatlán officially ended the uprising; had the revolt spread into central Mexico, it could well have destroyed the still weak Euro-Indo protostate.[85] The revolt made the point that in some cases indigenous loyalties to Christianity and to the Spanish state were pragmatic decisions in the face of power based on force.

Slowly Killing the Encomienda

For the European settlers, labor was more important than land, an acknowledgment of the frontier nature of the conquest. Several conflicting labor models came in contact after the conquest. Those who were able to demonstrate service sufficient to warrant an encomienda grant as well as land and who were able to maintain an armed reserve force in case of an Indian rebellion perceived their role to be that of natural nobility. As estate owners, they managed but did not work in the fields or directly supervise workers. Their social status as well as wealth depended on the distribution of Indians' labor in the form of tribute, as befitting the encomenderos' warrior status. Most Spaniards did not fall into this privileged category, functioning as farmers or herdsmen with a few indigenous laborers at times of peak necessity or as mine supervisors and tradesmen and subsequently as merchants.

Royal officials, well aware that the Laws of Burgos that had proved so disastrous in the Antilles could not be applied in Indio-Mexico, nevertheless understood the need for mandatory labor in the absence of a floating pool of wage labor. Consequently, the showdown between Spanish settlers and the Crown over the encomienda was deferred for an entire generation (twenty-nine years) before the Crown felt that it must act. Clerical opponents of the encomienda system, including Bartolomé de las Casas, successfully pressed the moral issue, providing a short-lived victory for the system's passionate critics. The unwillingness of Emperor Carlos V to address the issue indicated continued uncertainty over Spain's legal claim to proprietary rights in the New World and the emperor's pragmatism in allowing a lightly regulated encomienda to continue. The long delay in directly confronting the issue made the task much more difficult and politically dangerous. A worldview based on semifeudal privileges could not be easily displaced.[86]

The encomenderos and their descendants saw themselves as lords of the land, a political and socioeconomic position they believed to have been validated by the conquest. They were aware of the Crown's ambivalence concerning the encomienda but believed that their productive economic role directing Indians made them indispensable, a notion reinforced in 1536 when the Crown by the Law of Succession confirmed possession of an encomienda grants for two generations.[87] Subsequently, they were shocked when the encomienda came under an aggressive attack with the full support of the monarch. It became evident that Las Casas and those who opposed the encomienda system controlled the rhetorical environment that pushed Carlos V to react and overreach.

Las Casas focused on the political danger posed by New World *gran señores* while suggesting that if the emperor reacted positively to the needs of the natives of the land, the indigenous population would become loyal vassals; the implication that the Crown could not trust the encomenderos could not be missed and played to Carlos V's political insecurities. At a higher level, Las Casas noted that the real victims were Christianity and political legitimacy. Nevertheless, Las Casas proposed to make Spain's claims to sovereignty morally unassailable and consequently unquestionably legitimate. One can understand Carlos V's misreading of the situation, convinced that he could have a moral and political triumph. The Mixton War (1541–1543) demonstrated that the Crown perceived that dependence on self-directed individuals had come to an abrupt end. Pedro de Alvarado's arrogance, ill-fated bravado, and ignominious death symbolized the end of an era. Viceroy Antonio Mendoza dealt with the rebellion in an organized, deliberate fashion that demonstrated effective royal administration.

The New Laws of 1542, issued in Barcelona with subsequent additions in 1543, constituted a drastic change in both tone and policy. The turn toward regulation by the Crown indicated a much more confident monarchy that was no longer awed by those who had brought transoceanic kingdoms under the Spanish Crown; nevertheless, it turned out to be premature. The opening statement spoke of good intentions delayed but obstacles now put aside, allowing the monarch to devote full attention to New World affairs. He did so after convening a conference with representatives drawn from all ranks and many professions, religious and civil, suggesting that the New Laws had the same high political legitimacy as a matter decided by the Cortes. Clearly, the intent was to demonstrate that the emperor, fully informed and advised, now acted. In order to ensure that *los naturales* understood that the laws favored them, officials were ordered to reproduce copies of the New Laws in block letters and to distribute them across the Indies, with copies directed to clerics, who could then translate them into indigenous languages. In a pro forma first paragraph, the Audiencia was reminded of its judicial responsibility to protect the Indians and to punish those who were guilty of maltreatment. The Audiencia was to take into account indigenous law where possible and to prevent long, drawn-out suits by lawyers and render decisions promptly and summarily. From that point on, rhetorical niceties were dropped, and straightforward commands were issued without ambiguity. Indian slavery was prohibited for any reason including war, rebellion, and rescue from a potentially fatal situation (cannibalism), on the basis of the fact that Indians were subjects of the king on the same level as Spaniards.[88] The law ordered the release of all those who were currently held in unjust bondage, even if their owner produced a title. The Crown ordered judicial officials to take the initiative to investigate and summarily set individuals at liberty; a presumption of unjust captivity in all instances is evident.

Of most importance, the decree prohibited future grants of tributary Indians, and on the death of an incumbent holder, the grant would revert to the Crown. That old age had overtaken many of the original conquistadors meant that perhaps very soon their wives and children would be disinherited. The Crown ordered that some support for widows and children be provided from royal funds. The New Laws did not confiscate land but altered the labor market by eliminating involuntary work. The New Laws represented an attempt to bring the New World's land and labor regime into conformity with that of Spain. As a sop to the disinherited, they were to receive preference for positions within the Crown bureaucracy. New discoveries by sea required a permit from the Audiencia, which would set the terms. No Indians could be transported from new discoveries, and the governorship did not automatically fall to the expedition leader. A report on the new territory with an estimate of how much tribute the Crown could expect indicated that an incorporation procedure had evolved that subordinated the discoverer almost at the moment he sailed. In short, there were not going to be any more adventurers such as Cortés and Francisco Pizarro. Viceroy Mendoza, well aware of possible hostile reactions, used viceregal discretion to withhold publishing the New Laws.[89] His judgment proved correct, although the news spread throughout New Spain.

In the opinion of many settlers, Indian laborers worked only when coerced; consequently, those who were using workers could be subject to claims of mistreatment and lawsuits. The indigenous population had already taken to litigation and could rely on clerical support. Without tribute labor, particularly at harvest time or other peak periods, settlers insisted that they could not survive. Their profit margins, considering previously minimal labor costs, may have been another consideration. Whatever the actual reality, those who were dependent on tribute labor reacted hysterically to the New Laws, claiming that the Europeans would abandon the New World, return to Spain, and leave the land to revert to its pre-Spanish pagan state, suggesting an economic defeat as well as a reversal of Christian progress.

While the larger-than-life presence of Las Casas at the emperor's court carried the day, the battle could not be won outright. Many high officials including the president of the Council of the Indies, the Dominican cardinal García Loaysa, the bishops of Toledo and Seville, and a long list of others had reservation about the New Laws. The Franciscan friar Motolinía, one of the original missionaries, accused Las Casas of hypocrisy and exaggeration. Even Archbishop Juan de Zumárraga, who supported Las Casas on most moral issues, counseled the continuation of the encomienda. The archbishop, untroubled by possible moral contradictions, owned slaves and held an encomienda.[90] Many of Las Casas's opponents had no quarrel with his moral position but feared a political backlash that would sweep away all advances.

Las Casas, faced with ambivalent opponents, focused on moral issues as a way to goad the monarch into political action.[91] Carlos V proceeded, convinced that moral failures verged on undermining legitimacy and ignoring cautious advisers who were worried about the dangers of moving too fast.[92] The emperor overestimated his power to achieve voluntary obedience as well as the ability of royal officials to enforce compliance. The nearly rebellious reaction in Mexico and the full-scale rebellion in Peru shocked the royal bureaucracy and the monarch. In Peru, the hapless Viceroy Blasco Núñez Vela was defeated in battle, was beheaded, and had twine threaded through his lips, to be displayed as a macabre trophy. The beheading of a viceroy and talk of Gonzalo Pizarro marrying an Inca princess to establish the legitimacy of an independent Peruvian monarchy caused panic. The possibility of separate New World monarchies spoke once again to Spanish uncertainty about the legality of brushing aside the natural indigenous lords of the land.

The Duke of Alba and other close advisers of the monarch pressed for immediate revocation of Article 35, which ended the encomienda. The *comendador* of Castile raised the possibility of having to reconquer the Indies once again or to accept its loss, this time to rebellious Spaniards. The provincials of the major orders in New Spain, including the Dominican provincial friar Domingo de la Cruz, recommended perpetuity of tenure. The members of the municipality of the Mexico City also supported heredity grants. The emperor had little choice but to revoke Article 35 (1545), but that would not be enough, as it became evident that other articles could not be accepted, including the loss of an encomienda for abusing tributaries.[93]

The monarch and royal officials must have been displeased to learn that Mexico City set aside a day around Christmas as a holiday to celebrate the victory over Carlos V, with a bull fight and a decidedly European medieval pageant with courtly dances and 100 knights dressed in orange, blue, and white—all introduced with trumpet fanfares. Of course, Mexico City's municipal council carefully clothed their holiday proclamation with the customary formalities of obedience to their sovereign.[94] A disillusioned Las Casas, near the end of his life, complained in 1563 that Satan had invented laws to obscure evils that continued unrestrained.[95] Forcing the Crown to reverse an unpopular decision did not fully restore confidence in Madrid.

Economic and political reality prevailed between 1549 and 1550. In 1549, the Crown ruled that encomenderos could no longer govern the labor of their tributaries, although they could continue to receive tribute. The next step, specifying the amount of tribute owed, was taken in the 1550s: once a reasonable amount had been determined, both parties signed a legal agreement. Any violation could be taken to court. A Crown inspector, Diego Ramírez, in the early 1550s, reduced tribute and lodged charges against abusive offenders. Instances of forcing encomenderos to return tribute and arresting those charged with abuses had some impact. The affordability of labor posed another problem.

Encomendero resentment boiled over in 1563 when Hernán Cortés's son Martín arrived in Mexico. A conspiracy to place Martín on an independent throne resulted in arrests and the execution of two of the ringleaders. In the aftermath, Martín Cortés was returned to Spain. The growing number of Spanish farmers who resented the labor privileges of the encomenderos eventually created a different political dynamic. In the end, encomenderos retained some social prestige and large landholding—the origins of the hacienda. A mixed labor model, with Spanish farmers and herders who worked the land side by side with indigenous labor or African slaves, eventually emerged.

A transition to wage labor was inevitable as New Spain's economy expanded and the population dropped. In addition, urban growth had begun to pressure food supplies and prices. Silver mining, a priority of the Crown, employed a large labor force. Working conditions were difficult and, unlike agriculture, required year-round work. Miners, as an occupational group, were detached from village life and were natural urban dwellers. While the mining industry could afford high inputs, others could not. Continued doubts about the willingness of indigenous labor to hire out in the absence of coercion justified a compromise of sorts. Theoretically able to demand higher wages, scarce labor was subject to artificial wage manipulation with the creation of a revolving pool of mandatory but paid labor. The repartimiento, a system with Indo-Mexican antecedents, although modified, provided labor but paid at a rate set by the vice-regal government for unskilled labor, a category that applied to all agricultural workers. Wages were deducted for administrative expenses, likely another source of abuse. Individuals who were subject to repartimiento labor were divided into alternating groups to work for pay one week, followed by several weeks in between with no labor. Those who found such work onerous drifted away into the cities.

Not surprisingly, forced labor became less effective after the population decline of the late 1540s, further negatively impacted by the epidemic of the middle 1570s. The shortage of labor resulted in expanding the number of people subject to the labor draft, even drawing in Indian officials, further reducing the prestige of indigenous administrators. Technological advances made a rotating, unwilling labor force less practical. The trend to irrigated wheat cultivation required more labor and skills than a revolving pool of workers could reliably supply. Consequently, wheat farmers hired resident employees *(gañanes)* as a core workforce long before the end of the repartimiento. Less obvious technical advances in animal husbandry and in other activities including mining required resident labor for the same reasons.

Ironically, as compulsory labor declined, abuse of workers became rampant, perhaps in an effort to squeeze the last drops from a dying institution.[96] Vice-regal officials, *visitadores*, and clerics, well aware of the repartimiento's drawbacks and negative impact on Indian towns and villages, communicated their concerns to the Council of the Indies. Consequently, a decree issued by Felipe III (1601) attempted to end such labor; it abolished the use of repartimiento in all rural and urban activities with the exception of mining.[97] The decree allowed Indians to choose employers, a major step toward a free labor market. Unfortunately, the 1601 enactment proved premature and failed in the face of opposition, and in 1609, the prior procedures were reinstated. Finally, in 1633, the Crown ended the repartimiento, leaving judicial slavery for debt, common throughout Europe at the time, and the labor of convicts as the only legal forms of coerced labor. Such hapless individuals would have a place in wool workshops *(obrajes)*. Nevertheless, the repartimiento, while no longer legal, continued to function as customary law in isolated regions.

The perceived need to have directive control over permanent labor slowly changed the model to gañanes on large haciendas, augmented by sharecroppers and, if needed, hired day labor from nearby villages, a model that combined paternalism, profits, and for resident labor, a degree of social stability. The question of whether debt played a role in holding labor on haciendas has yet to be definitely decided, but the tentative answer would be no. The hacienda represented a rational form of large-scale exploitation of land: a prototype of the farm factory.[98] The charge against the hacienda that it absorbed Indian land during waves of pandemics appears to be valid, following Spanish law governing abandoned land.

The New Economy

Primitive economies develop naturally, slowly becoming more complex as people's needs and tastes widen. Intergroup trade accelerates economic growth and necessarily has a political component that seeks to direct consumption and to control supply in various ways. Indo-Mexico's economy had advanced far beyond the simple seizure of goods, but more as capital accumulation than commercial exchange. Voluntary trade avoided resource destruction and delivered a predicable supply. The workings of the preconquest economy depended on fixed assets that were only beginning to become more fluid, as land accumulation by the nobility suggests. The new Spanish arrivals equated land and property in general with wealth and could not accept a static situation. The collapse of Indo-Mexico's political system set off an economic struggle that resulted in a Europeanized economy that met transatlantic demand.

Both Indians and Spaniards sought land ownership under the laws of the successor state.[99] Indians could choose to direct their petition to indigenous courts that continued to function in the early colonial period, but most understood that the new rulers had the final decision. The advantages offered by Spanish law made a European court a logical choice, a preference that further delegitimized indigenous officials. Outright purchase of land in the initial organizing period could not meet demand; only after the epidemics of the 1540s did substantial abandoned land become available in the central basin. Renting land and then claiming that rent payments constituted purchase installments at times might work, but Indians did not hesitate to go to court. Pre-European law survived in the form of traditional customary practices at the village level and at times proved useful for Indians claiming historical rights to property. Shady practices and sales of land belonging to other villages by Indians preying on rival groups and eager Spanish buyers occurred. Sorting out legal transfers from the fraudulent ones was difficult. Forged documents, even painted codices alleged to date back to pre-Spanish times, might be presented as proof of ownership.

Fluid circulation of property could not be expected in Mexico, in part because of the strong attachment to a particular piece of land that appeared to embody the tribal spirit of a village. The initial reorganization after 1521, when the victors divided the spoils including available land, was soon over. Demand, however, was not static as the Europeans inserted themselves into the agriculture economy. Pastoral activities placed increased demands on land except in the depopulated Gulf Coast. Nevertheless, the impact of epidemics increased land availability. By 1620, some one-third of the land in the Valley of Mexico was held by people of European descent.[100]

Indo-Mexico prior to 1521 had many economic aspects similar to those existing in Euro-Asia and had demonstrated evolutionary adaptations along the lines of those in Europe, a process accelerated by Cortés's arrival. Nevertheless, restructuring the economy required a number of fundamental steps. Feathers and wild animal skins, both in high demand prior to 1521, ceased to have much value domestically or internationally. Those who were employed in supplying and reworking items that were no longer valued faced redundancy, and trade routes based on cultural economic demands were rerouted or abandoned. Foodstuffs, traditional clothing, copper, silver, dyes, and other trade or tribute goods continued to have a market and in the case of silver heightened demand. Economic and sociopolitical disruption caused by the changeover did not last long; the pochteca lost their monopoly on high-value trade, perhaps compensated for by the ability to trade freely without permission of the paramount chief. Moreover, they were able to flaunt their success.[101] Small-time traders entered commerce at will with the lifting of previous restrictions. Indigenous nobles likely continued to have a hand in interregional trade. Improved security reduced risks and costs. Status based on occupation was in a state of flux also.

Two distinct economies emerged, one based on European demand for silver and gold and some commodities and a domestic economy concerned with foodstuffs, traditional items, trade goods from Europe, and after 1565, silks and exotica from China via Manila. The transformative trade in new grains, an array of newly introduced animals and their meats, fibers and hides, such as horses, sheep, hogs, poultry, seeds, plants and more transformed the economy of the region known as New Spain.[102] The tribute in goods, the foundation of the Indo-Mexican economy prior to the arrival of the Europeans, still played a role in the early colonial period, but other consumers of tribute, including encomenderos and the state, preferred payment in labor and later in coin. What occurred was a quantitative expansion of items that entered the domestic market and fueled internal commerce. The transformation of the internal economy was one of the world's most rapid.

Large, centralized markets able to dispose of unwanted tribute surpluses were no longer necessary. Currency and credit also reduced costs, but not the value of trade; only one end of the exchange might be in material goods, in return for coin or credit. Transportation costs fell, especially once horses, mules, and oxen replaced porters and a road system developed. All of these changes made the restoration of the great Tlatelolco market unnecessary, while smaller regional markets flourished and took on political importance, a trend evident even before the conquest. The domestic market network became more geographically diverse than during the Aztec imperial administration. Smaller traveling markets functioned in certain locations on a fixed schedule, complemented by larger regional centers. Control of local markets, other than those in Mexico City, remained with Indian officials, while the larger ones were subject to interference by officials worried about price spikes, adequate supplies of staples, and food riots. A series of state warehouses dealt with the threat of potential food shortages.

The introduction of money and the establishment of a mint in 1535 may have had more to do with the transatlantic market, which, in part because of the high cost of transportation, required a shift to high-value items, particularly silver, to meet demands originating many thousands of miles away.[103] The use of coin initially met the needs of the newly established trade with Europe and then spread to the domestic economy in concentric rings around the Mexico City mint and into areas attuned to exports.

The domestic markets functioned as mixed ones of barter and currency in the form of cacao beans and coin.[104] Supplies of coin were inadequate initially, until the mint caught up with demand. Counterfeit coins circulated within two years of the founding of the mint, attesting to the general acceptance of Spanish currency. Copper coins, pegged to the value of cacao and other traditional items used to establish value, gained acceptance with minimal difficulty—not surprising, given how close to a monetary system pre-Spanish Indo-Mexico had come. The exchange rate of cacao beans to coin was 80–100 beans to one Spanish *real,* 640–800 to one *peso de oro común,* and so forth. A preference for cacao beans and low-value coins acted to control price inflation, met the need to store value, and enabled consumers to determine the market value of items offered.[105] Mixed barter, coins, and cacao currency continued to be used into the nineteenth century.

Transatlantic trade was much more controlled and complex. Spain, aware of the attraction of precious metals and the dangers posed by other European powers to its commerce with the New World, established a closed, controlled colonial system. The decision to do so was made with the relatively primitive island populations in mind and well before Indo-Mexico became a consideration. For Spain to secure its permanent possession, establishment of settlements along with the development of an economy, beyond gold washings, with commercial ties to Spain was necessary. The Casa de Contratación (Board of Trade), established in 1503, was charged with the task of encouraging trade as well as regulating it within the closed system. Its members, with direct access to the king, initially functioned more as advisers than as bureaucrats.

Merging the indigenous domestic economy of Indo-Mexico with the transatlantic economy proved more difficult. In the initial period, the importation of animals, seeds, Spanish plows and other agricultural implements, clothes, swords, and other items of European manufacture suggested the possibility of a reasonably healthy two-way trade. In the long run, the balance of trade favored New Spain. Most of the items offered by Spain, with the exception of luxury goods, could be copied and manufactured by Mexican craftsmen or, in the case of textiles, produced by traditional weavers. Wine, in limited demand by Spanish settlers, was too expensive; the traditional beverage pulque was affordable, and alcohol could be made from a number of readily available products, including sugar cane. Forced consumption by rural Indians, pressed on them by officials in league with small-time traders through the *repartimiento de comercio,* returned a minor living for both the principals but not much more. The distribution of goods included animals, not necessarily imported goods. Officials also engaged in legitimate trade using their position and status, perhaps with the collusion of Indian caciques (chiefs) to arrange profitable deals.

A network of small traders, including Indians, blacks, priests, Spanish farmers, officials, and others, serviced the countryside. The indigenous population, accustomed to trade and involved in home production of everyday items such as cotton clothing, pots, storage baskets, small devotional objects, and food, made for informed customers who were well aware of value and demand. They did not hesitate to complain to royal officials if it appeared to be to their advantage. To what extent Indians played the system is difficult to determine, but that they did is not contested. Local merchants dealt in retail trade but also bought and sold in large scale wool, hides, and other local commodities as well as animals of all sorts. The line between wholesale and retail was never a rigid one at any level; what mattered was profit. At the very bottom, traveling peddlers met individual consumers' personal needs in outlying haciendas, isolated villages, and tiny settlements. The entire complex commercial system relied on credit, although the amount and terms varied as one moved down the socioeconomic scale. Debt acted to mitigate competition but did not eliminate it.

The domestic economy relied on silver mining as the basic economic engine. A labor-intensive industry, mining paid high wages that had some impact on compensation levels. Part of workers' earning came in the form a self-collected share of the ore and consequently was well concealed from taxes, but it had local impact because the mine workers bought goods nearby. The industry, concentrated in the arid north, needed supplies of all sorts, from lumber to draft animals to food for animals and humans to clothing and much more. Mining camps functioned as temporary cities with demand for services as well as goods.

Other than precious metals, only a limited number of exports justified transatlantic transportation costs. In the latter half of the sixteenth century, with the discovery of productive silver veins, exports of precious metals rose rapidly. Mining remained the major driver of the colonial economy until the end of century, but as production slowed the bottom fell out in 1630: the number of shipments to Europe thirty years later in 1660 amounted to 10 percent of that of 1591; the exhaustion of easy-to-find surface veins was the likely cause.[106] In the eighteenth century, new technology—more expensive but able to penetrate deeply into silver veins—extracted silver ore at earlier high levels. Nevertheless, administrative cost and transportation expenses, including warships to protect the silver fleet, ate into the amount that ended up in the king's treasury.

Of more consequence for transatlantic trade, Spain became progressively impoverished by war and, as a result of overgrazing, soil exhaustion and erosion. Food shortages, malnutrition, and starvation became chronic problems, accompanied by demographic decline. Wheat yields fell, crops failed, and replacement supplies could not be easily found. Epidemics also took a toll, and food riots threatened political stability. To make matters worse, Spain invested the silver and gold extracted from the empire in unproductive ways.

Mexicans found uses for their own capital. Large merchant houses soon emerged as wholesalers. With capital at their disposal, they bought Spanish merchandise at the Jalapa trade fair when the once-a-year convoy arrived and then sold it at steadily rising prices until the next fleet arrived. In reality, the houses functioned as speculators, usually successfully. These merchants, the *almaceneros* (warehousemen), extended credit to regional distributors *(aviadores)*, who in turn sold items in the regional markets. Attempts by Crown officials to limit intracolonial trade failed. Ignoring restrictions and illegal trading with foreign ships reflected the reality that Spain's economy could not sustain a healthy two-way transatlantic trade.

Mexico City, the home of the almaceneros, became what Cádiz-Seville had hoped to be: the center of a Hispano-Indo-Mexican trading network. In reality, the two economies were not complementary; the ties that bound the two together were political and cultural (religion, language) more than economic.[107]

Animal husbandry benefited from depopulation. When the Spaniards stepped off the ship in 1519, their animals did so also. Horses, cattle, hogs, goats, sheep, and chickens followed almost immediately. In the central valleys, mixed animal husbandry along with crops led to disputes over crop damage; sheep and goats in particular were a problem because they cropped very close to the ground, denuding the land and causing erosion. Both Indians and Europeans engaged in animal husbandry; Indians in general did so communally and maintained small flocks. Operating a Spanish livestock *estancia* (ranch) required less labor than did crops and consequently attracted Spaniards who were concerned about the availability of Indian labor. Large animals increased the population's protein intake, but hides offered the most profit. Herds multiplied rapidly on native grasses, until these were inevitably replaced by European grasses that were carried in the digestive track of freshly introduced animals. Open-range herding was not suitable in agricultural regions. Spanish law allowed the grazing of animals on land after the harvest, but with year-round cultivation possible at lower elevations, the practice was destructive.[108] Regulations specified separation of animals from crops; however, enforcement tended to be after the fact if at all. Nevertheless, only a few locations in the central basin, in Toluca and Puebla, engaged in cattle herding.

A true cattle-ranching economy developed along the Gulf Coast. The indigenous Huastecas, defeated in the 1450s by Moctezuma I, were tributaries of the Aztecs. Prior to 1519, the entire region supported a relatively small population of some one million inhabitants, which stabilized at 12,000 after the epidemics had run their course (1532). African slaves, familiar with animal husbandry, provided the industry's workforce. Cattle, adapted by Andalucían settlers to the conditions in the Antilles and subsequently introduced into the Gulf Coast north of Veracruz, laid the foundation of a Mexican ranching economy. The skills transferred from the Antilles to the Huastecas represented one of the first of a number of multicultural hybridizations that occurred after 1521. The cattle industry eventually reached as far north as Tampico and inland to the foothills. Plentiful rainfall—some sixty inches annually—tapering off to the north and coastal swamps made for almost ideal conditions for cattle. The absence of a large resident population and limited crop cultivation allowed for open-range herding of domesticated and wild-range cattle. Horses raised in the Pánuco River delta supplied the cattle industry and the demand for horses across New Spain.[109] Hides shipped to Seville provided reasonable returns.

Self-regulation of the livestock industry by *estancieros* followed the practices in Castile and Andalucía, of regional and local (municipal) *Mestas*. A Mesta was formed in central Mexico in 1529. Their numbers increased along with the spread of cattle across New Spain. By 1563, the province of Michoacán in the southwest had a Mesta, as did most parts of New Spain. The Mexican organizations differed from the Spanish model, which functioned as a sheepherders association with the right to cross and graze on private land after the harvest as the animals moved from winter to summer pastures—a movement unnecessary in Mexico. In New Spain after 1574, Mesta members had to own private rangeland.[110]

The Imperial Political Pyramid

The Spanish monarchy had not envisioned a vast and distant new addition to what had up to 1519 been an assortment of island possessions. Even the larger islands such as Hispaniola and Cuba, with relatively sparse and primitive tribal populations, seemed manageable with little direct intervention by the Crown other than to respond to clerical critics and to rebuke overeager settlers for mistreatment of labor while at the same time encouraging gold washings. The philosophical issues could be resolved if necessary by handing the matter over to the *letrados* to debate.

The discovery of a vast mainland with millions of advanced civilized inhabitants and obvious wealth changed everything. The Crown could not avoid becoming deeply and directly involved. The monarchy, while encouraging the exploitation of silver and the religious conversion effort, understood the importance of extending Spain's political control in Indo-Mexico. That the kingdom of Castile, and not the other kingdoms that functioned separately in Spain, claimed sovereignty in the New World meant that Castile had a free hand to organize the political structure in the New World. Castile did not exclude migration from other Spanish kingdoms; consequently, from a sociocultural standpoint, a fusion of Iberian regional cultures occurred to a far greater degree in the New Word empire than in Spain.

Nevertheless, it was not the same monarchy as in 1492. With Juana la Loca's death, the Crown passed to a new dynasty in 1518, that of the Austrian Hapsburgs. Carlos I became the Holy Roman Emperor Carlos V the following year. Carlos V brought together a complex and diverse empire, each separate part of which had a distinct relationship with the ruler. In the Iberian kingdoms, his authority and hence power was institutionally restricted.

Internally, municipal governments functioned with distinct privileges and customs that were difficult to override. Queen Isabel previously established a measure of control with the appointment of a corregidor to head some municipal councils. In addition, self-governing corporations, from the Mesta (sheepherders) to the Consulado de

Comercio (large-scale merchant guilds), and lay religious organizations collectively constituted an influential political constituency.

These institutions and associations did not suddenly appear in New Spain, but with migration, some but not all slowly took root in the new frontier and eventually became a colonial political constituency with its own interests. The notable institutional exception in Indo-America was the absence of a Cortes, the consultative, quasi-legislative, and representative body that had to be called when the monarch needed revenues. The well-developed notion of popular sovereignty remained grounded in the municipality.

The municipal council served as a buffer between the vice-regal level and the population, maintaining sociopolitical stability. The initial territorial organization of New Spain relied on a modified Spanish organizational template inherited from Rome, not all that different from the pre-Spanish center-tributary network. Roman notions provided for provinces and a hierarchy of urban settlements in a descending chain of authority. Cities at the apex exercised authority over towns that in turn directed *villas* (small cities) that controlled subordinate villages *(pueblos),* and so on down to small places *(lugares).* Coupled with this structure, a designated urban center served as the administrative center *(cabecera).* Theoretically, instructions from the political top could be filtered down to the lowest levels, along with the responsibility for implementation. Hernán Cortés issued detailed instructions (August 5, 1519), just months following the collapse of Tenochtitlán, for the proper functioning of settlements that set the number of municipal officials who were to be named each year on the Day of the Circumcision of Jesus (January 1). Municipal officials who were responsible for assuring that weights and measures were correct, that butchers and fish sellers provided good products, that hours of commerce were appropriate, and more left little to local preference. Perhaps of more immediate utility, Cortés ordered that all settlers keep a lance, sword, and other weapons ready and be alert for trouble. Much of what he detailed would seem to be obvious and may have been issued to demonstrate his hands-on authority and ability to rule.[111]

Cities functioned as subterritorial units until the border of one municipality touched an adjoining one. Only major cities had municipal councils *(ayuntamientos)* recognized by the Crown. When the system was applied in Mexico over the course of the reorganizational period, planners struggled with Indo-Mexican complexity. The affected population rejected any perceived change in directive authority.[112] All three members of the defunct triple alliance protested the loss of their authority, insisting that only three cabaceras (head towns) existed prior to the conquest; lawyers pursued the matter with the Council of the Indies in Spain. Mexico-Tenochtitlán was designated a city in 1543, along with Texcoco. Eventually, Xochimilco and Tacuba achieved city status. On a practical level, Castile did not dislodge indigenous town governments, which continued to function, albeit aware of the broad requirements of the new overlords. As in Spain and previously under the indigenous calpulli, the municipal level interacted with the everyday life of the population. In Mexico City, two Indian *cabildos* (municipal councils) exercised authority along with a separate European council.[113] Lower-level authorities, directed by the municipality, carried out the basic functions of maintaining civic order, supporting local trade, assuring the supply of basic foodstuffs, providing common infrastructure, organizing celebrations, and regulating markets. While the institutional forms appeared to mirror those of Spain, they functioned differently in the Indo-American setting by imperial design.

Emperor Carlos V had faced the Revolt of the Comuneros, as discussed earlier. Consequently, he had no intention of re-creating troublesome institutions in New Spain, particularly the Cortes, which had caused him so much grief. He reestablished the Audiencia of Santo Domingo (a high court) in 1526, presided over by a governor with Crown-appointed judges; it seemed to work well enough in the islands. In Indo-Mexico, a much more complex situation, government by the Audiencia did not work as well. The second Audiencia of Mexico (1527) performed reasonably well; nevertheless, government by committee did not command sufficient respect from both Europeans and Indians accustomed to kings and paramount chiefs. The need for a strong and well-respected figure with a direct connection with the king and able to deal with the confusion of the early organizational period became apparent. The Council of the Indies turned to the organizational model of the kingdom of Naples, first employed by Aragón to manage its Mediterranean empire. Subsequently, in 1535, the Crown elevated Indo-Mexico to the status of a separate Kingdom of New Spain, one of many kingdoms under the emperor. As a kingdom, New Spain was entitled to the presence of the king or, in his absence, a viceroy. The rush to organize politically was in part to address the question of the Crown's right to exercise authority over the indigenous population and to bring the European settlers into a modified political system.

In reality, New Spain remained a frontier kingdom. Nevertheless, it had already developed a hybrid worldview, one that borrowed from the European experience but with indigenous modifications that fit their needs. To delay the imposition of Spanish governing institutions risked the creation of ad hoc frontier institutions. Moreover, the predatory conduct of Spanish settlers posed an immediate and pressing problem that might well lead to a rebellion. The need to fashion a reasonable balance between the needs of the settlers, of the Indians, and of the Crown was obvious.[114] Moreover, by extending protective institutions to the indigenous populations the monarchy created a counterbalance to the European settlers.

Antonio Mendoza, the first viceroy (1535–1550) dispatched to the New World, entered the former Tenochtitlán, now Mexico City, the capital of the Kingdom of New Spain, representing the monarch in his very person. Many settlers and natives might have preferred Cortés. Viceroy Mendoza, a member of Castilian high nobility, exercised the king's authority, subject to the king's pleasure and review at the end of his rule. Mendoza's family was one of the most important and active in Spanish politics and high society. As a young boy, Mendoza grew up in Granada, where his father served as the first Christian governor. His mother biologically represented all stages of Reconquista history with her mixture of Old Christian, Moorish, and Jewish blood; she was protected from intolerance by high status. As governor of Granada, Antonio's father on occasion wore Moorish dress, ate Middle Eastern food, and favored Arabic décor.[115] Not surprisingly, Antonio reflected his cosmopolitan upbringing and inherited a sense of command and gravitas necessary to overawe both the Spaniards and the indigenous population. In accepting the post, he relinquished a degree of political protection afforded by his high status. After the conclusion of the Mixton War, he was subject to investigation by a Crown-appointed visitador general de la Nueva España, Francisco Tello de Sandoval (1544), who had full powers to conduct a review. He did so in a hostile and unfair manner that forced the viceroy to spend time and money to clear his reputation.[116]

As viceroy, all the formalities expected by a monarch were rendered to Mendoza as the king's representative. The viceroy maintained a palace court with much of the ritual of an actual king. He demonstrated royal benevolence. Viceroy Mendoza patronized Mestizo schools and even confirmed their inheritances. He supported the Colegio de San Juan de Letrán, charged with teaching Mestizo boys a trade as well as being an asylum for Mestizo girls.[117]

Viceroy Mendoza worked with an array of institutions, each with a degree of traditional authority. The vice-regal executive level encompassed Crown appointees from a viceroy down to the Audiencia to alcalde mayores and corregidores on the secular side and, on the clerical side, archbishops and bishops. Viceroy Mendoza served as president of the Audiencia and vice patron of the church. Mendoza in most respects set the ideal model for subsequent viceroys.

All secular appointees had judicial responsibility, reflecting the monarch's primary responsibility to administer justice. The high clergy disciplined the lower clergy and served as replacements in case of an unexpected vice-regal vacancy. A special Crown judge *(juez de residencia)* with investigative authority conducted a review of a viceroy's conduct in office and reviewed accounts. Others, appointed to undertake a special task—such as Alonso de Zorita, who left an important account of his findings—were charged by an ever-cash-strapped monarchy to determine who should pay tribute. Audiencia judges also made inspection tours of the viceroyalty. New Spain functioned differently from the organization model of Spain; however, the quasi-democratic traditions established in Spain were not forgotten at the municipal level.

Earlier, Mexico City's municipal council requested that it be allowed to vote first in any meeting of municipalities, in effect as a Cortes. Carlos V responded positively but with the proviso that he did not intend it to meet as a group without royal supervision and control—in essence, an empty honor.[118] The emperor ignored the importance of a Cortes to vet reforms in advance of implementation. The municipal council of Mexico City, in the absence of a Cortes, assumed the oppositional philosophical responsibilities of that body. The city's accrued prestige as the former Tenochtitlán and then the capital of the viceroyalty allowed the council to act as a quasi-Cortes, although with a little more respect for Crown sensibilities.

The monarch acted as a judicial arbitrator willing to intervene if the balance between the settlers and the Indians became too injurious to his indigenous subjects or threatened to become politically disruptive. Royal officials did not move as fast as they should have in all cases, in part because of fear of resistance from Spanish settlers and the need to refer matters to Spain for consideration or perhaps even to a commission of university legal experts. In the initial establishment of the viceroyalty, the cooperation of the European settlers was vital.[119] In the event of a successful indigenous revolt, mounting a reinvasion would have been difficult, perhaps impossible.

The political devices available to the distant monarchy, while generally soft ones, in combination proved reasonably effective. The complex notion of Crown benevolence encapsulated a variety of concerns for the well-being of the king's subjects, mirroring those of a Christian heavenly kingdom. The process of making benevolence functional was a judicial one, including instructing the viceroy to make himself available to individual petitioners, legal services to Indians, and a special indigenous court, the *Juzgado de Indios.*[120] The well-known legalism of the monarchy allowed for an exhaustive examination of contentious issues and appeals that could last years. The judicial tendency to compromise in civil disputes and the passage of time worked politically in favor of stability. The one major exception, the hurried issuance of the New Laws of 1542, discussed earlier, caused turmoil across the empire. Less obvious than the immediate issues, the legal process allowed for the survival of indigenous customary law, encapsulated within Spanish forms, an accommodation that indicated the inevitable fusion of cultures.

CONCLUSION

NEW SPAIN'S MESTIZO culture as it developed appeared to be a confusing one and an incidental frontier creation, one difficult to accord respect. That it would become the culture of New Spain and of modern Mexico could not have been imagined in the sixteenth century. It eventually became a unifying culture, not a racial one.[1] Spain's approach was conditioned by its experience, which elevated other factors over race. Purity of blood was secondary to belief and culture. The Mediterranean region had long experienced significant miscegenation while retaining cultural differences. Merchants played a role, as did slavery and the slave trade. Enslavement resulting from defeat in war shifted people around the known world from the Roman west to Asia Minor to Syria to ports along the Arabian Sea. The legions of Pompey and Caesar between them enslaved at least 250,000 men, women, and children, who were sold immediately to far-ranging slave dealers. Civilization, trade, slavery, and miscegenation all went together in the Mediterranean world. Not surprisingly, the initial settlers in the New World toyed with indigenous slavery, only to be restrained by Christianity in the form of the papal charge. In contrast, the sexual conquest could not be controlled by religion in the face of human impulses.

Biological Mestizos in the early postconquest period were absorbed into European society with few social obstacles, dependent on the status of their fathers.[2] As their numbers grew, they became a separate group without secure social standing. Of more consequence, the progressive collapse of indigenous society created cultural Mestizos who, whether driven by rootlessness, choice, or necessity, sought to cope with the new reality by abandoning indigenous communities and moving into towns and cities. They did so within an imperial structure that functioned differently from that of Europe. The Spanish monarchy did not seek to destroy Indo-Mexico but sought to incorporate it and its acceptable institutions into a Christian world, a mixture of benevolent principle and self-interest that was difficult to balance. The papal charge made the monarch responsible for the well-being of his new subjects. Spain approached the New World with a mind-set that combined political economy and religion, a mixture that explains the agonizing debate over legitimacy, the toleration of men such as Bartolomé de las Casas, and exploitation coupled with benevolence. Nevertheless, Castile sought to impose an overarching European culture, although in the end, it could not do so fully in spite of the reality that Indo-Mexico could not freely select elements or openly reject others.

The small group of Spaniards, along with allied Indian armies, succeeded in establishing control over a large indigenous population with a well-established culture very different from that of Europe. Cortés and his men and those who followed functioned within an overarching Christian paradigm that conditioned how they viewed the indigenous population and the conquest and how they envisioned Indo-Mexico's future and the role of the Indian population in the new imperial creation. In short, the conquistadors had a ready-made plan. Thus, one of Cortés's first communications to the monarch requested the dispatch of missionaries to begin the conversion effort, an act that placed the pagan population in a European mental construct. The objective, to subordinate the indigenous population to the protection of a benevolent Christian emperor and his agents, constituted a preliminary claim to legitimacy. Christianity functioned as a juggernaut that kept the defeated and their gods off balance.[3] The new religious calendar officially aligned Indo-Mexico's ceremonial life with that of Europe and constituted a set of rules. Nevertheless, everyday rituals and periodic feast days on the Christian calendar obscured the survival of pre-Columbian elements that were barely disguised in religious pageants, celebrations, and slightly modified rituals. Spain, energized by Christianity and victory, put forth its construct as the preferred cultural paradigm but one unable to avoid fusion with pre-Spanish elements. At the lower levels, unarticulated notions remained as part of a village-based culture that on certain occasions reemerged mixed with European elements. Pope Gregory the Great would have understood the Indo-Mexican *rustici*'s difficulties separating religious belief. The religious similarities, disconnected from an understanding of the underlying theology, made confusion inevitable but facilitated amalgamation. Likely the Indo-Mexican conquest generation could not make more than pro forma accommodations, while post-1521 generations had little choice other than to accept an unfolding Mestizo reality.[4] Beyond the immediate, long-run permanence depended on the acceptance and demonstrated utility of Spain's culture across all aspects, from sociopolitical organization to economic activity to religious behavior. The material aspect of *mestizaje,* such as the spread of Spanish-style clothing, were easier to grasp than were the psychological and philosophical elements hidden within religion and language. Nevertheless, the introduction of European innovations jolted Indo-Mexico into modernity at an accelerated pace that was difficult to absorb or rationalize. The shock of European conquest accomplished what could not have been done internally.

Mexico City, the new center of authority and cultural dissemination, replaced Tenochtitlán, ending the string of city-based Mesoamerican civilizations that reached back to the Olmec and perhaps beyond. The decision to build a Spanish city on the rubble of the destroyed Tenochtitlán was much more than triumphalism. It demonstrated that the intruders had no intention of retreating with their plunder. The symbolism could hardly have been missed by the defeated. Building material extracted from the ruins, the placement of official edifices on sites used for similar purposes by the deposed, the building of the Cathedral of the City of Mexico within sight of the Great Temple, which would be leveled and filled over, made graphic points. The fickle Tezcatlipoca had joined with the gods of the intruders to humble the Aztecs and with them Mesoamerica. With the destruction of Tenochtitlán, Mesoamerica experienced a cataclysmic event at the hands of strangers, marking the end of an independent evolutionary process and the grafting on of one that had been formulated across the Atlantic. Destruction of Tenochtitlán, the discrediting of indigenous gods, and the onslaught of epidemic diseases allowed the intruders to consolidate their psychological-cultural control in the central valleys and subsequently across Mesoamerica. Christianization failed from a doctrinal standpoint but succeeded in disrupting the belief system.

The small numbers of friars and secular priests could not meet the challenge even with population decline. The rush to bring New Spain's religious institutions into conformity with those of Spain was premature. The evangelical phase that effectively ended with the introduction of the secular clergy in 1556, along with reluctance to allow for an indigenous priesthood, aborted what might have a more successful conversion. Predictably, incomplete conversion of Indians allowed for elements of both cultures to intertwine to meet individual needs. Underfunded and undermanned evangelization determined the survival of pre-European religious beliefs. Inevitably, a rich popular culture emerged to meet the needs of the indigenous population independent of European clerical oversight. Popular culture offered some sense of individual control, as it still does in modern Mexico through the devices of folk saints, home altars, and impromptu shrines.

In Indo-Mexico after the fall of Tenochtitlán, some twenty-five million indigenous people faced no more than 20,000 Europeans and black slaves.[5] A population of twenty-five million in 1519 would have been large enough not to be engulfed, but reduced to one million by disease and scattered across Indo-Mexico, it becomes a different matter. Confusion, disruption, and uncertainty were long lasting, made agonizingly so by the onslaught of epidemic disease. Disastrous epidemics changed Eurasia dramatically and did the same in Indo-Mexico. Indigenous Mexico, physically and psychologically weakened, reacted ineffectively. One should keep in mind that Spain continued to experience population losses from epidemic disease in the sixteenth century also, although by that time, social behavior and the economy had adapted to its impact, in contrast to Indo-Mexico. Those who fled the contagion in New Spain spread the disease to almost every corner. In order to regroup after epidemic disease had run its course, one had to have a workable grasp of what had become a different world. The demographic disaster coincided with the destruction of Indo-Mexico's organized spiritual world and its inadequate replacement by another religion formulated in a different historical time. Acculturation in all its complex facets follows the reality of numbers.[6]

Constructing a new political system is a difficult intellectual and psychological task that determines permanence and social cooperation.

That the existing system had to be modified to allow both the imperial power and its unwilling dependency to function was obvious. The monarchy supported the indigenous nobility's economic claims but did not recognize its political pretentions. The conquerors entrusted commoners with tasks that rightfully fell to nobles, creating political confusion but reflecting the Castilian distribution of authority across class lines. In order to avoid the charge of overthrowing legitimate rulers, Cortés bestowed titles of nobility on the family of Moctezuma II, subsequently confirmed by the Crown. The principal heirs of the discredited Aztec paramount chief (Isabel, Mariana, and Pedro, all provided with Spanish names) were recognized as *reyes naturales* (natural kings) but without a kingdom or the hope of one. Their existence served to reassure the Europeans that they had not unjustly deposed rulers. Over the course of the *antiguo regimen,* their descendants successfully defended property rights in Spanish courts but without regaining a political role.[7]

Some conquistadors envisioned establishing Hispano-Indo-Mexican noble houses through marriage into the high indigenous nobility; their hope for political power soon faded. Juan Cano, one of the original conquistadors, married Isabel Moctezuma, perhaps with that in mind.[8] A number of well-connected Mestizo offspring acquired honors based on service to the Crown but usually in Europe, not in New Spain. A hybrid Hispano-Indo nobility could not take roots without Crown support. Moreover, European settlers, hoping to become the new aristocracy, were natural opponents of the notion of indigenous nobility. It is not clear that the Crown ever considered a Mexican-based nobility, even though it found it necessary to confer the exalted title of the Marques del Valle de Oaxaca on Cortés, along with land and semifeudal rights; officials were careful to keep him and his son Martín in Spain.

The Alexandrine Bull of 1493 (*Inter cafeteria divine*) conveyed to Queen Isabel and her heirs and successors full lordship over the new discoveries even before the extent of the Western Hemisphere became evident. In turn, Carlos I in 1519 transferred title to the Crown as an institution the same year that Cortés landed in Indo-Mexico.[9] The amended papal charge allowed both Carlos I and his son Felipe II to make modifications in Mexico that they could not introduce in Castile: while traditional political forms were introduced, they performed differently on the American frontier. Carlos I adjusted the European political model in a significant manner, with important social and political implications. While in Spain influence rested on noble status, preferably ancient or achieved during the Reconquista by those of Christian roots, these elements were not present on the Indo-Mexican frontier. The conquest of Mexico had been too rapid to engender heroic generations of frontier warriors. Carlos I, relieved by his defeat of the Comuneros, the representatives of the cities of Castile who had demanded representative government, understood that it could well have gone the other way. To avoid such a possibility in New Spain, he refused to create a political nobility. However, he accepted the request of New Spain's cities to meet in a Cortes, provided that the king convened.[10] To assure that New Spain would not be philosophically contaminated by Castilian constitutionalism, Carlos I in 1523–1524 created a separate Council of the Indies, designated as supreme. The monarch appointed the new organization's membership, thereby separating it decisively from the experience of the Council of Castile. The Council of the Indies did not have a history and responded to the monarch's well-understood preferences. The council served as a preliminary screening device; once a situation had demonstrated its obvious importance, the Council of State dealt with the issue. The American empire would not have a separate legal code, although the Laws of the Indies were compiled; they dealt with problem-specific matters in many distinct locations across the Americas.

New Spain was a kingdom without functional nobles, separate *fueros,* and ancient privileges.[11] Nevertheless, those who went to New Spain during the conquest period had expectations of rich rewards. As Jerónimo Castillo de Bobadilla noted at the turn of the seventeenth century, the king recognized the great service that individuals had performed during the Reconquista in Spain and consequently divided the land between them and raised them to the nobility so that they became the "bone and sinew of the state."[12] The same circumstance seemly applied in Indo-Mexico. A sense of a just reward denied was difficult to ignore. Nevertheless, officials in Spain understood that a simple transference of Spain's political system might well encourage independent tendencies among those Europeans born in the New World (the Creoles) and took measures to counteract that possibility. The overarching political structure of the new Kingdom of New Spain placed authority and power in the hands of a viceroy and the high court (Audiencia), supported by a bureaucracy. The Crown controlled all upper-level governing institutions including those of the church. The difficulties that accompanied the New Laws of 1542, as discussed, were not forgotten. The regalist Juan de Ovando helped draw up reforms in 1568 and in 1571 and assumed the presidency of the Council of the Indies. His initiatives centralized control in the 1570s. A *letrado* bureaucracy assured that New Spain's civic life would be structured, but infused with notion of bureaucratic self-sufficiency. From the viceroy on down, they were less receivers of royal patronage than employees in the fashion of a modern bureaucratic state.

The absence of a Cortes and nobles in the American empire eliminated traditional counterforces to monarchist authority, leaving only municipalities in a position to object, but individually, not collectively.[13] Municipalities, as they had in Spain, provided a basic organizational and self-governing structure replacing the calpulli. Once in place, they functioned with little interference into modern times. The opposition of Mexico City's municipal body to the New Laws of 1542 was an example of the institution's ability to focus public opinion in defiance of the monarch; although in that case, it was not immediately effective. When the Crown backed down, the municipality's victory celebration had a "we told you so" aspect. Officials in Spain usually paid attention.

In the absence of traditional means that determined one's position in post-1521 imperial society, Castile initially settled on race and a caste system, unable to foresee the extent of miscegenation that would soon characterize New Spain and undermine race and class markers. At the same time, the place of the Indian in the imperial structure was set.[14] Spain's historical experience allowed for flexibility and varying accommodation and privileges across the class spectrum. Social equality was not essential as long as the king's subjects formed part of the Christian community under a guiding Catholic monarch. Predictably, the victorious intruders cultivated an aura of natural superiority in religious, social, and political matters in New Spain, reinforced by the facts of the conquest. Asserted superiority almost immediately provided incentives for individuals to adopt elements of Spanish culture, in effect becoming cultural Mestizos. The gap between those who were able to adopt a degree of Castilian culture and those who were unable to do so took some time to close, but even in isolated areas, workable adaptations had to be made.

Unlike the linguistic situation in Spain, the Crown sought to avoid the introduction of regional languages, mandating the use of Castilian; although other Iberian-language speakers remained free to use their own language in intragroup relations, they functioned in a Castilian world. Nevertheless, Mexico shared greater Spain's philosophical traditions. The deeply ingrained notion of popular sovereignty underpinned civic life and in the early nineteenth century enabled Mexico to take an active role in the attempt to save the Spanish world from Napoleon's destructive ambitions.[15]

A combination of practices including the tendency of *letrados* to seek compromise, indigenous immunity from correction by the Inquisition, the introduction of the secular clergy, and the accommodations required of parish priests effectively allowed the Indians to control much of their personal spiritual life, as they do in our own time. Replacing a polytheistic religion with a monotheistic one formulated in a different historical context is difficult, in spite of its shadow popular religious extensions. Indo-Mexico's polytheism did not draw a line between its core beliefs and peripheral extensions that in a monotheistic context would be viewed as heresy of dismissed as ignorant superstition. The failure of Christianity to allow sufficient personally initiated spiritual control over illness, productivity of crops, and other important personal concerns without the participation of the clergy guaranteed Indo-Mexican survivals in popular culture. While the destruction of pyramids impacted the state religion, at the lower levels of beliefs, which Hernando Ruiz de Alarcón, writing in the 1620s, called idolatries, superstitions and customs could not be rooted out.[16]

The Indo-Mexican frontier, as characteristic of most, if not all, frontiers, was socially leveling. The lowest level of honor, the *hidalguía,* conferred the title of hidalgo (gentleman), which carried some respect but in essence indicated an attachment to European culture, behavioral norms, and imperial authority. On the frontier, even the roughest immigrant claimed to be a gentleman, as did others of doubtful refinement. Only the viceroys, drawn from the high nobility in Spain, could assert aristocratic social privileges; however, viceroys did not function as a natural nobility but as the physical embodiment of a distant monarch, serving at his pleasure and subject to removal.

While New Spain responded to immediate realities as they unfolded internally, it also reacted to events across the Atlantic. Medieval Europe entered the early Renaissance almost at the moment that Tenoch-titlán fell, and a new dynasty and monarch inherited the Castilian throne in 1520. As a result of a web of inheritances, a Hapsburg became Carlos I of Spain. Broadly educated, thrilled to have spent time in Paris, he represented a new generation that was much more cosmopolitan than that of Isabel I. Carlos I, soon to be Emperor Carlos V of the Holy Roman Empire, reoriented Spain's internal focus to an external, pan-European one that reflected the monarch's broader ambitions. He would have to deal with the Protestant Reformation, a difficult situation that required a modified and flexible approach. Of more immediate consequences, Carlos V's extravagant expenditures using borrowed money, eventually at 49 percent interest, set the stage for financial disaster.[17] Between 1532 and 1556, he borrowed a staggering amount, backed by future revenues from the New World and augmented by random confiscation of silver remittances from New Spain.[18] Wars and unrest in Carlos V's checkerboard empire almost fatally victimized the Spanish monarchy. American silver, as production increased to impressive levels, allowed him to raise vast amounts of money to meet his perceived obligations, eventually leading to state bankruptcy. Spain faced the long, drawn-out Revolt of the Netherlands and passive resistance and troublesome revolts by the Moriscos that dragged on until 1571, when extremely harsh measures finally broke their resistance. Moreover, the cost of waging a European war doubled from 1547 to 1552 and then increased by a third again in 1572; by 1590, it had jumped 40 percent. By 1630, it cost five times as much to field a soldier as it had a century before.[19] Felipe II inherited an impossible situation from his father.[20]

Realistically, the colonial empire could expect only minimal attention from officials in Spain, while its silver fueled political designs on the other side of the Atlantic.[21] It is worth noting that a policy of "benign neglect" characterized English North America (subsequently British North America) also. Both monarchies faced colonial resistance when they ended that policy and actively interfered in the eighteenth century.[22]

Directed change met the needs of the conquerors but with advantages for those indigenous elements that were able to adjust. Nevertheless, the unplanned consequence of modifications likely caused confusion. Much of what Spain had to offer beyond its religious beliefs and political structure, such as pack animals, were additive, not transformative, and their utility could be grasped with little difficulty and with minimal modification needed on both sides. Before the European arrival, the indigenous economy relied on plunder, tribute, and trade, all elements quite familiar to Europeans. We do not know to what extent trade was voluntary, but we do know that severing economic ties constituted an act of war. Recall that these merchants were trained warriors and resource scouts as well as traders. They also had the backing of Aztec armies, an advantage when setting terms with trading partners but politicizing trade. To trade with powerful tribute empires must have been somewhat like riding on the back of a tiger.

Large marketing centers served consumers, but their initial macro function was to recycle tribute. Tributary networks, like spokes of a wheel, channeled goods into the imperial hubs to be priced, exchanged, or sold. Tribute required a central market to act as both a depot and a distributing point. The tributaries provided the agreed-on goods and the transportation, in effect, a major subsidy that drained resources from others. Pricing, without an idea of the actual cost of production, led to distortions and waste and impoverishment for many poorer people. The inefficient exploitive structure did not survive the European reorganization, which in effect returned resources to indigenous cities across New Spain.

What might be positive for some could not be considered immediately so for the Indian majority. Nevertheless, with the displacement of pre-Spanish socioeconomic restrictions, new opportunities and beneficiaries made for a more fluid society. Interest groups emerged in support of the material reality that followed the conquest. Economic transformation occurred with surprising speed as the monopoly of intertribal trade ended and new commodities and merchants entered the market. Even before the armed phase had concluded, Indian traders traveled down the coast aboard the same Spanish ships that just a few years earlier they thought were the floating temples of strange gods. The new regime enabled socioeconomic elements to pursue their material potential, but at the expense of the tribal community. The end of restrictions on the pochteca, permitting anyone to engage in trade, increased commerce and exchange. Introduction of coinage just over a decade after the fall of Tenochtitlán cut costs and increased capital. Opening trade and commerce to anyone inclined to participate made possible wealth at levels that could not have been conceived of prior to 1521. Consumption suggested the potential of a broader market and the formation of groups whose social positions, as in Europe, rested on disposable resources.[23]

While the peasantry's traditional task remained agricultural, the family manufactured pots, baskets, small clay items, cotton cloth, and clothing items for sale, as well vegetables, fruits, prepared foods, and other products, as they had before the arrival of the Europeans. But after 1521, they could sell them when and where they wished. Micromarketplace sales involved women who produced what they sold or the products of family agricultural plots. Village-based traders stimulated small, local market economies at prices that reflected the absence of high transportation costs. Their economic activities likely elevated village living standards and in turn added to commercial exchanges, creating a trading mind-set that is still in evidence today. The benefits of economic reorganization touched all, from the top to the bottom.

Land and labor relations were difficult and exploitive in the early decades. Survival on a frontier, the struggle for resources, the keen competition of those at the social bottom for wealth and status was just beginning in Indo-Mexico.[24] The Spanish intellectual construct placed the New World in a Christian context that ignored the amoral pragmatism of frontiers. Opportunism is survival on any frontier, made more so in the sixteenth century by the distance of those who claimed authority. The line between opportunity and abuse is murky, and both occurred. The peasantry (macehualtin), formerly closely controlled, made the most of the end of socioeconomic rigidity, including converting communal property into private holdings. Conversion of communal land into private property by peasants and nobles created transferable value and at the same time weakened social cohesiveness.

The inclusion of Europeans in an already settled land regime posed major difficulties. The Spanish monarchy did not question Indian communal property rights or dispute the validity of land distribution to the indigenous nobles. Limited property transfers in the absence of comprehensive indigenous land law required Spanish enactments to fill the legal vacuum. Displacing indigenous cultivators could only be done legally under well-defined circumstances. The notion of private property, well developed among the Indo-Mexican nobility, was further solidified by the Roman concept of property that emphasized ownership as a social and political value. Meanwhile, a land-grab mentality made it almost impossible to determine valid claims.[25] A confusing, often brutal situation lasted until epidemic diseases depopulated the countryside. Spain, having almost no experience with a feudal system, did not allow the indigenous nobility, on the verge of instituting a proto-feudal system, to impose one; and it eyed the encomienda as it functioned in Mexico with hostile suspicion for similar reasons.

The movement from symbolic money to coinage to a diversified market economy took place rapidly. Monetization of the Indo-Mexican economy resulted in a social transformation, just as it did in Europe. Metallic money doubled value, functioning as an artificial commodity that had not existed before.[26] Coins could be accumulated, functioning as ready capital when needed. Searching for buried caches remained a village pastime at least into the nineteenth century. The establishment of a mint in 1535 marked a successful transition even as minted coins coexisted with cacao beans. Coin usage drastically reduced transportation costs. Wheeled carts, horses, mules, donkeys, and oxen turned paths into primitive roads. While porters remained the backbone of the transportation network for some time, the carrying capacity of the system had increased substantially at lower cost.

The variety of retail activity ran from traveling peddlers to priests conducting business out of the rectory to small, medium, and substantial merchants. Contacts between commercial levels involved a host of secondary regional merchants. Silver mining, export-import businesses, and the exploitation of virgin resources created new wealth. The end of extractive tribute freed resources for local development or other lucrative activity across Mesoamerica. Commerce, wholesale and retail, carried implied social restriction imported from Spain but of uncertain currency. Temporary nobles, by function of high office, theoretically could not be involved in retail directly or other base activity.[27] Just how many accepted such social restrictions is impossible to determine, although it must be kept in mind that New Spain was as much an economic creation as a political one. Bourgeois traders, merchants, miners, and entrepreneurs, not neofeudal lords, characterized Mexico and accounted for much of New Spain's prosperity. In general terms, Indo-Mexico's economic trajectory aligned with that of Europe, but without the static semicorporate restrictions of Spain.

In New Spain, disease struck at a crucial time, when one might have expected a wide spread perhaps to rally a rebellion to expel the intruders.

More or less on schedule, a rebellion began on the western fringes. The Mixton War, had it spread across New Spain, would have been a major test that likely would have rearranged all the elements, material and otherwise, in ways not necessarily positive for the indigenous population, even if they succeeded in evicting the Europeans. There were other possibilities if Indo-Mexico had succeeded in expelling Spain: coastal raiding, plundering by European irregular soldiery with all the violence that it implies, a slave trade, perhaps a multinational picking apart of Indo-America, enclaves formed around silver deposits worked by slaves, and other predatory schemes. None of this happened.[28] Only European pirate activity in the seventeenth century hinted at violent alternatives, although pirates preyed on coastal cities, not the interior population, and had a localized impact.

Spain is often taken to task for conducting a violent and vicious conquest in the Americas as well as failing to deal with abuses in a timely manner: the essence of the Black Legend.[29] When the imperial power is a theocracy, self-doubt is rare. Spain in fact demonstrated ambivalence as it sought to establish legitimacy in Indo-Mexico. At the same time, it could not tolerate paganism. In the end, Spain remolded Indo-Mexico only partially; nevertheless, its cultural contribution represented modernity. The integration of the Western Hemisphere into the world civilization was accomplished by a Spanish monarchy responsive to the values embedded in Christianity. Consequently, in spite of moral lapses, even failures, and heavy costs to the indigenous population, Indo-Mexico survived as a vital component of the empire's Mestizo culture.[30]

The pulling of Indo-Mexico into the global economy also meant that it functioned as a part of an imperial system that offered some protection from international predators. Indirectly, New Spain had a seat at the western European table.[31] In our own time, at the upper social levels, the usable past is that of Hispano-Mexico representing modernity. As one moves down the class structure, it shades toward that of the Indo-Mexican, modified to fit the myths and remnants of a once great indigenous people. The historical experience and the processes of both Europe and Indo-Mexico are reflected in the culture of modern Mexico.

NOTES

PROLOGUE

1. Interestingly, Commander Mitso Fuchida of Admiral Nagumo's carrier group led the attack on Pearl Harbor as well as the one on Darwin, accounting for the planning similarities between the two successful raids.
2. Many Australian politicians viewed the United States as a disloyal and "errant British Dominion," ignoring its struggle for independence.
3. The sinking of the two capital ships, the HMS *Prince of Wales* and the HMS *Repulse*, represented a death blow for the British defense of the island.
4. With a central character modeled after a World War I aviator, *Captain Midnight* began as a radio show in 1938. When Japan attacked Pearl Harbor, the scripts began to emphasize the Secret Squadron's duty to fight the war. "War is terrible, Joyce," says Captain Midnight to a girl Secret Squadron member, "but if those rats win, then freedom loses."

INTRODUCTION

1. The economist Thorstein Veblen, in his *The Theory of the Leisure Class: An Economic Study of Institutions,* published in 1899 (reprint, ed. Martha Banta [Oxford: Oxford University Press, 2009]), coined the term "leisure class." His implied notion of an acceptable socioeconomic balance made his study more than a time-specific attack on wealth. Arthur Demarest views ideology as the underlying functional element, with religion at its core. Arthur A. Demarest, "Archaeology, Ideology, and Pre-Columbian Cultural Evolution: The Search for an Approach," in *Ideology and Pre-Columbian Civilizations,* ed. Arthur A. Demarest and Geoffrey W. Conrad (Santa Fe, NM: School of American Research, 1992), 1–14.
2. Robert Jackson correctly references Mestizos in the Valle Bajo (Cochabamba, Bolivia) as people who no longer "behaved like *Indios,*" who had private property

and no longer participated in farming communal lands. Robert H. Jackson, *Race, Caste, and Indians in Colonial Spanish America* (Albuquerque: University of New Mexico Press, 1999), 51. The American poet Stephen Vincent Benét describes the process of the New World's English settlers who take the first step toward being cultural hybrids: "And those who came were resolved to be Englishmen, / Gone to the World's end, but English every one, / And they ate the white corn kernels, parched in the sun, / And they knew it not, but they'd not be English again." Stephen Vincent Benét, *Western Star* (New York: Farrar and Rinehart, 1943), 116. Sophie Coe relates a similar moment taken from Diego Durán: when the Europeans offered the indigenous food as a test to see if they were gods or mortals, they waited suspiciously for their hosts to eat first. Sophie D. Coe, *America's First Cuisines* (Austin: University of Texas Press, 1994), 72.

3. Spanish America's Mestizo cultures vary substantially from one region or republic to the next but all are a part of a hybrid Spanish World created after 1521.

4. Agustín Yáñez, *El contenido social de la literatura iberoamericana* (Mexico City: Colegio de México, 1944), 21–22. Agustín Yáñez served as the head of the Mexican delegation to UNESCO in 1960, among other political offices he held. Otis H. Green, *Spain and the Western Tradition: The Castilian Mind in Literature from El Cid to Calderón,* vol. 3 (Madison: University of Wisconsin Press, 1968), 80–81. Different degrees of imperialism exist, conditioned, in part, by the nature of the targeted indigenous population, the extent of its isolation, and the historical experience of the imperial power. Thus, when the Portuguese, French, and British arrived in India, it was not a shock. Highly populated civilized societies selected what they wanted and rejected the rest.

5. The neomaterialist Marvin Harris makes a convincing case in his *Cannibals and Kings: The Origins of Cultures* (New York: Random House, 1977).

6. The World Conference on Cultural Policies held in Mexico (UNESCO, 1982) defined culture as a "set of distinctive spiritual, material, intellectual and affective features that [serves to] characterize a society or social group."

7. Edward Shils observes that "the past does not have to be remembered by all who reenact it; the deposit is carried forward by a chain of transmission and reception. To become a tradition, however, and remain a tradition, a pattern of assertion or action must be entered into memory." Edward Shils, *Tradition* (Chicago: University of Chicago Press, 1981), 167. The French concept of *imaginaire* could be used here.

8. Octavio Paz notes that "an invisible thread of continuity" runs from Aztec rulers to Spanish viceroys to Mexican presidents. Octavio Paz, *The Other Mexico: Critique of the Pyramid,* trans. Lysander Kemp (New York: Grove, 1972), 85, 111. Paz could have expanded this to include Rome, Roman Spain, and the Spanish Reconquista.

9. Mesoamerica (middle America) is a cultural-geographical designation bounded in the north by a line that runs from the Mexican cities of Tampico on the Gulf Coast across to Mazatlán on the Pacific, and in the south by western Honduras in Central America.

10. George L. Cowgill, "Towards a Political History of Teotihuacan," in Demarest and Conrad, *Ideology and Pre-Columbian Civilizations*, 87, 88.

11. Quoted in Maurice Keen, "Introduction: Warfare and the Middle Ages," in *Medieval Warfare: A History*, ed. Keen (Oxford: Oxford University Press, 1999), 4.

12. Charles Gibson notes that origin stories of separate tribes in Indo-Mexico tend to be the same in a standard form—in short, a collective myth. Charles Gibson, *The Aztecs under Spanish Rule: A History of the Indians of the Valley of Mexico, 1519–1810* (Stanford, CA: Stanford University Press, 1964), 9.

13. An example of complex technology that spread throughout Mesoamerica is paper manufacturing (*amatl* in Nahuatl, and *huun* in Maya). Paper was made from the inner bark of a species of fig tree, processed in a series of steps, and finally coated with starch or calcium carbonate to produce a smooth, white, glossy surface. Just where and when it originated are unknown, but it dates at least as far back as Teotihuacan and likely much earlier. See the interesting discussion in Frederick Peterson, *Ancient Mexico: An Introduction to the Pre-Hispanic Cultures* (New York: Capricorn Books, 1962), 231–232.

14. The difference between taxes and tribute (in my view) is that taxes are used within an independent political unit for its own needs, whereas tribute is the dispatching of resources to another independent entity to be disposed of as it wishes. Michael Smith defines taxes as regular payments collected on a set schedule. Michael E. Smith, *The Aztecs*, 3rd ed. (Malden, MA: Wiley-Blackwell, 2012), 156.

15. Bernal Díaz (del Castillo), *The History of the Conquest of New Spain*, ed. David Carrasco (Albuquerque: University of New Mexico Press, 2008), 169.

16. Jack Goody, *The Domestication of the Savage Mind* (Cambridge: Cambridge University Press, 1977), 27.

17. It should not be assumed, however, that needed adjustments and even significant changes could not be accomplished; they were but at a slower rate. Those who recited may well have made barely perceived modifications that over time might have become cumulatively significant. We know that Nahuatl, Maya, Mixtec, Zapotec, and other language groups attained an impressive level of expression able to convey shades of meaning and abstractions; it is unlikely that those who were skilled in public presentations could resist using these intricacies.

18. Jack Goody notes that a document exists independently of its author; it becomes depersonalized, subject to intellectual additions by those who use it. Goody, *Domestication of the Savage Mind*, 136–137.

19. Dennis Tedlock, trans., *Popol Vuh: The Mayan Book of the Dawn of Life* (New York: Simon and Schuster, 1995), 46. Tedlock provides illustrations.

20. Serge Grunzinski, *The Conquest of Mexico* (Cambridge, UK: Polity, 1993), 8–14, provides a succinct discussion of the painted books.

21. The introduction of the Roman alphabet in New Spain linked Indo-Mexico with the European struggle to record with all the mental adjustments that different written languages require. See Sir John Edwin Sandys, *Latin Epigraphy:*

An Introduction to the Study of Latin Inscriptions, 2nd ed., revised by S. G. Campbell (Cambridge: Cambridge University Press, 1927), esp. 34–58. There were other scripts used in Italy (based on different Greek alphabets). See Carl D. Buck, *A Grammar of Oscan and Umbrian* (Boston: Ginn, 1904). For the Greek alphabet, the standard work is L. H. Jeffery, *The Local Scripts of Archaic Greece: A Study of the Origin of the Greek Alphabet and Its Development, from the Eighth to the Fifth Centuries B.C.,* 2nd ed. (New York: Oxford University Press, 1990).

22. "Great Awakening" is a term employed to describe the religious revival movements in the colonial and early republican United States but is appropriate in the context of Indo-Mexico. Just why new religions emerge at a particular time and place remains unclear. That they are transformative, as in the case of Christianity and Islam, is obvious: the former emerged with the social uncertainty in Rome, and the latter during an unacceptable situation in Arabia.

23. Rudolfo A. Anaya, *Lord of the Dawn: The Legend of Quetzalcóatl* (Albuquerque: University of New Mexico Press, 1987), 17.

24. Some confusion existed as to the relationship among God, Jesus, and the Holy Spirit. Historical (Catholic) Christianity was thrown on the defensive by Islam and, subsequently, by Martin Luther and the Reformation.

25. Both Christianity and Islam were selective in borrowing from Judaism. Yoram Hazony notes that Christianity bypassed the notion that the Hebrew Bible represented God's law in order to use it to demonstrate God's miracles. Consequently, it is only marginally correct to view the Hebrew Bible as foundational of Christianity and Islam. See Yoram Hazony, *The Philosophy of Hebrew Scriptures* (New York: Cambridge University Press, 2012).

26. Garth Fowden, *Empire to Commonwealth: Consequences of Monotheism in Late Antiquity* (Princeton, NJ: Princeton University Press, 1993), 90. Fowden cites Matthew 28:19–20; Mark 16:15; Luke 24:47; Acts 1:8.

27. Consequently, one can write about a distinct Mexican Catholicism. Osvaldo Pardo, *The Origins of Mexican Catholicism: Nahua Rituals and Christian Sacraments in Sixteenth-Century Mexico* (Ann Arbor: University of Michigan Press, 2006), 16.

28. Clifford Geertz notes that when chaos threatens, it results from "a tumult of events" that cannot be interpreted because people are at the limit of their analytic capability and insights. Consequently, life becomes incomprehensible and without meaning. Clifford Geertz, "Religion as a Cultural System," in *The Interpretation of Cultures: Selected Essays* (New York: Basic Books, 1973), 100.

29. The terms *paganism* and *pagan* referred to people of non-Christian beliefs, as well as to those who had a weak grasp of Christianity; it implied backwardness in all its negative senses. It was not applied to Jewish or Muslim believers.

30. Fowden, *Empire to Commonwealth,* 6.

31. David Lupher examines the frame of reference. David A. Lupher, *Romans in the New World: Classical Models in Sixteenth-Century Spanish America* (Ann Arbor: University of Michigan Press, 2003). Just how harsh was the Roman conquest of the Iberian tribes is debatable; however, it is possible the tribes might well have been traumatized in a fashion similar to that of Indo-Mexicans. Greg Woolf observes that Rome succeeded in convincing those whom it incorporated that

"this was their world." The device of citizenship (not that of subjects) held the empire together through civil wars and rebellions in support of a favored emperor. Greg Woolf, *Rome: An Empire's Story* (New York: Oxford University Press, 2012), 222.

32. Frederick Jackson Turner, "The Significance of the Frontier in American History," *Annual Report of the American Historical Review,* 1894. Frontiers are seldom static; they follow demographics, either contracting or expanding with different levels of uncertainty and order at each stage.

33. The career of the influential Palafox included service as a councilor to the Council of Indies, bishop of Puebla de Los Angeles, interim viceroy of New Spain, archbishop of Mexico, and important posts in Spain. Saint Augustine's notion that pagan virtues were vices in disguise did not deter the bishop.

34. The Mayan experience differed. The conquest of the Maya occurred slowly, ending in modern times.

35. Américo Castro notes that in spite of "wide differences, cultural and psychic analogies are clearly evident." Américo Castro, *The Spaniards: An Introduction to Their History* (Berkeley: University of California Press, 1971), 175n3.

36. Goody approaches the issue with more caution. Goody, *Domestication of the Savage Mind,* 36.

37. Noam Chomsky, *Language and the Mind,* University of California Television (UCTV), Jan 10, 2008.

38. James Lockhart, "Double Mistaken Identity: Some Nahua Concepts in Postconquest Guise," *Of Things of the Indies: Essays Old & New in Early Latin American History* (Stanford: Stanford University Press, 1999), 98–119. Lockhart notes that each side presumed that in similar situations their concepts followed their own understanding. This was, in effect, "double mistaken identity."

39. Japan after Commodore Matthew Perry's intrusion in 1853 is an example of the rapid transformation of a developed society ready to grasp the utility of change but able to select and control cultural change, thus remaining in charge of its future.

40. Angus MacKay, *Spain in the Middle Ages: From Frontier to Empire, 1000–1500* (New York: St. Martin's, 1977), 125.

41. Ruth Pike, *Enterprise and Adventure: The Genoese in Seville and the Opening of the New World* (Ithaca, NY: Cornell University Press, 1966); John H. Parry, *The Spanish Seaborne Empire* (Berkeley: University of California Press, 1990), 39, 42–43.

42. Peggy K. Liss, *Isabel the Queen: Life and Times* (New York: Oxford University Press, 1992), 294–295.

43. Peggy K. Liss, *Mexico under Spain, 1521–1556: Society and the Origins of Nationality* (Chicago: University of Chicago, 1975), 44.

44. Cortés, to his credit, must have believed such a debate was necessary.

45. J. Jorge Klor de Alva, "The Aztec-Spanish Dialogues of 1524," *Alcheringa* 4 (1980): 56–193. Sahagún's account, written in 1564, represented a reworking of the exchange. Bernardino de Sahagún, *Coloquios y doctrina cristiana,* ed. Miguel León-Portillo (Mexico City: UNAM, 1986), 86–89; Kenneth Mills and William

B. Taylor, *Colonial Spanish America: A Documentary History* (Wilmington, DE: Scholarly Resources, 1998), 19–22.

46. During the planning of the 500th anniversary of the "discovery" of America in 1992, the trauma surfaced intellectually. Carlos Fuentes suggested that the government erect a monument to Cortés (on horseback): "Our father was Hernán Cortés, whether we like it or not." Octavio Paz agreed that a more balanced view of the conquest would be useful. Carlos Monsiváis declined to fight with the "ghost" of Cortés but noted that "culturally Mexico is Mestizo, but ethnically it is still an Indian country," and he stands with the majority. Monsiváis noted that his grandparents spoke Nahuatl. The *Los Angeles Times,* in an article titled "Mexico Confronts Cortes—Again" (written by Marjorie Miller, March 31, 1992, H5), gathered the anguished views together in a concise but admirable interpretive essay that sparked my concerns about how to view Mexican culture.

47. John Schwaller's term "conqueror-priest" separates the early clerics into two groups: those engaged in the conquest and missionaries more concerned about religious objectives. John Frederick Schwaller, *The Clergy in Sixteenth-Century Mexico* (Albuquerque: University of New Mexico Press, 1987), 226.

48. Robert Ricard, *The Spiritual Conquest of Mexico: An Essay on the Apostolate and the Evangelizing Methods of the Mendicant Orders in New Spain, 1523–1572,* trans. Lesley Byrd Simpson (Berkeley: University of California Press, 1966), 23. The establishment of a university (authorized in 1551 and inaugurated in 1553) could not ensure the training of sufficient priests. Many rural Mexicans, at least into the twentieth century, rarely saw a priest.

49. It seems unlikely that Spain would have tolerated a non-Christian state and some indigenous practices, particularly human sacrifice. Nevertheless, the sheer population numbers prior to the virgin-soil pandemics would have guaranteed Indo-Mexican cultural survival.

50. Alonso de Zorita, *Life and Labor in Ancient Mexico: The Brief and Summary Relation of the Lords of New Spain,* trans. Benjamin Keen (New Brunswick, NJ: Rutgers University Press, 1963), 125.

51. On the death of Carlos V in 1556, Indians and Spaniards participated in a joint funeral service and staged pageants that depicted both the indigenous past and the ancient history of Europe as the "twin antiquities of all New Spain." Liss, *Mexico under Spain,* 152.

52. Tzvetan Todorov, *The Conquest of America: The Question of the Other* (New York: Harper and Row, 1984), 80–81.

53. This is not to suggest that all Spaniards could read or write; many of those who took part in the conquest were illiterate. Rather, the term *literate* refers to a certain level of dissemination of knowledge in written form.

54. A modern depiction of the crowds in Tenochtitlán's streets romantically likened the scene to a group of Athenians in their cloaks. Jacques Soustelle, *Daily Life of the Aztecs on the Eve of the Spanish Conquest* (Stanford, CA: Stanford University Press, 1961), 132.

55. Gonzalo Fernández de Oviedo, *Historia general y natural de las Indias,* Biblioteca de Autores Españoles (BAE) 117–121 (Madrid: Ediciones Atlas, 1959); José de

Acosta, *Historia natural y moral de las Indias,* ed. P. Francisco Mateos, Biblioteca de Autores Españoles (BAE) 73 (Madrid: Ediciones Atlas, 1954).

56. Frances F. Berdan, *The Aztecs of Central Mexico: An Imperial Society* (Belmont, CA: Thomson Wadsworth, 2003), 65; Luis Weckmann, *La herencia medieval de México,* 2nd ed. (Mexico City: Fondo de Cultura Económica, 1994), 5.

57. Hernán Cortés, *Primera carta de relación* (Mexico City: Editorial Porrúa, 1960), 16.

58. Bartolomé de las Casas, *Historia de las Indias* (Mexico: Fondo de Cultura Económica, 1951). As Lupher notes, the Greeks and Romans were on hand for the conquest of Mexico as part of the mental baggage of "both the conquistadors and their critics." Lupher, *Romans in the New World,* 1. This suggests the possibility that the discoverers forced the previously unknown into a known context, beginning a string of basic misconceptions that were, in turn, built upon. This likely would have been the reaction of the other side also. To what extent were misconceptions subsequently corrected, or did they create a series of false working realities?

59. Gibson, *Aztecs,* 32.

60. Krishan Kumar, "Greece and Rome in the British Empire: Contrasting Role Models," *Journal of British Studies* 51, no. 1 (2012): 76–101, notes the consequence of the two models on the nature of empire. This suggests that modern imperialism cannot survive its self-constructed misconceptions. The victimization of nineteenth-century Africa, perhaps, is a case in point.

61. The longevity of Spain's empire in the Americas may have rested on acceptance of a distant monarch, out of sight and more of an abstraction than a reality, somewhat along the lines of the Aztec chieftaincy and the British monarch. T. O. Lloyd, *The British Empire, 1558–1995,* 2nd ed. (New York: Oxford University Press, 2008), v.

62. Bernardino de Sahagún, *Florentine Codex: General History of the Things of New Spain* (translation of and introduction to *Historia general de las cosas de la Nueva España,* 12 vols. in 13 books), trans. Charles E. Dibble and Arthur J. O Anderson (Salt Lake City: University of Utah Press, 1950–1982), 142, 64.

63. Diego Durán, *The History of the Indies of New Spain,* trans. Doris Heyden (Norman: University of Oklahoma Press, 1994), 399. His dates are close but are not correct. Cuba was conquered in 1512–1515; Sultan Selim I came to power in 1512, and Moctezuma II in 1502.

64. The medievalist Angus MacKay notes a certain sense of " 'déjà vu' in the New World as Spaniards . . . drew . . . and drew heavily—on the stock of experiences . . . of the medieval centuries." MacKay, *Spain in the Middle Ages,* 212.

65. It is unlikely that the early friars succeeded in making their political point. Costumed enactments and masking long predated 1519. Masking had a regional and local aspect. Indian groups, however, updated their masks—for example, the *negrito* mask after the introduction of African slavery by the Spaniards, and masks for the dance for the Battle of the Fifth of May (Cinco de Mayo, 1862). Barbara Mauldin, *Masks of Mexico: Tigers, Devils, and the Dance of Life* (Santa Fe: Museum of New Mexico Press, 1999), 1–7, 22, 23.

66. Among Carlos V's many titles, he numbered the kingship of Jerusalem. The friars who directed the play did not hesitate to mingle the sixteenth century

with Roman days, replacing the Roman emperor with Emperor Carlos V. To what extent they amused themselves while at the same time making their point is impossible to determine. Lupher, *Romans in the New World,* 40.

67. A memorable reenactment called "Las Morismas" (a multitude of Moors) in Zacatecas in 1910 required more than a thousand actors and lasted three days. Actors played the Moorish King Moor Muza, Don Juan of Austria, the Catholic kings, and so on; Moors could be identified by their turbans. The blending of historical figures without concern for chronology is obvious. The Morisma ceremony continues today in Zacatecas. Frances Toor, *A Treasury of Mexican Folkways: The Customs, Myths, Folklore, Traditions, Beliefs, Fiestas, Dances, and Song of the Mexican People* (New York: Crown, 1947), 347–349.

68. María Elena Martínez, *Genealogical Fictions: Limpieza de Sangre, Religion, and Gender in Colonial Mexico* (Stanford, CA: Stanford University Press, 2008).

69. Castro, *Spaniards,* 216. Castro makes the point that Spain, unlike any other European nation, had a centuries-long relationship with Islam and Judaism that made its worldview different from that of Europe in general.

70. Louise Burkhart's insightful contribution notes that early accounts are a record of contact rather than of precontact. Louise M. Burkhart, *The Slippery Earth: Nahua-Christian Dialogue in Sixteenth-Century Mexico* (Tucson: University of Arizona Press, 1989), 5. Nigel Davies laments the reality that the friars provided vivid descriptions of beliefs and rituals but not their meaning. Nigel Davies, *The Aztecs: A History* (Norman: University of Oklahoma Press, 1973), 168.

71. Leonard A. Churchin, *The Romanization of Central Spain: Complexity, Diversity, and Change in a Provincial Hinterland* (New York: Routledge, 2004), 12–14, offers a concise review of the acculturation model.

72. Edmundo O'Gorman, *The Invention of America* (Bloomington: Indiana University Press, 1961). O'Gorman's term "metaphysical wrestling" is from his "Letter on the North Americans," *American Scholar,* Autumn 1947, 461–463.

73. Modern Mexico clung to the notion of a Mestizo nation until 2004, when the president officially declared the nation to be based also on indigenous roots. Ironically, that is the definition of a Mestizo culture. The Mexican Constitution of 1917, Article 2, as amended in 2004, defined Mexico as a multicultural nation based on an indigenous foundation. Under that article, indigenous people, some ten million strong, have certain rights of self-regulation and cultural organization. What the 2004 declaration did was elevate indigenous-Mestizo culture to a position of equality with the Mestizo Mexico.

74. Alfredo López Austin suggests that religion and sovereignty are characteristic of a stage of sociopolitical development. Alfredo López Austin, *Hombre-Dios: Religión y política en el mundo náhuatl* (Mexico City: UNAM, 1973).

75. Gonzalo Aguirre Beltrán, *La población negrá de México* (Mexico City: Fondo de Cultura Económica, 1972). Beltrán used available census data to estimate that in 1570 Mestizos numbered 2,437. In my view, the estimate is too low to have warranted official attention, such as the decree of 1540, as well as being biologically doubtful.

76. Anglo-Indians in British India endured a similar situation. Putative racial superiority was an imperial tool, but certain individuals had unique skills.

Consequently, Anglo-Indians ran the Indian railways, occupied important secondary positions, and claimed a degree of respect.

77. Two major nineteenth-century figures were Mestizos. Benito Juárez was an Indian but a cultural Mestizo married to a Creole (second marriage); and Porfirio Díaz, part Zapotec, was a cultural-racial Mestizo also married to a Creole (second marriage).

78. As J. H. Parry puts it, "The story of conquest and empire in the Indies is comprehensible only against the background of the older story of conquest and monarchy in Spain." Parry, *Spanish Seaborne Empire,* 28. James Lockhart notes that "remarkable" similarities or "points of contact" exist between the cultures. James Lockhart, *The Nahuas after the Conquest: A Social and Cultural History of the Indians of Central Mexico, Sixteenth through Eighteenth Centuries* (Stanford, CA: Stanford University Press, 1992), 429.

1. MESOAMERICAN CIVILIZATIONS

1. Sea levels were 200 feet lower; consequently, the continental shelf land bridge would have been exposed. The low occurrence of type B blood among Native Americans, while more common in China, would seem to support the notion of successive waves of migrants. The Kon-Tiki expedition supports the Polynesian notion, as do some language similarities. Of course, multiple routes are possible.

2. A. Arnaiz-Villena et al., "The Origin of Amerindians and the Peopling of the Americas According to HLA Genes: Admixture with Asian and Pacific People," *Current Genomics* 11, no. 2 (2010): 103–114, corrected in *Current Genomics* 11, no. 6 (2010): 481; James C. Chatters et al., "Late Pleistocene Human Skeleton and mtDNA Link Paleoamericans and Modern Native Americans," *Science* 344, no. 6185 (16 May 2014): 750–754.

3. Chatters et al., "Late Pleistocene Human Skeleton"; Silvia González and David Huddart, "The Late Pleistocene Human Occupation of Mexico," *FUMDHA-Mentos VII,* January 2008, 236–259.

4. Frederick A. Peterson, *Ancient Mexico: An Introduction to the Pre-Hispanic Cultures* (New York: Capricorn Books, 1962), 20.

5. González and Huddart, "Late Pleistocene Human Occupation of Mexico."

6. Amber VanDerwarker, *Farming, Hunting, and Fishing in the Olmec World* (Austin: University of Texas Press, 2006).

7. Bernardino de Sahagún, *Florentine Codex: General History of the Things of New Spain* (translation of and introduction to *Historia general de las cosas de la Nueva España,* 12 vols. in 13 books), trans. Charles E. Dibble and Arthur J. O Anderson (Salt Lake City: University of Utah Press, 1950–1982).

8. For a recent analysis of the development of the Olmec and subsequent pre-Columbian civilizations in Mexico, see Alan Knight, *Mexico: From the Beginning to the Spanish Conquest* (Cambridge: Cambridge University Press, 2002); Richard A. Diehl, *The Olmecs: America's First Civilization* (London: Thames and Hudson, 2004).

9. Michael D. Coe, *Breaking the Maya Code,* 3rd ed. (London: Thames and Hudson, 2012).

10. Michael D. Coe and Richard A. Diehl, *In the Land of the Olmec,* 2 vols. (Austin: University of Texas Press, 1980).

11. Diehl, *Olmecs*; Lars Kirkhusmo Pharo, *The Ritual Practice of Time: Philosophy and Sociopolitics of Mesoamerican Calendars* (Leiden: Brill, 2013); Christopher A. Pool, *Olmec Archaeology and Early Mesoamerica* (Cambridge: Cambridge University Press, 2007); Martha J. Macri and Matthew G. Looper, *The New Catalog of Maya Hieroglyphs,* vol. 1, *The Classic Period Inscriptions* (Norman: University of Oklahoma Press, 2013).

12. Esther Pasztory, *Teotihuacan: An Experiment in Living* (Norman: University of Oklahoma Press, 1997); David Carrasco, Lindsay Jones, and Scott Sessions, *Mesoamerica's Classic Heritage: From Teotihuacan to the Aztecs* (Boulder: University Press of Colorado, 2002).

13. Richard A. Diehl, *Tula: The Toltec Capital of Ancient Mexico* (New York: Thames and Hudson, 1983); Nigel Davies, *The Toltecs: Until the Fall of Tula* (Norman: University of Oklahoma Press, 1977).

14. Enrique Florescano, *The Myth of Quetzalcoatl (El mito de Quetzalcóatl),* trans. Lysa Hochroth, ill. Raúl Velázquez (Baltimore: Johns Hopkins University Press, 1999); H. B. Nicholson, *Topiltzin Quetzalcoatl: The Once and Future Lord of the Toltecs* (Boulder: University Press of Colorado, 2001).

15. Nigel Davies, *The Toltec Heritage: From the Fall of Tula to the Rise of Tenochtitlan* (Norman: University of Oklahoma Press, 1980).

16. Eduardo Matos Moctezuma, *El Templo Mayor: Excavaciones y estudios* (Mexico City: INAH, 1982), 36–37.

17. Possible locations for the origin of the Mexica might be anywhere on the high table land of the Colorado plateau. It is unlikely that they originated on a seacoast. An interesting example of Indo-Mexico rewriting of history, even after the conquest, is the Mapa de Sigüenza, created in the sixteenth century as a pictograph showing the path of Mexica migration that details the stops along the way with the amount of time spent at each location until they reached the site of Tenochtitlán. A trail of footsteps adds a nice touch to what must have been an arduous journey. The map is at INAH and available online at the UNESCO World Digital Library.

18. Alfredo López Austin and Leonardo López Luján, *Mexico's Indigenous Past* (Norman: University of Oklahoma Press, 2001), 19; John Keegan, *A History of Warfare* (New York: Vintage Books, 1994), 125.

19. Agricultural people are dependent on cultivation, although they may gather wild foodstuffs and hunt as well.

20. Diego Durán, *The History of the Indies of New Spain,* trans. Doris Heyden (Norman: University of Oklahoma Press, 1994), 12, 19, 22.

21. Richard Krautheimer, *Three Christian Capitals: Topography and Politics* (Berkeley: University of California Press, 1983), 3–5.

22. Dennis Tedlock, trans., *Popol Vuh: The Mayan Book of the Dawn of Life* (New York: Simon and Schuster, 1995).

23. A chieftaincy has the potential to evolve into a state, as the example of Saudi Arabia in the 1920s demonstrated. Ibn Sa'ud retained tribal values as a socially

unifying force but encapsulated them within a personal state. Joseph Kostiner, "Transforming Dualities: Tribe and State Formation in Saudi Arabia," in *Tribes and State Formation in the Middle East,* ed. Philip S. Khoury and Joseph Kostiner (Berkeley: University of California Press, 1990), 226–249.

24. Robert Carneiro, "Point Counterpoint: Ecology and Ideology in the Development of New World Civilizations," in *Ideology and Pre-Columbian Civilizations,* ed. Arthur A. Demarest and Geoffrey W. Conrad (Santa Fe, NM: School of American Research, 1992), 187. Carneiro suggests that war played a key role in the development of chieftaincies.

25. Matricide and patricide among the gods act to dispose of outmoded functions.

26. Durán, *History of the Indies of New Spain,* 37. A human skin, after being carefully removed with sharp obsidian knives, was worn inside out, presenting a bloody spectacle with the hands left intact and hanging. The legs were removed and the skin then fitted to the priest with throngs in the back. Burr Cartwright Brundage, *The Jade Steps: A Ritual Life of the Aztecs* (Salt Lake City: University of Utah Press, 1986), 123–124.

27. Edward E. Calnek, "The Internal Structure of Tenochtitlán," in *The Valley of Mexico,* ed. Eric R. Wolf (Albuquerque: University of New Mexico Press, 1978), 288–291.

28. Eduardo Matos Moctezuma, "Aztec History and Cosmovision," in *Moctezuma's Mexico: Visions of the Aztec World,* ed. David Carrasco and Eduardo Matos Moctezuma (Boulder: University Press of Colorado, 2003), 3–98.

29. López Austin and López Luján, *Mexico's Indigenous Past,* 209–210. The authors suggest a population of 150,000 to 300,000, a range that seems too high but is not totally improbable.

30. Anthony F. Aveni, Edward E. Calnek, and Horst Hartung, "Myth, Environment, and the Orientation of the Templo Mayor of Tenochtitlan," *American Antiquity* 53, no. 2 (1988): 287–309.

31. Sahagún, *Florentine Codex,* book 9; Pedro Carrasco, "The Social Organization of Ancient Mexico," in *Handbook of Middle American Indians,* vol. 10 (Austin: University of Texas Press, 1971), 366.

32. Alonso de Zorita, *Life and Labor in Ancient Mexico: The Brief and Summary Relation of the Lords of New Spain,* trans. Benjamin Keen (New Brunswick, NJ: Rutgers University Press, 1963), 89.

33. Inga Clendinnen estimates that at the founding of the city, some fifteen calpullis existed, increasing to eighty when the Europeans arrived. Inga Clendinnen, *Aztecs: An Interpretation* (Cambridge: Cambridge University Press, 1991), 33.

34. Carlos Santamaría Novillos, *El sistema de dominación Azteca: El imperio Tepaneca* (Madrid: Fundación Universitaria Española, 2006); Zorita, *Life and Labor in Ancient Mexico,* 89.

35. Carrasco, "Social Organization of Ancient Mexico," 370; Pedro Carrasco, *The Tenochca Empire of Ancient Mexico: The Triple Alliance of Tenochtitlan, Tetzcoco, and Tlacopan* (Norman: University of Oklahoma Press, 1999).

36. Charles Gibson, *The Aztecs under Spanish Rule: A History of the Indians of the Valley of Mexico, 1519–1810* (Stanford, CA: Stanford University Press, 1964), 20.

37. Eduardo Matos Moctezuma, "Templo Mayor: History and Interpretation," in *The Great Temple of Tenochtitlán: Center and Periphery in the Aztec World*, by Johanna Broda, David Carrasco, and Eduardo Matos Moctezuma (Berkeley: University of California Press, 1987), 56.

38. This is similar to the Christian concept of layers of heaven and hell.

39. Louise M. Burkhart, *The Slippery Earth: Nahua-Christian Dialogue in Sixteenth-Century Mexico* (Tucson: University of Arizona Press, 1989), 47–48.

40. Evil is a social construct, although humans share basic notions of what constitutes evil.

41. Total replacement may be the only solution, suggesting an explanation for the disappearance of religions. Those religions that have interpretive flexibility may have an advantage.

42. Geoffrey W. Conrad and Arthur Demarest, *Religion and Empire: The Dynamic of Aztec and Inca Expansionism* (Cambridge: Cambridge University Press, 1984), 189. Imperialism may be a way of imposing an objective or logical structure.

43. Matos Moctezuma, "Templo Mayor," 56.

44. An obsidian knife could not cut through the sternum but could be used to skin victims for other rituals as well as for everyday use.

45. Burr Cartwright Brundage, *Fifth Sun: Aztec Gods, Aztec Worlds* (Austin: University of Texas Press, 1983), 36. The gender order is the same in Judaic-Christian-Muslim belief, following the male priesthood.

46. Recent scientific research suggests that life originated more than once. Five known die-offs have been identified: the Permian extinction some 252 million years ago and the Cretaceous extinction that killed the dinosaurs being among the most dramatic. The current estimates are that half of all living matter is underground up to a depth of five kilometers, deep enough to survive a surface catastrophe, unlike humans. For a discussion of these issues, see the work of Robert M. Hanzen of the Carnegie Institution for Science, whose ten-year project is devoted to understanding the chemical, physical, and biological roles on the Earth. Robert M. Hazen, "Exciting Frontiers Await at Scientific Boundaries: An Example from the Deep Carbon Observatory," *EARTH* 56, no. 7 (2011): 71. Hazen has also written a number of books and articles for the general public about scientific research relating to the evolution of our planet and life. See, for example, Robert M. Hazen, *The Story of Earth: The First 4.5 Billion Years, from Stardust to Living Planet* (New York: Viking, 2012).

47. Research suggests that the Earth has gone through five biological revolutions caused by geological disasters beginning with volcanic activity that accompanied the splitting of North America from Europe, followed in each era by the generation of new species. Jessica H. Whiteside, Paul E. Olsen, Timothy Eglinton, Michael E. Brookfield, and Raymond N. Sambrotto, "Compound-specific Carbon Isotopes from Earth's Largest Flood Basalt Eruptions Directly Linked to the End-Triassic Mass Extinction," *Proceedings of the National Academy of Science* 107, no. 15 (2010): 6721–6725.

48. Another possibility is a similar event off the west coast of what is now India. In South America, the Tupi Guarani lore notes destruction of the world by fire

followed by flood. Geographically widespread destruction lore suggests a collective universal experience and should not be dismissed casually as myth.

49. The physics is intriguing. Planets of the solar system do burn out. A recent theory by the physicist Roger Penrose of Oxford University suggests that a series of big bangs occurred. Evidence in support of the theory is imprinted on the cosmic microwave background (CMB), as reported by the physicist Vahe Gurzadyan of the Yerevan Physics Institute (Armenia). See Vahe G. Gurzadyan and Roger Penrose, "Concentric Circles in WMAP Data May Provide Evidence of Violent Pre-Big-Bang Activity," arXiv.org, November 16, 2010, http://arxiv.org/abs/1011.3706v1.

50. As Nigel Davies notes, this seem a contradiction; after all, if the world ended, so would life, including women-beasts, children-mice, and hapless men. Nigel Davies, *The Aztecs: A History* (Norman: University of Oklahoma Press, 1973), 95. See notes 53 and 54 for another possible explanation.

51. In Christianity, individual responsibility for sins, including those committed in secret, applied to all, including the ruler, with religious consequences; in contrast, the Indo-Mexican concept placed major responsibility on the collective, not the individual. Wigberto Jiménez Moreno, "Los indígenas frente al cristianismo," *Estudios de historia colonial* (Mexico City, INAH, 1983), 413.

52. Guilhem Olivier, *Mockeries and Metamorphose of an Aztec God: Tezcatlipoca, Lord of the Smoking Mirror,* trans. Michel Bession (Boulder: University Press of Colorado, 2003).

53. Sahagún, *Florentine Codex,* book 6, 175.

54. Ibid., 32.

55. By contrast, Candomblé in Brazil provides for possession of a devotee by a god in a public setting, thus affirming direct contact and a protective alliance between the two worlds.

56. Burkhart, *Slippery Earth,* 51, 53; David Herlihy, *The Black Death and the Transformation of the West* (Cambridge, MA: Harvard University Press, 1997), 60.

57. Burkhart, *Slippery Earth,* 51. Failure in one's designated social role resulted in being discarded rather than punished.

58. Sahagún, *Florentine Codex,* book 6, 115; book 2, 143. This realm is somewhat similar to the Christian concept of the outer ring of hell being reserved for unbaptized stillborn babies.

59. Durán writes of both an election and selection process conducted by the council in order to elevate a new ruler. In such a small group, a consensus would be the key. Durán, *History of the Indies of New Spain,* 70–71.

60. Doris Heyden, introduction to Durán, *History of the Indies of New Spain,* xix.

61. Zorita notes that in several other chieftaincies, the common people tested a candidate's ability to remain calm by loudly insulting him, even pushing him. If so, it would seem prudent to have done so in a restrained manner. Zorita, *Life and Labor in Ancient Mexico,* 93–94.

62. Nezahualpilli grew up to be an exceptional individual. He was a poet, an engineer, a scholar, and an astute politician. He maintained a large library and botanical garden. Miguel León-Portillo suggests that Nezahualcoatl and his son

Nezahualpilli disapproved of the warrior mentality and sought to move toward a revived Toltec culture. Miguel León-Portillo, *The Aztec Image of Self and Society* (Salt Lake City: University of Utah Press, 1992), 166–168.

63. Status rituals are important in all political systems. The high nobility of Castile had similar symbolic privileges in the presence of the king.

64. Diego Durán, *Historia de las Indias de Nueva España e islas de Tierra Firme,* vol. 2 (Mexico City: Porrúa, 1967), 317.

65. Conflicting accounts abound, strengthening the suspicion that Chimalpopoca was murdered. Domingo Francisco de Antón Chimalpahin, *Relaciones originales de Chalco Amaquemecan* (Mexico: Fondo de Cultura Económica, 1965), 190–191; Antonio Tovar, *Lingüística y filología clásica* (Madrid: Revista de Occidente 1944), 55.

66. Durán, *History of the Indies of New Spain,* 307, 382.

67. Ibid., 415.

68. Ibid., 411.

69. Ibid., 457.

70. Peter L. Berger, *The Sacred Canopy* (New York: Random House, 1967), 26.

71. Durán, *History of the Indies of New Spain,* 208–211.

72. A peaked roof may have been suggestive of a personal pyramid, infringing on state religious symbolism.

73. Jacques Soustelle notes that the governing pattern took the form a monarchy. It is not clear whether it was so recognized, but the trend had been set. Jacques Soustelle, *Daily Life of the Aztecs on the Eve of the Spanish Conquest* (Stanford, CA: Stanford University Press, 1961), 225.

74. The Inca protostate also resorted to rigidity to shore up its authority and power around the same time, reducing social mobility at the bottom to insupportable levels and setting off reactionary responses on the eve of the Spanish arrival. For a brief but insightful discussion of the vulnerabilities of the Inca regime, see Judith Drick Toland, "Discrepancies and Dissolution: Breakdown of the Early Inca State," in *Studies in Human Society: Early State Dynamics,* ed. Henri J. M. Claessen and Pieter van de Velde (Leiden: Brill, 1987), 138–153.

75. Absolute tribal equality does not exist. Individuals are elevated above others on the basis of intelligence, wise council, battle success, and access to supernatural sources, blood ties, and other factors. Such social differentiation may be at least, in part, the primitive origins of the state. Elman R. Service, *Origins of the State and Civilization: The Process of Cultural Evolution* (New York: Norton, 1975), 291.

76. Collection canoes were stationed around the city to collect waste matter, augmented by smaller collection units. Waste was used for fertilizer. No evidence of public health problems exist.

77. Pedro Carrasco, *Estratificación social en la Mesoamérica prehispánica* (Mexico: Instituto Nacional de Antropología en Historia, 1976), 115.

78. Belief in the signs of the Zodiac as a determining life factor appears to be a common feature in many civilizations, persisting into the present, but usually not as part of the formal religious structure.

79. Sahagún, *Florentine Codex,* book 6, chaps. 4 and 5.

80. Sahagún's detailed description of a theft seems unlikely. First, the robbers approached the location they intended to rob, dancing with an image of Quetzalcóatl in front, carrying an arm from elbow to hand of a woman who died delivering her stillborn first birth. The arm caused the household inhabitants to fall into a trance. The robbers ate, leisurely gathered up the valuable items, and left running. Ibid., book 6, chap. 31.

81. The friars' elevation of humility and poverty to the level of admired virtues also acted to undermine the indigenous political structure.

82. Durán, *History of the Indies of New Spain,* 80. Rewriting history had a along tradition in Indo-Mexico. See translator's notes in ibid., 81.

83. R. C. Padden, *The Hummingbird and the Hawk: Conquest and Sovereignty in the Valley of Mexico, 1503–1541* (New York: Harper, 1967), 98–99. On the death of a high noble, several hundred lower nobles were killed to serve him in death; presumably the number would be less as one moved down the status ladder. Such extravagance represented another unsustainable demand.

84. Peterson, *Ancient Mexico,* 292–293.

85. Durán, *History of the Indies of New Spain,* 420–423.

86. The tendency to equate cities with civilization is problematic. Mayan civilization flourished as a rural creation, although with impressive ceremonial centers—a reality that made it difficult to conquer, as both Indo-Mexicans and the Europeans understood. The Maya were not reduced to central authority until the late nineteenth century.

87. Durán, *History of the Indies of New Spain,* 283–286.

88. Clendinnen, *Aztecs,* 244.

89. Durán, *History of the Indies of New Spain,* 455.

90. Burr C. Brundage, The Jade Steps: A Ritual Life of the Aztecs (Salt Lake City: University of Utah Press, 1985), 192.

91. Nigel Davies, *The Ancient Kingdoms of Mexico* (New York: Penguin, 1982), 194–195.

92. How many is subject to speculation. Beyond a certain number, disposal of the bodies would have been a problem.

93. Octavio Paz's sense of macabre amusement prompted him to compare the flower wars to the modern blood bank as a reserve of the "sacred substance." Octavio Paz, *The Other Mexico: Critique of the Pyramid,* trans. Lysander Kemp (New York: Grove, 1972), 91.

94. Frances F. Berdan, *The Aztecs of Central Mexico: An Imperial Society* (Belmont CA: Thomson Wadsworth, 2003), 113.

95. Ritualized battles are not unique. The Assyrians, Egyptians, Chinese, and others engaged in them often, requesting the sites be prepared to exacting specifications. Keegan, *History of Warfare,* 172–173. Ross Hassig suggests that flower wars served to weaken an opponent—a slow chipping away that would eventually lead to its collapse. Ross Hassig, *Mexico and the Spanish Conquest* (New York: Longman, 1994), 30. Of course, it could weaken both sides.

96. Durán, *History of the Indies of New Spain,* 286.

97. The extravagant sacrifice of life possibly had its origins in primitive tribal times when food supplies were problematic at best. Juan Bautista Pomar, "Relación de Tezcoco," in *Nueva colección de documentos para la historia de México,* ed. Joaquín García Icazbalceta (Mexico City: Biblioteca Enciclopédica del Estado de México, 1975), 46–47. Nigel Davies observes that victims who shared the same language and deities were deemed more acceptable than barbarians. If so, it would indicate a nascent protoreligious nativism. Davies, *Aztecs,* 96.

98. Gary A. Anderson, *Sin: A History* (New Haven, CT: Yale University Press, 2010).

99. Sir Ernest B. Tylor's claim that dreams and visions play a role in the elaboration of religion seems well demonstrated. Ernest B. Tylor, *Primitive Culture: Researches into the Development of Mythology, Philosophy, Religion, Language, Art, and Custom* 2 vols. (London: John Murray, 1871).

100. Durán notes that the use of mushrooms almost immediately led to an altered state so frightening that some people committed suicide. Durán, *History of the Indies of New Spain,* 407.

101. Brundage, *Fifth Sun,* 80–81.

102. Ibid., 108.

103. David Carrasco, *Quetzalcoatl and the Irony of Empire: Myths and Prophecies in the Aztec Tradition* (Chicago: University of Chicago, 1984), 133–140.

104. This holds true for all dominant state religions as well as ideologies. See the suggestive insights of Jerome D. Frank, *Sanity and Survival: Psychological Aspects of War and Peace* (New York: Vintage Books, 1967), 97–102.

105. David Carrasco, *City of Sacrifice: The Aztec Empire and the Role of Violence in Civilization* (Boston: Beacon, 1999), 46–48. An omen is more concrete and immediate than generalized superstition, although superstition appears to be a subcategory of popular religion.

106. Queen Isabel I of Castile, around the same time, consulted the writings of the semimythical Merlin of King Arthur's Court, hoping for the long-dead sorcerer's postmortem assistance. Peggy Liss, *Isabel the Queen: Life and Times* (New York: Oxford University Press, 1992).

107. Brundage, *Jade Steps,* 97–125.

108. *Curandero* is modern Mexican usage that captures the process more accurately than the pejorative *witch doctor.*

109. Durán, *History of the Indies of New Spain,* 71, 91.

110. The Tartar chief Tamerlane (1336–1405), leader of the powerful Central Asian force, made skull pyramids for similar reasons. His brutality may have been necessary.

111. Durán, *History of the Indies of New Spain,* 316–317.

112. Zorita, *Life and Labor in Ancient Mexico,* 181.

113. David C. Grove and Susan D. Gillespie, "Ideology and Evolution at the Pre-state Level: Formative Period Mesoamerica," in Demarest and Conrad, *Ideology and Pre-Columbian Civilizations,* 23.

114. Zorita, *Life and Labor in Ancient Mexico,* 48.

115. Fernando Alvarado Tezozomoc, *Cronica mexicana,* ed. Manuel Orozco y Berra (Mexico: Editorial Porrúa, 1975), 668–669.

116. Frederic Hicks's definition of an integrated market is one in which retailers of all kinds, not involved in agriculture, meet steady demand for supplies of foodstuffs and everyday manufactured items available at all times. Such markets function as part of a continuous supply network. In addition, the authorities must have sufficient power to maintain order, adjudicate disputes, enforce contracts, and impose regulations. All these elements were present in Indo-Mexico. Frederic Hicks, "First Steps towards a Market-Integrated Economy in Aztec Mexico," in *Studies in Human Society,* vol. 2, *Early State Dynamics,* ed. Henri J. M. Claessen and Pieter van de Velde (Leiden: Brill, 1987), 92.

117. A load refers to the amount goods carried by one porter—from 70 to 100 pounds.

118. Frances F. Berdan and Patricia Anawalt, *The Essential Codex Mendoza* (Berkeley: University of California Press, 1997), 113, 120.

119. Soustelle estimates that cotton cloth alone represented the annual support of 100,000 people. Soustelle, *Daily Life of the Aztecs,* 83. Aggregating the value of all tribute, the figure is well in excess of 500,000 annual livelihoods.

120. An impressed Bernal Díaz supplies a vivid picture of the market. Bernal Díaz del Castillo, *The Conquest of New Spain,* trans. J. M. Cohen (Baltimore: Penguin Books, 1963), 232–233.

121. Hernán Cortés, *Five Letters, 1519–1526.* (New York: Norton, 1962).

122. A good example of a miscalculation is the gold rupee minted during the British Raj, which disappeared from circulation as it became a dowry item passed from one family to another without having its value tested in the marketplace, except for the collector who snaps up the occasional coin with no intention of returning it to circulation.

123. Mesoamerica understood the key monetary concept of value related to scarcity. Acceptance of the Pacific coast oyster shell as a protocurrency was based on a supply that occurred in deep water, thus limiting the number of shells in circulation, and that had few alternative uses.

124. Michael Harner, "The Ecological Basis for Aztec Sacrifice," *American Ethnologist* 4 (1977): 117–135; Stafford Poole, *Pedro Moya de Contreras: Catholic Reform and Royal Power in New Spain, 1571–1591* (Berkeley: University of California Press, 1987), 168.

125. Human sacrifice and cannibalism accompanied the evolution of civilization. Nevertheless, the consumption of human flesh in advanced civilizations was cloaked in ritual, thus avoiding the insecurity that would have been engendered by the random harvesting of humans as food. A common feature of cannibalism excluded the person responsible for killing the victim from eating the flesh. In the case of Indo-Mexico, the warrior who had taken the person in battle abstained. In a similar fashion, the Tupi Guarani in the Amazon excluded the executioner and utilized all parts with the exception of the brain.

In the case of the Tupi, cannibalism appeared to be the mechanism to ensure constant warfare by an act of disrespect, although the food value was not wasted.

126. A. P. Vayda, "On the Nutritional Value of Cannibalism," *American Anthropologist* 72 (1970): 1462–1463; Bernard R. Ortiz de Montellano, *Aztec Medicine, Health, and Nutrition* (New Brunswick, NJ: Rutgers University Press, 1991), 90–91.

127. Communion in Catholic theology suggests that it represents the body and blood of Christ: a reminder of the Son of God's physical sacrifice for one's sins.

128. Pulque had symbolic importance. The myth of its discovery involves a woman hunted by a man who escapes by yielding her potent gift. The connection with breast milk and sexual potency is obvious. See the discussion in Clendinnen, *Aztecs,* 245. The food value of fresh pulque could not be ignored.

129. See the appendix in Ortiz de Montellano, *Aztec Medicine, Health, and Nutrition,* 239–243.

130. Shelburne Cooke and Simpson Lesley Byrd, *The Population of Central Mexico in the Sixteenth Century* (Berkeley: University of California Press, 1948), 46.

131. Consumption of beef by Indians after 1521 caused supply concerns and complaints that they did not maintain sufficient herds for their own demands. Attempts to restrict consumption were not effective. Gibson, *Aztecs under Spanish Rule,* 345–346.

132. Ortiz de Montellano, *Aztec Medicine, Health, and Nutrition,* 88.

133. Durán, *History of the Indies of New Spain,* 238–241.

134. The existence of Indo-Mexican great estates with a resident labor force predating the colonial hacienda suggests an evolution toward large landholdings unconnected with the European land grants and the encomienda system's temporary assignment of indigenous labor. The difficulty of linking the encomienda to the emergence of the Spanish hacienda is explored by James Lockhart, "Encomienda and Hacienda: The Evolution of the Great Estate in the Spanish Indies," in *Readings in Latin American History: The Formative Centuries,* vol. 1, ed. Peter J. Bakewell, John J. Johnson, and Meredith D. Dodge (Durham, NC: Duke University Press, 1985), 51–66.

135. Motolinía, Toribio de Benaventa, *Las cosas de la Nueva España y los naturales* ed. Edmundo O'Gorman (Mexico: UNAM, 1971), 366–367.

136. Harmonizing a system that, for some reason, has fallen out of sync requires broad changes. See an interesting discussion in Wally Seccombe, *Millennium of Family Change: Feudalism to Capitalism in Northwestern Europe* (London: Verso, 1992); and Stephen D. White, *Re-thinking Kingship and Feudalism in Medieval Europe* (Aldershot, UK: Ashgate, 2005).

137. Imperial states at certain points consolidate psychologically through the use of ritual and ceremony. The assumption by Queen Victoria of the title of Empress of India in 1877 is a modern example, though certainly a less bloody one.

138. Durán, *History of the Indies of New Spain,* 228–229. The fall of Carthago Novo in 209 to the Roman general Scripto Africanus, followed by the slaughter of all

men, women, children, and animals, including dogs, cats, and birds, had a
similar shock effect.

139. Davies, *Ancient Kingdoms of Mexico,* 193.

140. Pathways were subject to being washed away or collapsing. In addition, the
defending party might block the path by transplanting rows of agave cactus
(century plants) to slow down a hostile army or to force them to take a
different route.

141. Hassig, *Mexico and the Spanish Conquest,* 15, 24. Logistics and distance as limiting
factors faced by Rome and others are discussed in Keegan, *History of Warfare,*
301–315.

142. The existence of multilingual confederations suggests that over time an
amalgamation into larger units would occur.

143. Durán, *History of the Indies of New Spain,* 281.

144. Divine status must be understood in the same sense as that of the imperial cult
of Roman emperors: as a way of strengthening legitimacy, not actual deification. It imposed an obligation to acknowledge the order offered by a divine
ruler.

145. Padden, *Hummingbird and the Hawk,* 100.

146. The Maya lowland's dense tropical forests constituted a natural invasion
barrier and, moreover, had limited food resources. Robert L. Carneiro, "A
Theory of the Origin of the State," *Science* 169 (1970): 733–738; Carneiro,
"Point Counterpoint," 189, 203.

147. See the discussion in Conrad and Demarest, *Religion and Empire,* 66–69.

148. Durán, *History of the Indies of New Spain,* 452–453.

149. León Portillo, introduction to *Broken Spears: The Aztec Account of the Conquest of
Mexico* (Boston: Beacon, 1966), 4–6.

2. THE FORMATION OF EURO-SPANISH CULTURE

1. The physical aspect of the peninsula is discussed in Leonard A. Curchin,
Roman Spain: Conquest and Assimilation (New York: Routledge, 1991), 10–15.

2. Christopher Kelly, in *The End of Empire: Attila the Hun and the Fall of Rome*
(New York: Norton, 2009), 288, compares the Huns' level of violence favorably
with that of Rome.

3. Adrian Keith Goldsworthy, *The Roman Army at War, 100 BC–AD 200* (Oxford:
Oxford University Press, 1998), 259–260. Medieval soldiers in the same fashion
had an opportunity to acquire wealth—looting the battlefield and holding
important captives for ransom. John Keegan, *The Face of Battle* (New York:
Penguin, 1978), 115.

4. Michael Mann, *The Sources of Social Power,* vol. 1, *A History of Power from the
Beginning to A.D. 1760* (Cambridge: Cambridge University Press, 1986), 278.

5. Quoted in C. R. Whittaker, *Frontiers of the Roman Empires: A Social and Economic
Study* (Baltimore: Johns Hopkins University Press, 1997), 131.

6. This process was similar to that of Indo-Mexico as the Chichimeca moved into
central Mexico from the arid north.

7. William V. Harris, *War and Imperialism in Republican Rome* (New York: Oxford University Press, 1979), 51.

8. Leonard A. Curchin, *Romanization of Central Spain: Complexity, Diversity, and Change in a Provincial Hinterland* (New York: Routledge, 2003).

9. Ibid., 131, 214.

10. Celtic religion appeared to privilege the moon over the sun.

11. S. R. F. Price, *Rituals and Power: The Roman Imperial Cult in Asia Minor* (New York: Cambridge University Press, 1984), 133–169, 170–233.

12. Curchin, *Roman Spain,* 162.

13. Muhammad also made that claim.

14. Myth and religion share the need to believe; inevitably, over time, basic Christian beliefs became encrusted with popular religious myth. See Alan Watts, *Myth and Ritual in Christianity* (Boston: Beacon, 1968).

15. Samuel N. C. Lieu, *Manichaeism in the Later Roman Empire and Medieval China,* 2nd ed. (Tübingen, Germany: Mohr Siebeck, 1992), 51–69; Garth Fowden, *Empire to Commonwealth: Consequences of Monotheism in Late Antiquity* (Princeton, NJ: Princeton University Press, 1993), 75.

16. Ramsay MacMullen, *Christianizing the Roman Empire (A.D. 100–400)* (New Haven, CT: Yale University Press, 1984), 46–48, 49–50.

17. Fowden, *Empire to Commonwealth,* 81–82.

18. Arians centered on the relationship between God the Father, God the Son, and God the Holy Spirit. Arians contended that Christ did not always exist but was created by God, and therefore he is separate and subordinate to God the Father—a biological approach.

19. G. W. Bowersock, *Julian the Apostate* (Cambridge, MA: Harvard University Press, 1978), 71, 82–83; Fowden, *Empire to Commonwealth,* 52–55.

20. Fowden suggests that the empire gave way to a commonwealth. Fowden, *Empire to Commonwealth,* 170. Extensive empires in decline have little choice except to allow a degree of federalization in the form of a de facto commonwealth.

21. Peter Brown, *Power and Persuasion in Late Antiquity: Towards a Christian Empire* (Madison: University of Wisconsin Press, 1992), 46–47.

22. Quoted in Fowden, *Empire to Commonwealth,* 87–88.

23. Bart Ehrman observes that being right was a unique concern of Christianity as heir to the truth. Once truth had been determined, it became orthodoxy. What one believed became all important. Bart D. Ehrman, *Lost Christianities: The Battle for Scripture and the Faith We Never Knew* (New York: Oxford University Press, 2003), 91–94.

24. Brown, *Power and Persuasion in Late Antiquity,* 38–41. The Gnostics offered an explanatory framework drawn from Greek thought. Following Plato, they held that a lesser deity (the demiurge) created the world. Christ was an enlightened emissary of a remote supreme God who brought esoteric knowledge (gnosis) to redeem an imperfect world. The notion of lesser deities creating the basic structure is similar to Indo-Mexica theology.

25. Crucifixion was the primary form of punishment for slave revolts. By the time of Jesus, it was used for sedition only. Reza Aslan, *Zealot: The Life and Times of Jesus of Nazareth* (New York: Random House, 2013), 220.

26. MacMullen, *Christianizing the Roman Empire,* 136–137.

27. Ramsay MacMullen, *Paganism in the Roman Empire* (New Haven, CT: Yale University Press, 1981), 8.

28. MacMullen, *Christianizing the Roman Empire,* 7.

29. Ibid., 38–39.

30. Mann suggests that the crisis was one of identity, generated by the success of the Roman Empire. Mann, *History of Power,* 309. A new identity was one of the outcomes but perhaps not the cause.

31. Aslan, *Zealot: The Life and Times of Jesus of Nazareth,* X.

32. Averil Cameron, *Christianity and the Rhetoric of Empire: The Development of Christian Discourse* (Berkeley: University of California Press, 1991), 178–188.

33. The Roman cult of heroes may have provided the model for Christian saints. Peter Brown, *The Cult of the Saints: Its Rise and Function in Latin Christianity* (Chicago: University of Chicago Press, 1981), 5–6, 113. Inga Clendinnen observes that the mass ceremonies performed in Mexico's main temples represented dramatizations that had more to do with state ideology than with "service to the gods." Inga Clendinnen, *Aztecs: An Interpretation* (Cambridge: Cambridge University Press, 1991), 68.

34. MacMullen, *Paganism in the Roman Empire,* 4.

35. A. H. M. Jones, *The Decline of the Ancient World* (New York: Pearson, 1975), 24–27.

36. In theory, everything other than the cardinal belief in one God should not have been a divisive, disqualifying issue. Rigidity and exclusion resulted from the deliberative work of the numerous religious councils charged with deciding orthodoxy. The emergence of a papal bureaucracy able to police orthodoxy and to elaborate dogma and rituals created a superstructure that collectively elevated ritual to a level on par with the belief in one God. Only political needs could prompt Rome to recognize different rites and independent patriarchs as acceptable.

37. MacMullen, *Christianizing the Roman Empire,* 98–99, 116.

38. The importance of tribal soldiers explains the cautious approach to suppression. Stephen McKenna, *Paganism and Pagan Survival in Spain up to the Fall of the Visigothic Kingdom* (Washington, DC: Catholic University of America, 1938), 42–43.

39. J. N. Hillgarth, "Popular Religion in Visigothic Spain," in *Visigothic Spain: New Approaches,* ed. Edward James (Oxford: Oxford University Press, 1980), 7.

40. McKenna, *Paganism and Pagan Survival,* 28–38.

41. Priscillianism's general notion recognized a duality—good and evil. Light and dark and elements that sprang from them were either good or evil. Moreover, it claimed that the soul is a portion of the divine essence that passed through seven heavens until cast into the body by the prince of evil. A variation is that

God created the souls to conquer the realm of darkness but failed, and the devil imprisoned them in physical bodies. Priscillianism also included belief in the signs of the zodiac and the notion that people acted under the control of the stars.

42. *Catholic Encyclopedia,* s.v. "Pope St. Gregory I ('the Great')," www.newadvent.org/cathen/06780a.htm (accessed February 20, 2013).

43. Rachel L. Stocking, *Bishops, Councils, and Consensus in the Visigothic Kingdom, 589–633* (Ann Arbor: University of Michigan Press, 2000), 157–160.

44. Jeffery Burton Russell, *Lucifer* (Ithaca, NY: Cornell University Press, 1984), 63.

45. Ibid., 71–72.

46. J. Charles Wall, *Devils* (London: Methuen, 1904), 88. Several other popes fell under suspicion, including John XXI (1276–1277), Benedict XII (1334–1342), and Gregory XII (1406–1415); Gregory XII was forced to respond to concerns at the 1409 Council of Pisa.

47. Believed to have been written at the end of the first century AD, the Book of Revelations was the last book accepted as part of the New Testament at the Council of Carthage of 397, but not without controversy.

48. Robert Muchembled, *A History of the Devil from the Middle Ages to the Present* (Cambridge, UK: Polity, 2003), 17.

49. Patricia Lopes Don, *Bonfires of Culture: Franciscans, Indigenous Leaders, and the Inquisition in Early Mexico, 1524–1540* (Norman: University of Oklahoma Press, 2010), 30–31.

50. Livy 28.12.12.

51. Curchin, *Roman Spain,* 128.

52. The slowness of voluntary acculturation beyond the cities is evident also in the case of Indo-Mexico.

53. Price, *Rituals and Power,* 93.

54. Benedict Lowe suggests that the continuous influx of circum-Mediterranean peoples made the peninsula a very active economic creation during the first millennium BC. Benedict Lowe, *Roman Spain: Economy, Society and Culture* (London: Duckworth, 2009), 166. The interior likely participated marginally except for mining.

55. Kenneth Harl, *Civic Coins and Civic Politics in the Roman East, A.D. 185–275* (Berkeley: University of California Press, 1987), 52–70.

56. The emergence of the modern state moved the temporal font of benevolence to the king as an agent of God. Nevertheless, networks of support and obligation remained important and passed through to Mexico.

57. MacMullen, *Christianizing the Roman Empire,* 10–24.

58. Visigoth history is subject to revision. Conflicting information, lack of material evidence, misdated transcriptions, inadequate archeological work, and hallowed myth all come into play. Roger Collins pours cold water over certainty in his *Visigoth Spain, 409–711* (Oxford, UK: Blackwell, 2004).

59. Ibid., 241.

60. The differences between the two versions of Christianity revolved around the nature of the relationship between God and Jesus. In addition, Arians practiced triple baptism, while the Catholic ritual, symbolic of unity, was a single baptism.

61. Luis A. García Moreno, *Historia de España visigoda* (Madrid: Ediciones Cátedra, 1989), 317–324.

62. *El Fuero Real de España,* in *Los códigos españoles, concordados y anotados,* vol. 1, ed. Antonio de San Martin, 2nd ed. (Madrid: Librero de los Ministerios de Estado, 1872), book 1, title 11, part 2; Walter Ullmann, *A History of Political Thought: The Middle Ages* (Harmondsworth, UK: Penguin, 1970), 21.

63. *El Fuero Real,* book 1, introduction.

64. Modern social science has resurrected to a degree the notion of Natural Law along the lines of Noam Chomsky's idea of hardwired human elements common to all peoples. Noam Chomsky, *Language and Mind* 3rd ed. (Cambridge: Cambridge University Press, 2006).

65. Bernice Hamilton, *Political Thought in Sixteenth-Century Spain: A Study of the Political Ideas of Vitoria, Soto, Suárez and Molina* (Oxford, UK: Clarendon, 1963), 120–134. The admirable intellectual ferment during this time is often unjustly overshadowed by the eighteenth-century Enlightenment.

66. Charles Homer Haskins, *The Renaissance of the Twelfth Century* (Cambridge, MA: Harvard University Press, 1927), 284–290.

67. Mónica Quijada, "From Spain to New Spain: Revisiting the *Potestas Populi* in Hispanic Political Thought," *Mexican Studies / Estudios Mexicanos* 24, no. 2 (2008): 198–199.

68. Lester K. Little, "Life and Afterlife of the First Plague Pandemic," in *Plague and the End of Antiquity: The Pandemic of 541–750,* ed. Little (New York: Cambridge University Press, 2007), 4.

69. John of Ephesus observed, "a sane person could no longer be easily found." Quoted in Michael G. Morony, " 'For Whom Does the Writer Write?': The First Bubonic Plague Pandemic According to Syriac Sources," in ibid., 78.

70. Little, "Life and Afterlife," 31; Jacobus de Voragine, *The Golden Legend* 6 vols., (London: Temple Classics, 1931), Vol. 2:202.

71. Little, "Life and Afterlife," 22.

72. Ibid., 18.

73. These are questions posed by Jo N. Hays, in "Historians and Epidemics: Simple Questions, Complex Answers," in ibid., 33–56. The extrapolations are mine.

74. Woodrow W. Borah and Shelburne Cook, *Aboriginal Population of Central Mexico on the Eve of the Spanish Conquest* (Berkeley: University of California Press, 1963).

3. MOORS AND CHRISTIANS

1. Roger Collins, *Visigoth Spain, 409–711* (Oxford, UK: Blackwell, 2004), 139.

2. Bernard Lewis, *The Arabs in History,* 6th ed. (New York: Oxford University Press, 1993), 134, 140–141.

3. Stanley G. Payne, *A History of Spain and Portugal*, 2 vols. (Madison: University of Wisconsin Press, 1973), 1:30. Payne mulls over the parallels between the caliphate and the much-later Habsburg Spain.

4. Kenneth Baxter Wolf, "Christian Views of Islam in Early Medieval Spain," in *Medieval Christian Perceptions of Islam,* ed. John Victor Tolan (New York: Routledge, 2000), 90.

5. The decision to declare deviations from the dominant orthodoxy as an acceptable rite was common in religions that were yet to be rigidly solidified. The decision to do so was political in all cases.

6. Joseph O'Callaghan traces the concept to the Hebrew scriptures, the foundation of both sides. Joseph F. O'Callaghan, *Reconquista and Crusade in Medieval Spain* (Philadelphia: University of Pennsylvania Press, 2003), 12.

7. O'Callaghan blames the massacre that followed the short-lived Christian victory on the French, rather than on the more accommodating Spaniards, who were more attuned to Moorish culture. Ibid., 27.

8. John Keegan suggests that military orders provided the model for the regimented units that emerged in the sixteenth century as monarchs took control of armies. John Keegan, *A History of Warfare* (New York: Vintage Books, 1994), 295.

9. J. B. Trend observes that religion would be made to support a political theory. J. B. Trend, *The Civilization of Spain*, 2nd ed. (Oxford: Oxford University Press, 1967), 33. The process can go in the other direction.

10. Quoted in Angus MacKay, *Spain in the Middle Ages: From Frontier to Empire, 1000–1500* (New York: St. Martin's, 1977), 40. Spaniards in the New World understood the soundness of that advice.

11. Julius Kline, *The Mesta: A Study in Spanish Economic History, 1273–1836* (Cambridge, MA: Harvard University Press, 1920).

12. MacKay, *Spain in the Middle Ages,* 37.

13. Ibid., 49.

14. Charles Tilly, *Coercion, Capital, and European States* (Cambridge, MA: Blackwell, 1990), 45; Herman Schwartz, *States versus Markets: History, Geography, and the Development of the International Economy* (New York: St. Martin's Press, 1994), 13–15.

15. That Spain became an early cradle of democracy may have been a result at least in part of the dependency of various small monarchies on freelance soldier-peasants who began the reconquest. See Jaime E. Rodríguez O., "Las revoluciones atlánticas: Una reinterpretación," *Historia Mexicana* 63, no. 4 (April–June 2014): 1873–1874.

16. Vicent García Edo, *Constituciones de los reinos hispánico en el Antiguo Régimen.* (Castellón:Universitat Jaume I, 2003), 108.

17. The canon law's rejection of forced conversion is clear. Pope Clement III forbade forced conversion but with sufficient ambiguity to allow for compulsion. Benjamin Z. Kedar, "Muslim Conversion in Canon Law," in *Proceedings of the Sixth International Conference of Medieval Canon Law* eds. S. Kuttner and K. Pennington (Berkeley: University of California Press, 1985), 321–332;

Benjamin Z. Kedar, *Crusade and Mission: European Approaches towards Muslims* (Princeton, NJ: Princeton University Press, 1984), 72–74.

18. The Castilian galley fleet was deployed in the Straits of Gibraltar during major offensives in order to head off reinforcements. MacKay, *Spain in the Middle Ages,* 130.

19. Castile could not risk a repeat of the 1263 revolt, preferring the security of expulsion in the absence of other acceptable options. The danger outweighed the negative economic impact. Castile must have been aware of Frederick II's solution following the Muslim revolt in western Sicily in 1220, but the numbers involved made that solution impossible. Frederick resettled the defeated insurgents on the Italian peninsula at Lucena, within 200 miles of Rome, to isolate them from possible reinforcements from North Africa. He used them as productive labor and as a military force in his own campaigns, while tolerating their Muslim beliefs. John Phillip Lomax, "Frederick II, His Saracens, and the Papacy," in *Medieval Christian Perception of Islam,* ed. John Victor Tolan (New York, Routledge, 2000), 175–197.

20. Henry Kamen's guess seems acceptable. Henry Kamen, *The Spanish Inquisition: A Historical Revision* (New Haven, CT: Yale University Press, 1998).

21. Jiménez de Cisneros remained a major political force into his eighties. Ibid.

22. Concerns that many conversos were in fact Marranos (secretly practicing Jews) added to the paranoia.

23. Population figures in this section are quoted from Payne, *History of Spain and Portugal,* 1:286,

24. María Elena Martínez, *Genealogical Fictions: Limpieza de Sangre, Religion, and Gender in Colonial Mexico* (Stanford, CA: Stanford University Press, 2008).

25. Nancy Bisaha, *Creating East and West: Renaissance Humanists and the Ottoman Turks* (Philadelphia: University of Pennsylvania Press, 2006), 2–3.

26. Letter from Pope Pius II to Mahomet II (1461). Pius's line of reasoning followed the notion of earlier observers, including William of Tripoli, a Dominican friar and resident of Acre, who wrote in 1273 that while Islam dealt in lies, it was close to the Christian faith and the path of salvation. The letter's importance is as an indication of Christian concerns that survival in the east appeared to be at dire risk, thereby endangering Rome and the west. Nancy Bisaha, "Pius II's Letter to Sultan Mehmed II: A Reexamination," *Crusades* 1 (2002): 183–200.

4. CREATING MESTIZO MEXICO

1. Not every landmass had been contacted by the Europeans. The Dutch officially "discovered" Australia in 1606, although the Portuguese may have done so secretly much earlier.

2. Columbus appears to have been totally disoriented. As suggested by Luis Weckmann, Columbus should be seen as the last of the "Great Medieval Travellers." He believed he had found an earthly paradise so rich that it could finance an army of 100,000 and 10,000 cavalry, sufficient to retake Jerusalem. He expected to see mythical life forms. Luis Weckmann, "The Middle Ages in the

Conquest of America," *Speculum* 26 (1951): 130–139. The indigenous population must have been equally as astonished.

3. Portuguese mariner-traders arrived on the Malabar Coast of the Indian subcontinent in 1498. They reported on an extensive and civilized population. Consequently, assuming incorrectly that Columbus had intruded into their sphere, albeit from the west, they contemplated arresting him when he entered Lisbon's harbor on his return trip in 1493. The Portuguese reaction may have played a role in the church's response.

4. The inaccurate term "the Indies" continued to be used to refer to the landmass until it was gradually replaced by "America," a term that acknowledged that it represented a new world for the Europeans.

5. Quentin Skinner, *The Foundation of Modern Political Thought,* 2 vols. (Cambridge: Cambridge University Press, 1978), 1:54; Mónica Quijada, "From Spain to New Spain: Revisiting the *Potestas Populi* in Hispanic Political Thought," *Mexican Studies / Estudios Mexicanos* 24, no. 2 (2008): 185; Anthony Pagden, *The Fall of Natural Man: the American Indian and the Origins of Comparative Ethnology* (Cambridge: Cambridge University Press, 1982), 38.

6. Paternalism as a psychological and attitudinal state is evident in clerical accounts.

7. Such a conveyance drew on precedent. Pope Adrian IV assigned Ireland to the English King Henry II and his successor in 1155 for the purpose of evangelization. The result was equally as dismal as that in the Antilles.

8. The notion that the New World's inhabitants had descended from a lost tribe of Israel offered another perspective.

9. For the text of the *Requerimiento,* see Juan Manzano Manzano, *La incorporación de las Indias a la Corona de Castilla* (Madrid: Ediciones Cultura Hispanica, 1948), 43–46.

10. The extent to which the indigenous population was vulnerable became evident after the fact—far too late. In Indo-Mexico, royal regulations took on a much more proactive approach.

11. Rafael Altamira, "El texto de los Leyes de Burgos de 1512," *Revista de Historia de América* 4 (1938): 5–79.

12. "From The Laws of Burgos (1512–1513): Royal Ordinances for the Good Government and Treatment of the Indians," trans. Franklin W. Knight, in *An Account, Much Abbreviated, of the Destruction of the Indies (with Related Text),* by Bartolomé de las Casas (Indianapolis: Hackett, 2003), 89–90.

13. Heinrich Mitteis, *The State in the Middle Ages: A Comparative Constitutional History of Feudal Europe* (Amsterdam: North Holland, 1975), 380.

14. The need to devise a new philosophical framework to place the Western Hemisphere in some sort of context made the term "New World" appropriate. It was a difficult task of invention that was never before encountered by Europeans. The distinguished Mexican intellectual Edmundo O'Gorman's book *The Invention of America* (Bloomington: Indiana University Press, 1961) lays out the process. In a similar fashion, Eviatar Zerubavel, using early maps, shows how Europeans began to discover just what Columbus had "discovered." Eviatar

Zerubavel, *Terra Cognita: The Mental Discovery of America* (New Brunswick, NJ: Rutgers University Press, 1992).

15. Colin M. MacLachlan, *Spain's Empire: The Role of Ideas in Institutional and Social Change* (Berkeley: University of California Press, 1988), 15.

16. Quijada, "From Spain to New Spain."

17. Richard Bulliet notes that the wheel was part of the culture being exported by Europe in the age of imperialism. Interestingly, the camel replaced the wheel for trade in North Africa and the Middle East, while wheels had other uses. Richard W. Bulliet, *The Camel and the Wheel* (Cambridge, MA: Harvard University Press, 1975), 227, 260. Horses and the wheel served the conquistadores in New Spain and expanded trade. The first recorded use of war dogs in the Indies occurred in 1494 on the Island of Jamaica. John Grier Varner and Jeannette Johnson Varner, *Dogs of the Conquest* (Norman: University of Oklahoma Press, 1983), 5.

18. Geoffrey Parker, in *The Military Revolution: Military Innovation and the Rise of the West, 1500–1800,* 2nd ed. (Cambridge: Cambridge University Press, 1996), notes the importance of redesigned forts and warships.

19. John Keegan, *The History of Warfare.* London: Hutchinson, 1993, 321, 331.

20. José Antonio Maravall, *Las comunidades de Castilla: Una primera revolución moderna* (Madrid: Revista de Occidente, 1963).

21. Miguel León-Portillo, introduction to *The Broken Spears: The Aztec Account of the Conquest of Mexico* (Boston: Beacon, 1966), 23–28.

22. Ross Hassig, *Mexico and the Spanish Conquest* (New York: Longman, 1994), 64–72, provides a gripping account of the epic battle. Diego Durán, *The History of the Indies of New Spain,* trans. Doris Heyden (Norman: University of Oklahoma Press, 1994), 522, omits discussion of the battle that preceded the crucial alliance.

23. Hassig, *Mexico and the Spanish Conquest,* 79, discusses the possibilities.

24. The enslavement of the survivors was controversial and soon reversed by the Crown. Cortés likely followed Pope Nicholas's bull of 1452 *Dum Diversas,* reaffirmed by a number of papal successors, that authorized both Spain and Portugal to invade and capture Saracens and pagans (possible converts to Islam) and subject them to perpetual slavery. The bull, issued on the eve of the fall of Constantinople to Muslim forces, was a desperate call for all-out war to stop what seemed unstoppable. In addition, the ancient rules of war permitted enslavement of the defeated. The Crown, well aware of the context of the bull and the rules of war, decided that it should not be applies to New World pagans.

25. The general explanation is that a weak, frightened Moctezuma had become emotionally paralyzed. Yet Moctezuma had acted to restructure social relations, dealt harshly with those who resisted his wishes, and was moving toward deification—a strong agenda that spoke to the issue of political consolidation.

26. Imperialism's use of technology against an unprepared indigenous population was in its early stages in 1521. A high point of sorts was reached by European powers in 1914, when 84 percent of the world's surface was under European control. Daniel R. Headrick, *The Tools of Empire: Technology and European*

Imperialism in the Nineteenth Century (New York: Oxford University Press, 1981), 3.

27. It is hard to imagine what the city looked like before its destruction. Contemporary accounts and those written after 1521 are of some help. Understandably overawed, these accounts might well have exaggerated. Bernal Díaz compared it to a dream. Subsequently, Vailliant portrayed the city as a gleaming island capital and Spengler as a world city. Soustelle is more measured. Bernal Díaz del Castillo, *The Conquest of New Spain*, translated by J. M. Cohen. (Baltimore: Penguin Books, 1963), 217. George Vailliant, Mexico: *Origin, Rise, and Fall of the Aztec Nation* (Baltimore: Penguin Books, 1960), 216. Oswald Spenglar, The *Decline of the West,* 2 vols (New York: Alfred A. Knopf, 1928–1929): vol. 2: Perspectives of World History, 44–45. Jacques Soustelle, *Daily Life of the Aztecs on the Eve of the Spanish Conquest* (Stanford, CA: Stanford University Press, 1961), 33.

28. Cortés in his letters to Carlos V stressed the economic (silver) opportunities.

29. The notion that the defenders lost because they sought to take prisoners alive in order to sacrifice them later rather than killing the attackers seems somewhat plausible. As time wore on, they must have become desperate as they realized they were losing. Inga Clendennin is on firmer ground when she notes the hatred between Tlaxcala and Tenochtitlán. The fateful alliance between the intruders and the Tlaxcalans made the difference. Inga Clendennin, *Aztecs: An Interpretation* (Cambridge: Cambridge University Press, 1991), 267–274.

30. Spain followed the Romans' view of a multipurpose land as wealth.

31. A sobering visual shock is provided by a map, prepared by John Chuchiak, showing the pacification campaign routes of Euro-Indian armies that brought Mesoamerica under imperial control. John F. Chuchiak IV, "Map 1: Indios Conquistadores in Spanish Expeditions of Conquest in New Spain, 1519–1620," in *Indian Conquistadors: Indigenous Allies in the Conquest of Mesoamerica,* ed. Laura E. Matthews and Michel R. Oudijk (Norman: University of Oklahoma Press, 2007), 2–3.

32. Peggy K. Liss, *Mexico under Spain, 1521–1556: Society and the Origins of Nationality* (Chicago: University of Chicago Press, 1975), 120–126.

33. Anthony Pagden, *Spanish Imperialism and Political Imagination: Studies in European and Spanish-American Social and Political Theory* (New Haven, CT: Yale University Press, 1990), 18–22.

34. Cortés to Carlos V, October 15, 1524, in *Colección de documentos para la historia de México,* vol. 1, ed. Joaquín García Icazbalceta (Mexico City: Librería de J. M. Andrade, 1858), 470–483.

35. J. H. Elliott, *Empires of the Atlantic World, 1492–1830* (New Haven, CT: Yale University Press, 2006), 89.

36. Lesley Byrd Simpson, *The Encomienda in New Spain: The Beginning of Spanish Mexico* (Berkeley: University of California Press, 1950), 109.

37. Mass sacrifices appeared to be more of a political event conducted by the chieftaincy with collective religious significance. Individual offerings were not so common. The new intruder regime suppressed such ceremonies, but

individual sacrifices may have continued for some time before eventually ending. Nevertheless, as noted by Fernando Cervantes, pious individuals performed clandestine sacrifices in the name of the collective community. Fernando Cervantes, *The Devil in the New World: The Impact of Diabolism in New Spain* (New Haven, CT: Yale University Press, 1994), 43.

38. Popular religion is dynamic and unconcerned with heresy and is thus open to religious invention. Santa Muerte, a recent Mexican creation, is portrayed as a skeleton but given a benevolent role somewhat like the Virgin Mary, although "La Flaca" is treated with more informal respect. The Catholic Church advertises on the Mexico City metro that it has no connection with the cult. This is correct technically but not from a cultural standpoint.

39. Robert Ricard, *The Spiritual Conquest of Mexico: An Essay on the Apostolate and the Evangelizing Methods of the Mendicant Orders in New Spain, 1523–1572,* trans. Lesley Byrd Simpson (Berkeley: University of California Press, 1966), 56–58.

40. Ricard notes that the Crown believed that only Castillian Spanish language could convey a complex theology. In addition, a common shared language would tie the American empire with Castile and eliminate the political difficulties posed by of so many different languages. Ibid., 51–52. It is possible that a pragmatic monarchy viewed the orders as too idealistic in the context of the harsh suppression of Arabic culture in Spain. It should be kept in mind that the various kingdoms of Spain had their own languages. Castile as the ruler of the New World specified its language, giving Indo-Mexico a unifying language, a situation that did exist in the Iberian Peninsula.

41. The possibility that both Indo-Mexico's and Inca Peru's populations had been traumatized cannot be dismissed.

42. Helen Rand Parish, introduction to *Bartolomé de las Casas: The Only Way* (Mahwah, NJ: Paulist, 1992), 35.

43. Negotiated truces, common during the Reconquista in Spain, provided an option in the New World also. A famous example was of shipwrecked black slaves who mixed with Indians in Esmeraldas (Ecuador) who could not be subdued and had to be dealt with diplomatically. A painting in the Museo de América, Madrid, shows three chiefs who visited Quito in 1599. See also Charles Beaty-Medina, "Between the Cross and the Sword: Religious Conquest and Maroon Legitimacy in Colonial Esmeraldas," in *Africans to Spanish America: Expanding the Diaspora*, ed. Sherwin K. Bryant, Rachel Sarah O'Toole, and Ben Vinson III (Urbana: University of Illinois Press, 2012), 95–113.

44. According to Lewis Hanke, "Subsequently, the King ordered the punishment of the revolting Indians, the Land of True Peace became even poorer, and the possibility of winning the Indians by peaceful means alone faded away." Lewis Hanke, *The Spanish Struggle for Justice in the Conquest of America* (Philadelphia: University of Pennsylvania, 1949), 81.

45. *Bartolomé de las Casas in History: Towards an Understanding of the Man and His Works,* ed. Juan Friede and Benjamin Keen (DeKalb: Northern Illinois University Press, 1971), 176–177.

46. Néstor García Canclini suggests that modern capitalism in our own time is finishing a process that began 500 years ago. Mexican nationalism attempts to provide a substitute structure. Néstor García Canclini, *Transforming Modernity: Popular Culture in Mexico,* trans. Lidia Lozano (Austin: University of Texas Press, 1993), 64–68.

47. Fintan B. Warren, *Vasco de Quiroga and His Pueblo-Hospitales of Santa Fe* (Washington, DC: Academy of American Franciscan History, 1963), 43–54.

48. The Portuguese employed the same reasoning with the Directorio dos Indios in the eighteenth-century Amazon, as did the Spanish Jesuits in Paraguay in the seventeenth century.

49. Patricia Lopes Don calls this process the "arbitration of avoidance." Patricia Lopes Don, *Bonfires of Culture: Franciscans, Indigenous Leaders, and the Inquisition in Early Mexico, 1524–1540* (Norman: University of Oklahoma Press, 2010), 14. Indigenous town government in Cuauhnahuac (Cuernavaca) endured into the independence period; Robert Haskett traces its evolutions. Robert Haskett, *Indigenous Rulers: An Ethnohistory of Town Government in Colonial Cuernavaca* (Albuquerque: University of New Mexico Press, 1991).

50. Haskett, *Indigenous Rulers,* 27.

51. Bishop Juan de Zumárraga on at least one occasion reportedly hurried to the scene to assist in smashing artifacts.

52. Richard E. Greenleaf, *The Mexican Inquisition of the Sixteenth Century* (Albuquerque: University of New Mexico Press, 1969), 8–14, 26.

53. Christian theology lent urgency to the conversion of the indigenous population to avoid its being excluded as the imminent end of the world approached.

54. James Lockhart, *The Nahuas after the Conquest: A Social and Cultural History of the Indians of Central Mexico, Sixteenth through Eighteenth Centuries* (Stanford, CA: Stanford University Press, 1992), 119. The adoption of surnames appeared to be restricted initially to the high nobility. In the seventeenth century, efforts were made to add surnames to Indian ones for official purposes. See Pedro Carrasco, "La introducción de apellidos Castellanos entre los Mayas alteños," in *Historia y sociedad en el mundo de habla española: Homenaje a José Miranda,* ed. Bernardo García Martínez. (Mexico City: El Colegio de México, 1970), 217–223.

55. In many respects, the controversy seemed to be a continuation of the ambivalent struggle to control organizational deviations in Europe, personified by Saint Francis and others. The difference was that in New Spain, the regular clergy functioned far beyond the traditional confines of monastic life.

56. John Frederick Schwaller, "The *Ordenanza del Patronazgo* in New Spain, 1574–1600," *Americas* 42, no. 3 (1986): 253–254.

57. The jurisdictional complexity of the situation, the lack of resources, and the fundamental weak authority of the archbishop is detailed in Stafford Poole, *Pedro Moya de Contreras: Catholic Reform and Royal Power in New Spain, 1571–1591* (Berkeley: University of California Press, 1987), 148–160.

58. The work of the orders has been well documented but not that of the secular clergy.

59. The hermit of the shrine of Our Lady of Guadalupe had two estates, one for cattle and the other for mules. John Frederick Schwaller, "The Secular Clergy in Sixteenth-Century Mexico" (Ph.D. diss., Department of History, Indiana University, 1978), 158.

60. Ibid., 160.

61. Ibid., 166–176.

62. Poole, *Pedro Moya de Contreras*, 135–136.

63. Ibid., 153.

64. Serge Grunzinski, *The Conquest of Mexico* (Cambridge, UK: Polity, 1993), 248–249.

65. William Beezley notes the difference between Indian and Mestizo home altars in our own time. William H. Beezley, "Home Altars: Private Reflections of Public Life," in *Home Altars of Mexico,* photographs by Dana Salvo, ed. Ramón A. Gutiérrez (Albuquerque: University of New Mexico Press, 1997), 93.

66. A number of distinguished Catholic scholars, including Stafford Poole, protested the canonization. Juan Diego was provided with a personal history, including a life span from 1474 to 1548 and continuous to live today as a saint. The selection of 1474 as his birth date coincides with Queen Isabel's assumption of the Crown of Castile. Our Lady of Guadalupe became a symbol of Mexican nationality and became known as "Patroness of the Americas." Stafford Poole, *The Guadalupan Controversies in Mexico* (Stanford, CA: Stanford University Press, 2006).

67. Fear played a role in Christianity but for one's life after death and with mitigating options.

68. The replacement of pre-Christian names followed the pandemics in Europe. David Herlihy, *The Black Death and the Transformation of the West* (Cambridge, MA: Harvard University Press, 1997), 79.

69. Rituals mix Catholic and folk religion among Indo-Mexicans. The use of copal for religious purposes in sickness and death and other ancient ceremonies were culturally ingrained but did not preclude Christian practices.

70. The tithe, the one-tenth of one's personal income that Christians paid the church for its maintenance, supported (barely) the secular clergy only. The friars depended on their own resources, and the mendicants relied on alms.

71. John Frederick Schwaller, *The Origins of Church Wealth in Mexico: Ecclesiastical Revenue and Church Finances, 1523–1600* (Albuquerque: University of New Mexico Press, 1985), 22–23.

72. José Miranda, *La función económica del encomendero en los orígenes del régimen colonial (Nueva España, 1525–1531)* (Mexico City: UNAM, 1965), 26–27.

73. Separate legal codes applicable only in the empire did not emerge, although the Crown created protective laws and tribunals exclusively for the Indians. "It is often asserted that the Indians were considered minors. That is not entirely correct. Spanish law, which was based on Roman law, distinguished between two forms of legal minority. The first, *infants* and *impúberes*—that is, persons sixteen years and younger—lacked legal independence and were supervised by a *tutor*. The second consisted of individuals younger than twenty-five years—the

age of legal maturity—and older than sixteen. They possessed the right to act independently on all legal matters, but they were supervised by a *curator* who protected them in case others 'abused their lack of experience, lack of malice, or incapacity.' The Indians of Spanish America were considered minors in the second sense. In their case, the king—that is, the monarchy—functioned as their curator." Jaime E. Rodríguez O., "The Emancipation of America," *American Historical Review*, vol. 105, no. 1 (February 2000), 131–152, quote 133, note 5.

74. By allowing settlers to create a de facto situation before imposing protective regulations, by then often not enforceable, the monarchy upheld its attachment to legalism, as well as its need to be viewed as a benevolent Christian monarchy.

75. Charles Gibson, *Aztecs under Spanish Rule: A History of the Indians of the Valley of Mexico, 1519–1810* (Stanford, CA: Stanford University Press, 1964), 257.

76. MacLachlan, *Spain's Empire,* 29.

77. The grant of an encomienda did not include land, although a separate land grant might also be awarded. In the 1530s, at the height of their power, thirty encomiendas with some 180,000 tributaries functioned in the Valley of Mexico. Gibson, *Aztecs under Spanish Rule,* 61; Silvio Zavala, *La encomienda indiana,* 2nd ed. (Mexico City: Editorial Porrúa, 1972); Simpson, *Encomienda in New Spain,* 56–83.

78. The relative unimportance of African slaves in Mexico may be explained, at least in part, by the low cost of Indian labor. Only in hot coastal areas did Africans have a significant presence.

79. Gibson notes the high ratio of workers to tasks. Gibson, *Aztecs under Spanish Rule,* 222.

80. Alonso de Zorita, *Life and Labor in Ancient Mexico: The Brief and Summary Relation of the Lords of New Spain,* trans. Benjamin Keen (New Brunswick, NJ: Rutgers University Press, 1963), 219–229, provides a long list of criminal practices.

81. Ibid.

82. Zorita, writing sometime after the Mixton War, nevertheless defended the encomenderos as "needed to hold the land and provide for its security." Ibid., 254.

83. The similarities with the Boxer Rebellion in China and other fantasy movements are obvious. A people's reaction against ill-understood imposed modernization at the hands of imperial intruders often results in a desperate attempt to rescue themselves at any cost.

84. Mendoza had military experience gained in Granada against the Moors. Arthur Aiton, with some justification, calls the successful Mixton campaign the second conquest of Mexico. Arthur Scott Aiton, *Antonio de Mendoza: First Viceroy of New Spain* (Durham, NC: Duke University Press, 1927), 156. Ida Altman presents a detailed account in *The War for Mexico's West: Indians and Spaniards in New Galicia, 1524–1550* (Albuquerque: University of New Mexico Press, 2010).

85. Aiton, *Antonio de Mendoza,* 137. José López-Portillo y Weber asserts that had the Mixton War succeeded, the Europeans would have been driven out of Mexico and all other parts of their still shaky empire. José López-Portillo y Weber, *La rebelión de Nueva Galicia* (Mexico City: Instituto Panamericano de Geografía e

Historia, 1939). What would have occurred next is speculation. It would seem impossible for indigenous groups to revert to a pre-European worldview. Perhaps something analogous to China's slow and difficult absorption of western European elements might have occurred while the Indians attempted to minimize the imperial incursions.

86. Cortés received *señorío* over vassals and pueblos, but the Crown reserved powers; consequently, institutional jurisdictions counterbalanced those of the conquerors. Juan Friede, "El privilegio de vasallos otorgado a Hernando Cortés," in Bernardo García Martínez et al., *Historia y sociedad en el mundo de habla española*; MacLachlan, *Spain's Empire*, 16.

87. The idea was to encourage permanence by allowing inheritance by surviving children or a widow. Simpson, *Encomienda in New Spain*, 115.

88. It is unclear how many slaves were rescued at the point of sacrifice, a pretext that was more believable in the Antilles. In Portuguese America, this pretext seems to have been used frequently to enslave individuals. Colin M. MacLachlan, "The Indian Directorate: Forced Acculturation in Portuguese America (1757–1799)," *The Americas* 28, no. 4 (1972): 357–387.

89. Liss, *Mexico under Spain*, 59.

90. Zumárraga in his will freed his Indian slaves, two black slaves and an East Indian cook from Calcutta (Kokata). Liss, *Mexico under Spain*, 180.

91. Las Casas skillfully manipulated a reactive monarchy by employing exaggerations followed by calmly presented solutions in a highly calculated process. MacLachlan, *Spain's Empire*, 52–57. Bartolomé de las Casas, *An Account, Much Abbreviated, of the Destruction of the Indies (with Related Text)*, ed. Franklin W. Knight, trans. Andrew Hurley (Indianapolis: Hackett, 2003). Knight supplies an intelligent appreciation of the work as well excerpts of the texts of the Laws of Burgos and the New Laws of 1542.

92. Simpson suggests that Carlos V may have coveted the wealth of the encomenderos. Simpson, *Encomienda in New Spain*, 129. It is not clear how much wealth they possessed other than land and sufficient working capital. It would seem that Indian tribute constituted their most valuable asset, an explanation of their passionate defense of the grants.

93. Hanke, *Spanish Struggle for Justice*, 83–102, provides a full account of the reaction.

94. *Actas de cabildo de la ciudad de México*, 12 vols., ed. Ignacio Bejarano (Mexico City, 1889–1900), 5:162. Cited in Hanke, *Spanish Struggle for Justice*, 102.

95. Bartolomé de las Casas,*Opúsculos, cartas y memoriales*, de *Obras escogidas de Fr. Bartolomé de las Casas*, ed. Juan Pérez de Tudela Bueso (Madrid:Biblioteca de Autores Españoles, tomo CX, 1958), 450b.

96. Gibson, *Aztecs under Spanish Rule*, 233.

97. The exception of mining indicates that the Crown approached the repartimiento issue in an unsentimental fashion. Conditions in the mines, the economic engine of the economy, were difficult and dangerous, making it hard to attract sufficient labor, in spite of allowing miners to collect a certain amount of silver ore on their own account.

98. Gibson, *Aztecs under Spanish Rule,* 253–254, notes that in Los Portales, one of the largest haciendas in the Valley of Mexico, some 300 workers owed 367 pesos (1778), with individual amounts running from a few reales to 28 pesos. At the same time, the hacienda hired nonresident weekly shifts of twice the number of debtors. Gibson notes that even in workshops, debt alone could not hold workers.

99. Susan Kellogg, *Law and Transformation of Aztec Culture, 1500–1700* (Norman: University of Oklahoma Press, 2005), 48.

100. Gibson, *Aztecs under Spanish Rule,* 277.

101. Initially, Spanish officials, worried about security, required indigenous merchants to obtain permission before leaving on a trading expedition, but they soon dropped the requirement.

102. Alfred W. Crosby, *The Columbian Exchange: Biological and Cultural Consequence of 1492* (Westport, CT: Greenwood, 1973).

103. Trade with Manila, also a part of the Spanish empire, connected New Spain with China and Asian goods. The Mexican silver peso was highly prized by Chinese merchants and was used in secondary trading.

104. José Luis de Rojas, *La moneda indigena y sus uso en la Nueva España en el siglo XVI* (Mexico City: Centro de Investigaciones y Estudios Superiores en Antropología Social, 1998).

105. Juan Suarez Peralta, *Noticias históricas de Nueva España (1589–90),* ed. Justo Zaragoza (Madrid, 1878), 166–167. In response to complaints about high prices in the Tlaxcala market, market prices were set by an Audiencia judge in 1545. The list of items is all in cacao beans, indicating that little if any coin was in use, although the coin equivalent was set at 200 beans per one *tomín* or 230 dried-out beans per *tomín.* "List of Market Prices Established by Judge, Tlaxcala, 1545," in *Beyond the Codices: The Nahua View of Colonial Mexico,* ed. Arthur J. O. Anderson, Frances Berdan, and James Lockhart (Los Angeles: UCLA Latin American Center, 1977), 209–213.

106. John H. Parry, *The Spanish Seaborne Empire* (Berkeley: University of California Press, 1990), 226–227. Parry suggests that labor shortages may have played a role in the decline, although it would seem that the high wages traditionally paid by mine owners would have pulled in workers even in times of labor scarcity.

107. A similar situation occurred in eighteenth-century Brazil. Gold bullion created a huge Portuguese trade deficit with Brazil and an equally as large surplus with England, as Portugal turned to that nation to buy goods in demand. In short, an unintended parasitic relationship existed. Colin M. MacLachlan, *A History of Modern Brazil: The Past against the Future* (Wilmington, DE: Scholarly Resources, 2003).

108. Gibson, *Aztecs under Spanish Rule,* 274.

109. Terry G. Jordan, *North American Cattle-Ranching Frontiers: Origins, Diffusions, and Differentiation* (Albuquerque: University of New Mexico Press, 1993), 86–97.

110. Ibid., 104; William H. Dusenberry, *The Mexican Mesta: The Administration of Ranching in Colonial Mexico* (Urbana: University of Illinois Press, 1963), 50–51.

111. Hernán Cortés, *Cartas y documentos* (Mexico City: Editorial Porrúa 1963), 341–353.

112. Gibson, *Aztecs under Spanish Rule*, 34–37, 50.

113. Andrés Lira, *Comunidades indígenas frente a la ciudad de México: Tenochtitlan y Tlatelolco, sus pueblos y barrios, 1812–1919* (Mexico City: El Colegio de México, 1983), 13–22.

114. Simpson notes that to a large extent the interest of the Crown and the settlers were the same, and under no circumstance did royal officials override their own material interests. Simpson, *Encomienda in New Spain*, 2.

115. Liss, *Mexico under Spain*, 56–57.

116. Aiton, *Antonio de Mendoza*, 161–171.

117. Liss, *Mexico under Spain*, 61.

118. MacLachlan, *Spain's Empire*, 25.

119. The political situation changed dramatically as a result of the pandemics; had they not occurred, the balance between the Europeans and the Indians would likely have favored the latter.

120. Woodrow W. Borah, *Justice by Insurance: The General Indian Court of Colonial Mexico and the Legal Aides of the Half-Real* (Berkeley: University of California Press, 1983).

CONCLUSION

1. The concept of a racial filter going through all possible combinations resulting from intermixing and finally ending up where it started represented a mind-set that accepted race as a fluid concept. Initially imposed racial designations went through a prolonged process of disintegration, eventually leading to self-identification in the eighteenth century. Magnus Mörner, *Race Mixtures in the History of Latin America* (Boston: Little, Brown, 1967), 45–46.

2. Robert C. Schwaller identifies elite Mestizos as a distinct group. Robert C. Schwaller, "Defining Differences in Early New Spain" (Ph.D. diss., Pennsylvania State University, 2010), 164.

3. John Darwin correctly notes that "the real secret of the Spanish blitzkrieg" in Mexico "was cultural and biological." John Darwin, *After Tamerlane: The Rise and Fall of Global Empires, 1400–2000* (New York: Bloomsbury, 2009), 59. The actual toppling of the Aztecs in 1521 and the extension of control was not that easy; to use a World War II analogy, it was more like the North African campaign, not the fall of France.

4. James Lockhart calculates that it took 100 years for Spanish elements to pervade all aspect of Indo-Mexican life within an indigenous framework, eventually leading to the fusion of the two cultures. James Lockhart, *The Nahuas after the Conquest: A Social and Cultural History of the Indians of Central Mexico, Sixteenth through Eighteenth Centuries* (Stanford, CA: Stanford University Press, 1992), 428.

5. Population estimates are crude and disputed. Food resources, the carrying ability of the land, would seem insufficient for such a large number. On the other hand, the *indígenas* appeared to make use of every edible item. War and mass sacrifice may have been a population-control device carried forward from primitive times.

6. With Rome's decline, its successors, the Visigoths, some 20,000, ruled over a million Hispano-Romans, a ratio of fifty to one. Predictably, Visigoth culture gave way to that of the Hispano-Romans. David Herlihy observes that in an overpopulated Europe, the Black Death broke the "Malthusian deadlock," allowing the rebuilding of society along different lines. The same could be said of Indo-Mexico. David Herlihy, *The Black Death and the Transformation of the West* (Cambridge, MA: Harvard University Press, 1997), 39.

7. Donald E. Chipman, *Moctezuma's Children: Aztec Royalty under Spanish Rule* (Austin: University of Texas Press, 2005).

8. Ida Altman, *Emigrants and Society in Estremadura and Spanish America in the Sixteenth Century* (Berkeley: University of California Press, 1989), 272–273.

9. Had Carlos I been aware of the fabulous silver deposits, he likely would have made different arrangements.

10. Carlos I, responding to a petition by the municipal council of Mexico City to vote first in any meeting of municipalities (in effect as a Cortes), granted the request but with the proviso that to do so required royal permission. Not quite an empty honor, it recognized the primacy of the city over all others. Jaime E. Rodríguez O., "La naturaleza de la representación en la Nueva España y México," *Secuencia: Revista de Historia y Ciencias Sociales* 61 (January–April 2005): 6–32.

11. In the eighteenth century, the wealthy were permitted to buy a patent of nobility and form-entailed estates. While a title could be inherited, an individual had to have sufficient resources to live a noble lifestyle, essentially equating money, as long as it lasted, with nobility. Nobles had social prestige but limited political influence. See Doris M. Ladd, *The Mexican Nobility at Independence, 1780–1826* (Austin: Institute of Latin American Studies, University of Texas, 1976).

12. Colin M. MacLachlan, *Spain's Empire in the New World: The Role of Ideas in Institutional and Social Change* (Berkeley: University of California Press, 1988).

13. Technically, immigration was restricted to Castilians only, but the restriction was not enforced. Had it been enforced, pressure for a Cortes might have been more evident.

14. Stafford Poole, *Pedro Moya de Contreras: Catholic Reform and Royal Power in New Spain, 1571–1591* (Berkeley: University of California Press, 1987), 11–15, 210–211.

15. See Jaime E. Rodriguez O., *"We Are Now the True Spaniards": Sovereignty, Revolution, Independence, and the Emergence of the Federal Republic of Mexico, 1808–1824* (Stanford, CA: Stanford University Press, 2012).

16. Hernando Ruiz de Alarcón, *Treatise on the Heathen Superstitions That Today Live among the Indians Native to This New Spain, 1629*, trans. J. Richard Andrews and Ross Hassig (Norman: University of Oklahoma Press, 1984).

17. Cortés, in his fourth letter to the monarch on October 15, 1524, observed that he would be sending 70,000 pesos of gold, as he had been informed that the monarch "must have it to carry on wars." Hernán Cortés, *Five Letters, 1519–1526*, trans. J. Bayard Morris (New York: Norton, 1962), 279.

18. Ramón Carande, *Carlos V y sus banqueros,* 3 vols. (Madrid: Sucesores de Rivadeneyra, 1968), 3:461.

19. See the chart in Geoffrey Parker, *The Military Revolution: Military Innovation and the Rise of the West, 1500–1800,* 2nd ed. (Cambridge: Cambridge University Press, 1996), 61.

20. Modesto Ulloa, *La hacienda real de Castilla en el reinado de Felipe II* (Madrid: Fundación Universitaria Española, 1977).

21. New Spain in the transition stage could not have utilized its silver wealth without creating out-of-control inflation. Had Spain reinvested a reasonable amount in New Spain, the longer-term economic situation would have been different, likely stimulating a more robust immigration from Spain with political, social, and cultural ramifications for both. Mexico still would have been a Mestizo nation, but the cultural mix would have been more complex. Carlos I's extravagant expenditures appeared evident even across the Atlantic, as noted by Cortés when he dispatched money.

22. See MacLachlan, *Spain's Empire in the New World,* 113–135.

23. The new rulers, with security in mind, initially prohibited Indians from carrying swords or using horses, an interesting example of fighting the last war. It is not clear how long the general prohibition lasted. On the Gulf Coast, cowboys initially could not own horses but could ride those of the estancia owner.

24. The violence that occurred in Peru—the bloody struggle between Pizarro and Almagro—did not happen in Mexico but the potential existed.

25. José María Ots Capdequí, *España en America: El régimen de tierras en el época colonial* (Buenos Aires: Fondo de Cultura Económica, 1959).

26. Material assets had a shadow monetary value, in effect doubling the economic impact on the initial purchase and starting a chain of profitable exchange.

27. John Schwaller notes that an aspirant (in the 1580s) for a council seat in Puebla who owned a *obraje* (likely a wool workshop) would be denied because he lacked the perceived nobility (social acceptability?) required for the office. John Frederick Schwaller, *Origins of Church Wealth in Mexico: Ecclesiastical Revenue and Church Finances, 1523–1600* (Albuquerque: University of New Mexico Press, 1985), 17. Likely personal politics had a role, but the weapon was effective.

28. What did not happen—counterfactual history—is a useful diagnostic device when examining events across time and place.

29. The Black Legend of Spanish cruelty implies that had another European monarchy discovered America, things would have been different—a doubtful notion.

30. Jared Diamond, *Guns, Germs, and Steel: The Fates of Human Societies* (New York: Norton, 1999), 328, notes the process across civilizations. Killing, disease, technology, and superior political organization all play a role in a harsh human drama that may be more animalistic than admirable.

31. John Tutino has recently argued that New Spain was responsible for *Making a New World; Founding Capitalism in the Bajío and Spanish North America.* Durham: Duke University Press, 2011.

Bibliography

Acosta, José de. *Historia natural y moral de las Indias.* Edited by P. Francisco Mateos. Biblioteca de Autores Españoles (BAE) 73. Madrid: Ediciones Atlas, 1954.

Aguirre Beltrán, Gonzalo. *La población negro de México.* Mexico City: Fondo de Cultura Económica, 1972.

Aiton, Arthur Scott. *Antonio de Mendoza: First Viceroy of New Spain.* Durham, NC: Duke University Press, 1927.

Alchon, Suzanne Austin. *A Pest in the Land: New World Epidemics in Global Perspective.* Albuquerque: University of New Mexico Press, 2003.

Altamira, Rafael. "El texto de los Leyes de Burgos de 1512." *Revista de Historia de América* 4 (1938): 5–79.

Altman, Ida. *Emigrants and Society in Estremadura and Spanish America in the Sixteenth Century.* Berkeley: University of California Press, 1989.

——. *The War for Mexico's West: Indians and Spaniards in New Galicia, 1524–1550.* Albuquerque: University of New Mexico Press, 2010.

Alvarado Tezozomoc, Fernando. *Cronica mexicana.* Edited by Manuel Orozco y Berra. Mexico: Editorial Porrúa, 1975.

Anaya, Rudolfo A. *Lord of the Dawn: The Legend of Quetzalcóatl.* Albuquerque: University of New Mexico Press, 1987.

Anderson, Arthur J. O., Frances Berdan, and James Lockhart, eds. *Beyond the Codices: The Nahua View of Colonial Mexico.* Los Angeles: UCLA Latin American Center, 1977.

Anderson, Gary A. *Sin: A History.* New Haven, CT: Yale University Press, 2010.

Arnaiz-Villena, A., C. Parga-Lozano, E. Moreno, C. Areces, D. Rey, and P. Gomez-Prieto. "The Origin of Amerindians and the Peopling of the Americas According to HLA Genes: Admixture with Asian and Pacific People." *Current Genomics* 11, no. 2 (2010): 103–114. Corrected in *Current Genomics* 11, no. 6 (2010): 481.

Aslan, Reza. *Zealot: The Life and Times of Jesus of Nazareth.* New York: Random House, 2013.

Aveni, Anthony F., Edward E. Calnek, and Horst Hartung. "Myth, Environment, and the Orientation of the Templo Mayor of Tenochtitlan." *American Antiquity* 53, no. 2 (1988): 287–309.

Barba, Cecilia. "Francisco Vitoria y Hernán Cortés: Teoría y práctica del derecho internacional en el siglo XVI." In *Memoria del II congreso de historia del derecho Mexicano,* 125–131. Mexico City: Instituto de Investigaciones Jurídicas, 1980.

Beaty-Medina, Charles. "Between the Cross and the Sword: Religious Conquest and Maroon Legitimacy in Colonial Esmeraldas." In *Africans to Spanish America: Expanding the Diaspora,* ed. Sherwin K. Bryant, Rachel Sarah O'Toole, and Ben Vinson III, 95–113. Urbana: University of Illinois Press, 2012.

Beezley, William H. "Home Altars: Private Reflections of Public Life." In *Home Altars of Mexico,* photographs by Dana Salvo, edited by Ramón A. Gutiérrez, 91–107. Albuquerque: University of New Mexico Press, 1997.

Bejarano, Ignacio, ed. *Actas de cabildo de la ciudad de México.* 12 vols. Mexico City, 1889–1900.

Benét, Stephen Vincent. *Western Star.* New York: Farrar and Rinehart, 1943.

Benton, Lauren A. *Law and Colonial Culture: Legal Regimes in World History, 1400–1900.* New York: Cambridge University Press, 2002.

Berdan, Frances F. *The Aztecs of Central Mexico: An Imperial Society.* Belmont, CA: Thomson Wadsworth, 2003.

Berdan, Francis F., and Patricia Anawalt. *The Essential Codex Mendoza.* Berkeley: University of California Press, 1997.

Berger, Peter L. *The Sacred Canopy.* New York: Random House, 1967.

Bierhorst, John. *The Mythology of Mexico and Central America.* New York: Morrow, 1990.

Bisaha, Nancy. *Creating East and West: Renaissance Humanists and the Ottoman Turks.* Philadelphia: University of Pennsylvania Press, 2006.

———. "Pius II's Letter to Sultan Mehmed II: A Reexamination." *Crusades* 1 (2002): 183–200.

Boone, Elizabeth Hill. *The Aztec World.* Washington, DC: Smithsonian Books, 1994.

Borah, Woodrow W. *Justice by Insurance: The General Indian Court of Colonial Mexico and the Legal Aides of the Half-Real.* Berkeley: University of California Press, 1983.

Borah, Woodrow W., and Shelburne Cook. *Aboriginal Population of Central Mexico on the Eve of the Spanish Conquest.* Berkeley: University of California Press, 1963.

———. *Essays in Population History.* 2 vols. Berkeley: University of California Press, 1973–1974.

———. *The Indian Population of Central Mexico, 1531–1610.* Berkeley: University of California Press, 1960.

Bowersock, G. W. *Julian the Apostate.* Cambridge, MA: Harvard University Press, 1978.

Brown, Peter. *The Cult of the Saints: Its Rise and Function in Latin Christianity.* Chicago: University of Chicago Press, 1981.

———. *Power and Persuasion in Late Antiquity: Towards a Christian Empire.* Madison: University of Wisconsin Press, 1992.

Brundage, Burr Cartwright. *Fifth Sun: Aztec Gods, Aztec Worlds.* Austin: University of Texas Press, 1983.

———. *The Jade Steps: A Ritual Life of the Aztecs.* Salt Lake City: University of Utah Press, 1986.

Buck, Carl D. *A Grammar of Oscan and Umbrian.* Boston: Ginn, 1904.

Bulliet, Richard W. *The Camel and the Wheel.* Cambridge, MA: Harvard University Press, 1975.

Bundy, David. "The Syriac and Armenian Christian Response to the Islamification of the Mongols." In *Medieval Christian Perceptions of Islam,* edited by John Victor Tolan, 33–54. London: Routledge, 2000.

Burkhart, Louise M. *The Slippery Earth: Nahua-Christian Dialogue in Sixteenth-Century Mexico.* Tucson: University of Arizona Press, 1989.

Cabello Balboa, Miguel. *Descripción de la provincia de Esmeraldas.* Edited and with an introduction and notes by José Alcina Franch. Madrid: Consejo Superior de Investigaciónes Científicas, 2001.

Calnek, Edward E. "The Internal Structure of Tenochtitlán." In *The Valley of Mexico,* edited by Eric R. Wolf. Albuquerque: University of New Mexico Press, 1976, 287–302.

Cameron, Averil. *Christianity and the Rhetoric of Empire: The Development of Christian Discourse.* Berkeley: University of California Press, 1991.

Cañeque, Alejandro. *The King's Living Image: The Culture and Politics of Viceregal Power in Colonial Mexico.* New York: Routledge, 2004.

Carande, Ramón. *Carlos V y sus banqueros.* 3 vols. Madrid: Sucesores de Rivadeneyra, 1968,

Carneiro, Robert L. "Point Counterpoint: Ecology and Ideology in the Development of New World Civilizations." In *Ideology and Pre-Columbian Civilizations,* edited by Arthur A. Demarest and Geoffrey W. Conrad, 175–204. Santa Fe, NM: School of American Research, 1992.

———. "A Theory of the Origin of the State." *Science* 169 (1970): 733–738.

Carrasco, David. *City of Sacrifice: The Aztec Empire and the Role of Violence in Civilization.* Boston: Beacon, 1999.

———. *Quetzalcoatl and the Irony of Empire: Myths and Prophecies in the Aztec Tradition.* Chicago: University of Chicago Press, 1984.

Carrasco, David, Lindsay Jones, and Scott Sessions. *Mesoamerica's Classic Heritage: From Teotihuacan to the Aztecs.* Boulder: University Press of Colorado, 2002.

Carrasco, Pedro. "La introduccíon de apellidos Castellanos entre los Maya alteños." In *Historia y sociedad en el mundo de habla española: Homenaje a José Miranda,* edited by Bernardo García Martínez et al., 217–223. Mexico: Colegio de México, 1970.

———. *Estratificación social en la Mesoamérica prehispánica* Mexico: Instituto Nacional de Antropología en Historia, 1976.

———. "The Social Organization of Ancient Mexico." In *Handbook of Middle American Indians,* vol. 10. Austin: University of Texas Press, 1971.

———. *The Tenochca Empire of Ancient Mexico: The Triple Alliance of Tenochtitlan, Tetzcoco, and Tlacopan.* Norman: University of Oklahoma Press, 1999.

Carter, Charles H. "The Informational Base of Spanish Policy, 1598–1625." *Cahiers d'Histoire Mondiale* 8 (1964): 149–159.

Casas, Bartolomé de las. *Opúsculos, cartas y memoriales, de Obras escogidas de Fr. Bartolomé de las Casas,* edited by Juan Pérez de Tudela Bueso (Madrid: Biblioteca de Autores Españoles, tomo CX, 1958)

———. *An Account, Much Abbreviated, of the Destruction of the Indies (with Related Text).* Edited and with an introduction by Franklin W. Knight. Translated by Andrew Hurley. Indianapolis: Hackett, 2003.

———. *Doctrina.* Edited by Agustín Yáñez. Mexico City: UNAM, 1951.

———. *The Only Way.* Edited by Helen Rand Parish. Translated by Francis Patrick Sullivan. Mahwah, NJ: Paulist, 1992.

Castañeda Delegado, Paulino. "Los métodos misionales en América: ¿Evangelización pura o coacción?" In *Estudios sobre Fray Bartolomé de las Casas,* edited by André Saint-Lu, 123–189. Sevilla: Universidad de Sevilla, 1974.

Castro, Américo. *The Spaniards: An Introduction to Their History.* Berkeley: University of California Press, 1971.

Castro, Daniel. *Another Face of Empire.* Durham, NC: Duke University Press, 2007.

Cervantes, Fernando. *The Devil in the New World: The Impact of Diabolism in New Spain.* New Haven, CT: Yale University Press, 1994.

Chamberlain, Robert S. "The Concept of the Señor Natural as Revealed by Castilian Law and Administrative Documents." *Hispanic American Historical Review* 19 (May 1939): 130–137.

Chomsky, Noam. *Language and Mind* 3rd ed. Cambridge: Cambridge University Press, 2006.

———. *Language and the Mind,* University of California Television (UCTV), Jan 10, 2008.

Chatters, James C., Douglas J. Kennett, Yemane Asmerom, Brian M. Kemp, Victor Polyak, Alberto Nava Blank, Patricia A. Beddows, Eduard Reinhardt, Joaquin Arroyo-Cabrales, Deborah A. Bolnick, Ripan S. Malhi, Brendan J. Culleton, Pilar Luna Erreguerena, Dominique Rissolo, Shanti Morell-Hart, and Thomas W. Stafford, Jr. "Late Pleistocene Human Skeleton and mtDNA Link Paleoamericans and Modern Native Americans." *Science* 344, no. 6185 (16 May 2014): 750–754.

Chevallier, François. *Land and Society in Colonial Mexico: The Great Hacienda.* Berkeley: University of California Press, 1972.

Chimalpahin, Domingo Francisco de Antón. *Relaciones originales de Chalco Amaquemecan* Mexico: Fondo de Cultura Económica, 1965

Chipman, Donald E. *Moctezuma's Children: Aztec Royalty under Spanish Rule.* Austin: University of Texas Press, 2005.

Christian, William A., Jr. *Local Religion in Sixteenth-Century Spain.* Princeton, NJ: Princeton University Press, 1989.

Chuchiak, John F., IV. "Map 1: Indios Conquistadores in Spanish Expeditions of Conquest in New Spain, 1519–1620." In *Indian Conquistadors: Indigenous Allies in the Conquest of Mesoamerica,* edited by Laura E. Matthews and Michel R. Oudijk, 2–3. Norman: University of Oklahoma Press, 2007.

Churchin, Leonard A. *The Romanization of Central Spain: Complexity, Diversity, and Change in a Provincial Hinterland.* New York: Routledge, 2004.

Clendinnen, Inga. *Aztecs: An Interpretation.* Cambridge: Cambridge University Press, 1991.

Coe, Michael D. *Breaking the Maya Code.* 3rd ed. London: Thames and Hudson, 2012.

Coe, Michael D., and Richard A. Diehl. *In the Land of the Olmec.* 2 vols. Austin: University of Texas Press, 1980.

Coe, Sophie D. *America's First Cuisines.* Austin: University of Texas Press, 1994.

Collins, Roger. *Visigoth Spain, 409–711.* Oxford, UK: Blackwell, 2004.

Colman, David. *Creating Christian Granada: Society and Religious Culture in an Old World Frontier City, 1492–1600.* Ithaca, NY: Cornell University Press, 2003.

Conrad, Geoffrey W., and Arthur Demarest. *Religion and Empire: The Dynamic of Aztec and Inca Expansionism.* Cambridge: Cambridge University Press, 1984.

Cook, Alexandra Parma, and David Noble Cook. *The Plague Files: Crisis Management in Sixteenth-Century Seville.* Baton Rouge: Louisiana State University Press, 2009.

Cooke, Shelburne, and Simpson Lesley Byrd. *The Population of Central Mexico in the Sixteenth Century.* Berkeley: University of California Press, 1948.

Cortés, Hernán. *Cartas y documentos.* Introduction by Mario Hernández Sánchez-Barba. Mexico City: Editorial Porrúa, 1963.

——. *Five Letters, 1519–1526.* New York: Norton, 1962.

——. *Primera carta de relación.* Mexico City: Editorial Porrúa, 1960.

Cowgill, George L. "Towards a Political History of Teotihuacan." In *Ideology and Pre-Columbian Civilizations,* edited by Arthur A. Demarest and Geoffrey W. Conrad, 87–114, Santa Fe, NM: School of American Research, 1992.

Crosby, Alfred W. *The Columbian Exchange: Biological and Cultural Consequence of 1492.* Westport, CT: Greenwood, 1973.

Cuevas, Mariano, ed. *Documentos inéditos del siglo XVI para la historia de México.* Mexico City: Talleres de Museo Nacional de Arqueología, Historia, y Etnología, 1914.

Curchin, Leonard A. *Romanization of Central Spain: Complexity, Diversity, and Change in a Provincial Hinterland.* New York: Routledge, 2003.

——. *Roman Spain: Conquest and Assimilation.* New York: Routledge, 1991.

Darwin, John. *After Tamerlane: The Rise and Fall of Global Empires, 1400–2000.* New York: Bloomsbury, 2009.

Davies, Nigel. *The Ancient Kingdoms of Mexico.* New York: Penguin, 1982.

——. *The Aztecs: A History.* Norman: University of Oklahoma Press, 1973.

——. *The Toltec Heritage: From the Fall of Tula to the Rise of Tenochtitlan.* Norman: University of Oklahoma Press, 1980.

——. *The Toltecs: Until the Fall of Tula.* Norman: University of Oklahoma Press, 1977.

Demarest, Arthur A. "Archaeology, Ideology, and Pre-Columbian Cultural Evolution: The Search for an Approach." In *Ideology and Pre-Columbian Civilizations,* edited by Arthur A. Demarest and Geoffrey W. Conrad, 1–14. Santa Fe, NM: School of American Research, 1992.

Demarest, Arthur A., and Geoffrey W. Conrad, eds. *Ideology and Pre-Columbian Civilizations.* Santa Fe, NM: School of American Research, 1992.

Diamond, Jared. *Guns, Germs, and Steel: The Fates of Human Societies.* New York: Norton, 1999.

Díaz del Castillo, Bernal. *The Conquest of New Spain.* Translated by J. M. Cohen. BaltimorePenguin Books, 1963.

——. *The History of the Conquest of New Spain.* Edited by David Carrasco. Albuquerque: University of New Mexico Press, 2008.

Díaz, Gisele, and Alan Rogers. *The Codex Borgia.* Introduction and commentary by Bruce E. Byland. New York: Dover, 1993.

Diehl, Richard A. *The Olmecs: America's First Civilization.* London: Thames and Hudson, 2004.

——. *Tula: The Toltec Capital of Ancient Mexico.* New York: Thames and Hudson, 1983.

Dominguez Ortiz, Antonio, and Bernard Vincent. *Historia de los moriscos: Vida y tragedia de una minoría.* Madrid: Alianza Universidad, 1997.

Duby, Georges. *The Early Growth of the European Economy: Warriors and Peasants from the Seventh to the Twelfth Century.* Ithaca, NY: Cornell University Press, 1974.

Durán, Diego. *Historia de las Indias de Nueva España e islas de Tierra Firme.* Vol. 2. Mexico City: Porrúa, 1967.

——. *The History of the Indies of New Spain.* Translated, annotated, and with an introduction by Doris Heyden. Norman: University of Oklahoma Press, 1994.

Duránd-Forest, Jacqueline de. "Cambio económicas y monada entre los aztecas." *Estudios de Cultura Náhuatl* 9 (1971): 105–124.

Dusenberry, William H. *The Mexican Mesta: The Administration of Ranching in Colonial Mexico.* Urbana: University of Illinois Press, 1963.

Edmonson, Munro, ed. *Sixteenth-Century Mexico: The Work of Sahagún.* Albuquerque: University of New Mexico Press, 1974.

Ehrman, Bart D. *Lost Christianities: The Battle for Scripture and the Faith We Never Knew.* New York: Oxford University Press, 2003.

El Fuero Real de España. In *Los códigos españoles, concordados y anotados,* vol. 1, edited by Antonio de San Martin, 2nd ed. Madrid: Librero de los Ministerios de Estado, 1872.

Elliott, J. H. *Empires of the Atlantic World, 1492–1830.* New Haven, CT: Yale University Press, 2006.

Fernández Castro, M. C. *Villas romanas en España.* Madrid: Ministerio de Cultura, Dirección General de Bellas Artes, Archivo y Biblioteca, 1982.

Fernández-Santamaria, J. H. *The State, War and Peace: Spanish Political Thought in the Renaissance, 1516–1559.* Cambridge: Cambridge University Press, 1977.

Florescano, Enrique. *The Myth of Quetzalcoatl (El mito de Quetzalcóatl).* Translated by Lysa Hochroth. Illustrated by Raúl Velázquez. Baltimore: Johns Hopkins University Press, 1999.

Font Ruis, José María. *Instituciónes medievales españolas: La organización política, económica y social de los reinos cristianos de la Reconquista.* Madrid: Colección Cauce, 1949.

Fowden, Garth. *Empire to Commonwealth: Consequences of Monotheism in Late Antiquity.* Princeton, NJ: Princeton University Press, 1993.

Frank, Jerome D. *Sanity and Survival: Psychological Aspects of War and Peace.* New York: Vintage Books, 1967.

Frankl, Victor. "Hernán Cortes y la tradición de las Siete Partidas." *Revista de Historia de América* 53–54 (June–December 1962): 9–74.

Freeman, Charles. *The Closing of the Western Mind: The Rise of Faith and the Fall of Reason.* New York: Vintage Books, 2002.

Friede, Juan. "El privilegio de vasallos otorgado a Hernando Cortés." In *Historia y sociedad en el mundo de habla española: Homenaje a José Miranda,* edited by José Miranda and Bernardo García Martínez., 69–78. Mexico City: Colegio de México, 1970.

Friede, Juan, and Benjamin Keen, eds. *Bartolomé de las Casas in History: Towards an Understanding of the Man and His Works.* DeKalb: Northern Illinois University Press, 1971.

Gallegos Rocafull, José M. *El pensamiento mexicano en los siglos XVI y XVII.* Mexico City: Colegio de México, 1951.

García Canclini, Néstor. *Transforming Modernity: Popular Culture in Mexico.* Translated by Lidia Lozano. Austin: University of Texas Press, 1993.

García Edo, Vicent. *Constituciones de los reinos hispánico en el Antiguo Régimen.* Castellón:Universitat Jaume I, 2003.

García Icazbalceta, Joaquín, ed. *Colección de documentos para la historia de México.* Vol. 1. Mexico City: Librería de J. M. Andrade, 1858.

———. *Nueva colección de documentos para la historia de México* 3 vols. (Mexico City: Editorial Salvador Chávez Hayhoe, 1941.

García Moreno, Luis A. *History de España visigoda.* Madrid: Ediciones Cátedra, 1989.

Geertz, Clifford. "Religion as a Cultural System." In *The Interpretation of Cultures: Selected Essays.* New York: Basic Books, 1973, 87–125.

Getino, Luis Alonso. *Influencia de los Dominicos en las leyes nuevas.* Sevilla: Escuela de Estudios Hispanoamericanos, 1945.

———. *Relecciones teológicas del Maestro Fray Francisco de Vitoria.* 3 vols. Madrid: Imprenta Católica, 1933–1936.

Gibson, Charles. *The Aztecs under Spanish Rule: A History of the Indians of the Valley of Mexico, 1519–1810.* Stanford, CA: Stanford University Press, 1964.

Gimenez Fernández, Manuel. *Bartolomé de las Casa: Delegado de Cisneros para le reformación de las Indias (1516–1517).* Sevilla: Escuela de Estudios Hispanoamericanos, 1953.

Gínes de Supúlveda, Juan. *Tratado sobre las justa causas de la guerra contra los Indios.* Mexico City: Fondo de Cultura Económica, 1987.

Goldsworthy, Adrian Keith. *The Roman Army at War, 100 BC–AD 200.* Oxford: Oxford University Press, 1998.

Góngora, Mario. *El estado en el derecho indiano: Epoca de fundación, 1492–1570.* Santiago: Instituto de Investigaciones Histórico-Culturales, Facultad de Filosofía y Educación, Universidad de Chile, 1951.

González, Silvia, and David Huddart. "The Late Pleistocene Human Occupation of Mexico." *FUMDHAMentos VII,* January 2008, 236–259.

Goody, Jack. *The Domestication of the Savage Mind.* Cambridge: Cambridge University Press, 1977.

Gorges, Jean Gérard. *Les villas hispano-romaines: Inventaire et problématique archéologiques.* Talence, France: Université de Bordeaux III, 1979.

Green, Otis H. *Spain and the Western Tradition: The Castilian Mind in Literature from El Cid to Calderón.* 4 vols. Madison: University of Wisconsin Press, 1968.

Greenblatt, Stephen. *Marvelous Possessions: The Wonders of the New World:* Chicago: University of Chicago Press, 1991.

Greenleaf, Richard E. *The Mexican Inquisition of the Sixteenth Century.* Albuquerque: University of New Mexico Press, 1969.

———. *Zumárraga and the Mexican Inquisition, 1536–1543.* Washington, DC: Academy of American Franciscan History, 1961.

Grove, David C., and Susan D. Gillespie. "Ideology and Evolution at the Pre-state Level: Formative Period Mesoamerica." In *Ideology and Pre-Columbian Civilizations,* edited by Arthur A. Demarest and Geoffrey W. Conrad, 15–36. Santa Fe, NM: School of American Research, 1992.

Gruen, Erich S. *Culture and National Identity in Republican Rome.* Ithaca, NY: Cornell University Press, 1992.

Grunzinski, Serge. *The Conquest of Mexico.* Cambridge, UK: Polity, 1993.

Gurzadyan, Vahe G., and Roger Penrose. "Concentric Circles in WMAP Data May Provide Evidence of Violent Pre-Big-Bang Activity." arXiv.org, November 16, 2010. http://arxiv.org/abs/1011.3706v1.

Haliczer, Stephen. *The Comuneros of Castile: The Forging of a Revolution, 1475–1521.* Madison: University of Wisconsin Press, 1981.

Hamilton, Bernice. *Political Thought in Sixteenth-Century Spain: A Study of the Political Ideas of Vitoria, Soto, Suárez and Molina.* Oxford, UK: Clarendon, 1963.

Hanke, Lewis. "The 'Requerimiento' and Its Interpreters." *Revista de Historia de América* 1 (March 1938): 25–34.

———. *The Spanish Struggle for Justice in the Conquest of America.* Philadelphia: University of Pennsylvania, 1949.

Harl, Kenneth. *Civic Coins and Civic Politics in the Roman East, A.D. 185–275.* Berkeley: University of California Press, 1987.

Harner, Michael. "The Ecological Basis for Aztec Sacrifice." *American Ethnologist* 4 (1977): 117–135.

Harris, Marvin. *Cannibals and Kings: The Origins of Cultures.* New York: Random House, 1977.

Harris, William V. *War and Imperialism in Republican Rome.* Oxford: Oxford University Press, 1979.

Haskett, Robert. *Indigenous Rulers: An Ethnohistory of Town Government in Colonial Cuernavaca.* Albuquerque: University of New Mexico Press, 1991.

Haskins, Charles Homer. *The Renaissance of the Twelfth Century.* Cambridge, MA: Harvard University Press, 1927.

Hassig, Ross. *Mexico and the Spanish Conquest.* New York: Longman, 1994.

Hays, Jo N. "Historians and Epidemics: Simple Questions, Complex Answers." In *Plague and the End of Antiquity: The Pandemic of 541–750,* edited by Lester K. Little, 33–56. New York: Cambridge University Press, 2007.

Hazen, Robert M. "Exciting Frontiers Await at Scientific Boundaries: An Example from the Deep Carbon Observatory." *EARTH* 56, no. 7 (2011): 71.

———. *The Story of Earth: The First 4.5 Billion Years, from Stardust to Living Planet.* New York: Viking, 2012.

Hazony, Yoram. *The Philosophy of Hebrew Scriptures.* New York: Cambridge University Press, 2012.

Headrick, Daniel R. *The Tools of Empire: Technology and European Imperialism in the Nineteenth Century.* New York: Oxford University Press, 1981.

Herlihy, David. *The Black Death and the Transformation of the West.* Cambridge, MA: Harvard University Press, 1997.

Herzog, Tamar. *Defining Nations: Immigrants and Citizens in Early Modern Spain and Spanish America.* New Haven, CT: Yale University Press, 2003.

Heyden, Doris. Introduction to *History of the Indies of New Spain,* by Diego Durán. Norman: University of Oklahoma Press, 1994.

Hicks, Frederic. "First Steps towards a Market-Integrated Economy in Aztec Mexico." In *Studies in Human Society,* vol. 2, *Early State Dynamics,* edited by Henri J. M. Claessen and Pieter van de Velde, 91–107. Leiden: Brill, 1987.

Hillgarth, J. N. "Popular Religion in Visigothic Spain." In *Visigothic Spain: New Approaches,* edited by Edward James, 3–60. Oxford: Oxford University Press, 1980.

Hirschberg, Julia. "An Alternative to Encomienda: Puebla's Indios de Sevicio, 1531–45." *Journal of Latin American Studies* 11 (November 1979): 241–264.

Homer, Sidney. *A History of Interest Rates.* New Brunswick, NJ: Rutgers University Press, 1963.

Hopkins, Donald R. *The Greatest Killer: Smallpox in History.* Chicago: University of Chicago Press, 2002.

Ingham, John M. *Mary, Michael, and Lucifer: Folk Catholicism in Central Mexico.* Austin: University of Texas Press, 1987.

Jackson, Robert H. *Race, Caste, and Status: Indians in Colonial Spanish America.* Albuquerque: University of New Mexico Press, 1999.

Jeffery, L. H. *The Local Scripts of Archaic Greece: A Study of the Origin of the Greek Alphabet and Its Development from the Eighth to the Fifth Centuries B.C.* 2nd ed. New York: Oxford University Press, 1990.

Jiménez Moreno, Wigberto. "Los indígenas frente al cristianismo." In *Estudios de historia colonial.* Mexico City: INAH, 1983.

Jones, A. H. M. *The Decline of the Ancient World.* New York: Pearson, 1975.

Jordan, Terry G. *North American Cattle-Ranching Frontiers: Origins, Diffusions, and Differentiation.* Albuquerque: University of New Mexico Press, 1993.

Kamen, Henry. *The Spanish Inquisition: A Historical Revision.* New Haven, CT: Yale University Press, 1998.

Kedar, Benjamin Z. *Crusade and Mission: European Approaches towards Muslims.* Princeton, NJ: Princeton University Press, 1984.

———, "Muslim Conversion in Canon Law," in *Proceedings of the Sixth International Conference of Medieval Canon Law* eds. S. Kuttner and K. Pennington Berekeley: University of California Press, 1985, 321–332.

Keegan, John. *The Face of Battle.* New York: Penguin, 1978.

———. *A History of Warfare.* New York: Vintage Books, 1994.

Keen, Maurice. "Introduction: Warfare and the Middle Ages." In *Medieval Warfare: A History,* edited by Keen, 1–10. Oxford: Oxford University Press, 1999.

———, ed. *Medieval Warfare: A History.* Oxford: Oxford University Press, 1999.

Kellogg, Susan. *Law and the Transformation of Aztec Culture, 1500–1700.* Norman: University of Oklahoma Press, 2005.

Kelly, Christopher. *The End of Empire: Attila the Hun and the Fall of Rome.* New York: Norton, 2009.

Kirsch, Jonathan. *God against the Gods: A History of the War between Monotheism and Polytheism.* New York: Viking, 2004.

Kline, Julius. *The Mesta: A Study in Spanish Economic History, 1273–1836.* Cambridge, MA: Harvard University Press, 1920.

Klor de Alva, J. Jorge. "The Aztec-Spanish Dialogues of 1524." *Alcheringa* 4 (1980): 56–193.

Knight, Alan. *Mexico: From the Beginning to the Spanish Conquest.* Cambridge: Cambridge University Press, 2002.

Kostiner, Joseph. "Transforming Dualities: Tribe and State Formation in Saudi Arabia." In *Tribes and State Formation in the Middle East,* edited by Philip S. Khoury and Joseph Kostiner, 226–249. Berkeley: University of California Press, 1990.

Krautheimer, Richard. *Three Christian Capitals: Topography and Politics.* Berkeley: University of California Press, 1983.

Kumar, Krishan. "Greece and Rome in the British Empire: Contrasting Role Models." *Journal of British Studies* 51, no. 1 (2012): 76–101.

Ladd, Doris M. *The Mexican Nobility at Independence, 1780–1826.* (Austin: Institute of Latin American Studies, University of Texas at Austin, 1976.

Lanyon, Anna. *The New World of Martín Cortés.* Cambridge, MA: Da Capo, 2004.

León-Portillo, Miguel. *The Aztec Image of Self and Society.* Salt Lake City: University of Utah Press, 1992.

———, ed. *Broken Spears: The Aztec Account of the Conquest of Mexico.* Boston: Beacon, 1966.

———. Introduction to *Broken Spears: The Aztec Account of the Conquest of Mexico.* Boston: Beacon, 1966, xxv–xxix.

Lewis, Bernard. *The Arabs in History.* 6th ed. New York: Oxford University Press, 1993.

Lieu, Samuel N. C. *Manichaeism in the Later Roman Empire and Medieval China.* 2nd ed. Tübingen, Germany: Mohr Siebeck, 1992.

Linz, Juan J. "Intellectual Roles in Sixteenth- and Seventeenth-Century Spain." *Daedalus* 101 (Summer 1972): 59–108.

Lira, Andrés. *Comunidades indígenas frente a la ciudad de México: Tenochtitlan y Tlatelolco, sus pueblos y barrios, 1812–1919.* Mexico City: El Colegio de México, 1983.

Liss, Peggy K. *Isabel the Queen: Life and Times.* New York: Oxford University Press, 1992.

———. *Mexico under Spain, 1521–1556: Society and the Origins of Nationality.* Chicago: University of Chicago Press, 1975.

Little, Lester K. "Life and Afterlife of the First Plague Pandemic." In *Plague and the End of Antiquity: The Pandemic of 541–750,* edited by Little, 3–32. New York: Cambridge University Press, 2007.

———, ed. *Plague and the End of Antiquity: The Pandemic of 541–750.* New York: Cambridge University Press, 2007.

———. *Religious Poverty and the Profit Economy in Medieval Europe.* Ithaca, NY: Cornell University Press, 1978.

Lloyd, T. O. *The British Empire, 1558–1995.* 2nd ed. New York: Oxford University Press, 2008.

Lockhart, James. "Encomienda and Hacienda: The Evolution of the Great Estate in the Spanish Indies." In *Readings in Latin American History: The Formative Centuries,* vol. 1, edited by Peter J. Bakewell, John J. Johnson, and Meredith D. Dodge, 51–66. Durham, NC: Duke University Press, 1985.

———. *The Nahuas after the Conquest: A Social and Cultural History of the Indians of Central Mexico, Sixteenth through Eighteenth Centuries.* Stanford, CA: Stanford University Press, 1992.

———. "Double Mistaken Identity: Some Nahua Concepts in Postconquest Guise," in *Of Things of the Indies: Essays Old & New in Early Latin American History* (Stanford: Stanford University Press, 1999), 98–119.

Lomax, John Phillip. "Frederick II, His Saracens, and the Papacy." In *Medieval Christian Perception of Islam,* edited by John Victor Tolan, 175–197. New York: Routledge, 2000.

Lopes Don, Patricia. *Bonfires of Culture: Franciscans, Indigenous Leaders, and the Inquisition in Early Mexico, 1524–1540.* Norman: University of Oklahoma Press, 2010.

López Austin, Alfredo. *Hombre-Dios: Religión y política en el mundo náhuatl.* Mexico City: UNAM, 1973.

López Austin, Alfredo, and Leonardo López Luján. *Mexico's Indigenous Past.* Norman: University of Oklahoma Press, 2001.

López-Portillo y Weber, José. *La rebellion de Nueva Galicia.* Mexico City: Instituto Panamericano de Geografía e Historia, 1939.

Lowe, Benedict. *Roman Iberia: Economy, Society and Culture.* London: Duckworth, 2009.

Lupher, David A. *Romans in the New World: Classical Models in Sixteenth-Century Spanish America.* Ann Arbor: University of Michigan Press, 2003.

Lynch, John. *Spain under the Habsburgs.* Vol. 1, *Empire and Absolutism, 1516–1598.* New York: Oxford University Press, 1965.

MacKay, Angus. *Spain in the Middle Ages: From Frontier to Empire, 1000–1500.* New York: St. Martin's, 1977.

MacLachlan, Colin M. "The Eagle and the Serpent: Male over Female in Tenoch-titlán." *Proceedings of the Pacific Coast Council of Latin American Studies,* 1976, 45–56.

———. *A History of Modern Brazil: The Past against the Future.* Wilmington, DE: Scholarly Resources, 2003.

———. "The Indian Directorate: Forced Acculturation in Portuguese America (1757–1799)." *Americas* 28, no. 4 (1972): 357–387.

———. *Spain's Empire in the New World: The Role of Ideas in Institutional and Social Change.* Berkeley: University of California Press, 1988.

MacLachlan, Colin M., and Jaime E. Rodriguez O. *The Forging of the Cosmic Race: A Reinterpretation of Colonial Mexico.* Berkeley: University of California Press, 1980.

MacMullen, Ramsay. *Christianizing the Roman Empire (A.D. 100–400).* New Haven, CT: Yale University Press, 1984.

———. *Paganism in the Roman Empire.* New Haven, CT: Yale University Press, 1981.

Macri, Martha J., and Matthew G. Looper. *The New Catalog of Maya Hieroglyphs.* Vol. 1, *The Classic Period Inscriptions.* Norman: University of Oklahoma Press, 2013.

Mann, Michael. *The Sources of Social Power.* Vol. 1, *A History of Power from the Beginning to A.D. 1760.* Cambridge: Cambridge University Press, 1986.

Manzano Manzano, Juan. *La incorporación de las Indias a la Corona de Castilla.* Madrid: Ediciones Cultura Hispanica, 1948.

Maravall, José Antonio. *Las comunidades de Castilla: Una primera revolución moderna.* Madrid: Revista de Occidente, 1963.

Martin, Norman F. *Los vagabundos en la Nueva España, siglo XVI.* Mexico City: Editorial Jus, 1957.

Martínez, María Elena. *Genealogical Fictions: Limpieza de Sangres, Religion, and Gender in Colonial Mexico.* Stanford, CA: Stanford University Press, 2008.

Matos Moctezuma, Eduardo. "Aztec History and Cosmovision." In *Moctezuma's Mexico: Visions of the Aztec World,* edited by David Carrasco and Eduardo Matos Moctezuma), 3–98. Boulder: University Press of Colorado, 2003.

———. *El Templo Mayor: Excavaciones y estudios.* Mexico City: INAH, 1982.

———. "Templo Mayor: History and Interpretation." In *The Great Temple of Tenochtitlán: Center and Periphery in the Aztec World,* by Johanna Broda, David Carrasco, and Eduardo Matos Moctezuma, 15–60. Berkeley: University of California Press, 1987.

Matthews, Laura E., and Michel R. Oudijk, eds. *Indian Conquistadores: Indigenous Allies in the Conquest of Mesoamerica.* Norman: University of Oklahoma Press, 2007.

Mauldin, Barbara. *Masks of Mexico: Tigers, Devils, and the Dance of Life.* Santa Fe: Museum of New Mexico Press, 1999.

McKenna, Stephen. *Paganism and Pagan Survival in Spain up to the Fall of the Visigothic Kingdom.* Washington, DC: Catholic University of America, 1938.

Melville, Elinor G. K. *A Plague of Sheep: The Environmental Consequences of the Conquest of Mexico.* Cambridge: Cambridge University Press, 1997.

Miller, Mary, and Karl Taub. *An Illustrated Dictionary of the Gods and Symbols of Ancient Mexico and the Maya.* London: Thames and Hudson, 1993.

Mills, Kenneth, and William B. Taylor. *Colonial Spanish America: A Documentary History.* Wilmington, DE: Scholarly Resources, 1998.

Miranda, José. *El tributo indígena en la Nueva España durante el siglo XVI.* Mexico City: Colegio de México, 2005.

———. *España y Nueva España en la epoca de Felipe II.* Mexico City: UNAM, 1962.

———. *La función económica del encomendero en los orígenes del régimen colonial (Nueva España, 1525–1531).* Mexico City: UNAM, 1965.

Mitteis, Heinrich. *The State in the Middle Ages: A Comparative Constitutional History of Feudal Europe.* Amsterdam: North Holland, 1975.

Monzón, Arturo. *El calpulli en la organización social de los Tenochca.* Mexico City: Instituto de Historia, 1949.

Moreno de los Arcos, Roberto. "Los cinco soles cosmogónicos." *Estudios de Cultura Náhuatl* 7 (1967): 183–210.

Mörner, Magnus. *La corona española y los foráneos en los pueblos de indios de América.* Stockholm, Sweden: Almqvist and Wilsell, 1970.

——. *Race Mixtures in the History of Latin America*. Boston: Little, Brown, 1967.

Morony, Michael G. "'For Whom Does the Writer Write?': The First Bubonic Plague Pandemic According to Syriac Sources." In *Plague and the End of Antiquity: The Pandemic of 541–750*, edited by Lester K. Little, 59–86. New York: Cambridge University Press, 2007.

Motolinía, Toribio. *Carta al Emperador: Refutación a Las Casas sobre la colonización española*. Mexico City: Editorial Jus, 1949.

——. *Las cosas de la Nueva España y los naturales*, edited by Edmundo O'Gorman. Mexico: UNAM. 1971.

Muchembled, Robert. *A History of the Devil from the Middle Ages to the Present*. Cambridge, UK: Polity, 2003.

Nicholson, H. B. *Topiltzin Quetzalcoatl: The Once and Future Lord of the Toltecs*. Boulder: University Press of Colorado, 2001.

O'Callaghan, Joseph F. *Reconquista and Crusade in Medieval Spain*. Philadelphia: University of Pennsylvania Press, 2003.

Offner, Jerome A. *Law and Politics in Aztec Texcoco*. Cambridge: Cambridge University Press, 1983.

O'Gorman, Edmundo. *The Invention of America*. Bloomington: Indiana University Press, 1961.

——. "Letter on the North Americans." *American Scholar*, Autumn 1947, 461–463.

Olivier, Guilhem. *Mockeries and Metamorphose of an Aztec God: Tezcatlipoca, Lord of the Smoking Mirror*. Translated by Michel Bession. Boulder: University Press of Colorado, 2003.

Ortiz de Montellano, Bernard R. *Aztec Medicine, Health, and Nutrition*. New Brunswick, NJ: Rutgers University Press, 1991.

Ots Capdequí, José María. *España en America: El régimen de tierras en el época colonial*. Buenos Aires: Fondo de Cultura Económica, 1959.

——. *Instituciones*. Barcelona: Salvat, 1959.

Otte, Enrique. "La flota de Diego Colón: Españoles y genoveses en el comercio transatlántico de 1509." *Revista de Indias* 24 (1964): 475–503.

Oviedo, Gonzalo Fernández de. *Historia general y natural de las Indias*. Biblioteca de Autores Españoles (BAE) 117–121. Madrid: Atlas, 1959.

Owensby, Brian P. *Empire of Laws and Indian Justice in Colonial Mexico*. Stanford, CA: Stanford University Press, 2008.

Padden, R. C. *The Hummingbird and the Hawk: Conquest and Sovereignty in the Valley of Mexico, 1503–1541*. New York: Harper, 1967.

Pagden, Anthony. *The Fall of Natural Man: the American Indian and the Origins of Comparative Ethnology*. Cambridge: Cambridge University Press, 1982.

——. *Lords of All the World: Ideologies of Empire in Spain, Britain and France, c. 1500–c. 1800*. New Haven, CT: Yale University Press, 1995.

——. *Spanish Imperialism and Political Imagination: Studies in European and Spanish-American Social and Political Theory*. New Haven, CT: Yale University Press, 1990.

Pardo, Osvaldo. *The Origins of Mexican Catholicism: Nahua Rituals and Christian Sacraments in Sixteenth-Century Mexico*. Ann Arbor: University of Michigan Press, 2006.

Parish, Helen Rand. Introduction to *Bartolomé de las Casas: The Only Way,* by Bartolomé de las Casas, translated by Francis Patrick Sullivan. Mahwah, NJ: Paulist, 1992, 9–10.

Parker, Geoffrey. *The Military Revolution: Military Innovation and the Rise of the West, 1500–1800.* 2nd ed. Cambridge: Cambridge University Press, 1996.

Parry, John H. *The Spanish Seaborne Empire.* Berkeley: University of California Press, 1990.

——. *The Spanish Theory of Empire in the Sixteenth Century.* Cambridge: Cambridge University Press, 1940.

Paso y Troncoso, Francisco del, comp. *Epistolario de Nueva España, 1505–1818.* Mexico City: Porrúa, 1939–1942.

Pasztory, Esther. *Teotihuacan: An Experiment in Living.* Norman: University of Oklahoma Press, 1997.

Payne, Stanley G. *A History of Spain and Portugal.* 2 vols. Madison: University of Wisconsin Press, 1973.

——. *Spain: A Unique History.* Madison: University of Wisconsin Press, 2011.

Paz, Octavio. *The Other Mexico: Critique of the Pyramid.* Translated by Lysander Kemp. New York: Grove, 1972.

Pérez, Joseph. *La revolución de las comunidades de Castilla (1520–1521).* Madrid: Siglo XXI de España, 1977.

Peterson, Frederick A. *Ancient Mexico: An Introduction to the Pre-Hispanic Cultures.* New York: Capricorn Books, 1962.

Pharo, Lars Kirkhusmo. *The Ritual Practice of Time: Philosophy and Sociopolitics of Mesoamerican Calendars.* Leiden: Brill, 2013.

Pike, Ruth. *Enterprise and Adventure: The Genoese in Seville and the Opening of the New World.* Ithaca, NY: Cornell University Press, 1966.

Pomar, Juan Bautista. "Relación de Tezcoco." In *Nueva colección de documentos para la historia de México,* vol. 3. edited by Joaquín García Icazbalceta. Mexico City: Biblioteca Enciclopédica del Estado de México, 1975.

Pool, Christopher A. *Olmec Archaeology and Early Mesoamerica.* Cambridge: Cambridge University Press, 2007.

Poole, Stafford. *The Guadalupan Controversies in Mexico.* Stanford, CA: Stanford University Press, 2006.

——. *Pedro Moya de Contreras: Catholic Reform and Royal Power in New Spain, 1571–1591.* Berkeley: University of California Press, 1987.

Powell, Philip Wayne. *Tree of Hate: Propaganda and Prejudices Affecting United States Relations with the Hispanic World.* New York: Basic Books, 1971.

Price, S. R. F. *Rituals and Power: The Roman Imperial Cult in Asia Minor.* Cambridge: Cambridge University Press, 1984.

Quijada, Mónica. "From Spain to New Spain: Revisiting the *Potestas Populi* in Hispanic Political Thought." *Mexican Studies / Estudios Mexicanos* 24, no. 2 (2008): 185–219.

Ricard, Robert. *The Spiritual Conquest of Mexico: An Essay on the Apostolate and the Evangelizing Methods of the Mendicant Orders in New Spain, 1523–1572.* Translated by Lesley Byrd Simpson. Berkeley: University of California Press, 1966.

Richardson, John S. *The Romans in Spain.* Hoboken, NJ: Wiley-Blackwell, 1998.

Robertson, Donald. *Mexican Manuscript Painting of the Early Colonial Period.* New Haven, CT: Yale University Press, 1959.

Rodríguez O., Jaime E. *The Independence of Spanish America.* Cambridge: Cambridge University Press, 1998.

———. "The Emancipation of America," *American Historical Review,* vol. 105, no. 1 (February 2000), 131–152

———. "La naturaleza de la representación en la Nueva España y México." *Secuencia: Revista de Historia y Ciencias Sociales* 61 (January–April 2005): 6–32.

———. "Las revoluciones atlánticas: Una reinterpretación." *Historia Mexicana* 63, no. 4 (April–June 2014): 1871–1968

———. *"We Are Now the True Spaniards": Sovereignty, Revolution, Independence, and the Emergence of the Federal Republic of Mexico, 1808–1824.* Stanford, CA: Stanford University Press, 2012.

Rodríguez O., Jaime E., and Colin M. MacLachlan. *Hacia el ser histórico de México: Una reinterpretación de la Nueva España.* Mexico City: Editorial Diana, 2001.

Rojas, José Luis de. *La moneda indígena y sus uso en la Nueva España en el siglo XVI.* Mexico City: Centro de Investigaciones y Estudios Superiores en Antropología Social, 1998.

———. *México Tenochtitlan: Economía e sociedad en el siglo XVI.* Mexico City: Fondo de Cultura Económica, 1986.

Ruiz de Alarcón, Hernando. *Treatise on the Heathen Superstitions That Today Live among the Indians Native to This New Spain, 1629.* Translated by J. Richard Andrews and Ross Hassig. Norman: University of Oklahoma Press, 1984.

Russell, Jeffery Burton. *Lucifer.* Ithaca, NY: Cornell University Press, 1984.

Sahagún, Bernardino de. *Coloquios y doctrina christiana.* Edited by Miguel León-Portilla. Mexico City: UNAM, 1986.

———. *Historia general de las cosas de Nueva España (Florentine Codex).* Santa Fe: School of American Research, 1950–1982.

Sánchez Agesta, Luis. *El concepto del estado en el pensamiento español del siglo XVI.* Madrid: Instituto de Estudios Políticos, 1959.

Sandys, Sir John Edwin. *Latin Epigraphy: An Introduction to the Study of Latin Inscriptions.* 2nd ed. Revised by S. G. Campbell. Cambridge: Cambridge University Press, 1927.

Santamaría Novillos, Carlos. *El sistema de dominación Azteca: El imperio Tepaneca.* Madrid: Fundación Universitaria Española, 2006.

Schroeder, Susan. *Chimalpahin and the Kingdoms of Chalco.* Tucson: University of Arizona Press, 1991.

Schroeder, Susan, and Stafford Poole, eds. *Religion in New Spain.* Albuquerque: University of New Mexico Press, 2007.

Schroeder, Susan, Stephanie Wood, and Robert Haskett. *Indian Women of Early Mexico.* Norman: University of Oklahoma Press, 1997.

Schwaller, John Frederick. *The Clergy in Sixteenth-Century Mexico.* Albuquerque: University of New Mexico Press, 1987.

———. "The Expansion of Nahuatl as a Lingua Franca among Priests in Sixteenth-Century Mexico." *Ethnohistory* 59, no. 4 (2012): 675–690.

———. "The *Ordenanza del Patronazgo* in New Spain, 1574–1600." *Americas* 42, no. 3 (1986): 253–274.

———. *The Origins of Church Wealth in Mexico: Ecclesiastical Revenue and Church Finances, 1523–1600.* Albuquerque: University of New Mexico Press, 1985.

———. "The Secular Clergy in Sixteenth-Century Mexico." Ph.D. diss., Department of History, Indiana University, 1978.

Schwaller, Robert C. "Defining Differences in Early New Spain." Ph.D. diss., Pennsylvania State University, 2010.

Schwarts, Herman. *History, Geography, and the Development of the Internationsl Economy.* New York: St. Martin's Press, 1994.

Seccombe, Wally. *Millennium of Family Change: Feudalism to Capitalism in North-western Europe.* London: Verso, 1992.

Seed, Patricia. *Ceremonies of Possession Europe's Conquest of the New World, 1492–1640.* New York: Cambridge University Press, 1995.

Service, Elman R. *Origins of the State and Civilization: The Process of Cultural Evolution.* New York: Norton, 1975.

Shiels, Eugene W. *King and Church: The Rise and Fall of the Patronato Real.* Chicago: Loyola University Press, 1961.

Shils, Edward. *Tradition.* Chicago: University of Chicago Press, 1981.

Simpson, Lesley Byrd. *The Encomienda in New Spain: The Beginning of Spanish Mexico.* Berkeley: University of California Press, 1950.

Skinner, Quentin. *The Foundation of Modern Political Thought.* 2 vols. New York: Cambridge University Press, 1978.

Smith, Michael E. *The Aztecs.* 3rd ed. Malden, MA: Wiley-Blackwell, 2012.

Smith, Ricardo. *Un humanista al servicio del imperialismo: Juan Ginés de Sepúlveda (1490–1573).* Córdoba, Spain: Talleres gráficos de la Penitenciaría de Córdoba, 1942.

Smith, Robert S. *The Spanish Guild Merchants: A History of the Consulado, 1250–1700.* Durham, NC: Duke University Press, 1940.

Soustelle, Jacques. *Daily Life of the Aztecs on the Eve of the Spanish Conquest.* Stanford, CA: Stanford University Press, 1961.

Spenglar, Oswald, *The Decline of the West* 2 vols. New York: Alfred A. Knopf, 1928–1929.

Spufford, Peter. *Money and Its Use in Medieval Europe.* Cambridge: Cambridge University Press, 1988.

Stocking, Rachel L. *Bishops, Councils, and Consensus in the Visigothic Kingdom, 589–633.* Ann Arbor: University of Michigan Press, 2000.

Stoetzer, O. Carlos. *The Scholastic Roots of the Spanish American Revolution.* New York: Fordham University Press, 1979.

Suarez Peralta, Juan. *Noticias histórica de Nueva España (1589–90).* Edited by Justo Zaragoza. Madrid, 1878.

Tedlock, Dennis, trans. *Popol Vuh: The Mayan Book of the Dawn of Life.* New York: Simon and Schuster, 1995.

———. *The Spoken Word and the Work of Interpretation.* Philadelphia: University of Pennsylvania Press, 1983.

Tilly, Charles. *Coercion, Capital, and European States.* Cambridge, MA: Blackwell, 1990.

Todorov, Tzvetan. *The Conquest of America: The Question of the Other.* New York: Harper and Row, 1984.

Tolan, John Victor, ed. *Medieval Christian Perception of Islam.* New York: Routledge, 2000.

Toland, Judith Drick. "Discrepancies and Dissolution: Breakdown of the Early Inca State." In *Studies in Human Society: Early State Dynamics,* edited by Henri J. M. Claessen and Pieter van de Velde, 138–153. Leiden: Brill, 1987.

Toor, Frances. *A Treasury of Mexican Folkways: The Customs, Myths, Folklore, Traditions, Beliefs, Fiestas, Dances, and Song of the Mexican People.* New York: Crown, 1947.

Tovar, Antonio, *Lingüística y filología clásica.* Madrid: Revista de Occidente 1944.

Trend, J. B. *The Civilization of Spain.* 2nd ed. Oxford: Oxford University Press, 1967.

Turner, Frederick Jackson. "The Significance of the Frontier in American History." *Annual Report of the American Historical Review,* 1894.

Tutino, John. *Making a New World; Founding Capitalism in the Bajío and Spanish North America.* Durham: Duke University Press, 2011.

Ullmann, Walter. *A History of Political Thought: The Middle Ages.* Harmondsworth, UK: Penguin, 1970.

Ulloa, Modesto. *La hacienda real de Castilla en el reinado de Felipe II.* Madrid: Fundación Universitaria Española, 1977.

Vailliant, George C. *Mexico: Origin, Rise, and Fall of the Aztec Nation.* Baltimore: Penguin Books, 1960.

VanDerwarker, Amber. *Farming, Hunting, and Fishing in the Olmec World.* Austin: University of Texas Press, 2006.

Van Kleffens, E. N. *Hispanic Law until the End of the Middle Ages.* Edinburgh: Edinburgh University Press, 1968.

Varner, John Grier, and Jeannette Johnson Varner. *Dogs of the Conquest.* Norman: University of Oklahoma Press, 1983.

Vayda, A. P. "On the Nutritional Value of Cannibalism." *American Anthropologist* 72: 6 (1970): 1462–1463.

Veblen, Thorstein. *The Theory of the Leisure Class: An Economic Study of Institutions.* 1899. Edited by Martha Banta. Oxford: Oxford University Press, 2009.

Voragine, Jacobus de. *The Golden Legend* 6 vols., London: Temple Classics, 1931.

Wall, J. Charles. *Devils.* London: Methuen, 1904.

Warren, Fintan B. *Vasco de Quiroga and His Pueblo-Hospitales of Santa Fe.* Washington, DC: Academy of American Franciscan History, 1963.

Watts, Alan. *Myth and Ritual in Christianity.* Boston: Beacon, 1968.

Weckmann, Luis. *La herencia medieval de México.* 2nd ed. Mexico City: Fondo de Cultura Económica, 1994.

———. *Las Bulas Alejandrinas de 1493 y la teoría política del Papado medieval.* Mexico City: Editorial Jus, 1949.

———. "The Middle Ages in the Conquest of America." *Speculum* 26 (1951): 130–139.

White, Stephen D. *Re-thinking Kingship and Feudalism in Medieval Europe.* Aldershot, UK: Ashgate, 2005,

Whiteside, Jessica H., Paul E. Olsen, Timothy Eglinton, Michael E. Brookfield, and Raymond N. Sambrotto. "Compound-Specific Carbon Isotopes from Earth's Largest Flood Basalt Eruptions Directly Linked to the End-Triassic Mass

Extinction." *Proceedings of the National Academy of Science* 107, no. 15 (2010): 6721–6725.

Whittaker, C. R. *Frontiers of the Roman Empires: A Social and Economic Study.* Baltimore: Johns Hopkins University Press, 1997.

Wolf, Kenneth Baxter. "Christian Views of Islam in Early Medieval Spain." In *Medieval Christian Perceptions of Islam.* Edited by John Victor Tolan, 85–108. New York: Routledge, 2000.

Wood, Stephanie. *Transcending Conquest: Nahua Views of Spanish Colonial Mexico.* Norman: University of Oklahoma Press, 2012.

Woolf, Greg. *Rome: An Empire's Story.* New York: Oxford University Press, 2012.

Yáñez, Agustín. *El contenido social de la literatura iberoamericana.* Mexico City: Colegio de México, 1944; Mexico City: Editorial Americana, 1967.

Zavala, Silvio. *La encomienda indiana.* 2nd ed. Mexico City: Editorial Porrúa, 1972.

———. *Los esclavos indios en Nueva España.* 3rd ed. Mexico City: Colegio de México, 1994.

———. *Poder y lenguaje desde el siglo XVI.* Mexico City: Colegio de México, 1996.

Zerubavel, Eviatar. *Terra Cognita: The Mental Discovery of America.* New Brunswick, NJ: Rutgers University Press, 1992.

Zorita, Alonso de. *Life and Labor in Ancient Mexico: The Brief and Summary Relation of the Lords of New Spain.* Translated and with an introduction by Benjamin Keen. New Brunswick, NJ: Rutgers University Press, 1963.

Acknowledgments

William Sater and William Beezley read earlier drafts of this work, and I am indebted to them for their constructive suggestions for strengthening the book. My deep thanks to Linda Alexander Rodríguez and Jaime E. Rodríguez O., who read the manuscript in all its versions and offered valuable criticism and insightful suggestions for improvement that helped to clarify and enrich my analysis of the formation and clash of empires. I am most grateful to Annelisa Romero, who encouraged, advised, and supported me and my work during a long and difficult illness. Finally, I thank Kathleen McDermott, who found my manuscript valuable and guided it judiciously during the evaluation and production process.

Index